More Praise for *Comprehension from the Ground Up*...

This is a book I have been waiting for since Sharon's first publication *On Solid Ground*. Again Sharon does not disappoint. It is filled with sensible, practical, and innovative ways to help students gain real meaning from what they read. Sharon is a master at understanding how children best learn the essentials of reading comprehension. This is a book that every K–3 teacher needs to read.

—Tony Stead, coauthor of *Explorations in Nonfiction Writing*

In many classrooms today instruction feels frenzied, superficial, and choppy. Sharon describes teaching that is focused, meaningful, and cohesive and reminds us that teaching is not about "covering" material, it's about *learning* the material. I wish every child could have Sharon Taberski for their teacher.

—Nell K. Duke, Michigan State University,
Literacy Achievement Research Center

This remarkable book *shows* teachers how to be knowledgeable and reflective. It brims with high-quality literacy practices that allow teachers to meet the goals of RTI or new standards on their own terms and in child-centered ways. Sharon provides the engaging, meaningful activities teachers need to differentiate their reading instruction throughout the day. *Comprehension from the Ground Up* will virtually change the face of comprehension and how it is addressed in schools—and teachers and children everywhere will reap the benefits.

—Mary Howard, author of *Moving Forward with RTI* and *RTI from All Sides*

Sharon Taberski provides K–3 teachers everything they need to know to simplify comprehension instruction while keeping it appropriate, rigorous, enjoyable, and always focused on the children. In *Comprehension from the Ground Up*, Taberski applies research and extensive teaching experience to re-envision, refine, and slow down the teaching of comprehension. She provides instructional specifics on skills and strategies, fluency, vocabulary development, independent reading, minilessons, conferences, guided reading groups, and much more. This "must-have-it" book for primary teachers provides a wealth of substantive ideas, explicit teaching strategies, and valuable text resources to support and inspire reading and writing across genres.

—Regie Routman, author of *Regie Routman in Residence:*
Transforming Our Teaching, DVD-based series

With this book, we can put aside programs and curricula that place undue pressure on our K–3 students and take them away from meaningful literacy. Taberski offers a remarkably wise set of practices and activities that facilitate children's development as engaged readers. She is a gentle mentor for other teachers, helping them teach with rigor and smartness while savoring the "now" of children's lives. What I really love about Sharon's work is that she is like a feisty big sister, readily calling to question practices that don't make sense, and replacing them with practices that do, all because she cares so deeply about children and teachers. This will be a treasured, foundational resource for years to come.

—Gretchen Owocki, author of *The RTI Daily Planning Book, K–6*

Sharon Taberski does it again, bringing simplicity, sanity, and sensitivity to the teaching of literacy in the early grades. In *Comprehension from the Ground Up*, Sharon helps teachers sift through the endless bombardment of instructional suggestions and mandates that come across their desks, demonstrating the importance of having a set of crystal-clear priorities. Along the way, Sharon surprises her readers with such inviting new practices as content-area literacy centers, synopsis texts, companion sets, teacher-tailored collections, and Ta-Da publications. An incredible work of scholarship and innovation.

—Shelley Harwayne, author of *Novel Perspectives*

COMPREHENSION
from the GROUND UP

COMPREHENSION
from the GROUND UP

Simplified, Sensible Instruction for the K–3 Reading Workshop

Sharon Taberski

HEINEMANN

PORTSMOUTH, NH

HEINEMANN

361 Hanover Street

Portsmouth, NH 03801–3912

www.heinemann.com

Offices and agents throughout the world

The author and publisher wish to thank those who have generously given permission to reprint borrowed material in this book:

Fig. 2-1: Excerpt from *Beezy at Bat* by Megan McDonald, illustrations by Nancy Poydar. Text copyright © by Megan McDonald. Illustrations copyright © 1998 by Nancy Poydar. Published by permission of Orchard Books, an imprint of Scholastic Inc. and Megan McDonald. Reprinted by permission of the publisher and author.

credits continue on page xv

Library of Congress Cataloging-in-Publication Data

Taberski, Sharon.

    Comprehension from the ground up : simplified, sensible instruction for the K–3 reading workshop / Sharon Taberski.

      p. cm.

    Includes bibliographical references and index.

    ISBN: 978-0-325-0-09819-7

    1. Reading comprehension—Study and teaching (Primary). 2. Reading (Primary)—Curricula. I. Title.

LB1525.7.T33 2011

372.47—dc22   2010030740

This text was previously published under ISBN: 978-0-325-00411-2

Editor: Wendy Murray

Production editor: Patricia Adams

Cover and interior design: Joyce Weston

Cover photographer: John Videler

Typesetter: Gina Poirier Design

Manufacturing: Steve Bernier

Printed in the United States of America on acid-free paper

23 22 21 20 19 GP 3 4 5 6 7

To my friend and editor Wendy Murray
for making it happen

Contents

Part Two: Refining Our Teaching

Please also see the Online Resources for a Study Guide and the Appendices.

Effective Practices

See these tabbed pages throughout the book.

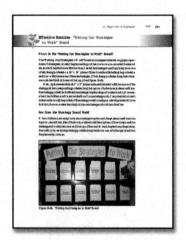

Appendices

Please also see the Online Resources for a Study Guide and the Appendices.

To access the online resources for *Comprehension from the Ground Up*, go to www.heinemann.com and click on the link in the upper right to **Log In.**

(If you do not already have an account with Heinemann will need to create an account.)

Register your product by entering the code: **COMPRE**

Once you have registered your product, it will appear in the list of My Online Resources.

Acknowledgments

This book has been a long time coming...a very long time coming. Many starts and stops and lots of chapter ones along the way. My dear friend Ann Marie often teased that I should just do a book of chapter ones and be done with it. I couldn't laugh then, but I can smile now and say quite emphatically—I'm glad it took so long to write this follow-up to *On Solid Ground* because it gave me much needed time to read, learn, grow, teach children, interact with colleagues, reflect, and revise how I think comprehension is best taught to K–3 readers. A topic as important as comprehension instruction can't be rushed. And it certainly wasn't.

And now I have a long list of folks to thank for helping me along this journey of discovery. As always, a huge thank-you to the staff, families, and children of the Manhattan New School for giving me the solid ground on which to teach and consider best practices. I'm forever grateful for having had the opportunity to work with you and learn from you. To founding MNS principal Shelley Harwayne and current principal Sharon Hill, you inspire excellence, and each of us whose life you touch is the better for it.

I want to thank all the children and teachers in whose classrooms I worked and those I interacted with at seminars and workshops. You gave me ideas, inspiration, and an ever-growing understanding of what's needed. A special thanks to the team of educators at Middlebrook Elementary School in Trumbull, Connecticut and PS 197 in the South Bronx for welcoming me into your very special teaching and learning communities—I am forever grateful.

I am especially grateful to my editors. First, to Leigh Peake who started me down the road to writing this book years and years ago. Thank you for believing I had something important to say and understanding that I couldn't be rushed. To my developmental editor Wendy Murray, who finally did "rush" me, words can't express how fortunate I feel to work alongside an editor as talented and as generous as you. You're a mentor to me in so many ways. To Patty Adams, production editor, I stand in awe at your ability to hold this all together when things were coming at us fast and furious and for helping me believe that we really did have things under control. To Rosanne Kurstedt, for your always sound advice and ability to sift through drafts and ideas for what's "right" and most helpful to teachers. A humble and heartfelt thanks to all of you.

Thank you to Heinemann Publishers and president Lesa Scott for giving me such a talented team to work with. Thank you Maura Sullivan for years and years of cheerleading and support. Thanks to all of you for believing in this project and backing it up unstintingly. You truly went above and beyond. From Doria Turner who kept sending me additional copies of books I owned but couldn't find, to Olivia MacDonald for overseeing the arduous job of procuring permissions, to marketers

Charles McQuillen and Elizabeth Valway for getting the word out, and manufacturing buyer Steve Bernier for coordinating a complex printing job on a challenging schedule.

To freelancer Judy Wallis for her work on the Study Guide, designer Joyce Weston for the gorgeous interior and cover design, typesetter Gina Poirier, and photographers Donnelly Marks and John Videler whose images are shown alongside some of my own classroom shots.

A very special thank-you to my family for always asking "How's the book coming?" and for allowing me to grumble when it wasn't and cheering me on whenever the muse paid a visit. To my wonderful children Ann and Paul, Matt and Clarisa, Danny and Jay, and my "adopted" daughter Ann Marie Corgill Ingram—thank you for helping me keep things in perspective and see the light at the end of the tunnel. I'm so proud of all of you and love you very much. To my grandchildren Jack, Sofia, Danny, and Eva for inspiring me and, most of all, for all the delicious snuggles and hugs. To Ted, the love of my life, thank you for fun times and happiness in the midst of it all.

—Sharon Taberski
September 2010

Credits, *continued from page viii*

Fig. 3-1: Figure from "Growth in Reading and How Children Spend Their Time Outside of School" by R. C. Anderson, P. T. Wilson and L. G. Fielding from *Reading Research Quarterly*, Summer 1998, 23(3), 285–303. Published by the International Reading Association. Reprinted by permission of the publisher.

Fig. 3-7: Excerpt from *Old Mother Hubbard's Hungry Family: An Adaptation of a Nursery Rhyme* by Carrie Smith, illustrated by Vincent Vigla. Copyright © 2008 by Benchmark Education Company, LLC. Published by Benchmark Education Company, LLC. Reprinted by permission of the publisher.

Fig. 3-8: "Pet Selection" from *Oh, Theodore! Guinea Pig Poems* by Susan Katz, illustrated by Stacey Schuett. Text copyright © 2007 by Susan Katz. Illustrations copyright © 2007 by Stacey Schuett. Published by Clarion Books, an imprint of Houghton Mifflin Harcourt Publishing Company. Reprinted by permission of the publisher.

Fig. 3-9: "Forever" from *Oh, Theodore! Guinea Pig Poems* by Susan Katz, illustrated

by Stacey Schuett. Text copyright © 2007 by Susan Katz. Illustrations copyright © 2007 by Stacey Schuett. Published by Clarion Books, an imprint of Houghton Mifflin Harcourt Publishing Company. Reprinted by permission of the publisher.

Fig. 3-13: Cover image from *Pran's Week of Adventure* by Tina Athaide, illustrated by Lisa Cinelli. Text copyright © 2003 by Tina Athaide. Illustrations copyright © 2003 by Lisa Cinelli. Published by Lee & Low Books, Inc. Reprinted by permission of the publisher.

Figs. 3-14 and 3-15: Excerpts from *Little Lion* by Carol Pugliano-Martin, illustrated by John Bennett. Copyright © 2004 by Benchmark Education Company, LLC. Published by Benchmark Education Company, LLC. Reprinted by permission of the publisher.

Fig. 4-6: Excerpt from *Author: A True Story* by Helen Lester. Copyright © 1997 by Helen Lester. Published by Houghton Mifflin Harcourt Publishing Company. Reprinted by permission of the publisher.

Fig. 5-1: Excerpt from *About Birds: A Guide for Children* by Cathryn Sill, illustrated by John Sill. Text Copyright ©1991, 1997 by Cathryn P. Sill. Illustrations copyright ©1991, 1997 by John C. Sill. Published by Peachtree Publishers. Reprinted by permission of the publisher.

Fig. 5-3: "Can I Have a Monkey?" from *Can I Have a Pet?* by Gwendolyn Hudson Hooks, illustrated by Lisa Cinelli. Text copyright © 2002 by Gwendolyn Hudson Hooks. Illustrations copyright © 2002 by Lisa Cinelli. Published by Lee & Low Books, Inc. Reprinted by permission of the publisher.

Fig. 5-4: Excerpt from *Adventures of Riley—Polar Bear Puzzle* by Amanda Lumry and Laura Hurwitz. Copyright © Eaglemont Press. Reprinted by permission of the publisher.

Fig. 5-5: Excerpt from *Hurty Feelings* by Helen Lester, illustrated by Lynn Munsinger. Text copyright © 2004 by Helen Lester. Illustrations copyright © 2004 by Lynn Munsinger. Published by Houghton Mifflin Harcourt Publishing Company. Reprinted by permission of the publisher.

continues on next page

Credits, *continued*

Fig. 5-8: Excerpt from *Horses!* by Gail Gibbons. Copyright © 2004 by Gail Gibbons. Published by Holiday House, Inc. Reprinted by permission of the publisher.

Fig. 6-5: Excerpt from *The Little Red Hen* retold by Brenda Parkes and Judith Smith. Illustrated by James Palmer. Copyright © 2009 Benchmark Education Company LLC. Published by Benchmark Education Company. Reprinted by permission of the publisher.

Fig. 6-7: Excerpt from *A Trip to the City* by Margaret Yatsevich Phinney, illustrated by Lokken Millis, from Mondo's Bookshop Literacy Program. Published by Mondo Publishing. Reprinted by permission of the publisher.

Fig. 6-14: Excerpt from *Johnny Appleseed: An American Tall Tale* by Gregory Brown, illustrated by Karen Leon. Copyright © 2007 Benchmark Education Company, LLC. Published by Benchmark Education Company, LLC. Reprinted by permission of the publisher.

Fig. 7-1: Excerpt from *Animals in Winter* by Henrietta Bancroft, illustrated by Helen K. Davie. Text copyright © 1997 by Henrietta Bancroft. Used by permission of HarperCollins Publishers.

Fig. 7-7 Excerpt from *Children Past and Present* by Matthew Frank. Copyright © 2009 by Benchmark Education Company LLC. Published by Benchmark Education Company. Reprinted by permission of the publisher.

Fig. 8-3: Excerpt from *Rainstorm* by Barbara Lehman. Copyright © 2007 by Barbara Lehman. Published by Houghton Mifflin Harcourt Publishing Company. Reprinted by permission of the publisher.

Fig. 8-5: "N" from *ABC* by Bruno Munari. Copyright © 1960, 2006 by Bruno Munari. Published by Chronicle Books. Reprinted by permission by the publisher.

Fig. 8-6: Excerpt from *AlphaOops! The Day Z Went First* by Althea Kontis, illustrated by Bob Kolar. Text copyright © 2006 by Alethea Kontis. Illustrations copyright © 2006 by Bob Kolar. Published by Candlewick Press. Reprinted by permission of the publisher.

Fig. 8-7: Excerpt from *The Worrywarts* by Pam Edwards, illustrated by Henry Cole. Text copyright © 1999 by Pamela Duncan Edwards. Illustrations copyright © 1999 by Henry Cole. Published by Harper-Collins Publishers. Reprinted by permission of the publisher.

Fig. 8-9: Excerpt from *The Bird Alphabet Book* by Jerry Pallotta, illustrated by Edgar Stewart. Text copyright © 1988 by Jerry Pallotta. Illustrations copyright © 1988 by Edgar Stewart. Published by Charlesbridge Publishing, Inc. Reprinted by permission of the publisher.

Fig. 8-10: Excerpt from *S is for Story: A Writer's Alphabet* by Esther Hershenhorn. Copyright © 2009 by Esther Hershenhorn. Published by Sleeping Bear Press, an imprint of Gale Cengage Learning. Reprinted by permission of Gale Cengage Learning.

Figs. 8-14 and 8-15: Cover image and "Words" from *Donkey-donkey* by Roger Duvoisin. Copyright © 2007 by Roger Duvoisin. Published by Random House. Reprinted by permission of the publisher.

Fig. 9-4: "Why Tornadoes Form" from *Storms* by Andrew Collins. Copyright © 2002 by The Hampton-Brown Company, Inc. Published by the National Geographic Society. Reprinted by permission of the publisher.

Fig. 9-5: Illustration from *Spotty* by Margret Rey, illustrated by H.A. Rey. Copyright © 1945, © renewed 1973 by Margret Rey. Published by Houghton Mifflin Harcourt Publishing Company. Reprinted by permission of the publisher.

Fig. 10-2: Excerpt from *Ducks!* by Gail Gibbons. Copyright © 2001 by Gail Gibbons. Published by Holiday House, Inc. Reprinted by permission of the publisher.

Fig. 10-4: Excerpt from *Corn Is Maize: The Gift of the Indians* by Aliki. Copyright © 1986 by Aliki Brandenberg. Published by HarperCollins Publishers. Reprinted by permission of the publisher.

Fig. 10-22: Excerpt from *A Week with Aunt Bea* by Judy Nayer, illustrated by Debbie Tilley, from Mondo's Bookshop Literacy Program. Text copyright © 1997 by Judy Nayer. Illustrations copyright © 1997 by Debbie Tilley. Published by Mondo Publishing. Reprinted by permission of the publisher.

Fig. 10-23: Excerpt from *Watch a Frog Grow* by Carol Pugliano-Martin. Copyright © 2007 Benchmark Education Company, LLC. Published by Benchmark Education Company, LLC. Reprinted by permission of the publisher.

Fig. 10-24: Excerpt from *Ants* by Mickey Daronco and Lori Presti. Copyright © 2001 Benchmark Education Company, LLC. Published by Benchmark Education Company, LLC. Reprinted by permission of the publisher.

Fig. 10-25: Excerpt from *Take a Bow, Winky Blue* by Pamela Jane, illustrated by Debbie Tilley, from Mondo's Bookshop Literacy Program. Text copyright © 1998 by Pamela Jane. Illustrations copyright © 1998 by Debbie Tilley. Published by Mondo Publishing. Reprinted by permission of the publisher.

Excerpt in Closing Thoughts: "A Lazy Thought" from *There Is No Rhyme For Silver* by Eve Merriam. Copyright © 1962, 1990 by Eve Merriam. Reprinted by permission of Marian Reiner.

Part One

....

Defining Our Teaching

What Really Lies at the Heart of Comprehension

 CHAPTER 1

Any book worth its salt is an argument. From the novelist's love story to the nonfiction author's account of a famous shipwreck, writers declare a deeply considered point of view. Their books are one big *This-is-how-I see-it* portrait and often explicitly or implicitly challenge other prevailing ideas. For me, I want to declare a way of teaching K–3 readers that is based on more than three decades of classroom experience as well as recent research. The feisty argument of this book that will help you teach? That teachers and children are trapped in a skewed metaphor of "five pillars" that grew out of the National Reading Panel Report of 2000, and as a result comprehension has been reduced to a pillar— a set of strategies—when it's actually what reading is all about.

I've been in too many classrooms across this country in the last couple of years, visited too many publishers' displays at state and national conferences, and had access to too many literacy programs where I see teachers continuing down the wrong instructional path as a result of this decade-old misrepresentation. So here's how I think the pillars notion we've bought into is distorted, and how with a little revision, the pillars of teaching reading become a pretty marvelous metaphor to have in mind as we plan and teach. Remember folks used to think the world is flat? Changing the pillars might not be as game-changing as showing the world is round, but I do think the paradigms we live by are powerful influences, and if we can correct the image, our daily teaching will come into focus and become sharper and more doable than we ever imagined.

Re-Envisioning the Pillars

Within a year of the National Reading Panel Report (2000), the professional literature and commercial teaching resources began referring to *The Five Pillars of Effective Reading Instruction*. While the report showed a strong research base for the following five areas of teaching reading, it never meant for these five to be championed at the expense of all other aspects of literacy, but wow, these five took hold—and their top billing in textbooks and educational resources made them even mightier. The five pillars heralded:

- phonemic awareness
- phonics
- fluency
- vocabulary
- comprehension

Don't get me wrong, each one of these five is important to children's reading. But it's an incomplete list and therefore problematic that these five became so sacred that other critical aspects of literacy got sidelined.

I remember when I first saw the five listed I almost fell off my chair. Imagine a doctor reading a report from the Surgeon General declaring the body's vital organs are: the brain, the heart, the collar bone, the kidneys, and the femur. *The collar bone? The femur? Are you kidding?* The Surgeon General would have been run out of town. The five pillars of reading forgot the lungs, so to speak—some of the essential experiences and skills children need in order to breathe as readers, including oral language development, writing, and background knowledge. And they elevated to pillar status skills, like phonemic awareness, that, although important, aren't pillar-worthy.

Granted, the panel's decision to include these five elements of reading instruction and not others rested on their mandate to only examine research having a broad empirical base. However, in doing so, they eliminated hundreds of reputable research studies and the knowledge and insight teachers have accumulated through years of experience.

In the New Thinking on the Pillars of Reading graphic, you will see how I re-envision the pillars to better reflect how children learn to read. The biggest change I make is that comprehension isn't a pillar at all—it's the overarching pediment, supported *atop* the pillars. Everything leads to the pinnacle—understanding what we read—and plays a part in children's comprehension development. And further, comprehension is far more than just comprehension strategies teaching, far more than the formula of phonemic awareness, plus phonics, plus fluency… = reading approach.

In this book, I offer the re-envisioned pillars to help you create a structure for teaching reading and writing that develops children's comprehension organically

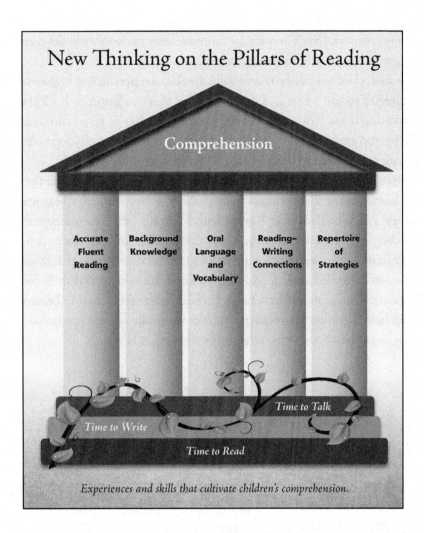

Experiences and skills that cultivate children's comprehension.

rather than in the hyper overdrive we've been experiencing for several years as a result of embracing "the big 5" with all its attendant pressure to get kids farther, faster. I share practical ideas so you'll know how to fill your days with rich literacy experiences. You'll find dozens of activities and practices, schedules, favorite books, photos of classrooms and students, management ideas, sample lessons—all of the details you need to teach reading in K–3 in a simplified, streamlined way.

I'll show you how to slow down, to not worry about checking children's reading rates constantly, or think that if you aren't teaching comprehension strategies 24/7, you're not teaching reading well. In too many classrooms I hear stories of how children call the fast readers the good readers, perpetuating a damaging misconception. In too many classrooms I get the sense that children are using the lingo of comprehension without truly engaging with and understanding the texts they are reading. We've all witnessed students rotely recording the text-to-text and text-to-self connections they've made, with all the thoughtfulness of writing "I will not run in the hallway" a hundred times. This is not what strategy-based instruction was ever intended to be.

In part, the distortion occurred because the pressures in education in recent years have not allowed teachers the "think" time to factor in the practicality and developmental appropriateness of their practices. As a result, our youngest readers, in grades K–3, are too often asked to apply strategies that are better suited for older, more mature readers. (See Chapter 10 for more about schoolwide developmentally appropriate comprehension strategy instruction.)

To be sure, children need to eventually develop a repertoire of higher-order cognitive strategies to use when and if needed, and this can begin in K–3 classrooms. But showcasing these strategies—to the extent that they're given too much weight and take up too much time—can distract us from teaching children *all* the skills and strategies they need to become better, comprehending readers.

Children in K–3 should leave school with minds brimming with all the information they learned from that great ocean animal book they read together, or smiling at the memory of Amelia Bedelia or Kevin Henkes' spunky Lily. And teachers should end the day feeling confident that children's interactions with Lily, Amelia Bedelia, and the great white shark (along with the comprehension instruction they so artfully embedded) have enhanced their children's developing reading achievement and their comprehension. These experiences should have brought children one step closer to becoming motivated, confident, self-improving readers, who automatically call up appropriate strategies when they sense their connection to a book's meaning is faltering.

Something to Consider

In 2009 Peter Dewitz, Jennifer Jones, and Susan Leahy published a study in *Reading Research Quarterly* called "Comprehension Strategy Instruction in Core Reading Programs" where they examined five of the most widely used core programs for how they recommended comprehension be taught in grades 3, 4, and 5. While each of these programs claimed to be "research-based," the study's findings showed that comprehension strategy instruction was implemented far *differently* in the core programs than in the original research. For the most part, the core programs:

- didn't provide for the same degree or amount of independent and guided practice as the original research
- didn't consistently follow the gradual release of responsibility model where teachers first demonstrate in whole-group settings and then gradually relinquish control to the point where students are applying the target strategy on their own

- neglected to consistently follow the guidelines for explicit instruction, which insist that teachers relate one strategy to another and make clear their impact on learning to read

Each of these aberrations is likely to impact the program's effectiveness and compromise children's developing ability to comprehend text.

Although Dewitz, Jones, and Leahy studied teaching and learning in the intermediate grades, we can extrapolate that similar use of core programs and distortions of the metacognitive strategies occur in the lower grades as well. Lost in translation are adequate time for independent and guided practice; explicit teaching of skills and strategies in a way that immediately highlights for children their connectedness to real literature; and scaffolded comprehension strategy instruction so that they carry it into their independent reading.

Literacy Essentials That Meet Children's Fundamental Needs as Readers, Writers, and Thinkers

In this book I offer a blueprint for a simpler and more developmentally appropriate approach to comprehension instruction. It's one that embraces a full range of experiences, skills, and strategies that lead not just to learning a set of meta-cognitive strategies to apply to texts, but to a richer, more genuine, reading experience.

In the chapters that follow I organize classroom routines and lessons around these fundamental needs of children:

> + **Children need us to be their advocates.** (See *Chapter 2: Five Child-Centered Principles to Guide You*)

I suspect that if you're reading this book, I'm preaching to the choir, but think about it: students in grades K–3 are between five- and nine-years-old. That's very young when you step back and consider how recently they were preschoolers just learning the alphabet. At home they're still getting lost with race cars and dollhouses, slumbering with stuffed animals and their nightlight on, and yet in school we expect them to read complex texts.

For example, asking all emergent readers to reach a fixed reading level by the end of kindergarten that we *know* is unlikely and inappropriate simply because that's where our core reading program sets the bar is harmful and demoralizing. Asking struggling first graders to take a fluency assessment every two weeks that bears little resemblance to the books they're reading in class—no pictures, no color, no supportive language structures, nothing that scaffolds their reading and makes them feel successful and motivated to read more—erodes students' self-confidence and makes them pull back. This is especially true of our English language learners.

If we truly want to differentiate instruction, then small groups and one-to-one teaching are the way to go. And it is simply wrong to withhold the precious time students need to delight in reading books from their just-right bag that will help them consolidate the skills and strategies they're trying to acquire because we've used up all our time with lengthy whole-group instruction.

At some point we're going to have to take a stand and truly stand up for children. We know that many of the things we're being asked to do in the name of "raising the scores" is neither in our children's best interests nor good for them. Therefore we must acquire knowledge of effective and sensible teaching practices and make our voices heard.

> + **Children need ample opportunities to read widely and across genres, to write texts for others to comprehend, and to engage in thoughtful conversation.** (*See Chapters 3, 4, and 5: Time to Read, Write, and Talk*)

Children need time to read, write, and talk. Without these basic experiences, the skills and strategies we so diligently try to teach cannot take root and grow. In "Effective

Practices for Developing Reading Comprehension," Nell K. Duke and P. David Pearson (2002) maintain:

> [C]omprehension instruction should be *balanced*. By this we mean that good comprehension instruction includes both explicit instruction in specific comprehension strategies and a great deal of time and opportunity for actual reading, writing, and discussion of text. (p. 207)

It's folly to think that it is sufficient to demonstrate reading skills and strategies without also giving children time to try them out on their own. If we want children to develop as readers, they must have abundant opportunities to write texts for others to comprehend. Children need to experience the meaning-making nature of written text from the inside out, empowering them to become more insightful and skilled readers. They also need to talk about books and pieces they're writing with other readers and writers to hear different points of view and ways of expressing ideas and information.

- **Children need to read accurately and fluently with comprehension.** *(See Chapter 6: Accurate Fluent Reading)*

We want students to read words accurately with appropriate speed, intonation, and emphasis so that they understand what they're reading. We want them to laugh at the funny parts and be moved to tears when things go badly for the characters. We want our young readers to learn new information about the world and ultimately about themselves. In her chapter "Fluency in the Classroom: Strategies for Whole-Class and Group Work," Melanie Kuhn (2003) reports:

> There is a general consensus that fluent reading not only incorporates automatic and accurate word recognition and expressive rendering of text, but it is also likely to be a contributing factor in a reader's ability to construct meaning from what is being read. (p. 128)

To achieve this level of engagement and understanding, children must develop accurate fluent reading, as it has everything to do with comprehension. Our brain has a limited amount of mental capacity in its working memory, and if most of it is directed at sounding out words, there isn't enough left to understand the ideas and information the author is trying to communicate.

- **Children need to acquire background knowledge to bring to texts they read.** *(See Chapter 7: Background Knowledge)*

Background knowledge, as I refer to it in this book, is our knowledge of the natural world that readers bring to text, a subpart of their all-inclusive prior knowledge. It's their firsthand experiences about a topic, the information they've acquired through reading and content-area studies, and the attitudes and opinions regarding this background knowledge that they hold. Because learning is actually connecting what we know with what we're learning, background knowledge plays a critical role in children's reading success.

In an *American Educator* article "How Knowledge Helps: It Speeds and Strengthens Reading Comprehension, Learning—and Thinking," cognitive scientist Daniel T. Willingham (2006) asserts:

> ...[B]ackground knowledge makes one a better reader in two ways. First, it means that there is a greater probability that you will have the knowledge to successfully make the necessary inferences to understand.... Second, rich background knowledge means that you will rarely need to reread a text in an effort to consciously search for connections in the text. (pp. 32–33)

The more a child knows about a topic, the easier it is to read, understand, and remember the important ideas. New information gets integrated into the child's existing understandings or schemata. For example, when a child first experiences or reads about a ladybug—when someone tells her about them, or she finds one herself, or when she sees a picture or reads a book—a "hook" forms. A concept is now in her brain. From then on, whenever she experiences ladybugs, either firsthand or vicariously, new information latches on to that hook. This becomes her background knowledge—the very knowledge that makes it easier for her to read and learn new information.

- **Children need to extend their oral language and vocabulary, and capitalize on how they enhance reading comprehension.** *(See Chapter 8: Oral Language and Vocabulary)*

Oral language, as it relates to reading comprehension, involves children hearing elaborative language that is spoken and read aloud. But most importantly, it is the spoken language of students as they articulate their own ideas and opinions and build their understanding of text through discussion. In *Exploring the Literature of Fact: Children's Nonfiction Trade Books in the Elementary School*, Barbara Moss (2002) explains:

> Literacy learning is socially constructed. Students do not learn to be literate in isolation, but through social interaction with others. By talking about the text they read, students collaboratively construct meanings around text. (p. 126)

Developing students' oral language and building their vocabulary go hand in hand. As children share their ideas out loud and hear how their classmates respond, they refine their understanding of how words convey meaning, transport information, and communicate ideas, and that talk lies at the very heart of comprehension and learning. Their growing vocabulary enables them to understand passages that would be incomprehensible without knowing the meaning of individual words and concepts.

> • **Children need to appreciate not only how reading impacts writing, but how their experience as writers enables them to adopt an insider's stance as they read.** *(See Chapter 9: Reading-Writing Connections)*

Reading and writing nourish each another and, in my experience, it's actually easier to teach them as mirror images than as separate entities. Reading-writing connections are the implicit and explicit relationships between these two reciprocal processes.

Children who read acquire knowledge and skills they can bring to texts they write. Through wide reading across genres, children gain information and new ideas, pick up on text features, appreciate the power of words to persuade, and understand the power of helpful phrases writers use to transition from one idea to the next. A child's stance as a reader trying to understand the written word makes him more aware that his job as a writer is to make *his* ideas understandable to others.

Likewise, when children are engaged in writing texts to share with others, they become more attentive readers. They notice punctuation, appreciate how a text is organized to help access information, and marvel at an author's word choice and how it helps create an image in their minds. The 2010 Carnegie Corporation report, *Writing to Read: Evidence for How Writing Can Improve Reading*, concurs:

> … [H]aving students spend more time writing has a positive impact on their reading, increasing how well students comprehend texts written by others. (p. 5)

Just as reading influences children's writing, writing influences students' reading comprehension in powerful ways.

> • **Children need to acquire a repertoire of meta-cognitive strategies to help them navigate difficult texts and reconstruct meaning when it breaks down. These strategies should be presented in a developmentally appropriate and systematic way throughout the elementary grades.** *(See Chapter 10: Repertoire of Strategies)*

Children need to know that when comprehension falters or when they face a challenge, there are things they can do to get through the rough spots. As Nell K. Duke and P. David Pearson (2002) advise in "Effective Practices for Developing Reading Comprehension":

> A large volume of work indicates that we can help students acquire the strategies and processes used by good readers—and that this improves their overall comprehension of text, both the texts used to teach the strategies and texts they read on their own in the future. (p. 206)

Thus, having a repertoire of strategies to rely on greatly enhances children's overall reading enjoyment and comprehension.

Ideally, schools should decide upon a repertoire of six or so kid-friendly, meta-cognitive strategies, e.g., visualize to experience, ask questions and wonder, set a purpose for reading, that they want their students to learn by the time they graduate, and then determine how to teach these strategies in developmentally appropriate ways across the grades. This type of schoolwide planning is the best way to ensure a cohesive curriculum.

In kindergarten and first grade, teachers can demonstrate these comprehension strategies as opportunities arise naturally during read-aloud and shared reading (always keeping the pleasure of book reading and literature center stage), and invite students to participate in this whole-class experience, knowing that some of these same strategies will resurface during guided reading.

Second- and third-grade teachers ought to plan focus strategy units where students attend to one strategy per two-to-three-week unit, with an opportunity to practice these strategies on their own and come together as a class to process how it went. Likewise, fourth- and fifth-grade teachers should offer integrated strategy units to help students become savvy about when to use these strategies and how they work in combination.

More than anything, we need to simplify comprehension instruction and, in doing so, increase its effectiveness. For not only must the text make sense, but our teaching must make sense as well.

> ✦ **Children need to engage in an assortment of carefully selected learning experiences presented in whole-class, small-group, and one-to-one settings.**

Just as it's essential that students integrate their use of comprehension strategies, deciding which one or combination will help them gain meaning that has been lost or is difficult to discern, teachers need to select a handful of practices from the thousands out there and do them well. They must reflect on what their students need to learn and match this up with practices to help get them there.

In addition to the dozens of highly engaging ideas and foundational practices described in Chapters 1–10, in Chapters 6–10—the chapters that focus on five key aspects of comprehension—you will also find a section called **Effective Practices**. From letter and sound searches, to Ta-Da Publishing Books, to content-area literacy centers, these effective practices, indicated by the tab on the page, can help enhance your literacy instruction repertoire.

Effective Practice: Content-Area Literacy Centers

What Are Content-Area Literacy Centers and Why Are They Important?

[body text]

Figure 7-8. Millie Velasquez's Dinosaur Center

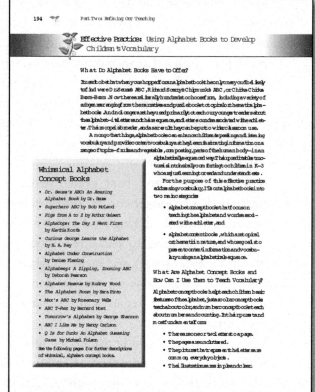

Effective Practice: Using Alphabet Books to Develop Children's Vocabulary

What Do Alphabet Books Have to Offer?

[body text]

Whimsical Alphabet Concept Books

- *Dr. Seuss's ABC: An Amazing Alphabet Book* by Dr. Seuss
- *Superhero ABC* by Bob McLeod
- *Pigs from A to Z* by Arthur Geisert
- *AlphaOops: The Day Z Went First* by Alethia Kontis
- *Curious George Learns the Alphabet* by H. A. Rey
- *Alphabet Under Construction* by Denise Fleming
- *Alphabeep: A Zipping, Zooming ABC* by Deborah Pearson
- *Alphabet Rescue* by Audrey Wood
- *The Alphabet Room* by Sara Pinto
- *Max's ABC* by Rosemary Wells
- *ABC T-Rex* by Bernard Most
- *Tomorrow's Alphabet* by George Shannon
- *ABC I Like Me* by Nancy Carlson
- *Q Is for Duck: An Alphabet Guessing Game* by Michael Folsom

See the following pages for further description of whimsical, alphabet concept books.

What Are Alphabet Concept Books and How Can I Use Them to Teach Vocabulary?

[body text]

These are some Effective Practices highlighted in later chapters.

Effective Practice: Idea Books

What's an Idea Book?

[body text]

Why Idea Books and Not Writer's Notebooks?

[body text]

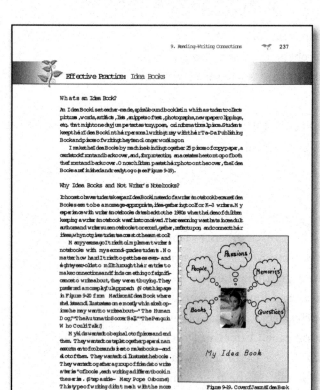

My Idea Book

Figure 9-19. Cover of Jason's Idea Book

Effective Practice: Ta-Da Publishing Books

What Are Ta-Da Publishing Books?

[body text]

How Do I Get Started with the Ta-Da Books?

[body text]

Julia's Publishing Book 2003–2004

Figure 9-26. Cover of Julia's Ta-Da Book

Cultivating Readers

The title of this book, *Comprehension from the Ground Up*, and its companion DVD, *Lessons from the Ground Up* (2011), express my conviction that to develop young readers who understand texts and enjoy reading we have to recognize that comprehension is like a bright green shoot that grows after we nourish children's varied experiences with text. Reading, writing, talking (and the skills and strategies involved in accurate fluent reading, background knowledge, oral language and vocabulary, reading-writing connections, and a repertoire of strategies)—they all cultivate comprehension.

In each chapter I want you to take what I say and think about your students. Not just your class as a whole, but about particular students—those who amaze you with their reading progress and the ones who keep you up at night with concern.

Children today are learning to read, write, ride bikes, do cartwheels, and ask questions in a world that is more anxious than it was a decade ago. Many adults are not as sure-footed or optimistic as they were in earlier generations, and so all the more reason to teach in a manner that is nurturing and highly responsive to each child.

Children need us teachers on so many levels. Let's not forget to be warm and funny and model our own enthusiasm for reading, writing, and thinking. Sure, we can be rigorous, but that doesn't mean rigorous in our service to external test scores. It means rigorous in our service to children, to using our expertise to know where each of them is as a reader, a writer, and a thinker and where to take them next.

No matter how you're teaching now, I assure you the practices I outline in this book are worth the effort of taking them on. In time you will become more accomplished at integrating them into a cohesive whole. The same slow and steady approach to teaching I advocate in the next chapter also applies to your professional development: give yourself the time to grow at a pace that is right for you.

 CHAPTER **2** The Text, Our Teaching—
They've Got to Make Sense

When I was twelve I wanted to wear lipstick. My father refused to allow this, stating simply: "If you wear lipstick when you're twelve, what are you going to want to do when you're thirteen?" As annoying as this pronouncement was to me as an adolescent, I keep returning to its intrinsic wisdom: It's better to take things slowly, better to savor the "now" of where you are and anticipate steps along the way, than to rush headlong toward a destination without pausing to see how things will add up.

When I meet with families at my first curriculum meeting of the year, I share with them this "slow-and-steady" conviction. Gathered in the classroom awaiting a description of how the year will unfold, most families hope I'll be nurturing with their kids, get them to work hard and, most of all, move them *up* considerably in reading levels.

So I get right to the point: "I know you want your child to become a better reader. So do I. I also know that you want him to move quickly to higher and higher reading levels." I pause for emphasis, for here, quite literally, comes the punch line: "But it's my job to stop him." A few parents wince as if I've punched them in the gut, but most of them are still smiling, taking notes, whispering to one another to see if perhaps they misheard me. (She couldn't have said *that!*) They look at me cautiously, waiting for me to say, "Just joking." Instead I repeat: "You want your children to get to higher and higher levels, faster and earlier, but it's my job to stop them."

To explain my rationale, I show the families an overhead of a running record I took when reading with second-grader Emmy, who asked for a conference at the start of the year to see if a book she wanted for her independent book bag was too hard. Emmy's running record showed that on the first three pages, she miscued on two proper names. She also failed to look all the way through to the end of several of the words, substituting words that were close but not exact matches. (See Figure 2-1 for two pages of the text Emmy was reading and the running record notations.)

Emmy had developed a pattern of not looking all the way through to the end of words in first grade—in *my* first-grade class, in fact! And I earnestly tried to help her overcome this habit. However, at least now in second grade, I could take some comfort in the fact that she was looking through *more* of the word. Emmy was on her way—slowly and steadily.

As the families and I reviewed Emmy's running record, I explained that, considering two of her miscues were proper name-related, her word accuracy was close enough to the 97–99 percent range required of independent reading text for me to have her continue reading this book, perhaps even giving her more books of the same type. That is—had I not dialogued with her about the meaning of the text and learned that Emmy was having trouble *comprehending* what she read.

Figure 2-1. Pages from Beezy at Bat

Just how much difficulty was Emmy having? A significant amount, I explain to the families. It was a funny book. Author Megan McDonald hoped to make the reader laugh, but Emmy didn't think the book was funny. In fact, when I asked her to indicate the "nuts" to which Mr. Gumm was referring, she pointed to the basket of nuts on the porch, not recognizing that Mr. Gumm was teasing Beezy and Gran, calling *them* "nuts." Emmy couldn't enjoy this story, as McDonald intended, because she didn't understand what she was reading. The book was too hard.

The families, eager to better understand my thinking, shower me with more questions. They aren't ready to accept that students like Emmy, perhaps even their own children, must take their time to progress through the stages on the reading continuum. I explain why it's important for children's reading to plateau before ascending higher, why it's important for them to read widely and across genres, and how this will ultimately support comprehension. And because some of these books may be easier for them to decode, they can put more of their attention into understanding meaning.

The families slowly begin to understand my rationale. I see it in their expressions. Over the weeks and months after this meeting, I know I will have to keep reassuring them that their children will "get there," slowly and steadily. Some parents will never relax, I know, because the current for speed and instant results is running fast in our society, but we still need to advocate for this approach with our students.

Take It Slow and Steady

Our job is to do what's best for children and not give in to wayward trends. We must set our sights on deep, sustained learning, where transfer of knowledge, skills, and strategies are the hallmark of success. We must gauge our success not merely on the level at which our children read, but whether or not they choose to read for their own pleasure.

This same meaning-making imperative that applies to Emmy's reading also holds true for our teaching in general. My resolve in following this standard has been inspired and buttressed by the words of Myrtle Simpson, best known for her work with the New Zealand Department of Education and her book *Reading in Junior Classes*. Simpson (1985) writes:

> A child's school day should make sense. It should be about something. Ideally, the various components of the day should work together building upon one another for some purpose.

> A teacher's day should also make sense. Teachers who can see a wholeness and simplicity in their teaching have an easier task of organizing their day than those who are frustrated or intimidated by what they interpret as the increasing complexity of the curriculum demanded of them.

While the importance of making sense, of seeking wholeness and simplicity in our teaching, rings true, there's little doubt that the curriculum has indeed become even more complex than it was in 1985 when Simpson wrote these words.

Too much is being asked of us these days. There's too much stuff in our teaching lives—too many assessments, too many forms to fill out, too many meetings to attend, too much material to cover, too many skills and strategies to teach, too many emails to respond to. Too much, too fast. We're led to believe that more is better, but in our heart of hearts we know that's simply not so. It's time to slow down, think about what we're trying to accomplish, and do that well.

Five Child-Centered Principles to Guide Your Teaching

Toward this end, I've identified five principles that guide my decision making and my interactions with students. They support my planning and give me the courage to prioritize my teaching to make room for what's most important.

1. It's Better to Do Fewer Things Well Than Many Things Superficially

When I visit classrooms I'm troubled by the frenzied pace I see teachers trying to keep. They hurry from activity to activity, frustrated by their inability to accomplish all that "needs to be done." They agonize over how they're going to fit in all their guided reading groups, move their struggling readers to higher reading levels, and challenge students who are already doing well. They test and retest students, yet haven't the time to analyze the data they've so painstakingly collected to figure out how to best put it to use. They move from one reading unit to the next, from one dis-jointed writing project to the next, yet sense that while they're doing things—lots of things—they may not be doing many of them very well. This feeling of failure is unfortunate because it is ultimately our successes, not our failures, that inspire each of us to do more and be better—whether it's teaching or learning. This is especially true for our youngest, most impressionable students.

You may already be familiar with the teaching goals I describe in my book *On Solid Ground: Strategies for Teaching Reading K–3* (Taberski 2000). Rather than use a scope and sequence, which I've internalized over the years, I prefer to plan and structure my teaching around several comprehensive goals—goals that serve the needs of students *across* the elementary grades—and then flesh out how to best achieve them with my particular class of students. The following box outlines my reading and writing goals.

My Goals for *Readers*	My Goals for *Writers*
• I want children to acquire skills and strategies for figuring out words and understanding text.	• I want children to acquire skills and strategies to communicate information and ideas.
• I want children to become more skilled reading a variety of genres.	• I want children to become more skilled writing in a variety of genres.
• I want children to write and talk about what they read.	• I want children to read and talk about what they write.
• I want children to love to read, choosing to read when they don't have to.	• I want children to love to write, recognizing its purposes and the power it can hold in their lives.

The fact that I have only four goals for reading and four for writing, and not forty, doesn't concern me in the least because each goal embodies so many others. This is how our brain works—flooded with too much data, it chunks information so that we have the mental capacity to use what we know in meaningful ways. I can recall these four goals when I'm conferring with students, when I'm reading aloud, when I'm ordering books for the classroom, when I'm meeting with families, when I'm designing my classroom. Four are memorable in a way that forty could never be, and therefore they're functional.

Embedded within each goal are numerous objectives (subgoals) that surface as I reflect on these four main goals and the instructional options I have available to achieve them. For example, the planning web in Figure 2-2 details some of the skills, strategies, and teaching practices I might choose to help children read a variety of informational text (part of Goal 2), but I'm under no illusion that I can, or even should, address them all.

One might argue that, reformatted, this web would resemble a more traditional scope and sequence. But there are real differences.

+ First, a web does not imply a linear progression as does a scope and sequence. Instead it invites us to factor in children's needs, interests, and abilities in deciding what to teach, and when.

+ Second, my web includes not only skills and strategies children need to acquire, but the teaching practices I might use to help them get there. It paints an entire teaching-learning landscape from which I can pick and choose where it's best to position myself on any given day.

Note: If you're a novice teacher or not confident taking on "goal-setting" on your own, you might start with your Common Core Standards or whichever language arts standards you're using and work from there. For example, your standards document might set as an objective to "help children recognize key ideas and details in informational text," and so you'd list "reading," "writing," "talking," "content areas," etc.,

It's ALL About Comprehension

Comprehension is the overarching goal that gives direction to each of these four reading and four writing goals. My goal is for kids to understand texts they read and make sense of texts they write, not become adept at every skill or strategy along the way.

It doesn't matter if students arrive at improved comprehension by directly acquiring a particular set of skills and strategies, by becoming savvy readers and writers of a variety of genres, by learning about reading from the writing they do, or simply because they love to read and write and so they read and write frequently.

The point is that it's all about comprehension. Each goal, each strategy, each skill, each facet of our teaching should be helping students refine their ability to make sense of what they read and write. Helping them becoming better at making meaning is my purpose, my primary focus.

Planning Web for Subgoal of Goal 2

I want kids to become more skilled reading informational text.

Instead of starting with a to-do list, I prefer to web various ideas and practices as an array of possible ways to achieve this goal. From here I select the ones that are most likely to help children achieve the end-of-year district and state standards.

Reading
- Expose kids to nonfiction during read-aloud, shared and guided reading, independent reading, and writing
- Different types of nonfiction texts, i.e., expository, narratives, blended texts
- Interest surveys
- Expose kids to a range of topics (content-area and personal favorites)
- Nonfiction text features (use large formatted books for read-aloud so kids can see text features up close)

Background Knowledge
- Build background knowledge and academic vocabulary
- Help children access their background and prior knowledge
- Remember and remind children: The more they know the more they'll understand
- Tons of nonfiction in the classroom and time to read them

Writing
- Use mentor texts for nonfiction writing, e.g., topics, organization, text features
- Mini-lessons to encourage kids to read about what they're writing and write about what they're reading
- Let kids write about what they're learning throughout the day
- 50% of what kids write should be nonfiction
- Illustrations convey a lot of information

Talking
- Engage kids in conversations about nonfiction topics they're reading about or ones you're studying together
- Introduce fact logs and then encourage them to write more, illustrate, and "say more" as they share with classmates
- Concept circles as an alternative to literature circles
- Be sure to include nonfiction titles in book talks

Skills, Strategies, and Practices

Skills and Strategies
- Main ideas and details
- Ask and get kids to ask analytical "how" and "why" questions
- Help kids consider their purpose for reading nonfiction
- Attend to how texts are organized and their text features
- Demonstrate how to use background knowledge to infer

Classroom Organization
- Cluster books by topic
- 50% of books should be nonfiction and a large number of them expository
- Attractively display nonfiction texts
- Assemble nonfiction companion texts to accompany children's guided reading selections

Time
- Give kids lots of time to read, write, and talk about what they're learning
- Encourage nonfiction reading at home, trips to library, and bookstore visits
- Send short articles home for families to read about the importance of background knowledge
- Encourage families to read nonfiction to and with their children

Content Areas
- Integrate content-area topics into the literacy block
- Field trips
- Reader's Theater
- Be sure to select high-quality books on content-area topics—those without concept and academic vocabulary overload
- Nonfiction books about content-area topics for independent reading

Figure 2-2. Here are some skills, strategies, and practices that help children become more skilled reading nonfiction.

as sub-categories on your web. As you fill in ideas for each category of how you might achieve this, you'll recognize the connection among these aspects of literacy, and how a skill that traditionally comes under "reading" can also be addressed effectively during writing and as children talk about what they've learned.

With this approach I'm not weighed down or distracted by decontextualized or misappropriated "outcomes" that may or may not match the needs of my students. Instead, I can be more fully responsive to what I see students need. In their 2007 updated edition of *Grand Conversations: Literature Groups in Action*, Ralph Peterson and Mary Ann Eeds make the case for responsive teaching:

> We don't work out in advance what is going to happen when we teach. Instead, we prepare ourselves carefully to respond to what might happen within a living encounter. We rely on timing and our ability to seize the moment, always realizing that if one moment passes unrecognized, another is on its way. Responses flow out of what we believe and know. (p. 17)

Common Core State Standards

As this book goes to press the new Common Core State Standards have recently been released across the country, and none of us know just how they'll play out or where they'll take us. Educators are returning to school after summer break and finding these new standards awaiting them with their new crop of students. What these standards represent is a set of desired outcomes. We can only hope that these goals will be implemented with more sensible nuance and realism than we experienced with No Child Left Behind. To achieve these outcomes, schools and teachers need to be realistically resourced, and incentives need to be supportive, not punitive.

And just as we should not lose sight of our end goals, we must never forget a basic tenet of teaching and learning: *We need to start where the children are* if we are to have any hope of moving them farther along. We can't ignore the fact that many of our students live in poor, distressed households that find it difficult to impart the rich background of language and experience that economically advantaged families can more readily provide. It's difficult to learn when you're hungry or afraid to walk the streets of your neighborhood. We can't ignore

that children from immigrant families will often first have to struggle in school learning English, and that it will take time for them to acquire the academic language, concepts, and the confidence they'll need to succeed. We can't ignore the fact that the special needs of some children are quite real and must be addressed honestly and fully. All these considerations, along with questions of how attainable the standards actually are (either set too high or too sparse) for our particular population of students as a whole will have to be factored into our efforts if we are to successfully educate our children.

We must also remember that while the Common Core State Standards set the goals, they are not a prescription for how to achieve them. That's up to us. We need to use our talents, our knowledge of best practice, and our experience to bring them to life. This book offers an array of conceptual and practical tools to help teachers in the early grades achieve success in one section of the standards—literacy. Whatever success we achieve here provides the grounding for further success in the upper grades and the gateway to the broader fields of learning defined in the Common Core State Standards.

Some Questions to Consider as You Reflect on Your Goals

- Can I articulate my goals so that they're memorable when selecting books for the classroom, talking with families, conferring with students, etc.?
- Are these goals reflected in my classroom environment, my materials, and my schedule?
- How might each of the balanced literacy components help me achieve these goals?

- How will I know whether or not my students have achieved them?
- Do I understand how these goals incorporate the skills and strategies students need to acquire and that I need to teach?
- What practices might I need to eliminate so that I have more time for what's most important?

In the following box are some questions regarding the several goals you'll hopefully set for yourself and for your students. Take time to reflect on one or two of them. Read through them and discuss several of them with a colleague. Or bring them with you to your next staff meeting to get folks thinking about where they're headed or where they want to be.

2. Balanced Literacy Is a Menu, Not a Checklist

Imagine yourself sitting down to dine at a fine restaurant. You've been saving your appetite all day so you can enjoy this meal. The waiter hands you a menu and when you look inside you can hardly believe your good fortune. Entrée upon entrée of delectable dishes, including many of your favorites. How will you ever decide? However, you know you have to choose.

So, when the waiter returns to take your order, you select an appetizer and an entrée (and hold off until later to tell him that you'll most definitely order the key lime pie for dessert). Although you would have also loved to sample other dishes, you look forward to returning to this restaurant another time to try them out.

Balanced Literacy

Now imagine yourself opening a different menu—a balanced literacy menu. Only this time you don't know it's a menu because all the reading items are *listed* on one side and all the writing items are *listed* on the other (Figure 2-3). The reading and writing components aren't clustered under categories, such as "whole-group activities," "small-group activities," "one-to-one experiences" as were the appetizers, entrées,

Reading	Writing
Read-Aloud	Modeled Writing
Shared Reading	Shared Writing
Word Study	Interactive Writing
Guided Reading	Spelling and Conventions
Small Skill & Strategy Groups	Small-Group Writing
Book Talks/Literature Circles	Independent Writing
Independent Reading	Writing Conferences
Partner Reading	
Reading Conferences	

Figure 2-3. A List of Reading and Writing Balanced Literacy Components

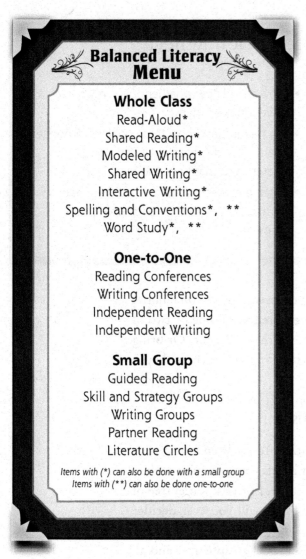

Balanced Literacy Menu

Whole Class
Read-Aloud*
Shared Reading*
Modeled Writing*
Shared Writing*
Interactive Writing*
Spelling and Conventions*, **
Word Study*, **

One-to-One
Reading Conferences
Writing Conferences
Independent Reading
Independent Writing

Small Group
Guided Reading
Skill and Strategy Groups
Writing Groups
Partner Reading
Literature Circles

Items with (*) can also be done with a small group
Items with (**) can also be done one-to-one

Figure 2-4. A Menu of Whole-Class, Small-Group, and One-to-One Experiences

and desserts. And so you perceive it as a checklist to make your way through, item by item. After all, aren't lists like that?

With your anxiety rising at the magnitude before you, you hope that you could do a read-aloud in 10 minutes if you read really quickly (check), a shared reading in 15 minutes keeping the same pace (check), guided reading groups in 45 minutes, if you really move the kids along, next, next, next (check, check, check). And then you try to do the same thing with writing.

And all the while you're thinking to yourself, "This is madness." Well you're right. It is madness to think that you can do each and every item on the list, or even many of them, in rapid succession, and do them well. You can't. Just as you couldn't eat all you would have liked from your dining menu, you have to see the various components of your balanced literacy program as a menu (Figure 2-4), not a checklist, and select several practices each day (some whole group, some small group, and some one-to-one) that will help you achieve the four or five comprehensive goals that you've set. *That's* how we're nourished, *that's* how children are nourished. The "I'll-have-all-of-the-above" approaches don't work. What works is to make informed selections each day on behalf of our kids.

3. The Parts of Our Balanced Literacy Should Work Together as a System

I'm all for systematic teaching. However, not the kind that lays out for teachers what must be taught and in what order to teach it. I'm convinced that neither our mind nor our teaching work well when confined to a micromanaged and linear progression. Rather, our teaching must be systematic in the sense of an organic whole of interrelated parts that can be adjusted as needed to support our desired outcomes.

An eloquent metaphor to keep in mind for growing our instruction day to day and week to week is the synergistic farming method that Native Americans developed to grow corn, beans, and squash. Instead of planting each crop in a separate field, they planted a corn plant, a squash plant, and a bean plant together in a mound of earth called a *milpa* (see Figure 2-5). They did this because they learned from experience how they worked together: The corn stalk grows tall and becomes the "pole" around which the beans twine; the flat, wide, and low-to-the-ground squash leaves help to keep water from evaporating from the soil; and the beans give off nutrients both above and below the ground.

Here are two examples of being systematic in our literacy teaching:

+ During a conference with Pierce, I noticed that his reading was choppy. So I explained that he needed to "chunk words into phrases" instead of reading word by word. I knew that I had a lot more teaching to do when he asked point-blank, "but how do you know…how do you know which words go together?" (Hmm…I thought. How does a six- or seven-year-old know?)

  I made a few attempts to show him how to read his text fluently by running my finger under the phrase instead of pointing to each word. I decided that I needed more time and a different venue to get this point across to Pierce and others in class needing this same instruction.

  So the next day in a mini-lesson related to a big book we'd been reading, I described to the class what had occurred during Pierce's conference and used this shared reading opportunity to demonstrate how to read fluently and chunk words together. I dramatically swept my pointer under the phrases, emphasizing the phrases rather than single words. I could tell that Pierce (and others) seemed to be getting the idea this time, but knew that in order for the children to master this skill, I needed to redemonstrate this many times over and provide them with opportunities to read from their own bag of just-right books.

+ By anticipating an upcoming social studies unit on New York City, its geography, neighborhoods, and how it's changed over time, I began reading aloud books on that topic during our literacy block the week prior to starting the unit to provide students with background to build on, instead of waiting to introduce the children to the topic on day one of the unit. I adjusted the elements of my teaching to support each other in an optimizing and systematic way, rather than confining the topic to the social studies time of day.

Figure 2-5. A Milpa

Throughout this book I provide examples that will highlight the connection between the various components of balanced literacy.

4. We Learn Through Multiple Exposures Over Time

Think of a lesson you did last week. It may have been the one you obsessed over for your annual observation. You made certain to follow protocol and included the necessary objectives, materials, procedure, and enrichment activities. And it went well—a tad unrealistic (well actually, hugely unrealistic) for day-to-day teaching and planning purposes—but well.

Or it may have been the lesson you initiated in response to a question a student asked. And, in contrast, this lesson required very little planning. You simply needed to locate a book to help answer and extend the child's question. But once you and the kids got talking, one thing led to another and before you knew it, many more students had something to contribute to the conversation.

No matter how planned or impromptu the lesson, it is disconcerting, humbling even, to realize that only some children "got it." Only some children even heard you! That's because learning involves the participation and engagement of the learner as well as the teacher. The students must value what you have to offer and be ready to partake. We can't make children learn. We can create a conducive environment, provide appealing materials, and present effective and explicit demonstrations, but all that won't be enough if the child's not needing, not wanting, or not ready to learn. That's the peculiar thing about teaching and learning.

Repetition and Practice Are Key

So how do we increase the odds in favor of learning? By repetition and practice. We introduce compelling ideas, concepts, skills, and strategies *multiple* times—and over time. And then we give children abundant opportunities to practice so that eventually they're able to effectively and naturally transfer what's been demonstrated to their own work. That's how we learn.

Consider, for example, how we learn words. According to researcher Stephen Stahl (1999):

> We live in a sea of words. Most of these words are known to us, either as very familiar or at least as somewhat familiar. Ordinarily, when we encounter a word we don't know, we skip it, especially if the word is not needed to make sense of what we are reading. . . . But we remember something about the words that we skip. This something could be where we saw it, something about the context where it appeared, or some other aspect. This information is in memory, but the memory is not strong enough to be accessible to our conscious mind. As we encounter a word repeatedly, more and more information accumulates about that word, until we have a vague notion of what it "means." As we get more information, we are able to define that word. (p. 14)

Here's another example: Early in the year you teach children about adding the suffix *-ed* to base words. And then you revisit this skill several weeks later because you see from your students' writing that most of them aren't applying what you've taught. When you remind them that you've taught this before, those same students look at you like you're crazy. Like they've never heard this before in their life! For a moment you think you might, in fact, be losing it. To confirm your sanity you rummage through your charts for proof that you did indeed teach them about *-ed* endings. Yep, you taught it, but only some got it! And it appears that the rest of them, for a variety of reasons, ranging from sleepiness to the task being out of their zone of proximal development, didn't take it in.

As frustrating as this may be, the realization can be quite liberating! Knowing that children need to hear and engage with words, skills, and strategies many times before they internalize and use them should lead us to prioritize our teaching, selecting the most important skills and strategies to highlight repeatedly throughout the course of the year. It is our hope that each time we revisit them, the children will hear more of it, build a memory hook on which to hang this information, and eventually get what we've taught—and taught and taught.

5. Our Practices Should Be Developmentally Appropriate

This fifth and final principle underlies the previous four: The children come first. In the push to get children reaching higher standards faster and earlier, schools are often more concerned with raising reading scores than with the appropriateness of their practices. They want children to move up in levels and they want it to happen quickly. Regardless of the child's age, regardless of the point from which he's starting, regardless of his early childhood experiences (at home or at school), regardless of second-language issues with which he may be dealing, regardless of his individual growth patterns, we want him to be on "grade level" by third grade. The implicit assumption here is that if his scores and levels go up, so will his comprehension. That, we have seen, is not necessarily the case.

Far too many of us are required to ask children to independently perform tasks that are beyond their reach. We have kindergarten and first-grade students writing book reports with directions to spell and punctuate correctly. We have second graders talking with one another about how they synthesize a text—a skill that's challenging for even fourth graders. We have third graders making endless (and often rote) connections between their lives and what they're reading at the expense of other comprehension-building conversations about the text.

My personal experiences with our youngest readers has led me to be pleased with just getting them to discuss the *same* book or acknowledge that their comment has already been made by another classmate (probably several others)! At the start of the year, I am even gratified when kindergartners can make it back to their seats with their own bag of books in tow. These youngsters should not be treated like something they're not. For the most part, children in kindergarten and first grade are one-dimensional. They think in the present and don't do well when asked to reflect back on the past or think about what's yet to come. They are egocentric and have difficulty taking multiple perspectives.

This doesn't mean they can't do smart reading and writing work. It doesn't mean that they shouldn't be challenged to think deeply. It doesn't mean that teaching children, even young children, to comprehend text shouldn't be a top priority. It just means that the goals we set for *all* children (our youngest and oldest) and the practices we use to teach them should be more closely aligned with what's developmentally appropriate. In the following box, I describe how the learning theories of Jean Piaget, Lev Vygotsky, and Jerome Bruner inform our thinking in this regard.

When children are asked to behave and think like older, more mature learners, it's frustrating all around. Frustrating for them, frustrating for the teachers, and frustrating for their families.

In the Gesell Institute's series of age-specific books on child development, e.g., *Your Five-Year-Old: Sunny and Serene, Your Nine-Year-Old: Thoughtful and*

Theorists Who Advance Our Understanding
of What "Developmentally Appropriate" Means

JEAN PIAGET posits that there are discrete biological stages through which children pass as they develop and grow. While individual children may certainly exhibit characteristics outside their "stage," the stages themselves represent characteristics of the majority of learners within that stage and must be factored into our practice.

LEV VYGOTSKY says that we must also consider the importance of children's social interactions with more accomplished mentors as they develop as learners. Children can do more complex tasks *with* them than they can do alone. The learning task should be within the child's *zone of proximal development*.

JEROME BRUNER maintains that we can teach fundamental concepts early, continually spiraling back to these concepts and going deeper each time, as long as we proceed in intellectually honest ways.

Mysterious, Louise Bates Ames (1981) advises parents not only to make certain that their child starts school at the proper age, and not too early, but to also insist that once he does start, his teachers not treat him like he is older than his actual years.

The importance of discerning the cognitive differences between a seven-year-old and a five-year-old is demonstrated in the following two examples of reading aloud a beloved picture book. A second-grade teacher reads Kevin Henkes' *Lily's Purple Plastic Purse* (1996) with her class and then discusses it successfully. The kids love it and beg to read it on their own. The lesson worked because seven- and eight-year-olds can take multiple perspectives in both real life and in book situations. They can see why Lily was so upset with her teacher for taking away her purple plastic purse when she couldn't stop playing with it, and why her teacher was justified in doing so. They are also capable of discerning Lily's embarrassment, to be reprimanded by a teacher she admires so, so much. Lily goes home beside herself with emotion, and second graders get it. They've "been there, done that."

In contrast, a well-intentioned kindergarten teacher reads aloud the same book and tries to launch right into a discussion, but her five-year-old students look confused. Most of them just aren't ready to understand and appreciate these multiple perspectives. The teacher might move onto another book, and another, and never quite recognize that her students are going along with her like ducklings following their mama, but their comprehension of the picture books is low. We have to choose books wisely and then be sure to scaffold children's reading, providing lots of time for them to think, discuss, and interact.

We need to think ahead to what we (the collective whole staff "we") want students to know by the end of their elementary school years, and then think back to how teachers at each grade can do their developmentally appropriate part to support these goals. Teachers of grades K–3 lay the *groundwork* for the development of skills and strategies that make sense and build on one another.

Comprehension: Clearing the Way for New Thinking

I would like to think that I've always known how to teach comprehension well and that I've always recognized the importance of matching children with books they can read and then scaffolding their understanding in ways that make sense for their age and stage of reading development. But that would be very far from the truth. The fact is 30 years ago I did things far differently than I do now, a lot of us did. We all have had to learn by trial and error, and a whole lot of professional study, which practices work and should therefore be enhanced and expanded upon, and which practices are best left by the wayside.

However, thanks to the hard work and dedication of researchers and practitioners such as P. David Pearson, Stephanie Harvey, Nell Duke, Ellin Keene, Richard Allington, Debbie Miller, Lucy Calkins, Regie Routman, Michael Pressley, Anne McGill-Franzen, Irene Fountas, and Gay Su Pinnell, we know so much more now than we did then. We know that there's no one silver-bullet approach to teaching children to read with meaning. We know that what works for one child may be ineffective with another. We know that there are many teaching practices and experiences that must be actualized so that children can get the most out of what they read. These experiences need to begin in the earliest grades and build as children mature.

Do What Works for Your Students—First and Always

As you read this book, consider the practices that resonate and can be integrated immediately into your practice, and others that will require a bit more contemplation and planning. But always consider the children *first*. We must adopt new and effective practices, and adapt or replace old ones, based on how much sense they make to our students and for our teaching.

Generally speaking, if you feel like you're working too hard to get your message across, then it's probably the wrong message or the wrong methodology. If you find yourself comparing teaching to pulling teeth or declaring that you feel like pulling your hair out, then stop pulling. Instead guide your students, nurture them, acknowledge who and where they are, and figure out how you can motivate them to engage and to learn. Slow down, do fewer things but do them well, consider what's developmentally appropriate, consider what's most important, and spend the bulk of your time there.

Teaching, as does learning, needs to be joyful. And I'm convinced it's all become far too complex and contrived. It's time to pull back and do what works. Comprehension should be our top priority, and that means teaching it wisely and well. With that goal in mind, we must acknowledge that in addition to teaching the meta-cognitive strategies, we must also provide students with time to read, time to write, and time to talk. We need to teach accurate fluent reading skills, build background knowledge, develop children's vocabulary and oral language, make reading-writing connections, and help students acquire a repertoire of strategies to use. Because in the end, both the text and our teaching have got to make sense.

 CHAPTER **3** Time to Read

Getting Independent Reading Right

We all want to make the most of children's independent reading time. To do this we need to put aside a few misconceptions about what it means to be engaged with a text, so that we go in with reasonable expectations. The ideal image of a class of children independently reading without a whisper or a shuffle of a chair is just that, an unrealistic ideal, a fantasy. Let's face it, it's hard for any of us to sit and read for an extended period of time.

Chances are that since you sat down to read this book, you've been up and about to check email, grab a snack, or attend to some other distraction. Even on those rare occasions when we sink deep into a couch and get caught up in a novel, there's probably more coffee-refilling and window-gazing than we think. So when we envision independent reading in the primary grades, we need to accept that our kids won't stay settled for too long. And that's okay.

Our brains—children's and adult's alike—are not wired for deep concentration over many minutes and are, in fact, poorly suited for nonstop attention (Jensen 1998). This is especially true when that attention is directed at something that's moderately stressful, which learning to read most certainly is. As a rule, the number of minutes children can concentrate on academic tasks pretty much matches their age. If they're five, they can attend to something that's moderately stressful for 5 minutes, if they're six, 6 minutes is on target, and so on. It's interesting to note, however, that when children are doing something they find particularly pleasurable or for which they are highly motivated, their ability to focus seems boundless.

One weekend when my seven-year-old granddaughter Sofia was visiting my husband Ted and me in Connecticut, I arose early on Sunday morning to get a head start on a report that was due. Sofia heard me crickity-creak down the stairs of our 1810 farmhouse and decided to follow. And of course, immediately the task-oriented side of me is thinking—there goes my head start! But Sofia and I struck a deal—she would let me write, and I would let her work on the jewelry box craft project I had given her the prior evening. Sofia was thrilled and couldn't wait to get started matching the sparkly jewels to the colored squares on the box. Yet, I was a bit skeptical as to how long she'd remain engaged.

The reading workshop model I describe in this chapter and throughout this book supports independent reading and nudges children to read for longer and longer stretches. It also recognizes that children do many things "alongside" their actual reading that hone their reading skills. Specifically, they respond to text, work on strategy sheets and reading logs, and engage in reading-related literacy center work.

Well, to my amazement, Sofia worked for two solid hours, scrutinizing the color key to make sure that each gem she attached was in its proper place! What kept Sofia engaged for so long on this project when she and other seven-year-olds have such a hard time attending to their reading for more than 7 minutes? Was it because she'd have something to show for her efforts that kept her going, something both practical and sparkly? Was it that her craft project was challenging, but not so hard as to make her struggle or fail? I believe it had much to do with the fact that Sofia felt capable of success throughout. And because of this, the experience brought her pleasure.

When I reflect on that morning with Sofia, I want to translate as much as I can of her sustained engagement into advice for independent reading time. How can we make it "sparkle" so that children will read for increasingly longer periods of time? What can we do to make children feel they can succeed, *moment to moment*, so they stay with it, consolidating the skills and strategies they'll need to become proficient? How can we provide independent reading experiences that are more fun than frustrating so students feel successful and find reading intrinsically pleasurable?

Cognitive scientists reinforce this need to strike the right balance between the effort we expend and mastery. In his book *Why Don't Students Like School? A Cognitive Scientist Answers Questions About How the Mind Works and What It Means for the Classroom*, Daniel T. Willingham (2009) explains that thinking about new problems or information, as inevitably occurs when children read, is not automatic. It requires effort, and it is slow and uncertain.

Yet, humans are naturally curious and enjoy a challenge. Problem solving is intrinsically pleasurable *if* we sense that there's a good chance of success. As Willingham amplifies, "...we choose problems that pose some challenge but that seem likely to be solvable, because these are the problems that lead to feelings of pleasure and satisfaction" (p. 14). The inference he draws for teachers is that "from a cognitive perspective, an important factor is whether or not a student consistently experiences the pleasurable rush of solving a problem" (p. 15).

Reading can't be pleasurable or engaging if children are asked to read books that are too hard or books they've had no hand in selecting. It's unrealistic to expect them to enjoy reading books that are so easy that they are boring, or so difficult that they are disheartening. While there must be some disequilibrium for any real learning to occur, the challenge must be moderate enough that students can envision themselves succeeding.

Why It's Important to Get Independent Reading Right

Independent reading has the potential to be one of the most important components of our balanced literacy program. It's not an "extra" as it seems to have been deemed years ago—something to fill in the time before or between the real work—but a vital and integral part of our balanced literacy program. Done right:

- **Independent reading promotes accurate fluent reading.** When children read books repeatedly—books to which they've been matched by their teacher because they're "just right" or books from their book bag to read after their guided reading group concludes—they are developing their sight word vocabulary and consolidating their phonics skills. This is a prerequisite for reading comprehension since it frees up space in their working memory to attend to meaning. And increased familiarity with a text strengthens children's comprehension as well as their fluency. The better they understand, the more fluently they read; the more fluently they read, the better they understand.

- **Independent reading builds background knowledge.** When children read informational text during independent reading or simply learn things about the natural world by looking at the pictures, they build background knowledge that they can then use to read and understand additional texts. Once again a cycle ensues—the more background knowledge children have, the more they comprehend. And the better they comprehend, the more they read and acquire new information.

- **Independent reading improves vocabulary.** Children who read habitually become acquainted with more contextualized vocabulary than children who do not. Thus independent reading enhances vocabulary, especially for students in third grade and higher because older readers, unlike their nascent counterparts, are likely to meet words in texts that are not part of their listening and speaking vocabulary. Up until third grade (or second grade for our more accomplished readers), most of the words in children's independent reading texts are words they already know.

- **Independent reading enhances familiarity with literary language structures.** When children read, they're exposed to language patterns they don't typically encounter during their daily interactions. Take, for example, this opening passage from Keiko Kasza's *The Dog Who Cried Wolf* (2005):

Moka was a good dog. He and Michelle loved to be together. Life was perfect, until one day, she read a book about wolves. "Look Moka," said Michelle, "you're kinda like a wolf."

This passage is an example of literary "every day" and "one day" time. Every day—Moka was a good dog. Every day—he and Michelle loved to be together. Every day—life was perfect. Until one day.... This is book language, not because the words are fancy, but because the context and problem are established in just a few sentences to thrust the story and reader forward. Children are exposed to such patterned language techniques when they read.

- **Independent reading provides a time when children can practice the skills and strategies we teach them.** Children need to practice what we've been demonstrating and want them to learn. Even the best teaching in the world will falter without adequate amounts of practice time to back it up.

- **Independent reading helps children fall in love with books.** We want our students to cheer when we announce it's time to read and groan when it's time to stop. Therefore, in addition to the leveled books we provide because they're "just right," we must also introduce students to books they'll be tempted to stash somewhere so only *they* will know where to look for them the following day. See the box below for professional books that will lead you to books your children will love.

It's nearly impossible to overrate the role of independent reading in children's reading development. As a teacher for 35 years, I've seen children grow by leaps and bounds because of their ready access to books and daily time to read them on their own. However, I need to state emphatically that maximizing the potential of independent reading involves *far more* than setting children up with a few books and letting them read as I did years ago when uninterrupted Sustained Silent Reading (SSR) and Drop Everything and Read (DEAR) were in vogue. In the chart on the next page, I compare and contrast the uninterrupted SSR and DEAR time of old to the more instructionally-informed approach I now advocate.

Professional Books That Suggest Great Kids' Books

Beyond Leveled Books, Second Edition by Franki Sibberson, Karen Szymusiak, and Laura Koch

The Read-Aloud Handbook: Sixth Edition by Jim Trealease

Learning Under the Influence of Language and Literature: Making the Most of Read-Alouds Across the Day by Lester L. Laminack and Reba M. Wadsworth

Books Kids Will Sit Still For 3: A Read-Aloud Guide by Judy Freeman

SSR and DEAR Time	A Re-Envisioned Independent Reading
Children are free to choose their own book to read at this time and can select from a variety of genres.	Children's book selections are monitored by the teacher as students meet with her one to one for a reading conference.
Children read silently, with distractions and interruptions kept to a minimum.	Children read alone or with a partner and respond to text in a variety of ways. They keep a reading log, write responses, engage in Reader's Theater practice, work on strategy sheets, etc.
The teacher may choose to read at this time, providing an adult reading model for students.	The teacher meets with students for reading conferences or small-group reading and provides feedback and guidance that serve children well as they read independently.
Uninterrupted SSR (and DEAR time) is kept separate from other reading work that is done during class time. It typically occurs at the start of the day.	Independent reading works with the other components of the reading workshop, and feeds and is fed by them.

The uninterrupted SSR and DEAR design simply provided time for children to read for a set 20 minutes a day. (Don't get me wrong, I'm not saying this was bad. It's just that, when done right, independent reading is capable of accomplishing so much more.) The children selected any book they wanted—hard, easy, one from home, whatever. As long as they read something, anything, that was all that mattered. However, once they chose a book they couldn't get up to exchange it for another. One chance was all they got. They couldn't interact with fellow students. There was no—"Hey, will you look at this turkey vulture! Gross!" or "Wanna read together? I'll read a page, then you read one." Nope. None of that—no talking. Reading was sustained and silent. Back then independent reading was kept separate from the rest of our literacy program. It was considered an extra, and once that 20 minutes was up, we could get down to the real business of teaching kids to read. What a mistaken notion!

Some days I even used to add a second DEAR time. Actually it was more of a "DEAR ME!" time. The kids returning from lunch were just too wired to settle down to work. So I let them read for a while to help them recover while I girded myself for the long afternoon ahead.

I'm impatient with any remnant of the controversy over whether or not in-class independent reading is a good use of school time. The research verifies that it *does* make a difference. Numerous studies document that children who read more, read better. One such study by Anderson, Wilson, and Fielding (1988) cited in Figure 3-1, shows that children reading at the 90th percentile read 33.4 minutes a day compared with students at the 10th percentile who read 1 minute a day. While this study examined independent reading done at home, the same correlation likely applies when kids read in school. Scores of studies like this one, plus 35 years of teaching experience and common sense, suggest that children—all of us—have to practice whatever we're trying to learn. And that's enough evidence for me. It's not independent reading *itself* that needs scrutiny, but rather the *type* of independent reading we provide.

Ramping Up Our Guidance and Feedback: Spotlight on Kyle

The necessity of providing children with time for independent reading *with* teacher guidance and feedback is amply demonstrated by a conference I had with Kyle, a student in Deirdre Cerulli's second grade. I asked Kyle, who at midyear was reading pretty much on grade level, to meet with me because I'd noticed he loved reading informational text, but was far less enamored with fiction. I wanted to shake things up a bit.

When I asked Kyle how he felt his reading was coming along, he said things were going pretty well, that he was reading both fiction and nonfiction and showed me his books. Predictably, the informational texts far outnumbered the fiction. Kyle confessed that he was reading several nonfiction books at once, as he likes to "learn a lot of facts." While it's safe to say that reading several books at once in any genre can be overwhelming for even a transitional reader like Kyle, I let this go for the moment since with informational text it is possible to dip in and out without too much trouble. And besides, I was more interested in learning how his fiction reading was progressing.

Kyle had three short chapter books in his personal reading basket (the children in his class used book baskets instead of bags)—two that he selected himself and one that he was reading mostly at home for his literature circle. Although he assured me he was only reading one fiction book at a time, and not several as with his informational texts, our conversation soon revealed that Kyle had actually started and stopped *both* of his self-selected chapter books without ever getting past the first few pages. As I looked through his reading folder, I found a *blank* main events strategy sheet he'd been assigned a couple of weeks earlier to accompany a fiction book he was reading. (See Figure 3-2 or Appendix 1 online for a sample "Main Events: Fiction" sheet.)

Variation in Amount of Independent Reading

Percentile Rank	Minutes/Day (books, magazines, newspapers)	Words/Year
98th	67.3	4,733,000
90th	33.4	2,357,000
70th	16.9	1,168,000
50th	9.2	601,000
30th	4.3	251,000
10th	1.0	51,000
2nd	0.0	——

Anderson, R. C., P. T. Wilson, and L. G. Fielding, 1988. "Growth in Reading and How Children Spend Their Time Outside of School." Reading Research Quarterly. Vol. 23, 285–303.

Figure 3-1. Variation in Amount of Independent Reading Outside of School

All Appendices are available online for classroom use.

Therefore, as Kyle and I conferred:

- I expressed my concerns about his near-exclusive reading of nonfiction and suggested that he needed a more balanced reading diet. I also asked him why he hadn't completed the "Main Events" sheet he'd been given earlier.
- I then asked Kyle to commit to finishing *Buffalo Before Breakfast* (Osborne 1999), the Magic Tree House book he had started, complete his strategy sheet, and ask for a conference so I could talk with him about how it went.
- To help him remember, I wrote a note in his assessment notebook (Figure 3-3) reminding him to do just that.

Now consider a scenario where Kyle's independent reading is kept *separate* from the rest of the reading workshop. Imagine what it would be like if Kyle, and others like him, read a book of their own choosing each day without having to talk to anyone about it, without ever being offered a better way to proceed.

Kyle needed that conference. He needed to use that strategy sheet (which had been demonstrated earlier during a whole-class read-aloud). He needed time to talk with Deirdre or me about commitment and the importance of balancing fiction with informational text. He needed a note reminding him of what to do. Without these scaffolds, Kyle is likely to have continued reading in this misguided way. And without the reading conference, I would have missed this golden opportunity to show him how to get better. (See "My Post-Conference To-Do List" box for the actions I took in *response* to Kyle's conference.)

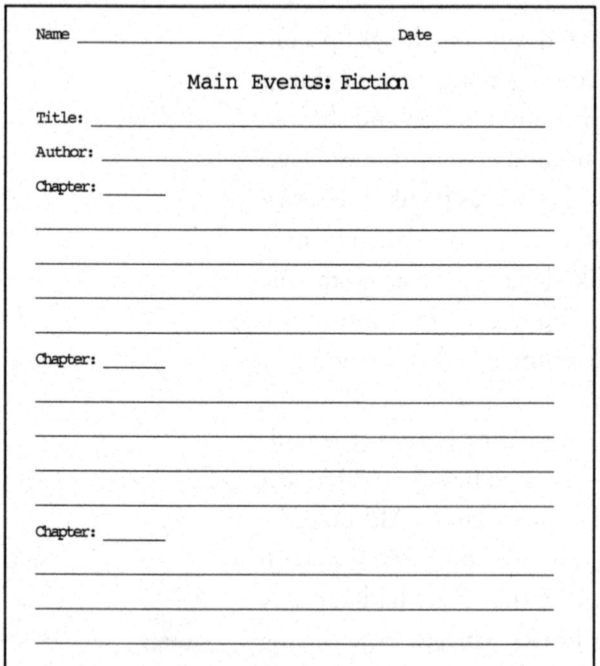
Name ______ Date ______

Main Events: Fiction

Title: ______

Author: ______

Chapter: ______

Chapter: ______

Chapter: ______

Comprehension from the Ground Up © 2011 by Sharon Taberski (Heinemann: Portsmouth, NH)

Figure 3-2. Main Events: Fiction Strategy Sheet

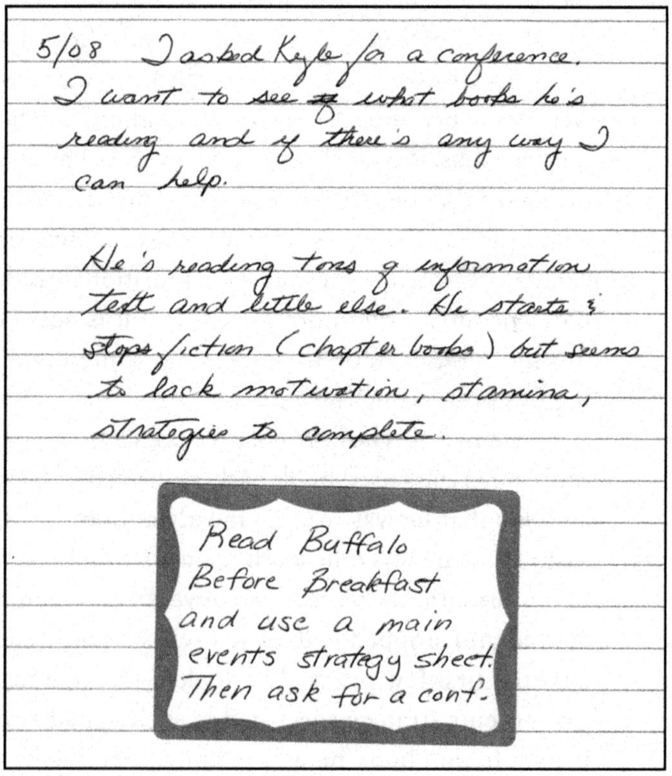
5/08 I asked Kyle for a conference. I want to see what books he's reading and if there's any way I can help.

He's reading tons of information text and little else. He starts & stops fiction (chapter books) but seems to lack motivation, stamina, strategies to complete.

Read Buffalo Before Breakfast and use a main events strategy sheet. Then ask for a conf.

Figure 3-3. Assessment Notebook Reminder to Kyle

My Post-Conference To-Do List

Not only did Kyle's conference help him to change his reading behaviors, it also left *me* with a "to-do" list to help Kyle and other students like him more effectively engage with chapter books. I had to:

1. Find additional short, high-quality chapter books that grab students and inspire them to commit to reading, without overwhelming them. Magic Tree House books, although fine for starters, soon grow old without a healthy assortment of additional texts with which to alternate. See the list on the following page for some noteworthy short chapter books.

2. Check my professional library for instructional practices and strategies that would help my chapter book "newbees" become more successful reading them. One such book is Nancy L. Roser and Miriam G. Martinez's *What a Character! Character Study as a Guide to Literary Meaning Making in Grades K–8* (2005). See Figure 3-4 for how I used the character journal practice described in Marjorie R. Hancock's chapter "Students Write Their Own Understanding of Characters—and Their Understanding Soars" to demonstrate how students can connect more personally to a book when they respond in the first person (as if they were the character) instead of in the more objective third-person voice.

{Character Journal Writing}

Chapter 1:
I've been shy for as long as I can remember. My mother is always trying to get me to make friends with kids. I say I don't want to, but I really don't know how.

Chapter 2:
I turned eight in July. My parents gave me a beagle. She is absolutely the prettiest dog in the world.

Instead of students writing a couple of sentences to summarize what happened in the chapter as they would on a typical "Main Events: Fiction" strategy sheet, this character journal practice as described in Martinez and Roser's What a Character! *invites students to respond in the first person as though they were the character. So instead of the third-person response: "Bobby Quinn had been shy for as long as he could remember," the child would write "I've been shy for as long as I can remember." This response helps students identify with character and become more engaged with the story.*

In this chart here I'm demonstrating this for students on large chart paper during a mini-lesson.

Figure 3-4. Character Journal Writing

List of Short, High-Quality Chapter Books

- ***The Most Beautiful Place in the World***
  by Ann Cameron
  Abandoned by his mother, Juan lives with his grandmother and, to help out, shines shoes for coins. He desperately wants to attend school, but fears Grandmother will say no. Finally gathering his courage, he is surprised when she not only agrees to send him to school but also chides him about the importance of standing up for himself.

- ***Fantastic Mr. Fox*** by Roald Dahl
  Mr. Fox is surrounded! He's going to have to come up with a truly fantastic plan to dig himself out of trouble this time. A fun, fast-paced read that gives kids plenty to talk about—like who are the "good guys" and who are the "bad guys" when many of the characters are both. Who should a reader side with?

- ***Akimbo and the Lions*** (and other books in the series) by Alexander McCall-Smith
  Akimbo, who lives with his family on an African game reserve, goes with his father to trap a lion who's been killing local cattle. But instead of the lioness, his dad captures her cub who Akimbo decides to care for until he can return it to the wild. This adventure teaches Akimbo an important lesson about friendship and sacrifice.

- ***Ruby Lu, Empress of Everything*** (and other books in the series) by Lenore Look
  In this second book in the series, Ruby Lu has a lot to handle when her cousin Flying Duck, who is deaf, emigrates from China to live with her family. Readers will enjoy learning how Ruby Lu handles this and other challenges to which eight-year-olds can relate.

- ***Alvin Ho: Allergic to Girls, School, and Other Scary Things*** by Lenore Look
  The first thing you should know about Alvin is that he's afraid of everything. Trains, girls, school—you name it. Young readers will con-

nect with Alvin's humorous adventures in this book and its sequel, *Alvin Ho: Allergic to Camping, Hiking and Other Natural Disasters*.

- ***Smarter Than Squirrels*** (and other books in the Down Girl and Sit series) by Lucy Nolan
  This book about two canines, Down Girl and Sit, will tickle the funny bone of kids beginning to read chapter books as these two friends describe the world as only "man's best friends" could. Ink-and-wash pictures pepper the text, adding to the fun.

- ***The World According to Humphrey***
  (and other books in the Humphrey series)
  by Betty Birney
  Humphrey, the class guinea pig, gets to sleep at a different student's house each weekend. This book is rollicking fun for middle-age readers as they learn how Humphrey helps each of them out.

- ***Horrid Henry*** (and other books in the Horrid Henry series) by Francesca Simon
  These four stories about Horrid Henry and his brother Perfect Peter are just what reluctant readers need to make them ask "When's it time to read?" Readers will be chomping at the bit to hear about Henry's perfect day, his dance class, his holiday, and how he meets his match with Moody Margaret. And they'll be comforted to know that after they finish *Horrid Henry*, there are five more books in the series. Now that's anything but horrid!

- ***Sophie the Awesome*** by Lara Bergen
  Sophie knows she's awesome, but how can she prove this to everyone else? Readers will love learning about Sophie's attempts to live up to her name, and what she finally does to earn her name and become a hero too.

- ***Ghost Horse*** by George Edward Stanley
  The last thing Emily expected to find in the backyard of her new house was a ghost horse.

But that's what she got. Emily makes the mistake of telling kids in her new school that she has a horse—a real one. How will Emily ever work her way out of this mess? And how will she find out why the ghost horse is haunting her house?

- ***The Boy That Ate Dog Biscuits*** by Betsy Sachs

  Billy wants a dog more than anything else in the world. As he helps out the local vet, he meets the most wonderful dog in the world. Now all he has to do is convince his parents that he's responsible enough to have one before someone else adopts him.

- ***Not My Dog*** by Colby Rodowsky

  Ellie finally gets a dog—but her great aunt's fully-grown dog, Preston, isn't exactly what she'd been hoping for. Readers will identify with her disappointment, and enjoy learning how Preston finally wins her over.

- ***Frankly Frannie*** by AJ Stern

  Frannie wants nothing more than to grow up and work in an office. So when she learns that the radio host of the local radio station her class is visiting is nowhere to be found, she jumps in to help out. But trouble ensues as she misinterprets callers' questions, and one chaotic event leads to another, leaving the entire town in turmoil.

- ***The Green Ghost*** by Marion Dane Bauer

  Marion Dane Bauer's ghost story is tender, moving, and a page-turner—not an easy task for a book that's just 86 pages. Children will be captivated by the string of events that lead Kate, whose family car becomes stranded while driving to visit her grandmother on Christmas Eve, to help a ghost connect with her sister, who's still one of the "breathing folks." Goosebumps and tears galore.

- ***Maybelle in the Soup*** (a Flip Book) by Katie Speck

  What could be cuter than a story about a plump, food-loving cockroach named Maybelle sharing a home with Myrtle and Herbert Peabody, who hate bugs? And once readers have laughed their way through this story, they can flip the book over and read *Maybelle Goes to Tea.*

- ***Uncle Pirate*** by Douglas Rees

  Move over Mr. Popper. You thought you had problems. Not only does a penguin—and a talking one at that—visit Wilson and his family, but a full-blooded pirate to boot. There's fun galore as kids read about how these feisty houseguests try to help out at home and at school.

The independent reading I'm proposing works *with* the other components of the reading workshop (and balanced literacy when you consider how read-aloud, shared reading, and writing interface), not in isolation, and provides children with guidance and feedback. It's heads and shoulders above the uninterrupted SSR and DEAR time of old when students read on their own without teacher intervention. So when I hear policy makers put down independent reading, when I hear recommendations that we not let kids read independently in school, but rather focus all our attention on direct instruction, I realize they haven't seen effective independent reading practices at work.

Becoming the kind of reader who will one day get lost in a book for hours on end doesn't happen in a day—or even a year. Especially for those kids who don't do a lot of reading at home, it's crucial that we provide time in school for children to develop this capacity with our help. Instead of just having kids read on their own, let's instead look to independent reading for all it can be and find ways to boost its effectiveness so that the experience will, in fact, sparkle for young readers.

Practices That Boost the Effectiveness of Independent Reading

Now, let's be sure to set realistic expectations for a K–3 independent reading time: Don't expect a hush to fall over the room once independent reading begins. Children in kindergarten and first grade need to subvocalize as they read, and a classroom full of twenty readers subvocalizing at once is bound to be noisy and make a teacher think he or she is failing at managing this time. Some noise is natural.

Even older readers need breaks from their reading and are likely to start up a conversation with a friend sitting alongside them when their independent reading time has maxed out at ten or fifteen minutes. Moreover, breaks are not wasted time. Brain research tells us that children need this down time to process the skills, strategies, and information they're trying to acquire (Jensen 1998). We have to change our mindset so that so called off-task behavior is valued more favorably as processing time.

Embrace the questions and challenges you face when trying to establish an independent reading time that works. And consider the recommendations I present here to ramp up your independent reading.

Design a Workable and Grade-Appropriate Schedule

Design a reading workshop schedule that's appropriate for children's age, grade, and abilities, and one that balances opportunities for children to confer with you, work in small groups, *and* spend a considerable amount of time reading independently. Later in this chapter, I will describe *how* reading conferences and small-group reading play a central role in supporting children's independent reading efforts. Now I'll discuss how all the components of a reading workshop—the mini-lesson, conferences, small-group work, independent reading, and reading share—might play out in kindergarten and first grade (Figure 3-5) and in second and third grade (Figure 3-6).

A Kindergarten and First-Grade Reading Workshop Design

Katy Howard, a first-grade teacher at PS 197 in the South Bronx, helps children develop stamina for reading and elevates their enjoyment and motivation to read by dividing the 60 minutes allotted for the reading workshop into two 25-minute mini-workshops with a 10-minute reading share at the end. Consequently, each day there are:

+ *two* mini-lessons
+ *two* independent reading sessions
+ *two* opportunities for the teacher to confer with students one-to-one or meet with small groups of readers
+ *one* reading share

Katy's mini-workshop variation on a typical 60-minute reading workshop design that has only *one* mini-lesson, *one* independent reading time (where conferences and small-group reading also occur), and a reading share at the end is both sensible and

A Kindergarten and First-Grade Reading and Writing Workshop Schedule

(Read-aloud or shared reading typically precede the reading workshop.)

A 60-Minute Reading Workshop *(Divided into two 25-minute mini-workshops and a 10-minute reading share.)*

First Mini-Workshop *(25 minutes)*

Mini-lesson #1 This mini-lesson often relates to the read-aloud or shared reading that preceded the reading workshop that day. It addresses whole-book skills and strategies. It may last up to, but should not exceed, 10 minutes.

Reading conferences or small-group reading The teacher meets one to one with three-to-five children to advise them on what they're doing well and what they might do better, and to match them with books for their independent reading book bag. Or…

The teacher meets with one small group of readers to guide them through a text that would be too difficult for them to read on their own. Or she might work with a small group for interactive read-aloud or word study.

Independent reading #1 (partner reading) The children work with a partner to read books from their bag. This experience helps to scaffold their reading for the second independent reading time when they'll read on their own.

Second Mini-Workshop *(25 minutes)*

Mini-lesson #2 This mini-lesson may also relate to the read-aloud or shared reading that preceded the reading workshop. It addresses word skills children need to acquire, and typically lasts 10 minutes.

Reading conferences or small-group reading (Same as during the first mini-workshop.)

Independent reading #2 (children reading alone) The children read from their bag of just-right books. They may also have a reading log or response sheet to work on.

Reading Share *(10 minutes)*

Several children volunteer or are asked to share something about the reading they did that day. They may share a book they liked and want to recommend, or share something they did that worked well.

Writing Workshop

A writing workshop that includes a mini-lesson, conferences or small-group writing, independent writing, and writing share follows the reading workshop. Spelling and handwriting are also addressed at this time.

© S. Taberski and K. Howard (2010)

Figure 3-5. A Kindergarten and First-Grade Reading Workshop Schedule

A Second- and Third-Grade Daily Reading and Writing Schedule

First Independent Reading *(20 minutes)*

Children read books from informational-text baskets and other book baskets around the room. They don't have their book bags of just-right books during this time and can select any book they want. The teacher does small-group reading or word work with her most "at-risk" readers.

Meeting (Whole-Group Session) *(50 minutes)*

Children share informational text learning from the first independent reading time that is often related to content-area studies and do "Words Words Words" vocabulary.

The teacher does interactive read-aloud, shared reading and phonics, or shared writing with a strategy or skills focus.

Reading Workshop *(60 minutes)*

Mini-lesson (often a recap of the skill or strategy demonstrated during read-aloud, shared reading, and so on).

Reading conferences or small-group reading The teacher meets one to one with three-to-five children to advise them on what they're doing well and what they might do better, and to match them with books for their independent reading book bag. Or. . .

The teacher meets with small groups of readers to guide them through a text that would be too difficult for them to read on their own. She might also work with small groups for interactive read-aloud, literature circles, or word study.

Second independent reading The children read books from their book bag, work on their reading log, response sheets, or response notebook. They might also do reading-related center activities.

Reading share The reading share is often launched with a prompt like, "What did you learn about yourself as a reader? What worked so well today that you might try to do it again?"

Writing Workshop *(45 minutes)*

The workshop includes a 10-minute mini-lesson (typically a recap of a skill or strategy that has been previously taught at greater length), a 25-minute independent writing time for independent writing, conferences or small-group work, and a 10-minute writing share. During the writing share, the teacher explores such questions as, "What did you learn about yourself as a writer? What worked so well that you may try to do it again? (See Chapter 4 for a more detailed description of the writing workshop.)

© S. Taberski (2010)

Figure 3-6. A Second- and Third-Grade Reading Workshop Schedule

practical for kindergarten and first-grade students. It takes into account children's shorter attention span and provides them with much needed movement between whole-group, small-group, and one-to-one learning situations. It also directs a teacher's attention to providing daily mini-lessons that address *both* whole-book strategies and word skills.

- **First Mini-Lesson: Focus on a Whole-Book Reading Strategy**

  Katy's first 10-minute mini-lesson kicks off the reading workshop and relates to a whole-book strategy. (See the following box for more on mini-lessons as they apply to the K–3 reading workshop.)

A Word About Mini-Lessons

Please note that in the K–1 and 2–3 reading workshop schedule both read-aloud and shared reading occur *outside* the 60-minute reading workshop. Both offer abundant opportunities to teach essential reading skills and strategies and must not be rushed by trying to fit them into a 10-minute mini-lesson. It's best to see read-aloud and shared reading as components of balanced literacy separate from the workshop, and the mini-lesson as a review or recap of a skill or strategy that's been previously taught at greater length.

The mini-lesson might summarize what's been demonstrated during the read-aloud or shared reading that day, or it might reinforce a lesson that occurred earlier in the week. Since children need multiple exposures over time to a skill or strategy before they can independently transfer it to their reading, the mini-lesson provides yet another exposure to those skills and strategies children have already experienced.

When the teacher sends children off to read at the end of the mini-lesson, she may *recommend* that they try what she's just demonstrated. However, she shouldn't insist that they follow through as a matter of protocol. This would require that students all be reading texts that lend themselves to a particular skill or strategy application. In addition, some readers who struggle more than others may not be a good match with the strategy. It's better to recognize that while some students will likely try out what you showed them, others will put it in their storehouse of skills and strategies to try at another time.

In other instances that occur with second- and third-grade classes, a teacher might be doing a strategy unit and use a portion of the independent reading time for guided practice, giving students a brief amount of time, say 15 minutes, to try out a skill or strategy she has demonstrated, and then gathering them to discuss how it went. In this case, the teacher makes sure that children have books and materials that lend themselves to the skill or strategy she wants them to try.

Having read Carrie Smith's Reader's Theater big book *Old Mother Hubbard's Hungry Family* (Benchmark Education 2008) with her students during shared reading over the past several days, Katy now directs the children's attention during the mini-lesson to the book's host of characters—Mother and Father Hubbard, Dog and Cat, and, of course, the omniscient Narrator—and how each is introduced at the beginning of the book (see Figure 3-7). She spends time discussing how Father, Dog, and Cat are alike (they are all hungry) and different (they like different foods).

Knowing that attending to characters is a primary consideration for reading comprehension at any age, Katy then suggests that when children return to their seats to read the books in their bag, they pay close attention to what the characters in their books are like (are they cheerful, sad, mean, angry?) and how they act. She may make Post-it notes available to students who wish to write a descriptive word that most applies to a character in their book. For example, Grandpa in Margaret Yatsevitch Phinney's *A Trip to the City* (Mondo 2004) would definitely be considered *silly*. However, there are no strategy sheets or assignments to accompany children's reading. For now, it's enough for them to know that "character" is one of the things readers think about. Katy is fully aware that children will likely need years to grow into this strategy. (See more about differentiating comprehension strategy instruction across the grades in Chapter 10.)

✦ First Independent Reading Session: Partner Reading

During the first independent reading session, Katy's children read with a partner. Children are often paired because they are at a similar stage of reading development, and are likely to have copies of the same guided or independent reading title

Figure 3-7. Pages from Old Mother Hubbard's Hungry Family

in their book bag. (Teachers may provide partners with a separate "buddy bag" to ensure that each child has a copy of the same book.) Occasionally, Katy partners a more fluent and less fluent reader so that the child who needs more assistance can get it from his more proficient partner. However, the gap between the buddies' reading abilities should not be so wide that the more fluent reader is bored or the more struggling one is embarrassed by his "developing" reading skills.

This cooperative reading experience eases children into a second independent reading session where each child will read alone. Since a child and his partner have already read some of their book bag books together, they are more familiar with the books, enabling them to read the books more accurately and fluently on their own. For more information on partner reading, check out Allyson Daley's *Partner Reading: A Way to Help All Readers Grow* (2005).

Reading Conferences and Small-Group Reading

While children read independently, a teacher may choose to confer with students one to one or work with small groups of three-to-five readers. Each teacher must decide for himself how to balance conferences and small-group work, and how that balance will play out over the course of weeks and months.

Katy chooses—at least for now—to use each of her 15-minute independent reading sessions to meet with students for guided reading. She also meets with one or two additional groups daily during developmental play and center time, and often manages to work in a conference or two with her more struggling readers. Katy's decision to schedule as many guided reading groups as possible and forego allotting more time for reading conferences reflects her understanding of how essential small-group work is for developing readers.

As much as Katy would love to have time to schedule in both small-group reading and one to one conferences during her reading workshop, she simply can't work it out under her current circumstances. Not with 27 first graders, many of whom are ELLs, and no assistant to help out. Therefore, she has to choose between doing more guided reading groups or conferring with students one to one.

Katy exemplifies how we teachers have to triage every day. And although reading conferences are highly beneficial, there may be weeks when we find we can't get to them often enough. The key is to see our workshop evolving and not beat ourselves up. Look forward to bringing more conferences in when both you and your students are on more solid ground.

Second Mini-Lesson: A Focus on Skills

Katy's second mini-lesson is skills-based and here she focuses on how the author uses exclamation marks to draw the reader's attention to Father Hubbard's, Dog's, and Cat's very distinct food preferences. Katy demonstrates how the statement, "I like cookies," would sound with and without the exclamation mark and the excitement it signals. She puts highlighting tape on the exclamation marks in the big book, and then has children reread portions of the text with proper expression.

Then, as Katy sends children off to read, she explains that at the end of the workshop she'll ask several of them to share examples of encounters they've had with exclamation marks. Again, Katy doesn't insist that all children go back and look for the punctuation marks in their texts, but provides a way to celebrate the kids who do and give students additional exposure to this skill. Bottom line—Katy wants her students to understand that punctuation conveys meaning—it's not just to pretty up a sentence.

Note: Since Katy selected this big book, which spans reading Levels C–J, to engage her class in Reader's Theater and allow a range of readers at different levels to work together, her skills mini-lesson focused on reading fluently, i.e., using punctuation to read with expression. However, she just as easily could have focused on helping children learn letter-sounds or sight words, as described in the Accurate Fluent Reading Effective Practices in Chapter 6.

- **Second Independent Reading Session: Children Read on Their Own**

During the second 15-minute independent reading session, Katy's children sit apart from one another and read books from their bag. They may use a portion of this time to respond to a book they've read or work on their reading log, but not for so long that it distracts them from Katy's main goal—to increase the amount of reading her children do. An appropriate balance between reading and responding must be maintained.

- **Reading Conferences and Small-Group Reading**

Since Katy has opted to focus on guided reading and let her conferences slide for now, she meets with a group of three-to-five readers to guide them through a text that would be too difficult for them to read on their own. While she doesn't target her mini-lesson topic (using exclamation marks to read more expressively) during the guided reading group, she would certainly call students' attention to any exclamation marks they serendipitously encounter.

- **Reading Share**

At the end of the workshop, Katy gathers her children at the meeting area for 10 minutes to allow several of them to share what they've learned, noticed, or tried. Two children have found exclamation marks in their independent reading books and ask Katy if they can share. Another child spontaneously volunteers to share something totally unrelated. This is fine, too. These three children take turns sitting in the reader's chair (the "reading" version of the author's chair) to share what they've done.

On another occasion, Katy may ask a student or two to share what they've worked on in their small group or have a child she's conferred with talk about what the conference centered on, allowing the entire class in on an individual child's reading experience. In each instance, Katy selects children to share *before* they gather at the meeting area and instructs them to bring to the meeting the book that relates to what they're sharing.

◆ ◆ ◆

Notice that in the flow of lessons and activities in this 60-minute reading workshop, Katy attends to both the "big and small" of reading—the skills and strategies involved in discovering the content and the wonderfully solitary act of reading, as well as its social aspect. And her first graders grow stronger from these multiple entryways to reading.

A Second- and Third-Grade Reading Workshop Design

While it's not uncommon for second and third graders at the end of the school year to take a book from their book bag and read for a hefty portion of their 40-minute independent reading time, you can be sure they didn't start out like this. Children's ability to sustain their independent reading develops over time and under the right conditions.

But because they're older and more seasoned, second- and third-grade students can manage one longer independent reading time rather than needing it broken into two shorter segments. Their books are longer, the genres are more varied, the plots and topics are more engaging, and their reading skills are more developed. The reading workshop design at this stage reflects children's growing maturity and stamina. In addition, students can take a "break" from their reading by filling in their reading log, responding to text, or working on a strategy sheet.

In a second- and third-grade reading workshop, students are likely to:

- Read diverse books from their bag—just-right books, "look" books, and easy books—simply because they're interested in reading them. (See "Just-Right Books, 'Look' Books, and Easy Books" box for a description of each category.)
- Read books related to a fiction, nonfiction, or poetry genre unit in which their class is engaged.
- Read books that relate to a two-to-three-week-long focus strategy unit in which the class is involved. (See Chapter 10.)

- **Mini-Lesson**

  The reading workshop begins with a 10-minute mini-lesson. Let's say I'm working on a three-week-long "text structure" strategy unit where I'm helping children recognize the importance of zeroing in on a text's organization— its bones—to show how it establishes a framework on which to hang new ideas and information.

  So over the course of *several* days, I use Susan Katz's *Oh, Theodore! A Collection of Guinea Pig Poems* (2007) for mini-lessons to show children how even a collection of poems can tell a story in much the same way as the chapters in a novel move a story along. My steps:
  - I write on chart paper the titles of the poems, e.g., "Pet Selection," "Name," "Danger," "Roommates," "Morning," "Breakfast," to show how they hint at the "story's" progression.
  - I recite a few poems out loud and highlight how they chronicle a boy's transition from wanting any pet *but* a guinea pig, to caring for the

guinea pig, to losing and then finding him, to finally knowing he'll love him forever. See Figure 3-8 for the poem "Pet Selection" and Figure 3-9 for the poem "Forever."

+ And because we don't typically expect such chronology from a poetry book—we expect the poems to relate to a theme, but not in a time-ordered sequence—I challenge students to consider how they might read this collection of poems differently from other poems in more traditional collections.

+ To demonstrate I sketch a graphic organizer on chart paper (Figure 3-10) to represent what I *see* when I think of these collective poems and think aloud about how this helps focus my reading.

+ I refer children to the poetry books I've assembled that are similar to *Oh, Theodore!* in that the poems *together* tell a single story. See the "Poetry Collections That Tell a Story" box on the next page for several time-sequenced poetry collections that second and third graders might enjoy.

+ **Independent Reading**

After the mini-lesson, the children get their reading folder and bag of books, and settle in for their 40-minute independent reading time. During this time, I confer with four-to-five readers or meet with two groups of three-to-five readers for 20-minute small-group sessions.

When the children are engaged in a focus strategy unit as the one I'm describing, the mini-lesson often exceeds the usual 10-minute allotment.

Figure 3-8. Pages from Oh, Theodore!—*"Pet Selection"*   *Figure 3-9. Pages from* Oh, Theodore!—*"Forever"*

When this happens, the independent reading time (and the conference and small-group time) needs to be shortened to factor in the longer mini-lesson.

I might ask children to sketch a graphic organizer in their reading notebook when they read independently to represent how the book they're reading is organized or to jot down how attending to a text's organization helps them understand and remember what they're reading. I ask them to be ready to share it at our reading share.

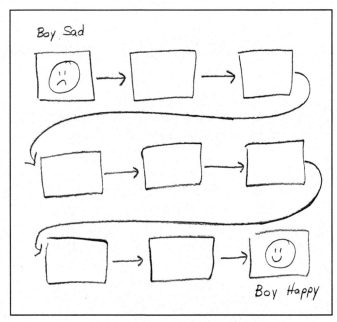

Figure 3-10. Graphic Organizer for How I Envision Oh, Theodore!

+ **Reading Conferences and Small-Group Reading**

Since the scenario I'm describing relates to a focus strategy unit on text structure, as does my mini-lesson, I reinforce the same strategy when I confer with students or meet with them in small groups. Using their book bag books and guided reading texts, we examine how attending to text structure supports their reading and comprehension.

+ **Reading Share**

The children reconvene at the meeting area at the end of the workshop to share some of the things they did that helped them get better at reading.

If I'm working on a focus strategy unit such as *text structure*, I ask students to center their sharing around that comprehension strategy. For example, during the workshop, students may have taken a card from the *think about text structure* pocket on the Putting Our Strategies to Work Board and recorded how using that strategy helped them read better. I may call on them to share

Poetry Collections That Tell a Story

Where I Live by Eileen Spinelli

My Name Is Jorge by Jane Medina

Oh, Theodore! A Collection of Guinea Pig Poems by Susan Katz

Vacation: We're Going to the Ocean by David Harrison

Moving Day by Ralph Fletcher

Today and Today by Issa

America, My New Home by Monica Gunning

Daddy Calls Me Man by Angela Johnson

Amber Was Brave, Essie Was Smart by Vera B. Williams

Scheduling Conferences and Small-Group Work

Making time in your literacy block for both reading conferences and small-group reading is the best way to provide children with the guidance and feedback they need to maximize the effectiveness of independent reading.

The decision about how to do this is best made by classroom teachers and school personnel based on the number of students in each class, the grade students are in, students' level of proficiency, and the instructional personnel available to assist. However, here are some guidelines to consider when designing a reading workshop schedule. When possible try to schedule:

- **A conference with each student every two weeks, or as needed.** These conferences are less formal and take less time (5-to-8 minutes) than the benchmark conferences held to obtain a child's reading level and note his progress, and are likely to begin with a friendly "How's it going?" or "What's happening in your reading?" They're used in our day-to-day teaching to help move children's reading forward.

- **Four-to-five 15-minute small-group lessons per week with each group of kindergarten and first-grade students.** These include guided reading groups, small-group interactive read-alouds, book talks, or skill and strategy groups.

- **Three-to-four 20- to 30-minute small-group lessons per week with each group of second and third graders.** These include guided reading groups, literature discussion groups, or skill and strategy groups.

- **And here's the kicker:** Children who struggle need to meet for conferences and small-group instruction even more frequently than their higher-achieving counterparts if we ever hope to bridge the gap between them. They will need double or triple the amount of interventions and small-group work the other children receive (Allington 2009a; Howard 2009).

what they wrote. (I'll describe this board in more detail in the Repertoire of Strategies Effective Practice section in Chapter 10.)

I often ask children what they did that day that worked so well that they would likely do it again. Children can also share books they enjoyed and want to recommend, as well as strategies they used to improve their reading.

Make Time to Confer

A teacher may wonder where she'll find the time to meet with students one to one, or how she can even justify spending time with one student when there are so many that need help and so much to do. Nonetheless, reading conferences remain a key component of the reading workshop and should be given full consideration in any reading workshop design. In fact, they may be the single most important factor in determining the success or failure of our independent reading time:

- Reading conferences provide opportunities for teachers to *scaffold* a child's independent reading by showing him what he's doing well and how he might improve. It's this instructional underpinning that helps to make this brand of independent reading vastly different from uninterrupted SSR and DEAR time.

+ Reading conferences also provide us with moments to *monitor* the texts that children read during independent reading and help them select additional books for their book bag.

Scaffolding Children's Reading

My primary goal during reading conferences is to have children leave the conference with new insight and knowledge of how to read the books in their book bag. I may take an informal running record, especially if the child is an emergent or early reader, to note any patterns in the child's miscues to which I might call her attention. I may listen to her read the first few pages and, if I see that she's struggling too much, I may suggest we find an easier book for her to read. Or I may walk her through an entire book to scaffold her reading.

Zeba, a Developing Reader After listening to her read a few pages of Syd Hoff's *Sammy the Seal* (2000), I realized that Zeba, whose native language is Urdu, wasn't adding an /s/ sound to the end of words to make them plural. When the text said, "The *lions* ate their meat," "The *elephants* ate their *hay*," "The *monkeys* ate their *bananas*," Zeba read *lion, elephant,* and *monkey*. She wasn't attending to either the letter sounds all the way through to the end of words or to conventions of English grammar. I showed Zeba how in English we often add *s* to the end of words to show "more than one." And I alerted her to how she should be more attentive to looking all the way through words as she reads. I even wrote her a note in her assessment notebook to remind her to do this (see Figure 3-11).

Jessie, a More Proficient Reader When I met with Jessie I didn't need to take a running record. It was clear from the onset of our conference that he wasn't happy with the books in his bag. He simply didn't like them and wanted others. However, I couldn't immediately draw out from Jessie precisely *why* he didn't like them. Was it the topic? Perhaps he wasn't interested in reptiles or ocean animals? Were they too hard? While they seemed to be at his just-right independent reading level (he was quite a proficient third-grade reader), perhaps there were challenges to Jessie I wasn't aware of.

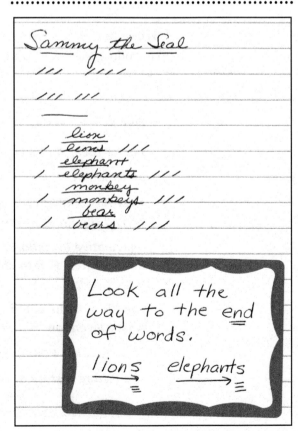

Figure 3-11. Note I Left for Zeba in Her Assessment Notebook

After speaking with Jessie a few minutes longer and pressing the "why" issue, he confessed that he hates reading about animals—books most kids simply devour—and that he's more interested in how things work. He loves reading about how water faucets turn on and off, what makes all the parts of a bicycle work in sync, or how elevators move up and down. And Jessie was fascinated by the men and women who created these marvelous inventions, hoping one day he'd invent something cool himself.

So while at the start of this conference I thought I was going to teach Jessie something he needed to know, it ended up that first he needed to teach me about his reading preferences. Then I could set out to find the books he wanted to read. Thus a new book basket titled "Inventors and Their Inventions" sprang to life. Initially, it had only a few volumes, but gradually as the year progressed, more and more books found their way into "Jessie's basket" and other readers wanted to learn more about the topic that so fascinated Jessie. (See box below for some titles that will tickle an inventor's fancy.)

And you should have seen the look on Jessie's face when he read the following opening lines of Judith St. George's *So You Want to Be an Inventor?* (2005):

> Are you a kid who likes to tinker with machines that clink and clank, levers that pull, bells that ring, cogs that grind, switches that turn on and off, wires that vibrate, dials that spin? You watch TV, ride a bike, phone friends, pop popcorn in a microwave, go to the movies. Inventions! And you want to be an inventor, too?

His face said loud and clear: "How did she know?" And I felt proud for being the one to introduce Jessie to this author who clearly understood his passion.

Books to Inspire Young Inventors

I Is for Idea: An Inventions Alphabet by Marcia Schonberg

Invention by Lionel Binder

They All Laughed . . . From Light Bulbs to Lasers: The Fascinating Stories Behind the Great Inventions That Have Changed Our Lives by Ira Flatow

Imaginative Inventions: The Who, What, Where, When, and Why of Roller Skates, Potato Chips, Marbles, and Pie (and More!) by Charise Mericle Harper

The Kid Who Invented the Popsicle: And Other Surprising Stories About Inventions by Don L. Wulffson

Mistakes That Worked by Charlotte Foltz Jones

The Picture History of Great Inventors by Gillian Clements

Monitoring Children's Text Selections

So how do we make sure that the right books get into the right children's hands? How do we make certain that the books children read will be a combination of leveled books and those that inspire them to read more and develop stamina? Aside from the reading preference inventories we ask students to fill out, our best shot at learning about what children need and want to read occurs when we sit face to face with them during reading conferences.

Instructional Tips When I confer with students I want to help them find independent reading books that they can and want to read. If they're reading books that are too hard, they won't get much out of the experience. If they're not enjoying the text, they won't sustain their reading for very long either. And remember how Kyle avoided reading fiction and only read informational text? It's our job—our very important job—to help get the right books into students' bags and into their hands.

Our ultimate goal, of course, is to teach students how to select their own books. As with everything else, children learn this skill through multiple exposures over time. And it's during reading conferences that these "how-to-choose-a-book" conversations pick up where the whole-group mini-lessons on book selection leave off.

+ **Make Sure Kids Have a Combination of Just-Right Books, "Look" Books, and Easy Books**

   Another goal I set for myself during reading conferences is to send children away with a bag filled with old (and easy) favorites, new (and just-right books), and some "look" books to help keep them engaged. This way, when they need to take a break from their just-right books, they have other books on which to fall back.

+ **Insist on a Balance Between Old and New**

   Children usually ask for a conference "to get new books." And quite frankly, many of them would like nothing more than to turn in all the books in their bag for new ones. However, they know I won't allow that. Instead I guide their exchange of books—insisting they only return a few and keep others.

   During reading conferences, I talk with children about which books they'd like to keep and which they'd like to replace. If I have any question about the ones they're returning, I may ask them to read a page or two to get a sense of whether or not their decision was a wise one.

   I typically encourage children to keep half of their books and exchange the other half for new ones. I offer much more guidance to emergent and early readers in selecting books for their book bag than I offer transitional and fluent readers. I go with them to the book baskets, browse along with them, and suggest several books in addition to one or two they've selected themselves. Then as children become more skilled at reading, I step to the side (just a bit), handing more of this decision making over to them. The "How I Level My Books" box gives more information on how to level books, and Figure 3-12 lists some

Just-Right Books, "Look" Books, and Easy Books

- **Just-right books** are books at students' independent level. They're books they can read with around 97 to 99 percent word accuracy. If, for example, a child is reading a book with 100 to 150 words on a page and 95 percent is the cutoff, as is sometimes recommended, she would have difficulty with between three to six words on every page. A book like this would simply be too difficult to read and understand (Allington 2009b). However, if she were an emergent or early reader, she's likely to read books for independent reading that fall a bit outside the 97 to 99 percent range since there are so many words she doesn't yet know and is in the process of learning.

  Therefore, we must keep an eye on the books our children are marching off with to read each day. Most likely many of the books kids have in their book bag or basket are far more difficult than we imagined. Not only must we make sure that these books are just right, but also that they're the very best just-right books we can find and that there are other supports in place.

  I resist ordering complete classroom libraries from any one publisher. Instead I prefer to pick and choose the best of the best. I recognize that the books may cost a little more this way than had I ordered in bulk. But I don't teach in bulk, nor do I do my ordering that way. I want books that I'll love to use and that children will love to read. It makes little sense to have a classroom full of books and only ever use a portion of them. It's kind of like shopping for clothes: Buy fewer items, but ones you know are classic.

- We also want to provide children with **"look" books.** These are books children can't read on their own because they're too difficult, but they're books children can look through and learn from. Take Steve Jenkins' *Down, Down, Down: A Journey to the Bottom of the Sea* and imagine a child paging through it, captivated by the sail fish that live close to the surface and the vent octopus that live in the depth of the sea. Sit a child with a couple of informational books on topics she loves and she's set to go. Even if she can't read the full text, she can study the pictures, read the captions, examine the charts, and learn a whole bunch of interesting facts!

  And what about wordless books? They certainly fall into the "look" book category. Readers need to tell a story by looking closely at the pictures. Read aloud Aesop's tale of "The Lion and the Mouse," and then buddy two children up with a copy of Jerry Pinkney's *The Lion and the Mouse* and see what happens. We need to give wordless books a more prominent place in our elementary classrooms. They appeal to children of all ages, running the gamut from Tomie dePaola's *Pancakes for Breakfast* to David Wiesner's *Flotsam*. The Effective Practice: Using Wordless Books to Support Literacy in Chapter 8 will provide you with more information about how to use them and some titles you'll want for your classroom.

- The **easy books** are those that students know well and can read quite effortlessly. They're books children have read often with pleasure or books that "speak to them" in a personal way.

characteristics of readers at different stages of development to keep in mind when matching kids with books.

Second and third graders often go to the leveled book baskets to select books on their own. Since they're typically more proficient in reading and more experienced in selecting just-right books, they're more likely to make good choices. However, I still ask these transitional and fluent readers to show me what they've chosen. They, too, need feedback regarding their selections and perhaps recommendations of books that might better suit their reading needs and preferences. Reading conferences give me the opportunity to provide children with this much needed individual guidance and feedback.

How I Level My Books

I place a colored label at the upper-right-hand corner of each book to indicate the stage of reading for which the book is best suited: blue for the emergent stage, yellow for early, red for transitional, and green for fluent. This draws my attention to the reading stage and characteristics of readers at different stages of development. I then write the level, e.g., Fountas and Pinnell, Reading Recovery, DRA, on the colored label (Figure 3-13). This helps me differentiate between the range of books at each stage, but also keeps my thinking centered on the broader characteristics of readers at different stages of reading development.

Emergent readers are:

- Using pictures to predict meaning
- Learning to track print
- Learning sight words
- Learning the names of letters and their sounds
- Beginning to problem solve words using visual, syntactic, and semantic cues together
- Developing fluency with familiar texts

Early readers are:

- Relying more on text than pictures
- Adding to their sight word vocabulary and knowledge of letter-sound relationships
- Expanding and consolidating word-solving skills and strategies
- Self-monitoring for meaning
- Beginning to read longer texts and a variety of genres

Transitional readers are:

- Learning to select appropriate texts
- Gaining mastery of skills and strategies
- Focusing most of their attention on comprehension
- Maintaining interest over an entire book
- Developing strategies for understanding a variety of genres
- Refining and extending their use of text features

Fluent readers are:

- Moving beyond a literal to a deeper understanding of text
- Writing about texts to heighten comprehension
- Engaging in conversations about texts to gain a new and broader perspective
- Independently applying comprehension strategies as needed

Figure 3-12. Some Characteristics of Readers at Different Stages of Development

Figure 3-13. Book Cover of Pran's Week of Adventure *(Bebop Books) with Leveling Label*

♦ Avoid an En Masse Book Exchange

I'm not a fan of book shopping days where children go off group by group to exchange *all* of their books for new ones. Where the only guidance they receive is the leveled basket in which the books are placed. While this may seem efficient—it certainly takes less time than matching kids with books during their reading conference—there are considerable drawbacks for K–3 readers.

For one, when kids replace *all* of their books at one time, it leaves them without familiar titles. They no longer have easier books that invite rereading and help them consolidate their skills and strategies and practice fluency. Second, when kids in K–3 choose many books at once, they're likely to choose some that are too hard, which can leave them frustrated. Even though they are selecting from their leveled basket, it's likely that many of the books in that basket are too hard, containing many unfamiliar high-frequency and other words. It's better to confer with the child, help him select several books to return, and recommend others he may try, or go with him to the baskets to help him find them.

No matter how confident we are that we've identified children's independent reading level and how confident publishers are that their books meet leveling specifications, the books in children's bags may still be too hard. Book levels are just not that perfect a system. Teachers are indispensable in helping children weed out the wrong books and make better selections for their bag, and in providing scaffolds and feedback to help children read those books.

Make Time for Guided Reading

Done right, guided reading can greatly enhance children's independent reading, sending kids off with books in their book bag they can read well and arming them with skills and strategies to apply to new texts. However, with teachers pressed to cram more and more into the school day, we tend to meet with guided reading groups less frequently than we should. And there's often little differentiation in procedure among groups, regardless of the children's needs relative to what the book has to offer. A book is introduced, the title and cover are discussed, students take a picture walk through the book as the teacher identifies challenging vocabulary, and then they read. Even in the upper grades, there's a stifling sameness from book to book and from group to group.

Furthermore, often these groups don't reconvene until much later in the week or even the following week, resulting in long intervals between sessions and students missing out on the repetition and reinforcement required for genuine learning to occur. Sensing this, a teacher is likely to resignedly introduce a brand-new guided reading selection the next time she and a group meet and embark on yet another "day one."

So instead of students going off at the end of a series of tightly clustered sessions knowing the guided reading selection inside out and being more familiar with reading skills and strategies they can apply to other books, they have yet another book in their bag that's a struggle and stretch for independent reading.

My advice to teachers for improving the overall quality of guided reading and maximizing its impact on independent reading is to:

+ Schedule *frequent* guided reading sessions with each group throughout the week.
+ Be sure to *know* your guided reading books well so you can use them effortlessly to teach readers what they need to learn.

Let's look now at how to make these two things happen.

Guiding Readers Through a Text over Multiple Days

Teachers in kindergarten and first grade should meet with each guided reading group four or five times a week for 15-minute sessions, and teachers in second and third grade should meet with each group three or four times a week for 20- to 30-minute sessions. Meeting less frequently than that precludes our ability to engage students in the variety of learning experiences guided reading can offer.

Ideally, each guided reading lesson should include text reading and discussion, word study, and writing. Incorporating all three components into one relatively brief lesson presents a challenge to even the most veteran teacher, but it's a goal worth striving for. At the very least, you should try to include two of these three elements at every lesson and all three within the course of your weeklong series of guided reading sessions. (*Note:* It's possible for some writing to occur when kids return to their seat *after* their lesson. Even writing words or a sentence on a wipe-off board at the beginning or conclusion of a lesson counts as writing.)

Increasing the number of guided reading groups you meet with each week will require you to rethink your schedule and eliminate other less essential practices. Remember, you can't do it all—no one can. You need to prioritize.

Teaching a Wide Range of Skills and Strategies

To make guided reading instruction more incisive than just sorting children into book-level groups and teaching generic lessons:

+ Take time to know the characteristic of readers at various stages of reading development (Figure 3-12) so you can make informed decisions about what to teach.

+ Take time to become book-savvy. I've found my teaching is not only more powerful but more relaxed when I go into a school year knowing the guided reading titles inside and out. That is: I know how each one functions in terms of illustrating the skills and strategies I will likely need to teach. For example, one title may be perfect for helping focus students' attention on how a character's personality impacts the story. Another illustrates how we use background knowledge to make inferences. Yet another is useful for demonstrating how to use the various nonfiction text features to pinpoint key information an author wants to share.

Take, for example, Carol Pugliano-Martin's *Little Lion* (Benchmark Education 2004) about a lion cub who wants to be any color but golden brown. I know this book well because I've used it many times.

+ I know that during the first half of the book Little Lion is wishing (three times) that he's a different color (Figure 3-14), and that during the second half he learns (three times) how his golden color keeps him safe from predators and allows him to hunt for food (Figure 3-15). Therefore, I can guide students to hold off on making predictions from just the cover and demonstrate that we need to discern when we have enough information to make a good prediction and when we do not. It takes skill and practice to know when it's a smart time to predict, and this book helps demonstrate this strategy. See Figure 3-16 for some predictions students wrote on Post-it notes halfway through the story.

+ I know I can also use this book to highlight story grammar, specifically problem and resolution. By midbook, students have no doubt regarding Little Lion's frustration and can then read on to find out how he'll handle his dissatisfaction.

+ Spend a planning day poring over some guided reading books. Take notes or devise your own grid so you have a memory-jogging reference for a significant number of books. Or maybe work with a grade-level buddy to build your knowledge together. This prep work will help you form groups and choose texts that are powerfully customized to the very skills and strategies your students need.

Figure 3-14. These pages from Little Lion *show that he wants to be blue like the fish in the pond.*

Figure 3-15. These pages from Little Lion *show where he learns why it's good for him to be golden brown.*

And by being at the top of your game with guided reading books, you are well-positioned to help match students to the right books for their independent reading, as we'll explore in the next section. After all, leveled books and literature for independent reading are not mutually exclusive. There's an overlap, and you never know which book is going to be "the one" that suddenly turns a child into an enthusiastic reader.

Bring in Books That Sparkle

While there is no magic bullet to a successful independent reading time, there are magic books—single titles that for mysterious reasons make a particular child a reader. To create the possibility of as many of these "love matches" between book and child as possible, we need to fill our classrooms with all sorts of books, so each year we can walk away with accounts like the following.

Figure 3-16. Children predict how Little Lion will solve his problem.

Quincy

Six-year-old Quincy fell in love with Leslie Fotherby's *The Cat Who Came to Stay* (1994)—so much so that whenever we conferred and I asked which books she wanted to return (hoping she'd finally let go of this one and find a replacement),

Quincy insisted on keeping her "cat book" right where it was, all safe and sound in her book bag. She kept it, in fact, from September through June, reading it each and every day—growing stronger and more self-confident every step along the way!

At the end of the year and in anticipation of Quincy and her family moving away, I gave her this book, suggesting that when she grows up she share it with special children in her life because, as I inscribed on the title page: "This is the book that taught six-year-old Quincy to read."

Ana Maria

I recently visited a kindergarten classroom where children were reading at tables around the room while their teacher, Carolyn Fields, was working with a guided reading group. As I sat alongside Ana Maria, I asked her to read out loud the book she had been whisper reading so intently. (Ana Maria's attention to her reading reminded me of Sofia's engagement when making her jewelry box. Both girls looked serious and intent—like they were doing something extremely important—and seemed removed from things happening around them.)

Ana Maria began reading *The Very Busy Spider* by Eric Carle (1989) loud enough for me to hear. I was impressed by the fact that although the words she read didn't exactly match those in the book, her rendition of the story conveyed its meaning and maintained its pattern. When Eric Carle wrote: "Moo! Moo! said the cow. Want to eat some grass? The spider didn't answer. She was very busy spinning her web," Ana Maria read: "The cow said do you want to play? The spider didn't say anything. He was too busy spinning his web." When Eric Carle wrote: "Baa! Baa! said the sheep . . . Neigh! Neigh! said the horse," etc., Ana Maria stuck to her own version!

And Ana Maria wasn't the only one. There were many other students in this kindergarten class doing the same thing. Dwayne was reading Patricia Hubbell's *Cars: Rushing! Honking! Zooming!* (2010) and kept tugging at my sleeve to get me to look at the police car, the limousine, the taxi, so he could tell me all about them. And Armando was reading about Allosaurus and Brachiosaurus and talking with a friend about the differences between the two dinosaurs. It was obvious that Carolyn had read these books aloud to the class countless times, and as a result these five-year-olds were primed to "read" them on their own.

Like my granddaughter Sofia bejeweling that box for two hours straight, these kindergartners were remarkably engaged because of that moment-to-moment feeling that they were being successful as readers. The books they had access to and Carolyn's teaching were responsible for that—like ice on a pond that's thick enough to hold the weight of skaters, both the books and explicit teaching allowed these kindergartners to sparkle and glide as readers.

To best match the book and the reader, consider setting up a chart like the one that follows where you link categories of books in your classroom, even specific titles, with kids that may enjoy reading them. Children love knowing that a book's been hand-selected for them and are certain to give it extra special attention.

Books	Students Who Might Like These Books	Other Notes
Mysteries	Kayla because she keeps reading the A to Z Mysteries series; Josh because he's always trying to figure out how stories will end...	
Humor	Lydia because she is always asking for books that make her laugh...	
Books Boys Tend to Like	John because he refuses to read books whose lead character is a girl...	Suggest Alvin Ho or Zach Files series
For Girls Who Think Pink	Eva who dreams of becoming a ballerina, princess, or anything beautiful...	
Books for Sports Lovers		Try to partner up Billy and Nate since they're both huge soccer fans
Books About Kids Who Dreamed Big		Tomie dePaola John Audubon Snowflake Bentley Michael Jordan
Books for Dog Lovers	Danny because he just got a Wheaten Terrier... Maria because "dogs" are all she writes about...	Gather all my fiction and nonfiction "dog" books and introduce kids to how they can write about a topic in different genres
Books for Big Brothers and Sisters	Doria because her mom is having a baby...	

Struggling Readers Need More of the Good Stuff

We all worry about our readers who struggle, readers who for whatever reason are having a difficult time getting the hang of reading and writing. We worry about our ELLs and empathize with how difficult it must be to learn a new academic language and to be pushed to do it quickly—fast, fast, fast. We want to make sure that we're providing them with the very best practices, materials, and opportunities to learn.

Yet, in our desperation to make our children who struggle learn it now—"yesterday" would be even better—we default to practices that are more likely to make them dislike reading and resist learning to read.

Worksheets are still in vogue despite the fact that we know they provide little genuine practice and even less in terms of motivation. Programs that provide too much direct instruction and too little time to practice are blocking the very readers who need to read more and widely. Assessments that provide data, but little in the way of directing teachers' efforts to teach better, are still standard and highly regarded. Those who say "you can't get more milk by weighing the cow" have it right. More teaching, more sound responsive teaching, and less of everything else is what's needed.

Therefore, instead of loading these strugglers down with tons of leveled books and little else, or grade-level texts they can't read, we need to make sure that even the kids who struggle—especially the kids who struggle—are getting opportunities to read materials that inspire and motivate them to read more. Books they can look through and learn from. And books they will reread scores of times, because of how the books speak to them.

Strugglers need more one-to-one conference time with teachers. They also need more small-group reading to bridge the gap between them and others in class who are more advanced in their academic skills. If everyone in class is getting 15 minutes of small-group work, then the strugglers need 30 to 45 minutes each day. It's fool-hearty to think that the gap can be closed any other way (Allington 2009a).

In addition, the instruction must be the good stuff—not the skill and drill kind that beats the life out of any one who comes near, but the kind that we know is wise and the kind that's been proven to work. And bear in mind, it's not only the experimental research that yields accurate and replicable results, it's also the practices that good teachers the world round know work—one-to-one time with students, matching them with just-right books, working with them in small groups, knowing the skills and strategies that need to be taught, but being willing to put that aside at any moment to respond to what a child may actually need. These practices—all of them—are what struggling readers and all children need.

Provide Choice Between Reading and Responding to Text

Although providing kids with time to read is a top priority, I'm satisfied if they read for only half of the independent reading time I provide. It's not that I have low standards. Or that I acquiesce to children taking frequent trips to the bathroom or lounging on the floor during their independent reading "down times." (Whenever I stumble—often quite literally—upon a lounger, I simply ask him affectionately, "What cruise are you on?" He always gets the message!) It's that I need to be realistic about what I can expect from children, for my own sanity and theirs.

I want children to be motivated to read, grow in their ability to choose books on their own, and feel successful reading the ones in their bag. I want them to read more and, as counterintuitive as it may seem, this means I have to provide opportunities for them to take natural breaks from their reading so they can process the new information, skills, and strategies they're learning.

The written responses I'm recommending children do during their downtime do not include worksheets or questions for children to answer at the end of each book or chapter they read. Assignments like these are often busywork that prevent students from engaging in authentic reading work that will add up. Thus they carry a high opportunity cost.

Rather, in addition to smart literacy center work, a teacher may provide opportunities for children:

+ to record the titles of the books they're reading and reflect on their process
+ to record their thinking about the books they read on response sheets or in a reading notebook
+ to work on strategy sheets that help them apply a strategy to a text they're reading

Opportunities such as these make children think more concretely about text and prompt them to reread, reflect, and revise their first impressions. Together with reading, they help fill out the picture of what independent reading can and should look like.

Reading Logs

Children across the grades can keep a record of some of the books they read, providing information about the type of books they most enjoy and giving them a sense of accomplishment.

Kindergarten and First Grade   Since developing readers and writers take longer to do things—writing their name, recording the title—it's better for them to spend more of their independent reading time engaged in reading and reading-related activities, such as making spelling pattern words with magnetic letters or rereading poems from their poetry folder, than to keep a daily log. Therefore kindergarten and early first-grade readers need only fill in a reading log two or three times a week. See Appendix 2 online for a kindergarten or early first-grade reading log adapted from Anne McGill-Franzen's *Kindergarten Literacy: Matching Assessment and Instruction in Kindergarten* (2005).

By the middle of first grade, when children can quite easily record the title and author of one book they've read each day and categorize it as fiction, informational text, or poetry without taking time away from their reading, it's reasonable to require them to keep a daily log (Appendix 3 online).

Second and Third Grade   In addition to recording the title, author, and genre, second and third graders know that by the end of the week, they will also need to hand in a reflection sheet (which is attached to their reading log) where they record what

Reading Log

Monday | Here's What I Think:

Title:

Author:

Genre: ◯ ◯ ◯ ◯ ◯

Tuesday | Here's What I Think:

Title:

Author:

Genre: ◯ ◯ ◯ ◯ ◯

Wednesday | Here's What I Think:

Title:

Author:

Genre: ◯ ◯ ◯ ◯ ◯

Reading Log, cont.

Thursday | Here's What I Think:

Title:

Author:

Genre: ◯ ◯ ◯ ◯ ◯

Friday | Here's What I Think:

Title:

Author:

Genre: ◯ ◯ ◯ ◯ ◯

Draw or write about something you learned.

◯ ◯ ◯ ◯ ◯

Reflection Sheet

This week I was successful at

Next week I plan to:

◯ ◯ ◯ ◯ ◯

Figure 3-17. Front and Back of Second- and Third-Grade Reading Log and Reflection Sheet

they were successful at that week and what their reading plans are for the coming week (Figure 3-17). This consolidates children's accomplishments and maps a course for them to follow. See Appendix 4 online for the log and reflection sheet.

Children quickly learn that they must keep up with their daily log. (It's no fun, and ineffective, to scramble on Friday to come up with book titles for Monday, Tuesday, Wednesday, etc.) And they also realize (when I call them on it) that it defeats the purpose of a reflection sheet to record what they were successful at early in the week before their reading has had time to unfold.

In addition, teachers soon recognize that a cursory introduction to these tools at the start of the year won't suffice to demonstrate the ins and outs of these materials and keep children on track. Rather, they'll need to revisit these materials regularly to demonstrate (via the mini-lesson) how to use them properly and highlight various ways to record their reading process.

Response Sheets and Notebooks

Teaching children early on that reading is an active process and that their thinking and understanding of a text occurs before, during, and after reading is integral to the reading process. Response sheets and notebooks help students take an active reading stance from the very beginning. The type of responses to text students make varies with age and grade. Teachers need to go slowly when introducing response sheets and reading notebooks and provide several whole-class demonstrations before asking children to go it alone. And it's likely that teachers will need to redemonstrate how to respond to text throughout the year to help students expand and refine their responses.

Kindergarten and First Grade   Kindergarten children may simply draw a picture of their favorite part of the book and then, as they're able, add a word or sentence to elaborate. A simple box with room to draw a picture and several lines at the bottom to write a word or two will suffice (see Appendix 5 online).

The responses of first graders typically include both a picture and text. Children might describe their favorite part of a book (and why they like it), what they learned, or what the book reminds them of. The response sheet in Figure 3-18 and Appendix 6 online requires the child to check off which of the three prompts he's using and then write his response on the lines. This type of response is most appropriate from the middle to the end of first grade.

---

10   Appendix 6

Name _____ Date _____

Title: _____

Response Sheet

☐ My favorite part is ...

☐ I learned ...

☐ This book reminds me of...

Draw a picture to show your thinking.

Comprehension from the Ground Up © 2011 by Sharon Taberski (Heinemann Portsmouth, NH)

Appendix 6, cont.   11

Name _____

Response Sheet, cont

_____

_____

_____

_____

_____

_____

_____

_____

_____

_____

_____

Comprehension from the Ground Up © 2011 by Sharon Taberski (Heinemann Portsmouth, NH)

Figure 3-18. Front and Back of a Mid-to-End of First-Grade Reading Response Sheet

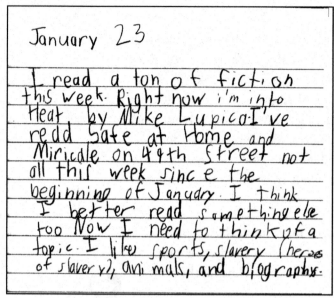

January 23

I read a ton of fiction this week. Right now i'm into Heat by Mike Lupica I've redd Safe at Home and Miricale on 49th street not all this week since the beginning of January. I think I better read something else too Now I need to think pf a topic. I like sports, slavery (heros of slavery), animals, and biographs.

Figure 3-19. Page from Jack's Reading Notebook

We must never downplay the important role that children's illustrations play in their ability to flesh out the details of a text and convey meaning. They should be encouraged and honored as long as children don't use them to avoid writing and the time they spend on them doesn't displace too much of their independent reading

Second and Third Grade The reading responses of second and third graders should offer insight into the kinds of books they enjoy and their reading process. Most second and third graders record their responses in a reading notebook (Figure 3-19). How frequently they respond is determined by what else the teacher is asking them to do and how accomplished they are as readers and writers. More proficient readers and writers can be asked to respond more frequently than those who are just developing since their responses are less likely to take too much time away from their reading.

Strategy Sheets

Strategy sheets scaffold children's use of a specific comprehension strategy, such as accessing prior knowledge or thinking about text structure, and provide a place to record their thinking. In fact, it's their permanence—whatever is written can be read, reread, and reflected upon—that's part of what makes strategy sheets (as well as reading logs, reading response sheets, and notebooks) so valuable. See Figure 3-2 for a "Main Events: Fiction" strategy sheet. Also see Appendix 1 online.

We often send second and third graders off to try out a strategy we've demonstrated without giving them a medium (e.g., a notebook, a strategy sheet, a Post-it note) on which to think and record. In such instances, we're expecting too much of them. Even adults would be hard put to follow through on a directive: "Be sure to think about what you already know about a topic before you start reading," or "Consider your purpose for reading in order to determine how you'll read a book" without something concrete on which to ground their thinking.

♦ ♦ ♦

These response intervals where children record titles in their log and write responses and work on strategy sheets are not "breaks" in the sense that children stop working and take a rest (not that that's a bad idea either from the standpoint of how our brain optimally works). Rather they are a *shift* in activity. Children read a bit, respond a bit, read a bit, fill in their reading log, read some more, work on a strategy sheet to help them process what they're doing and make their learning more tangible. And before you know it, they've done 20 minutes of reading and 20 minutes of responding, promoting their reading achievement. And, of course, there's some fooling around too! Because they're kids! Correction—because they're human!

Discussing Reading with Classmates

Children need to talk with other readers about what they're reading and learning. Just as we rush to phone a friend about the latest and one of the best books we've ever read—as I did upon completing Elizabeth Strout's *Olive Kitteridge* (2008)—children need to tell their friends about their great reading finds. We can provide a formal time for this by scheduling book talks where children take turns telling just enough about a new favorite to make the listener bite, or we can encourage kids to sit alongside a partner for a portion of the reading workshop as Katy did with her first graders so they can read, talk, and discover together.

◆ ◆ ◆

In order for independent reading to flourish, we must consider it in light of our entire balanced literacy program. Independent reading is not a stand-alone. It works best when it works together with all the other literacy work students do. Just as the Native American's corn, beans, and squash grew better when they were planted together so that they could intertwine for nourishment and support, the same is true for independent reading in relation to all the other components of the reading workshop. Giving students time to read is the core around which all other literacy flourishes and intertwines. If kids don't have time to read, to practice what we're trying to teach, to consolidate their skills and strategies, then nothing we teach can take root and grow.

CHAPTER **4**   Time to Write

Children's Writing Nourishes Their Reading Growth

Some of you may remember *The Mary Tyler Moore Show* and how the pompous but loveable news anchor Ted Baxter opened his baritone monologue with "it all started in a small 5,000-watt radio station in Fresno California." Well, for me, "it all started in a small classroom of the Horace Mann building at Teachers College in New York City" when I attended a Saturday workshop given by Donald Graves. Until then I knew little about teaching writing. But after Don's workshop, well... let's say I was inspired!

My three children were all under the age of seven back then, so it wasn't typical for me to leave them at home to attend a Saturday workshop, and yet I was compelled by a description about The Writing Process on a flyer posted in the teacher's lounge that was so unlike anything I'd ever read:

"...All children, even our youngest ones, can write"... *hmm*..."young children can invent the spelling of unfamiliar words as they work toward conventional spelling ... it's better to first help them focus on getting their ideas on paper"... *hmm* ... "children are natural communicators and, in fact, love to write...."

That may have been the hook, because up to that point my experience teaching writing most certainly did not support this claim. The children I taught disliked writing. They couldn't spell.

They didn't seem to have a clue what to write. They wrote a couple sentences and then "The End" as a signal not to bother them any further.

It now seems ludicrous to even say that I was teaching writing back then. This is what I was doing: Assigning topics like "Write a story about how it feels to be a pencil"; writing words on the board that children might want to use and therefore need to know how to spell; giving children a day or so to record their ideas (granted, there were very few ideas—what would you write in response to prompts like that?); taking their papers home to correct, in red ink, of course; returning their papers the following day for them to copy their story on "good" white paper (the "bad" paper was yellow—imagine being so judgmental about paper!).

Then, as if this weren't already painful enough, after the children had made their corrections (with brand-new mistakes), I would carefully erase and correct their most recent errors, in handwriting that resembled their own, so that their final papers looked perfect. Then up on the bulletin board they'd go, and I wouldn't need to think about writing again for another month when a new bulletin board display was due. The End.

Don Graves' workshop ended my "teaching-writing-by-assignment" era and began my career-long journey into the process approach to literacy. I immediately tried to implement Don's writing workshop suggestions and, I must say, got pretty good at it with the help of my newly acquired friends and colleagues at the Teachers College Writing Project—Shelley Harwayne, Lucy Calkins, Ralph Fletcher, Georgia Heard, and JoAnn Portalupi, to name a few. With an all-star lineup like that, you're probably wondering how could she *not* get it right! (See p. 85 for my writing workshop schedule.)

Fabulous mentors aside, what I loved most about the workshop approach was how it rang so true to what motivates children to write:

+ Trust kids to have their own ideas for writing.

+ Encourage longer, richer elaboration and self-confidence by refraining from correcting every piece of writing.

+ Demonstrate the use of writing conventions with mini-lessons so children see that writers use spelling, punctuation, and the like as meaning-making tools, but keep the energy of teaching and learning on helping children develop the ideas they want to convey.

+ Structure time so children can write every day, which gives them opportunities to grow as writers, far more than once-a-month writing assignments could ever do.

It wasn't long before I asked myself: If this workshop model/process approach works so well for writing, how might it work for reading? So after a great deal of professional reading and reflection, I eventually set up a reading workshop that mirrored my writing one, complete with mini-lessons, reading conferences, small-group reading, independent reading, and reading share. Now I had two workshops in place, a reading workshop and a writing workshop. The next step was finding how they work together: How reading informs writing, and how writing nourishes children's reading growth.

I've spent the last 25 years discovering and refining my understanding of teaching these two processes so that young children can "hear their harmony" as they learn to read and write. This exploration culminates in much that I share in this book.

Bringing Writing Back from the Brink

Learning to write well is an essential skill and must be taught throughout all the school years. While most children will not grow up to be published authors of novels, biographies, or poetry, they will certainly need to know how to write, and write well. None of us quite knows where the Internet revolution is taking us and how the new media forms of blogs, emails, Facebook, Twitter, and video will drive our teaching in new directions.

We don't yet know how digital storytelling, graphic novels, and other new narrative forms will trickle down into how we teach reading and writing in the elementary grades. We are in the eye of the storm and may not see it clearly for another generation—but it's safe to say that those who write well will do well.

However, schools are still under pressure to raise reading scores, and far too often writing takes a backseat to reading. And even when it is taught, it is very often to help raise students' scores on standardized tests. As teachers, we have to teach reading and writing with more balance. And we have to remind ourselves of how naturally children take to both when we explore reading and writing as engaging forums to communicate and to know the world.

In *Holding on to Good Ideas in a Time of Bad Ones: Six Literacy Principles Worth Fighting For*, Tom Newkirk (2009) shares stories of how writing and other important content areas have become poor cousins of reading. He writes:

> A couple of years ago, I was speaking with teachers in a Fresno school and they informed me that they had received a "waiver" for science. I had never heard of such a thing. A waiver, it turned out, was an informal agreement that time used for science might now be used for reading. Writing also gets crowded out, particularly the daily writing workshops that Don Graves argued for in the 1980s. (p. 55)

This "rob Peter to pay Paul" approach is misguided on so many counts. First of all, the degree to which we read well and comprehend what we read depends largely on the knowledge and experiences we bring to text. If schools reduce the amount of time given to science and social studies to devote more time to reading, they're shrinking opportunities for students to engage with critical information sources that provide invaluable background knowledge on which reading comprehension depends.

Additionally, when schools fail to actually teach writing, really *teach* it as I'm advocating, instead of simply training children to take tests, or using children's writing pieces to pretty up a bulletin board, they miss the opportunity to demonstrate the *relationship* between the two processes and seamlessly reinforce the very strategies they're working toward in reading.

Our job is not to steal from Peter to pay Paul but to integrate our teaching so that both reading and writing are taught well, in conjunction with other essential subjects like social studies and science. Our goal should be to make the interface between reading and writing palpable and its classroom application exciting and fun.

In March 2010, the Carnegie Corporation of New York published *Writing to Read: Evidence for How Writing Can Improve Reading* (Graham and Herbert 2010), a report that examines and summarizes high-quality research regarding the impact of children's writing on reading. The recommendations of this statistical review of research (meta-analysis) are presented in the "Recommendations" box, but I urge you to read the report in its entirety by googling "Writing to Read Report."

The Recommendations

Carnegie Corporation's *Writing to Read* Report

I. HAVE STUDENTS WRITE ABOUT THE TEXTS THEY READ. Students' comprehension of science, social studies, and language arts is improved when they write about what they read, specifically when they

- **Respond to a Text in Writing (Writing Personal Reactions, Analyzing and Interpreting the Text)**
- **Write Summaries of a Text**
- **Write Notes About a Text**
- **Answer Questions About a Text in Writing, or Create and Answer Written Questions About a Text**

II. TEACH STUDENTS THE WRITING SKILLS AND PROCESSES THAT GO INTO CREATING TEXT. Students' reading skills and comprehension are improved by learning the skills and process that go into creating text, specifically when teachers

- **Teach the Process of Writing, Text Structures for Writing, Paragraph or Sentence Construction Skills (Improves Reading Comprehension)**
- **Teach Spelling and Sentence Construction Skills (Improves Reading Fluency)**
- **Teach Spelling Skills (Improves Word Reading Skills)**

III. INCREASE HOW MUCH STUDENTS WRITE. Students' reading comprehension is improved by having them increase how often they produce their own texts.

(Graham and Herbert 2010, p. 5)

Two Writers, Two Opportunities to Connect Reading to Writing

"Wow Alice! You're writing! Read me what you wrote." In just a few words, my friend Karin Johnson conveyed the essence of the reading-writing connection to her two-year-old granddaughter when Alice handed her a story she had just written (Figure 4-1). On the surface, it's not much more complicated than that. Writers record their ideas and information, and readers read them. But in another sense, the reading-writing connection is quite profound.

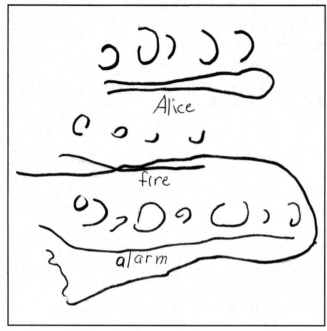

Figure 4-1. Alice's Writing

We're more savvy about how a child's reading impacts his writing than we are about how his writing impacts his reading, yet we often fail to make this basic reading-to-writing connection explicit so children can reap the rewards. We need to say things like "This book here that I'm reading aloud may actually start some of you thinking about topics you may want to write about?" Or "Look here, this *-ed* letter search we're doing is going to help you know what letters to write when you hear a /t/, /d/ and /ed/ sound at the end of words. How cool is that!"

In this same vein, we need to be highly attuned to how a child's writing impacts his reading comprehension and engagement. While this writing-to-reading "half of the circle" is less apparent than the reading-to-writing one, it is every bit as important. We need to understand and demonstrate how these two processes *together* are greater than the two working alone. We may know it in our head, but we've got to feel it in our bones and layer it into our lessons.

While it would have been silly for Karin to explain the link between reading and writing to two-year-old Alice any more than simply acknowledging its existence, our elementary-grade students are developmentally ready for it. Just sit alongside a child busy at work, talk with him about what he's doing, and the power of the reading-writing connection and the opportunities we have to mine its potential will hit home.

Webster's Writing Conference

Millie Velazquez sat alongside Webster, a student in her first-grade class, to see how she could help him with a piece of writing he was laboring over. Webster was trying to write the sentence "I make muscle words," and was having a hard time getting the letters to match the sounds. (Webster was writing about school and what he does throughout the day. "Muscle words" were the classroom term used for the high-frequency words the children were learning.)

Slowly…slowly…Millie guided Webster through the sentence, word-by-word, letter by letter, encouraging him to listen for and write what he heard and affirming his attempts. Throughout, Millie prompted Webster to reread the sentence from the beginning to give himself a running start on the next word, get his mouth ready to say the word, ask what would come at the end of the sentence, ask "Does that make sense to you?" Sounds like reading, right? And that's the point. Reading and writing are reciprocal processes, and we must let children know this. By the end of the conference Webster was beaming. He had been successful, his approximations were good ones, and he felt like a writer.

I hope Webster felt like a reader too, since his one-to-one time with Millie and their work during the writing workshop will also enhance his reading comprehension:

- Since Webster was attending so closely to writing the letters that match the sounds in words, he's likely to bring this attentive stance to other authors' texts.

- The letter sounds he encodes as he writes are the same ones he will decode as he reads. Learning to write and read these words accurately and automatically will help him develop fluency so he can direct more of his attention to the message the author is conveying.

- Because he's punctuating his piece to make it clear to a reader, he'll note the same conventions when he reads.

- Since he's rereading his writing to make sure it makes sense, he'll know to reread the sentence, paragraph, or page he's reading when meaning breaks down.

- And since Millie so wisely and frequently asked him, "Does this make sense?" Webster will ask himself the same question when he reads.

This reading-writing *comprehension* connection is huge. Because in addition to seeing the reciprocity between encoding and decoding and the mechanics of it all, Webster's gaining insight into the fact that there's a writer behind the stories and texts he reads. And that there are ideas and information for *him* to understand.

Lucas' Writing Conference

Second-grader Lucas asked me for a writing conference so I could check the fiction piece he had begun that morning. I suggested that before I took a look he read it over to see if it made sense, and then we'd talk. I had just introduced an editing checklist the week before, and editing circle #1—"Does it make sense?"—at the bottom of

Lucas' paper, remained untouched. (See Effective Practice: Editing Checklist in Chapter 9.) In suggesting this, I wanted him to recognize the meaning-making nature of both reading and writing. What we write has to make sense so that the reader can understand it.

Then Lucas and I read the piece together. We talked about his title, what he had written so far, and what he might write next. I decided that the most useful course to take in our conference was to help him identify the story's problem and draft a table of contents to outline how his "not-yet-decided-upon" events might unfold. A pretty heady assignment for an eight-year-old, wouldn't you say?

Authors are like architects, and the more we help children see reading and writing as beautiful structures of ideas, crafted by a real person, the more confident they will be in navigating each realm.

Like so much we do in teaching, we live in the moment and use our knowledge of each student to showcase something we know they are ready to take in and learn. I was under no illusion that Lucas was driven enough or skilled enough as a writer to develop a workable table of contents and craft a full story from it, but I *did* know that he was ready to think about the role of a workable table of contents in fiction and nonfiction.

By inviting Lucas to look at a favorite series book as a planning tool for his own writing, I wanted to plant a seed that writers, and in turn readers, rely on these organizational features to help them hang their ideas in a pleasing, understandable order. Chapters, headings, a writer's list of ideas jotted in a sequence—all these tools help fiction writers build the story's problem and resolution, and nonfiction writers organize their information.

I wanted him to anticipate these helpful features and use them to get his bearings and enter the text, much as one who approaches and enters a house is helped by walkways, foyers, and hallways to navigate their way. Authors are like architects, and the more we help children see reading and writing as beautiful structures of ideas, crafted by a real person, the more confident they will be in navigating each realm.

Teachers and students should view the reading workshop and the writing workshop as a reading-writing collaboration, where each process complements and reinforces the other. Teachers should call children's attention to the synergy between the two and invite them to discover new dimensions of this reading-writing kinship on their own.

Bringing the Reading-Writing Connection Full Circle

It's important to note that in all I've said so far about the reading-writing connection, I've given writing equal billing. I'm convinced our children's literacy gets stronger when we push our own thinking on how writing impacts reading.

So in this chapter I want to make clear what writing brings to the reading table, to clarify that the connection goes *both* ways. Children who read become stronger, more accomplished writers, and children who write become more proficient, better comprehending readers.

In "Effective Practices for Developing Reading Comprehension," a chapter in *What Research Has to Say About Reading Comprehension,* Nell K. Duke and P. David Pearson (2002) argue that writing helps children's reading flourish and recommend that readers spend:

> lots of time writing texts for others to comprehend. Again, students should experience writing the range of genres we wish them to comprehend. Their instructions should emphasize connections between reading and writing, developing students' abilities to write like a reader and read like a writer. (p. 208)

When you think about it, it's difficult to imagine it any other way. Writers understand the meaning-making nature of the writing process because they've lived it. As a result writers can appreciate and anticipate the work they must do as the reader when they approach a text someone else has written. (See box below.)

They've experienced what's involved in bringing a text from conception to publication and are better able to anticipate the challenges that reading entails. Then when these writers go off to read, something beautiful happens: they bring all of their experiences with writing texts to reading. And because they're writers, they'll be better readers.

For example, when Nilou first wrote her nonfiction piece on the blue shark, it lacked organization with general statements and details mixed in together. But her revision (Figure 4-2) more logically opens with a general statement and then moves to the details. Nilou realized that this was a more sensible way to organize her piece, and I'm counting on her carrying this experience over to her reading, looking for how authors have similarly structured their pieces.

Mimi's "Islands" poem (Figure 4-3) demonstrates her understanding of how content and illustrations work together to convey meaning. Her poem alone would be effective enough, but written on "land" with water all around reinforces her

A Writer's Job Is to . . .

- Research their topic to make sure the information they're sharing is complete, accurate, and up-to-date.
- Attend to how their text is organized, knowing that a better organized piece is easier to understand. They may decide to include a table of contents to give the reader the lay of the land.
- Anticipate parts that may be confusing to a reader and do what's necessary to present their ideas and information in a cohesive way.

- Define a word or include a text feature to illustrate a point they're making, or strive for more precise language to describe a scene. (Strong nouns and active verbs are the gold standard.)
- Anticipate how an audience might react. After all, it's not only the teacher who will read their work. During share time and peer conferences they read for an audience of peers and receive feedback about how to proceed, and during celebrations and publication their writing goes out to the world.

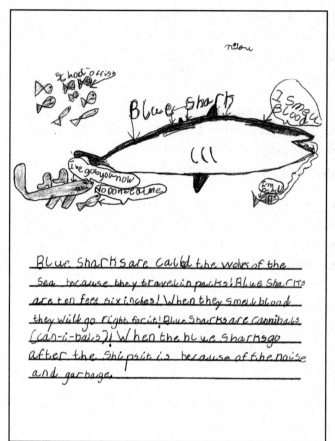

Blue sharks are called the wolves of the sea because they travel in packs! Blue Sharks are ten feet six inches! When they smell blood they will go right for it! Blue Sharks are cannibals (can-i-bals?)! When the blue sharks go after the ships it is because of the noise and garbage.

Figure 4-2. Nilou's Blue Shark Piece

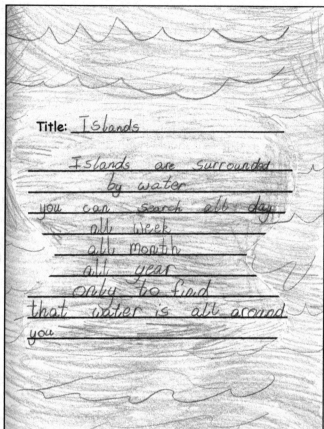

Title: Islands

Islands are surrounded by water you can search all day all week all month all year only to find that water is all around you

Figure 4-3. Mimi's "Islands" Poem

message. When Mimi goes to read, she'll be on the lookout for these same text and illustration connections. Both Nilou's and Mimi's experiences writing will scaffold their reading.

Children Who Write Are Insiders

When Ted and I first moved to New York City from upstate New York I became enchanted by the theater and the actor's life. On the rare occasion that we could afford tickets to a Broadway play, I would insist that we wait outside the stage door after the performance to see the actors and stage crew exit in street clothes and dash off to their lives outside the theater. It all felt very glamorous.

I wasn't looking for an autograph, although I often asked for one to justify my gawking. I was simply hoping to see the actors up close and get a glimpse of what was *inside* the stage door—a world I could only imagine. I wanted a peek at the dressing rooms where the actors did their make-up for performances and received kudos from fans afterward. (And did the dressing room doors really have a star on them like in the movies?) I wanted to see where the costumes were stored and how they were kept so that the butler didn't show up wearing a gangster suit. I wanted to know what it would be like to be them, to walk in their shoes. I wanted to be an insider.

When children write for real purposes in a workshop setting, they acquire a backstage pass to how published authors live their lives and craft their pieces. They learn what it's like to collect ideas in a notebook or file them in a shoebox in the hope that one might spark an idea for a new poem, informational piece, or story. They learn what it's like to work for days getting their ideas down on paper and then additional days getting them right. They understand the effort and skill it takes to communicate ideas so that their readers experience vicariously what the writer wants them to know or consider.

However, what we're trying to teach our students isn't necessarily about living a life of a novelist or biographer, but about setting them up to succeed in this age where writing, more than ever, gets things done, and where we are all writing for more audiences than ever, whether it's via electronic print or hard copy. One twenty-something entrepreneur I met asked me what I did for a living, and when I told him I was writing this book he replied, "Oh, so you're an information architect." That phrase struck me as wonderful and fresh, and underscored for me that the interplay between knowing how to write well and read well—the ability to toggle between the two and to have a trained eye for the *design* of well-ordered ideas—is going to be more and more important in the generations to come. All this begins in K–3.

Children Who Identify Themselves as Writers Feel a Kinship with Other Writers

While browsing through books at the Steinbeck Center in Monterey, California, I discovered Susan Shillinglaw's *John Steinbeck: Centennial Reflections By American Writers* (2002) and got a rush when I read that Richard Russo, another of my favorite authors, found in Steinbeck a kindred soul. Russo writes:

> In its [*Cannery Row*] opening paragraph, where the narrator describes the Row's residents, I sensed a kinship that was both thrilling and reassuring: "Its inhabitants are, as the man once said, 'whores, pimps, gamblers and sons of bitches,' by which he meant Everybody. Had the man looked through a different peephole he might have said, 'Saints and angels and martyrs and holy men,' and he would have meant the same thing.'" Well, this was pretty much my view of things in a nutshell, and to discover in a great writer such philosophical affinity sustained me then and sustains me still. (pp. 84–85)

Now take a look at eight-year-old Jared's "About the Author" page (Figure 4-4) that he wrote at the end of his book *The American Goldfinch*. Jared appreciates author Dan Greenburg (of the Zack Files fame) just as Russo does Steinbeck. And look at the "comments" page in Figure 4-5, for how Jared's classmates, also writers, feel a connection to Jared. It's almost like he has his own cheering section of peers who know just how hard it is to write, and yet how rewarding it can be. Oh, and note Jared's "good work" kudo to himself. That just about says it all!

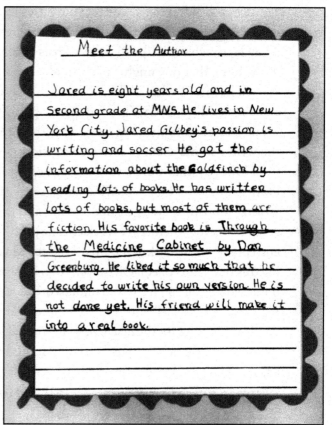

Jared's Bird Book

Meet the Author

Jared is eight years old and in Second grade at MNS. He lives in New York City. Jared Gilbey's passion is writing and soccer. He got the information about the Goldfinch by reading lots of books. He has written lots of books, but most of them are fiction. His favorite book is Through the Medicine Cabinet by Dan Greenburg. He liked it so much that he decided to write his own version. He is not done yet. His friend will make it into a real book.

Figure 4-4. Cover of Jared's Bird Book and the "Meet the Author" Page

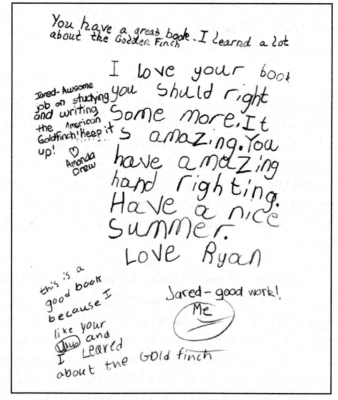

You have a great book. I learned a lot about the Golden Finch

I love your book you shuld right some more. It's amazing. You have amazing hand righting. Have a nice summer. Love Ryan

Jared- Awsome job on studying and writing the American Goldfinch! Keep it up! ♡ Amanda Drew

this is a good book because I like your and I Leared about the Gold finch

Jared- good work! Me

Figure 4-5. "Comments" Page from Jared's Bird Book

Literacy Lesson (3–5 days)

....

Using a Favorite Author to Model Writing Craft (A Mini-Author Study)

1. Select an author you love, such as Kevin Henkes, and one book he's written that's your absolute favorite.

2. Tell the children why it's your favorite. Is it the language, the way the author describes the characters, the way the illustrations and text work together, how he uses text features to extend what's written, etc.? For example, I simply love how Kevin Henkes portrays Lily in *Lily's Purple Plastic Purse*. She, as all of Henkes' characters, has a distinct personality that's revealed by what she says and how she says it.

3. Read the book to the class, finding, sharing, and discussing examples of one of these qualities of good writing that you admire, e.g., word choice, text features, the introductory "hook," character depiction.

4. Challenge the children to try out this quality of good writing during the writing workshop and call on them to share at the end.

5. Later, give children opportunities to share their favorite authors. Maybe even have them do a mini-author study as you just did, explaining why they like the author and giving examples from the text to support their assertions.

Teaching Point: Authors Write About What Matters Most to Them

Children love to hear stories. It doesn't matter whether it's a fairy tale like "Sleeping Beauty" or the real incident when author Patricia Polacco mistakenly took the wrong bag, leaving her keeping quilt and jewel box in Eeyore's Bookstore on Madison Avenue in NYC. Even though the following is a true story, let me—for story's sake—begin with "Once upon a time…."

Shelley Harwayne, my dear friend and founding principal of the Manhattan New School, invited teachers to walk over to Eeyore's with her after school to meet Patricia Polacco who would be signing books there. As great fans of *The Keeping Quilt* (2001), *Thunder Cake* (1997), *Meteor!* (1996) and just about anything else that Patricia Polacco wrote, we were delighted to go along.

After we chatted a bit (and giggled a lot) with Ms. Polacco, and after she autographed copies of the books we towed from school, she made an abrupt exit to an awaiting car taking her to La Guardia Airport where she would fly to her next book-signing event. Ms. Polacco got into the car, waved good-bye as any celebrity would, and was off. And so, we started to gather our belongings to head home.

Well, when teacher Joan Backer picked up her bag (or what she thought was her school bag) it felt different. Lighter, for one thing, and softer. And when she looked inside, she saw—not school books or homework papers—but Patricia

Polacco's very own keeping quilt and her jewel box, complete with a piece of the meteor that actually did land in the front lawn of her grandfather's farm in Michigan, becoming the inspiration for her book *Meteor!*

Can you imagine our disbelief? And can you imagine Patricia Polacco's panic when she looked inside Joan's bag? We waited...no more than a few minutes... for her call. Then... "Oh, my God! Thank goodness you have it! We're turning around right now to come back to pick it up! Thank you...thank you...THANK YOU!"

The children love that this true story, like fairy tales, had a happy ending. And from a writing perspective, I want them to appreciate the fact that writers care very much about their topics, which more often than not come from real-life experiences. Patricia Polacco wrote about her family's heirloom keeping quilt because it was an important part of who she is and the family to which she belongs. She doesn't write about topics she cares little or knows little about; the power of her stories is that they ring true. Children, like adults, find it difficult to write well about topics that fail to interest or engage them. Writers select topics carefully because the right choice can make all the difference in the world.

So what are some ways we can we help students select topics they care about? See the box below.

Ways to Help Kids Select a Topic They Care About

1. Read a personal narrative picture book, such as Patricia MacLachlan's *All the Places to Love*, Maribeth Boelts' and Noah Z. Jones' *Those Shoes*, or Susan Jeffers' *My Pony*. Then give students time to share experiences in their own lives that the book reminds them of.

2. Read books where the message is that you can write well about things you know best, such as Eileen Spinelli's *The Best Story* and Amy Schwartz's *Begin at the Beginning*. Have children discuss the book and how it relates to their experiences selecting a topic.

3. Have students keep a list of topics in their writing folder or Idea Book (see the Effective Practice: Idea Books in Chapter 9). Remind them, however, that just because they've listed a topic doesn't necessarily make it a good one.

4. Have students read through their list of topics and draw a "heart" alongside the ones they would *most* like to write about. Set aside time for them to occasionally write why this one may be a better choice than the others. Give them time to share their thinking with classmates.

5. Advise students to ask for a conference when deciding between two topics so you can guide their decision.

6. Give students time to tell stories about things that have happened to them so that they can begin to distill topics that might lead to good writing.

7. Find and share examples of how published authors find ideas for their writing. Show children how to Google their favorite authors to find their Web page.

Literacy Lesson (2–3 days)

Authors Write About What They Care Deeply About

1. Read a book that demonstrates the author cares deeply about the topic. I often read *When We Go Camping* by Margriet Ruurs. In this simple yet beautiful book, a brother and sister recount their experiences going camping with their parents. It's obvious Ruurs loves the outdoors because of the mood her evocative language creates, e.g., "the lake softly laps us to sleep," "the eagle glides across the sky like a kite without a string."

2. Ask students to listen carefully to the story as you read it aloud and think about what may have motivated the author to write it.

3. As you read, think aloud during parts that show a particular emotion or mood that conveys the author's feelings—which for this particular book is almost every page.

4. When you finish reading, ask students what they think. Engage them in a conversation about why they think the author wrote the book. Comments usually include things like camping is fun, she wants to remember the things she saw.

   Reflect on students' comments by bringing all the ideas together by saying, "So it sounds to me like you think she wrote about camping because she loves and respects the outdoors." Then add, "Writers often choose to write about things that matter to them."

5. Ask students what they know and care deeply about and begin a list of these topics. You may find that some items on the list are broad like "family," while other ideas are specific like "when my grandma takes me to the candy store." Accept all suggestions, then in future lessons discuss why narrowing the topic down promotes better writing.

Teaching Point: Writing Is Hard Work

I love explaining to children how hard it is to write well, perhaps because this lesson resonates with my own experience putting pencil to paper (or fingers to keyboard). I tell them that I never imagined myself writing a book, let alone two. Not when I'd always professed that the two things I don't do are: wash windows and write. (I still don't wash windows!)

However, I still find it excruciating to labor for hours over a couple of paragraphs and then find I'm disappointed in the result. So when I tell children how Helen Lester, author of the famed Tacky, the Penguin series, also finds writing difficult, I feel reassured and hope they will, too.

In Helen Lester's *Author: A True Story* (1994), an autobiographical account for the five- to eight-year-old crowd, she explains that as a child she had trouble writing, at first in the most basic of ways. She was a "mirror writer," writing her letters from right to left on the page. And then, to quote Lester:

> Thanks to a lot of help, I was finally
> able to write in the proper direction.
> But writing stories was so HARD for me!

Often I couldn't come up with a single idea,
and my stories got stuck in the middle,
and I couldn't think of a title,
and I had trouble making the changes my teacher
wanted me to make,
and I lost my pencils,
and I wondered why I was doing this,
and I got very very VERY frustrated.

And here's the part I simply love. Lester goes on to explain, starting with a bit of a tease (see text below and Figure 4-6), how even as an author, writing is still hard.

So here I am. An author!
And every time I sit down to write, perfect
Words line up in perfect order and WHOOP—
A perfect book pops out of the computer.

Figure 4-6. Page from Helen Lester's Author: A True Story

Well, not exactly.
Sometimes writing stories is so HARD for me!
I can't come up with a single idea,
and my stories get stuck in the middle,
and I can't think of a title,
and I have trouble making the changes my
editor wants me to make,
and I lose my pencils,
and I wonder why I'm doing this,
and I get very very VERY frustrated.

Need I say more about how all of us, young and old, should take Helen Lester's words to heart?

So what are some things writers can do when the going gets tough and the writing hard?

What to Tell Kids to Do When the Writing Gets Hard

1. Read to refuel your ideas. Sometimes just spending time with a book can open up possibilities for your own writing.

2. Take a break from writing. Go to your Idea Book for a while to play around with topics you may write about at a later date. (See Effective Practice: Idea Books in Chapter 9.)

3. Take a look at what other writers in class are doing.

4. Talk to someone about what's giving you trouble.

5. Read over what you've written.

6. Freewrite for a while—something will come.

7. Skip the part where you are stuck and move on.

8. Write something else about the topic.

Literacy Lesson (A Mini-Lesson)

Getting Unstuck: A Model Conference

1. Before the lesson ask a student who is stuck if he is willing to have a conference in front of the class so together you and he can model a strategy that might help him and other writers get "unstuck."

2. Explain to students that sometimes writers get stuck (as I'm sure they already know). Continue by explaining that there are different strategies writers use to get their creative juices flowing and that today you and a student will model one strategy writers use to help flesh out their ideas.

3. Ask the student what he is stuck on. Suppose he says, "I have nothing else to say." Ask the student to tell you about what he is writing without reading what he wrote. Repeat what you hear him say and ask any clarifying or need-more-information questions. You may even want to write down some points you heard or record notes on chart paper.

4. Then ask the student to read what he wrote. Chances are there were many details in his oral retelling that are not in his written piece. Encourage the student to include more of those details.

Remember, writing is a process, so if a student is *really* stuck on a piece of writing, maybe he should put it away for a while and begin a different piece. There will be many opportunities to revisit that piece if he wants.

Teaching Point: Writing Can Help Fix Things

Writing gives us power over our lives. We can take what was bad and shape it into something good. We can mend hurts, bridge relationships, understand what was once incomprehensible, turn a narrative into a persuasive piece, take a hurtful experience and turn it into something empowering. While these are sophisticated concepts for K–3 children to grasp, they can certainly understand how getting sad or wonderful events out and on paper makes us see them more objectively and perhaps even fixes things just a bit.

In *The Boy on Fairfield Street: How Ted Geisel Grew Up to Become Dr. Seuss,* Kathleen Krull (2004) explains how Ted Geisel turned painful childhood experiences as a German American living in Springfield, Massachusetts during World War I into a message of tolerance and hope. His classmates and neighborhood children tormented him because of his family's ethnicity—their customs, food, language—and this saddened him deeply. As a child, it must have been difficult for him to understand or make sense of such injustices, and perhaps there was little he could do but endure the experience. But as an adult, or more precisely, as an adult writer, he could give the experience a different spin and more harmonious resolution.

You remember how Sylvester McMonkey McBean scams the Sneetches by charging money to either give them stars or remove them with his Star-Off, Star-On Machine, until neither the Star-Belly nor Plain-Belly Sneetches knew who was who? He then drives away with a truckload of cash, quite content with his trickery and the Sneetches' silliness.

In the end, Dr. Seuss/Ted Geisel has the last word. The Sneetches ultimately learned that their exterior differences were unimportant compared to the community they share.

Likewise, writing can help kids handle difficult situations, such as these examples from my class:

+ When Kolbein wrote about how his dog Pretzel was hit by a car—the same Pretzel he had written numerous poems and stories about—you could tell by the expression on his face that just his classmates acknowledging how he must feel made it easier for him to handle the experience. See Figure 4-7.

+ When Bobby wrote and shared his piece about how unfair it was that his new baby brother was getting all the attention, he felt relieved when his audience of peers agreed that this was indeed unjust.

Figure 4-7. Kolbein Sharing a Poem About His Dog Pretzel

How K–3 Students Write to Fix Things

1. Encourage students to write about topics they're passionate about. It might be saving the environment or persuading their parents to buy them a pet, or it might be to get an extra 5 minutes of recess. Whatever it is, give students opportunities to write about topics of their own choosing.

2. Model various purposes for writing (e.g., to sell, to persuade, to keep in touch). Use books like *I Wanna Iguana* by Karen Kaufmann Orioff and *ABC Philadelphia: Travel Guides for Kids* by Matthew G. Rosenberger as examples.

3. Celebrate and support students' opinions and ideas. Ask them to share and talk about how it feels to write about something they care deeply about and how it impacts the quality of their writing.

4. Encourage them to write thank-you notes and apology letters to let people know how they feel.

 # Literacy Lesson
(Mini-Lessons done over a week)

Introducing Students to Writing with the Intent to Fix Something

1. Building on the idea that writers write about topics they care deeply about, it's important to let children know that writing about these topics can serve many purposes. People can write to share an emotion or a fun time with others. Or they may write to change something or get something done.

2. Share with students letters to the editor, advertisements, and books that have a "call to action," such as books on the environment or animal rights. Ask students to figure out what the author is trying to fix.

3. Make a list of these topics and then generate a list of topics about which students might write (e.g., wanting a pet, less homework, better playground equipment), continually focusing students on things they want to change.

4. Share different forms of publishing that children's writing might take. They can make a poster, write a letter, do a photo essay, create a newsletter—there are all sorts of publishing possibilities for you to model and children to write.

Please remember that "writing can help to fix things" is a sophisticated concept. And while it is important to introduce students to the variety of purposes for writing, it is not necessary that all students write to fix something. Instead, consider this an open invitation for students to widen their writing repertoire as well as providing them with insights into reading. Furthermore, you may have a passionate group of students who together want to change something in their community. If that is the case, support students' collaborative efforts in any way you can. You can be sure there will be writing involved!

+ When Carmen wrote about her grandma dying—the one who made sugar cookies for her whenever she visited—she felt better when Anna, one of her classmates, asked if she had the cookie recipe and suggested that maybe she could make them and think of her grandma. Carmen did, in fact, have the recipe, and went one step further by making the cookies with her mom for the class to sample and giving each student a copy of the recipe written in Carmen's own handwriting.

Children Learn That Writing, Like Reading, Takes Time

When you share with your students stories of how writers spend their day and the routines they follow, the two most consistent features among them are that they write daily and seek feedback from other writers. These facets of their writing process are as much a part of their artistic survival as nourishment, sleep, and exercise are to their physical and mental well-being.

Making Time to Write

Young writers, as do their adult counterparts, thrive on a writing schedule that offers consistency and predictability. If one day a child is having trouble coming up with a topic, just knowing he will write the following day and the next and the next pushes him to mull over topics when he's at home, on his way to the soccer field, or reading about a topic he loves. If a student is having a difficult time organizing his piece of writing, when he reads he'll be more aware of how published authors organize their information, knowing that he'll have the opportunity to apply these observations to his own piece of writing during the writing workshop.

Notice how my writing workshop schedule shown on the next page parallels my reading workshop schedule (see Figures 3-5 and 3-6). The symmetry communicates to children that both writing and reading are important and complementary endeavors. I say *endeavors* because if we can embrace writing and reading as pleasurable pursuits, as opposed to seeing them through a joyless skill-building lens, then it's easier to promote the reading-writing connection—and give writing an *equal* star-studded billing.

A Sample Writing Workshop Schedule

My daily writing workshop includes a mini-lesson, conferences or small-group writing, independent writing, and writing share. In the daily schedule on the next page I describe each of these practices within a recommended time frame.

Reading and writing workshop both occur daily, and there's no hard and fast rule regarding which should come first. While I typically schedule the reading workshop for 9:30 after our morning meeting, with the writing workshop following on its heels, in January I'm likely to move either writing or reading to the afternoon to give math the morning prime time it often needs. This is because I'm less skilled at teaching math than literacy and sometimes like to do it in the morning when I'm fresh.

A Daily 45-Minute Writing Workshop Schedule

- **Mini-lesson or writing share** (10 minutes)
  The teacher uses literature or samples of children's writing to offer examples of the skill or strategy she's demonstrating. She might also decide to start the workshop by having several children share a piece of writing and give them feedback on what they might do that day to improve the piece or to give other students ideas for topics they might write about.

- **Writing conferences or small-group writing** (25 minutes)
  The teacher meets one to one with three-to-four students to advise them on what they're doing well and how they might improve a piece. Or...

  The teacher meets with small groups of writers that she's gathered together because they're dealing with similar writing issues, e.g., finding a topic, organizing a piece of writing, or editing a piece before they publish.

- **Independent writing**
  The children not working with the teacher (above) use this time to write stories, poems, and informational text. Sometimes they select their own writing topics, and at other times they may be asked to write in the genre the class is studying. They might also work in their Idea Books and Ta-Da Publishing Books, edit pieces of writing, or work on spelling or handwriting.

- **Writing share** (10 minutes)
  The writing share is often launched with a prompt like, "What did you learn about yourself as a writer? What worked so well today that you might try to do it again?"

The most important scheduling consideration regarding reading and writing is to make sure you schedule them daily and give each of them the time they deserve. Then make visible the synergy that exists between the two processes.

Children Learn the Tools of the Trade

Craftspersons—carpenters, painters, knitters, sculptors, etc.—require tools to work, and this also holds true for writers who need a place to collect, imagine, record ideas, and draft and revise pieces of writing. Having the right tools can make all the difference in the world to writers trying to communicate their ideas and to teachers who are helping children see the connection between reading and writing.

Writing Folder

The writing folder, like the reading folder, offers students the opportunity to focus on process as well as product. Its heft and contents reflect the work that's involved in writing texts for others to comprehend and reinforces the connection between reading to understand and writing to be understood.

The writing folders, stored in plastic bins alongside my rocking chair, are distributed at the beginning of the writing workshop and returned at the end. Each folder (see Figure 4-8) contains:

- several pieces of writing a student may be working on (it's not at all unusual for a student to begin a second, or even third piece, before deciding which one to focus on and make better)

- a writing assessment notebook where I record observations regarding a student's needs and the progress he's making

- a Word Book containing basic high-frequency words and spaces to add additional words the child may want to remember how to spell

- a topic list on which a student records topics about which he may want to write

- a handwriting notebook to teach or refresh children's handwriting skills. (*Note on handwriting:* I teach children in a mini-lesson how to form new letters and later encourage each student to identify, in his own pieces of writing, the letters he needs to practice and perfect.)

- a personalized editing checklist consisting of the five circle labels attached to the inside of each folder. (I will discuss this further in the Effective Practice: Editing Checklist in Chapter 9.)

In addition to these standard materials housed in the children's writing folders, each child has additional tools that support his writing process, some of which I'll describe below.

Figure 4-8. Writing Folder

Idea Book

Two months into the school year, I transition children into using an Idea Book (see more on this in the Effective Practice: Idea Books in Chapter 9) where they gather pictures, word lists, artifacts, word and character webs, as well as topic lists to jump-start their writing. Each Idea Book is made by spiral-fastening together 20 to 30 sheets of printer paper between an oaktag front and back cover.

During mini-lessons I demonstrate how to use the Idea Books by sharing how published authors gather ideas for potential stories. An excellent source of information on well-known children's authors' lives and their writing process is Richard C. Owen's Meet the Author series. This series contains the autobiographies of well-loved authors such as Cynthia Rylant, Seymour Simon, Laura Numeroff, David Adler, and Patricia Polacco. Author Web sites are also a great way to learn about authors.

By using an Idea Book, children learn that stories don't just happen. A lot of hard work and planning goes into the finished product, and it may take published authors years to go from idea to publication. Seeing this and participating in this collection process primes children to appreciate the efforts of the authors whose books they're reading.

Ta-Da Publishing Book

In addition to their self-selected topics, the children and I work on four genre units throughout the year. These may include personal narratives, informational text writing, poetry, persuasive writing, pourquoi tales (folk stories that explain why or how aspects of the natural world came to be), and fiction. We typically include a personal narrative as the first published piece in their Ta-Da Book (aptly named to showcase their personal bests, Ta-Da, look at these!) since students just naturally seem to begin their year writing these. During these units I present mini-lessons that demonstrate skills, strategies, and techniques needed to write in that genre.

After each several weeklong unit concludes, the children publish and illustrate their piece in their hardcover Ta-Da Publishing Book in Figure 4-9. (See more on this in the Effective Practice: Ta-Da Publishing Books in Chapter 9.) Their illustrations may be quite elaborate as when publishing an informational piece or less elaborate when publishing a persuasive text.

Sophie's Publishing Book
2004–2005

Figure 4-9. Ta-Da Publishing Book

Project Folder

In addition to the blue writing folder children use for their daily writing, they also have a project folder that contains a piece they may be working on for their Ta-Da Book or their thinking and work around a genre unit the class is investigating. For example, if we're writing a class ABC book on New York City, each child keeps his NYC writing in the project folder, separate from his other writing, so that he can easily locate it when he needs to work on the project.

♦ ♦ ♦

Compare the "bad and good paper" I used to provide for my students during their "for-the-bulletin-board-writing" with the tools and materials I now provide during the writing workshop. In the "bad paper/good paper" scenario the children never got to experience the actual process and work of writing. They were never asked to think long and hard about a topic that most interested them, rehearse their ideas, share drafts of writing, apply what they learned from reading to their writing, reread their writing for meaning, and revise to make it better. They were asked instead to simply write, without being taught how to write with any depth or engaging in the process or tools writers typically use.

Now, children engage in the real work involved in bringing an idea to fruition. They see that writing is hard. That writers often labor for days, weeks, and months to communicate their ideas. And in seeing and experiencing this for themselves, they gain new insight and appreciation for the work the writers of the texts they're reading have done to bring them the story, information, etc. And because of these first-hand experiences and insights, they're more likely to work harder when they read to understand what the author has to say.

In *Of Primary Importance: What's Essential in Teaching Young Writers*, Ann Marie Corgill (2009) explains her reasoning behind the Writing Journey Folders she's developed to help make visible to families, friends, classmates, and teachers who attend her class' writing celebrations (and also as a reminder to the writers themselves) the steps involved in producing a finished piece of writing. She states:

> For years I secretly wished that the people at those celebrations could see every part of the work that went into creating each "perfect" published piece. What they always saw were the beautifully watercolored, well-crafted, correctly spelled, neatly handwritten published pieces of writing. (p. 36)

So in response to her frustration and to spotlight both product and process, Corgill designed a special folder to include the child's self-reflection on his piece, rough drafts of his work, letters to families about the study, comments sheets, and a photograph or copy of the final piece. For more on Corgill's Writing Journey Folder, see *Of Primary Importance*.

◆ ◆ ◆

I'm not the first to say that children's composing, revising, and reading their work and the work of their peers strengthens their reading. What I want to be "new" here is an appeal for you to start small and discover what works for you and your students. If you need to work up to having children write every day, that's fine. If you aren't familiar with children's authors and picture books, or feel uneasy about mining them for writing mini-lessons, pair up with a colleague or the school librarian to help you.

As I write, the image of a Slinky, that classic children's toy, comes to mind as a metaphor for how children's writing helps them spring into their reading. Picture metal spirals, slinking back and forth, back and forth, between open palms. Imagine the springy quality, the great clinking sound, the shifting of its weight, back and forth. I encourage you to find your own metaphor for how you can move between writing and reading, reading and writing, each day, so the flow between the two is indeed a flow rather than just a bell ringing or a clock striking a new hour.

 CHAPTER **5**

Time to Talk

Giving Children the Chance to Put Words
to Their Thoughts

When I work in schools, teachers will often pull me aside to confide that their students don't seem to be able to open up and talk when asked to share what they think about a topic or book they're reading. These teachers bemoan: "You read a book, ask the kids to talk about it, and they have little, if anything, to say. They look at you pensively. Then some generous souls take pity and offer a few comments, but nothing that would make you burst into the teachers' lounge—shouting, 'You'll never believe what my kids just said!' What are we doing wrong?"

As we talk, these teachers eventually come to realize that perhaps their students are picking up on the pressure we've been feeling as educators in recent years. They see our tight jaws, hear our sighs, or detect our impatience when a classmate seems to take too long to give an answer. They sense how intently we are listening for the right answer, as if our jobs depended on it. They see us glancing up at the clock, worried we are falling off schedule. They note when we don't laugh or even smile when something funny happens in class, and know when a laugh is forced. We need to break through these negative perceptions by creating a comfortable time and space for authentic conversation.

Cathryn Sill, author of the acclaimed "ABOUT" series of informational texts—*About Mammals: A Guide for Children* (2007), *About Birds* (1997), *About Penguins* (2009), etc.—has a consistent style in communicating information to readers that should be the paradigm for how to teach and provide time for kids to talk.

On each double-page spread, Sill juxtaposes a richly colored, full-page picture of birds, amphibians, fish, etc., alongside a white page on which there is written just one brief sentence or phrase (Figure 5-1). In doing so, she invites readers to luxuriate in the picture and consider what's written. This allows them to then add to it their own experiences, questions, and connections to their lives. In a sense, Sill invites readers to coauthor the book by filling in the white space she's left.

That's how our classrooms should look, feel, and sound. A richly colored palette of gorgeous and engaging reading materials, comfy places to read and write alongside a friend, and time to talk and share ideas and information. We need to say less and leave plenty of white space for kids to say more—to meander about, wonder in, and talk about what they know and are learning.

Baby birds hatch from eggs.

PLATE 2
American Robin

Figure 5-1. Pages from Catherine Sills' About Birds: A Guide for Children

Why Oral Language Development Is Important

In their landmark study, *Meaningful Differences in the Everyday Experience of Young American Children*, Betty Hart and Todd Risley (1995) found startling differences in the early language experiences of children from more economically advantaged families and less advantaged ones.

> In four years . . . an average child in a professional family would have accumulated experience with almost 45 million words, an average child in a working-class family would have accumulated experience with 26 million words, and an average child in a welfare family would have accumulated experience with 13 million words. (p. 198)

That's a gap of 30 million words between children at the top of the socioeconomic ladder and those at the bottom, and the gap continues to widen each year.

Hart and Risley also learned that not only were there differences in the *quantity* of words children were exposed to, but also a difference in the *quality* of the language children experienced. Children from lower socioeconomic-level families were more likely to hear *restrictive* language, while those from more advantaged homes heard more *elaborative* talk.

Children who come to school having engaged in rich and stimulating language experiences during their early years are better equipped to succeed in school. They've been spoken to and read to a lot and have begun to internalize much of the vocabulary and language structures that show up in academic text. Consequently, while all students, regardless of their socioeconomic status, need schools to provide rich language experiences, vocabulary development, and time for accountable talk, schools need to work even harder to help students from the lower socioeconomic levels bridge the language-experience gap that hinders their ability to learn.

> *And here's the sad irony. In our current educational climate, we teachers, tired and stressed from all the curricular demands we've been handed in the name of raising students' test scores and reaching prescribed benchmarks, resort all too often to the very same restrictive language practices that occur in less advantaged socioeconomic households.*

And here's the sad irony. In our current educational climate, we teachers, tired and stressed from all the curricular demands we've been handed in the name of raising students' test scores and reaching prescribed benchmarks, resort all too often to the *very same* restrictive language practices that occur in less advantaged socioeconomic households. In our struggle to do more and more, faster and earlier, we catapult from topic to topic, reading unit to reading unit, assessment to assessment, activity to activity.

In the trade-off, we sacrifice opportunities to *elaborate* and be *explicit*—to explain to students why we've selected a particular poem or big book to share, what led us to choose the skill or strategy we're modeling, and how the demonstration will help them read or write better. We also are often too rushed to engage students in meaningful discussions that will elevate their thinking and reading to higher ground.

If comprehension is our goal, then we need to create "talking" classrooms, not silent ones. We need to encourage and support students to participate more fully in thoughtful conversations with us and with their classmates. (The Effective Practices in Chapter 8 will offer some concrete ideas on how to bring more talk into your classroom, as will the suggestions provided in this chapter.)

Why Isn't There More Talk in Our Classrooms?

Despite the fact that oral language plays a central role in children's reading comprehension and, in fact, sets the ceiling on it (Biemiller 2003), oral language seldom gets the attention it deserves. Schools typically focus their energies on reading and writing, and pay lip service to children's oral language development.

So why aren't schools scrambling to get their hands on materials that enhance children's abilities to express their ideas orally and hear what others have to say? Why aren't district leaders advocating for more time for kids to talk? Mandating it even? Why aren't we explaining to families the importance of "time to talk" and enlisting their support for promoting more of it? Let's explore some possible reasons for this neglect in the hope that increased awareness will motivate a shift in practice.

The Need to Feel in Control

I spent my first years of teaching trying to maintain order, and I must admit, I got pretty good at it. Back then, my idea of a well-functioning classroom was to have students working quietly at their seats on an assignment I'd given. I would weave in and out of the clusters of desks, bend over occasionally to check on a student, and then continue walking until it was time to collect the papers and move on to the next activity and assignment. How proud I felt if the principal or a colleague stopped by and saw how well I had things under control.

But however competent I looked, however well-structured my classroom appeared on the surface, there were serious flaws in my approach that undermined my children's ability to learn. I didn't know enough to factor in purposeful talk so students could interact with one another as they made sense of things. It didn't register that talk is an essential part of literacy and an important life skill. Fortunately, we know so much more today than ever before about how oral language development relates to learning.

Eric Jensen, a pioneer in the field of brain-compatible learning and author of *Teaching with the Brain in Mind* (1998), sheds light on the conditions that enhance or detract from learning, maintaining that learning involves both *external input* and *internal processing*. External input occurs when the learner receives information from an outside source, e.g., a book, a firsthand experience, a conversation. Internal processing is when the learner uses the external input to create new meaning. If either the external input or the time for internal processing is missing, learning cannot occur. Both must be present.

Jensen challenges the imbalance that typically exists between the amount of time teachers spend trying to get and keep students' attention and the time they allow for kids to process new information, ideas, and concepts. He posits:

> What if getting [students'] attention ought to be the exception—not the rule? What if we're placing inappropriate and often unreasonable demands on students, and the more that a teacher has a student's attention, the less genuine learning can happen? (p. 41)

> You can either have your learner's attention or they can be making meaning, but never at the same time. (p. 46) … It may actually be the down time, which we know is not really "down" that's most important for information processing. (p. 47)

With this in mind, let's provide instruction that's more balanced, where children have opportunities to both receive *and* make sense of new information. All instruction, regardless of whether it relates to oral language development, reading, math, etc., should involve:

+ demonstrations of skills and strategies students need to know
+ time for students to practice these skills and strategies
+ time for students to discuss with their teacher and peers what they learned and to hear what others have to say

Accountable Talk Takes Time

Helping children comprehend text by boosting their oral language experiences should be among our top priorities. To do this we need to eliminate some of our less effective and time-consuming practices and modify some of the "keepers"— the components of balanced literacy and the reading workshop we can tweak a bit to create opportunities to nurture rich dialogue. The box below and the chart on the next page walk you through some of these possibilities.

Freeing Up Time to Talk

- *Choose* from your balanced literacy menu the components that will most likely help you reach your goals. Don't try to do them all. Doing fewer practices well—with time for kids to talk— is better than silencing children as you rush to check off items on your teaching to-do list.

- Be *explicit* when addressing students. *Tell* them what you want them to know and do—and *why*. Avoid engaging in dead-end question-answer banter. (See "Questioning Techniques" box on p. 102.)

- Ask fewer, but higher-level, questions that lead students to think and dialogue. (Again, see the "Questioning Techniques" box.)

- *Balance* the type and *limit* the number of written responses to text you ask kids to make. In addition to requiring fewer responses in general, the responses children do make should include opportunities for them to work with partners and share their thinking with the class.

- Be *selective*. When kids turn and talk, you don't need to hear what they have shared each and every time. Just the fact that they're getting their ideas out, and hearing what their partner has to say, is huge.

- *Rethink* worksheets (and dramatically scale back on them) so that they are a better use of children's time. In her new book, *Moving Forward with RTI: Reading and Writing Activities for Every Instructional Setting and Tier*, Mary Howard (2010) offers some generic activity forms that get children thinking and talking about texts they're reading, rather than filling in worksheets that often amount to little more than busywork.

- *Prepare* and copy a Weekly Homework Sheet to send home on Monday, listing the homework for each day. This saves children from spending class time copying homework assignments from the board. On the back of the sheet, include any needed explanations for the homework, reminders of upcoming trips and events, deadlines to note, vocabulary words kids are learning in class, etc. (See Appendix 7 online for a sample homework sheet.)

You're Already Doing . . .	So Instead . . .
Read-Aloud and Shared Reading	*Make them interactive.* Instead of simply reading aloud to kids or sharing an engaging text ask analytical "how" and "why" questions that get students thinking.
	Balance the amount of fiction you read aloud and share with equal amounts of informational text. I've found that students are more likely to ask questions and engage in conversations in response to informational texts than to fiction.
	Read aloud short, high-quality chapter books instead of long ones. When our read-alouds take too long, we don't leave enough time for the children to discuss what we've read.
	Read aloud picture books (even in the upper grades) to give kids time to discuss the ideas and information. Since the texts are shorter, there'll be more time for talk.
	Select large-formatted informational texts to read aloud and share. Because children can see the pages up close—the photos, diagrams, charts, scale drawings, captions—they're more likely to ask questions or initiate a conversation around what they see than when the book's a smaller, standard-size trade book.
Guided Reading	*Vary the type of small-group work you do.* In addition to guided reading groups, you can work with small groups of readers for interactive read-aloud, literature circles, and book clubs.
	Keep your groups brief. Kindergarten and first-grade groups should last 15 minutes, and second- and third-grade groups should last between 20 and 30 minutes.
	Select short texts for guided reading. Since it's preferable not to have children's reading of a single title extend beyond a week, it's wise to select shorter texts for guided reading, which allow time for kids to talk.
Reading Conferences	Instead of having an agenda when you confer with students, open with questions like, "So how's it going?" and "What can I do to help?" This will make your conference look and feel more like a conversation and will encourage students to express what's on their mind. This will also help you to identify and respond to students' needs.
	Limit the amount of time you meet with each student so that your conferences and workshop don't extend beyond the allotted time. You should aim to teach just one new skill or strategy during each conference. Conferences with emergent or early readers typically last between 7-to-10 minutes since you'll want to help them select a couple of books for their book bag and perhaps take an informal

continues

You're Already Doing...	So Instead...
Reading Conferences, *cont.*	running record of a book-bag book they're reading. Conferences with transitional and fluent readers last around 5 minutes and most often do not involve taking a running record.
Independent Reading	*Acknowledge that students need "downtime" built into their independent reading.* Since children can only attend to their reading for modest amounts of time, provide opportunities for them to talk with other students about what they're reading and learning. Partner reading with time to talk afterward is one way to do this.
Reading Share	Let's face it: Although reading share is on your reading workshop schedule, it's likely that you cancel it more often than you'd care to admit because you've run over on other parts of the workshop.
	Therefore, *structure your reading workshop schedule (and keep to it) so you can have kids share daily.* Preserving the time for reading share is a surefire way to give kids a chance to say what's on their mind, discuss strategies they're using, and learn from one another.
Writing Share	Once or twice a week, move writing share to the beginning of the writing workshop, instead of at the end. This way you won't run out of time, and children will have the opportunity to talk about a piece they're writing and receive feedback from classmates.
	Let children gather in groups of three so each child reads his piece to two of his peers, gets to talk about it, and receives feedback. This is instead of having a couple children read their piece to the entire class at the beginning or end of the workshop.
Writing Mini-Lesson	Design mini-lessons that give children opportunities to share ideas. For example, when doing a series of mini-lessons on selecting a writing topic, allow students to sit in a circle and discuss how they find topics or have them state topics they're writing about and why they chose them.

Over-Reliance on Measurable Outcomes

The children are on the edge of their seats as I finish reading a chapter from Kate DiCamillo's *The Miraculous Journey of Edward Tulane* (2009) about a china rabbit that appears incapable of giving love even though he receives it in abundance—especially from Abiline, the ten-year-old girl who owns and adores him. As I close the book and look at the students in anticipation for how they might respond, I'm expecting them to comment on why Pelligrina, Abiline's grandmother, whispered the words, "You disappoint me" into Edward's ear as she pulled the bedsheets up to his whiskers. And sure enough my students zero in on this question of character.

Alexis jumps in first: "I knew it. I knew it all along. Something's weird about Pelligrina. The way she told that creepy story about the princess and the warthog." Jeffrey chimes in: "Yeah, and how about the way she stared into Edward's eyes when she read about the princess…you know…who didn't care about love or anything, even when everybody loved her? Freaky!" Many of the children agree; while others remain neutral for now, not yet ready to take a stand.

I'd been reading this book for a couple of days, and had paused now and then to ask children to turn and talk with their partner to sort out what was happening. I wanted to help them flesh out what Edward was like at the beginning of the book so that they could appreciate how he changes at the end, and reflect on and discuss how each experience along the way moves Edward one step closer to becoming a transformed rabbit.

As I read I explained, as unobtrusively as possible, a few, but not all, of the unfamiliar words, such as *jaunty* and *condescending*, knowing full well that children would need to encounter them many times over before they actually own them. On some days I encourage kids to write or sketch what they're thinking in their journals. But not every day—and not today.

While a written assignment would indeed produce both tangible documentation and a grade, it would preclude opportunities for students to learn from one another. Answering questions on paper won't give voice to their classmates' take on Pelligrina. It won't let them experience the multiple perspectives that are surfacing. They won't see alternatives to their own way of thinking or how they might think differently in the future. These readers saw that Edward was headed down a self-destructive path and rejoiced in his redemption.

It's not that accountability and a tangible record of children's learning aren't important. They most certainly are. No one is saying that we must never assign a grade to a child's written response, or that we devalue in any way the learning that occurs as children commit their ideas to paper, or that using a rubric or checklist to evaluate a child's participation in a discussion should be avoided. (See Figure 5-2 here and Appendix 8 online for a literature discussion form that might be used to keep notes on children's participation.)

Rather, we need to recognize the difference between engaging students in tasks that promote learning, and assigning work because it provides data. It undermines learning to reduce instructional practices to whether or not they render numbers to post, compare, and analyze. Talk is a pre-eminent means for helping children understand texts and their lives. In fact, the time kids have to talk about books can help shape their lives.

Literature Discussion Group Record

Title: _____

Date: _____

Students Name	Prepared to Discuss	Listened as Others Spoke	Engaged in Discussion	Quality of Responses	Additional Comments

Comprehension from the Ground Up © 2011 by Sharon Taberski. (Heinemann Portsmouth, NH.)

Figure 5-2. Form to Evaluate Children's Participation in Discussion

I witnessed a real-life instance of this deep learning when six-year-old Robert, spoken to for teasing a classmate during recess, admitted: "I was being like Claude [the bully in Rosemary Wells' *Timothy Goes to School* (2000)], when I should have been more like Timothy." Einstein had it right when he said: "Everything that can be counted does not necessarily count; everything that counts cannot necessarily be counted."

Lack of Knowledge of Protocol

Part of the challenge, I think, in sustaining rich conversations in our classrooms is that the American culture does not promote meandering, intellectually stimulating conversations over lunch or dinner. In addition, most teachers today did not have the benefit of book talks or literature discussion groups when they were in school. I know I never did.

I sat all day and listened as the teacher went through the drill, as she expounded on topic upon topic. I listened and watched the clock, greatly anticipating the end of the school day. My teachers may have gotten better at expressing their ideas through all their talking, but we kids didn't. I never got to see what a good literature circle or book talk looks like, let alone experience them myself. That's why I had to go to sources like those I list below for models of how to sharpen my oral language focus when teaching a new generation of students:

+ *Comprehension Through Conversation: The Power of Purposeful Talk in the Reading Workshop* (2006) by Maria Nichols

  Synopsis: As the title suggests, this books offers suggestions for how teachers can encourage purposeful talk in their classrooms. Maria Nichols lays the groundwork by discussing the importance of developing children's ability to think and communicate in today's world, discusses how our environment can enable purposeful talk, and describes practices that will "grow" accountable talk in the day-to-day life of our classroom.

  Why I Love It: In addition to the fact that it's packed with practical suggestions for how to promote talk in our classrooms, such as developing reading partnerships, using shared reading to increase the depth of students' thinking, and engaging students in reading, thinking, and talking experiences around fiction and informational text, I love that the book itself is short, allowing teachers who are already stretched for time to easily access important ideas and information they can use right away, and perhaps even talk with colleagues about what they learned.

+ *Choice Words: How Our Language Affects Children's Learning* (2004) by Peter Johnston

  Synopsis: To say this book is important is an understatement. It's an absolute necessity for teachers. Peter Johnston reveals how the language we use has a powerful effect on how students feel about themselves as learners and their willingness to put forth their ideas. For example, asking a writer or a reader, "What problems did you come across today?" reveals the expectation that learners *will* encounter problems and acknowledges that problems are a necessary part of learning and growth. Johnston's book is packed with examples like this that we can implement right away by simply changing the way we talk.

Why I Love It: Johnston took something that should be obvious—the words we use when addressing students do indeed matter—and demonstrates how to replace our often careless language with choice words that affirm and empower students.

* *Reading for Real: Teach Students to Read with Power, Intention, and Joy in K–3 Classrooms* (2008) by Kathy Collins

Synopsis: Kathy Collins' book takes us into the world of reading clubs, shows us how they support accountable talk, and demonstrates how to implement them. The appendices are filled with partnership contracts, note-taking sheets, reading club to-do lists, and planning guides. It's a practical reference for primary-grade teachers who want to get reading clubs up and running.

Why I Love It: I love Collins' playfulness in regards to reading clubs and how she insists there is no one right or wrong approach. Instead, she challenges us to be creative and flexible, to change our procedure from group to group as our needs and the needs of our students change, highlighting the importance of being responsive to students' strengths, needs, and interests.

Creating an Environment to Develop Oral Language and Vocabulary

Our environment, which includes the physical setup of our classroom, our materials, the daily schedule we keep, as well as the tone we set, can work for or against us achieving our goals. Its thrust should be interactive, promoting opportunities for students to share ideas and to converse with one another.

In Technical Report #512, "Developing Expertise in Reading Comprehension," P. David Pearson et al. (1990) assign "interaction" a starring position in helping students become comprehending readers, and thus states:

We can no longer think of reading comprehension as a series of discrete skills that can be summed to achieve comprehension ability. Instead, we see comprehension as a complex process involving interactions between readers and texts in various contexts for various purposes. (p. 6)

The photographs and schedule on the following pages demonstrate ways to make your classroom more interactive and how to enhance talk as a tool for comprehension.

1. My classroom is designed with inter-action in mind.

   Children work at tables instead of at assigned desks. Many of the tables are low to the ground, enabling children to sit on the floor instead of on a chair. Had I provided a desk and chair for each of the 25 students, there would have been little room left for students to move around and interact.

   Whole-group instruction takes place at the meeting area where children sit up close to me and alongside one another so they can more readily talk and engage with the text.

   There are a couple of small meeting areas around the room where children gather to work and talk.

2. Guided reading gives children the chance to talk with their teacher and group members about the text they're reading in a small-group setting.

4. When children share their writing with the class, they get to hear from their peers what worked well and ideas for how they might make a piece better.

A Second- and Third-Grade Daily Reading and Writing Schedule

First Independent Reading (20 minutes)

Children read books from informational-text baskets and other book baskets around the room. They don't have their book bags of just-right books during this time and can select any book they want. The teacher does small-group reading or word work with her most "at-risk" readers.

Meeting (Whole-Group Session) (50 minutes)

Children share informational text learning from the first independent reading time that is often related to content-area studies and do "Words Words Words" vocabulary.

The teacher does interactive read-aloud, shared reading and phonics, or shared writing with a strategy or skills focus.

Reading Workshop (60 minutes)

Mini-lesson (often a recap of the skill or strategy demonstrated during read-aloud, shared reading, and so on).

Reading conferences or small-group reading The teacher meets one to one with three-to-five children to advise them on what they're doing well and what they might do better, and to match them with books for their independent reading book bag. Or...

The teacher meets with small groups of readers to guide them through a text that would be too difficult for them to read on their own. She might also work with small groups for interactive read-aloud, literature circles, or word study.

Second independent reading The children read books from their book bag, work on their reading log, response sheets, or response notebook. They might also do reading-related center activities.

Reading share The reading share is often launched with a prompt like, "What did you learn about yourself as a reader? What worked so well today that you might try to do it again?"

Writing Workshop (45 minutes)

The workshop includes a 10-minute mini-lesson (typically a recap of a skill or strategy that has been previously taught at greater length), a 25-minute independent writing time for independent writing, conferences or small-group work, and a 10-minute writing share. During the writing share, the teacher explores such questions as, "What did you learn about yourself as a writer? What worked so well that you may try to do it again? (See Chapter 4 for a more detailed description of the writing workshop.)

© S.Taberski (2010)

---

3. In addition to the spontaneous conversations that arise throughout the reading and writing times of day, my literacy block schedule provides three distinct opportunities for students to talk about their reading and their writing and to dialogue with one another.

   • after the first independent reading
   • the reading share
   • the writing share

5. Informal conversations occur throughout the day as children collaborate on their reading and writing.

6. Part of the fun in reading is having someone to share it with. Children love to sit close together so they can chat about what they're reading.

7. Talk about a captive audience! These children listen intently as a classmate reads aloud.

8. Children can't get enough of these content-area literacy centers where they can buddy up with a classmate to read, write, and learn about a topic they're both interested in. First-grade teacher Millie Velazquez's Dinosaur Center, shown here, is widely popular with her students and admired by her colleagues.

9. Reading and writing conferences allow us to get up close and personal. They're the perfect time of day for the children to learn from us what they do well and consider what they may need to work on. Ideally, we teachers also learn from our students information that will impact our teaching.

Questioning Techniques

There are questions and then there are questions. Some questions feel like an interrogation, don't they? Even in professional and social circles, we come across people who seem to ask questions that are somehow more for their benefit and power. We feel like we are being tested, that the questions are after our weaknesses rather than our strengths. In these cases, we feel it's best to play possum. These are the questions that don't belong in K–3 classrooms because they shut children's hearts and intellects down in no time flat.

Then there are other questions that open us up and invite us to reflect and say more. They feel safe and nonthreatening because we sense that the person asking the question is genuinely interested in hearing more of what we have to say. We can tell by the way they lean in close so as not to miss a word. We can see in their face that they're not being judgmental. That they're not looking for a right or wrong answer, just prompting us to think and consider what's on our mind.

This type of questioning technique is more like a Socratic dialogue. Rather than eliciting a correct response, the purpose is to *engage* students in conversation and dialogue that helps them articulate and clarify their thoughts, drawing from them their own knowledge, examples, experiences, and insights.

In the rush to cover curriculum and pressure to make sure our students are "getting it," it's all too easy to default into an interrogatory line of questioning. It's something we have to guard against. Here's how an exchange of this nature might go:

"Boys and girls, what's the name of the story we started to read yesterday?" (The teacher asks this while holding the book in her hands so it's obvious to all that this is not a real question.) A child answers. "And who's the main character?" Another child answers. "Who remembers what happened in chapter one?" A child answers, often several more, because the teacher may not be satisfied with the first answer that was given.

Then the teacher again—"What do you think will happen now?"

And it may go on like this for several more minutes, with the likely result that the students are no longer interested in hearing more of the story. Their curiosity and motivation have been dampened. Unintentionally, this teacher's questioning technique has set up a barrier between her and her students. The dead-end questions led to dead-end answers, ruining any hopes of serious communication and dialogue.

Now consider this scenario where instead of looking for a *right* answer, the teacher is getting students to think. She sits holding the book on her lap:

Teacher: Boys and girls I just can't wait to read more of *Absolutely Lucy.* I felt sorry for Bobby, didn't you? It must be really hard to be so shy and not have any friends. I keep wondering though how he's going to fix his problem. I'd love to hear some of your ideas.

Child: I think maybe Bobby's not going to be shy at the end.

Teacher: What makes you say that?

Child: 'Cause stories have happy endings.

Teacher: Can you say more about what you mean?

Child: Well, all the books I read turn out happy. Gloria and Officer Buckle were friends again at the end.

Teacher: Hmmm . . . so you're saying that most books you read have a happy ending. Interesting.

Teacher: Anyone want to add on to what [child] has said about books having happy endings, or how *Absolutely Lucy* might turn happy at the end?

Child 2: I think the dog on the cover is going to help Bobby.

Teacher: I'm curious to know why you think this?

continues

Questioning Techniques, *cont.*

And the conversation continues. Here the children's thinking is guided by the questions the teacher asks. Not any old questions, but ones that elicit answers that in turn generate new questions and new thinking.

Here are some Socratic-type questions and prompts that elicit conversation and dialogue:

- What makes you say that?
- Can you give me an example?
- Why do you think this is so?
- What do you think caused that to happen?
- Can you say that another way? I'm not sure I understand what you mean.
- I'd love to hear your thoughts.
- Tell me more.
- What's another way to look at that?
- How do you know this?
- How are _____ and _____ similar?
- Why do you think I'm asking you this question?
- How does that connect with what we learned before?

"Can it be, Ischomachus, that asking questions is teaching? I am just beginning to see what is behind all your questions. You lead me on by means of things I know, point to things that resemble them, and persuade me that I know things that I thought I had no knowledge of."

—Socrates Quoted in Xenophon's *Oeconomicus*

Believe me, I don't arrive home after teaching, plunk down on my couch, and pull Socrates off the shelf as a habit, but I found this quote a potent reminder that there is an art to posing questions. Asking any old question (and lots of them) is not teaching. It's autopilot and a bad habit. Instead, the questions we ask must lead the learner out of himself (*educare*, to lead forth, as in "educate") and help him learn.

Vocabulary Learning Goes Hand in Hand with Verbal Exchanges of Ideas

It's almost too basic to say, but I'll say it: we need to have an expansive vocabulary in order to be expansive in our thinking about topics and texts. Vocabulary, you could argue, *is* thought. Not only does the gift of words lead to a gift of gab, word learning generates better comprehension. Children must know the meaning of most of the words in a text or passage to understand it. Ever try reading a passage that's packed with vocabulary or technical terms you don't know the meaning of? Perhaps a report on recent medical research findings or a financial analysis in the *Wall Street Journal*? While you're able to enunciate the words, you may be hard pressed to explain what it all means.

Children feel like this as well when they sit with a book that's too hard or outside the realm of their experience. We need to do everything we can to help them navigate these texts and ensure that their vocabulary continues to grow. Children need a rich oral and written vocabulary so they can understand what they're reading and communicate their ideas to others.

In *Vocabulary Development*, a volume in the From Reading Research to Practice series, Steven Stahl (1999) elaborates:

> "A richer vocabulary does not just mean that we know more words, but that we have more complex and exact ways of talking about the world, and of understanding the ways that more complex thinkers see the world." (p. 1)

Thus, helping students enhance their vocabulary should be a top priority, especially because of how it scaffolds comprehension.

How Children Acquire Vocabulary

My grandson Jack has been read to since birth. From the time he was born, he and his mom would settle in for their bedtime reading with a stack of books, which he, as a two-year-old, called "a cupla books." A favorite that we read repeatedly was Clunes' *Who Lives in the Wild?* (2003). Throughout these re-readings, Jack was introduced to the fact that penguins huddle together to keep warm.

At first, he didn't know what *huddle* meant or for that matter what a penguin was (although the photographs and Ann's responses to his mantric query "Wuz zat?" most certainly helped). Later, he put that experience together with what he heard sitting alongside his dad watching football—that the team called a huddle. This concept was reinforced even further when he saw the movie *Happy Feet* and all those adorable huddling penguin chicks tripping over each other to get to the coveted middle. Jack now understands the multiple meanings of huddle and the contexts in which it is used. He can use it to express himself both orally and in writing.

Children like Jack, who come to school with rich oral vocabularies, have a leg up on those who do not. But that's just the beginning of vocabulary acquisition. All children, regardless of their background, need to learn thousands more words between kindergarten and ninth grade. Isabel Beck, Margaret McKeown, and Linda Kucan (2002) estimate the number to be around 7,000 Tier 2 words, or 700 a year.

Beck, McKeown, and Kucan define Tier 2 words as the high-frequency words for mature language users that show up regularly in *written* text, as opposed to basic

What Not to Do

It should be noted that vocabulary researchers caution against assigning children ten words a week to look up in a dictionary, use in a sentence, and be tested on each Friday. That's simply not how we acquire vocabulary that leads to better comprehension.

In *Creating Robust Vocabulary: Frequently Asked Questions and Extended Examples*, Beck, McKeown, and Kucan (2008) report:

Mezynski's (1983) review of eight studies and Stahl and Fairbanks's (1986) meta-analysis of about 30 studies concluded that instruction that succeeded in affecting comprehension included three features: more than several exposures to each word, both definitional and contextual information, and engagement of students in active, or deep, processing. (p. 4)

Tier 1 words, such as *clock* and *baby*, that children learn quite effortlessly because of their high *oral* language exposure to them. Nor are they the domain-related Tier 3 words, such as *meteorite* and *constellation* that surface primarily when reading about a specific content-area topic. Tier 2 words are words such as *fortunate*, *scold*, and *desperate* that mature language users need to know.

There are many ways to introduce children to new and interesting words and give them the multiple exposures that are necessary before they can own them. Some of these exposures involve explicit instruction, while other exposures are more incidental.

Incidental Vocabulary Acquisition

Incidental vocabulary experiences are those that are not planned and, in fact, can't be. They originate from our purposeful attentiveness to what's happening around us, to the texts children are reading and writing, and to the oral conversations occurring in our classroom.

Rich Oral Language Exposure and Experiences Children who begin their formal education equipped with more language, more vocabulary, and more information have an easier time learning to read than children who start with less. This "rich-get-richer" phenomenon, commonly referred to as the "Matthew Effect" (taking its name from a passage in the Gospel of Matthew), suggests that children who lack these early childhood experiences—the "poorer" ones—often require intensive and extensive interventions from the school community to help bridge this ever-widening vocabulary gap.

Fortunately, regardless of children's early literacy experiences, teachers can adopt practices that will enrich all students' language experiences and ratchet up their ability to learn. Many of the school experiences that expose children to new vocabulary occur incidentally during conversations with teachers who are mindful of the teaching opportunities their purposeful interactions with students provide. Here are two examples of incidental, yet purposeful, vocabulary encounters that occurred in Millie Velazquez's first-grade classroom:

As John met with Millie for a conference, he commented on a page in his book: "Look Ms. Velazquez, it says the squirrel is *scattering* nuts." Millie's response was not a quick "yes, he is," but rather one that presumed John might not know the meaning of *scattered* even though he could read it. While running her finger over the picture of the ground where the squirrel is scattering nuts, she said, "Yes, John, he certainly is *spreading* them all around the yard." By elaborating on the meaning of *scattered*, Millie showed that she understands the importance of giving students impromptu explanations of words to help develop their language and vocabulary.

On another occasion Millie met with children on the rug to discuss the "stone soup" they would be making. After reading Heather Forest's retelling of *Stone Soup* earlier in the week, the children were eager to try their hand at making their own. Millie sat with them to go over what they needed to do: "Boys and girls, let's *generate* a list of *ingredients* we will need for our soup." And as she did she began listing foods the students named—potatoes, onions, carrots, etc.

Millie might have considered that the words *generate* and *ingredients* were too advanced for first graders and used words like *make* and *things that will go into the soup* instead. However, she knew that the context of their conversation would scaffold their understanding of the words. She knew that children learn these more mature words by hearing them, reading them, and speaking them repeatedly in authentic situations.

In each of these examples, the opportunity to enhance children's vocabulary would have been missed had Millie been unaware that using these higher-level Tier 2 words in our daily interactions with students is perhaps the first of many exposures to these words that they'll receive on their way to owning them.

Voluminous Reading   It is widely recognized that one of the most effective ways to enhance children's vocabulary is to increase the amount of reading they do. Although this sounds simple enough, there's a rub. Since most children's reading comprehension does not match their oral comprehension until *well past* third grade (Biemiller 1999), we cannot rely on children's independent reading alone to improve their language development in the primary grades.

Up until third grade children are likely to be reading books in which the author has controlled, to a greater or lesser extent, the words she used. These authors favor more common words children already know and avoid the more sophisticated words that students may have a hard time decoding. For example, as effective as Gwendolyn Hudson Hooks' *Can I Have a Pet?* (Figure 5-3) is for helping children learn to read,

Can I have a monkey?

3

Figure 5-3. Page from Can I Have a Pet?

it doesn't enhance their vocabulary or their oral language development. Justifiably, the words and language patterns in beginning-level independent reading books like this one need to be ones children already know through their oral language exposure to them.

At the other end of the primary-grade spectrum we have children reading books from Dan Greenburg's Zack Files and Nancy E. Krulik's Katie Kazoo Switcheroo series and informational-blended books (*ala* "Magic School Bus style") such as Amanda Lumry and Laura Hurwitz's *Polar Bear Puzzle* (2007) and *South Pole Penguins* (2007) from the Adventures of Riley series. These readers will invariably meet new and interesting words (see Figure 5-4) and infer the meaning of many of them from their context. But still not enough to account for the thousands of words they must eventually learn.

This is where read-aloud comes in. To boost the vocabulary development of all K–3 readers, but especially that of emergent and early readers or students who avoid reading because they don't like to or don't do it well, we will have to provide much of this wide voluminous reading exposure from texts we *read aloud*.

In his *Reading Research Quarterly* article, "Vocabulary Acquisition from Listening to Stories," Warwick Elley (1989) reports on research he conducted in elementary classrooms in New Zealand, in which teachers read aloud stories and

Figure 5-4. Page from Polar Bear Puzzle

then measured students' vocabulary growth. His findings confirmed that children do indeed learn vocabulary words simply by listening to stories, and that vocabulary growth was even greater when:

+ stories were read multiple times
+ teachers explained the meaning of unfamiliar words
+ words occurred several times in the story
+ the illustrations enhanced the meaning of the words
+ the context supported children's understanding of the words

Elley's research suggests that if I read Helen Lester's *Hurty Feelings* (2004) once to students, they would learn some of the Tier 2 words like *sturdy, rude, resemble, compare, weep,* and *wail* just from hearing the story read aloud and from being shown the pictures. However, if I, briefly as an aside, explain the meaning of some of the words, and read the story multiple times, then children would learn even more, especially since Lester's illustrations and storyline so strongly support the word meanings (see Figure 5-5). In addition, many of the focus words, such as *sturdy, weep,* and *wail,* occur multiple times throughout the story.

We need to make sure that all students receive rich exposure to high-end vocabulary in the early grades so they can use these newly acquired words to understand and learn additional words, and ultimately increase their ability to better comprehend what they read.

Figure 5-5. Pages from Helen Lester's Hurty Feelings

Explicit Vocabulary Instruction

Explicit vocabulary instruction involves the teacher preselecting the Tier 2 words she wants to expose students to and then initiating practices such as the Effective Practice: "Words Words Words" in Chapter 8 to help students learn them. Note that the goal here is not mastery, but additional exposures to words that will eventually lead children to understand and use them effortlessly. Teachers should also help students infer the meaning of unknown words from context.

Interactive Read-Alouds to Boost Vocabulary Learning   During interactive read-alouds, teachers model their thinking and the strategies they use to comprehend text, and engage students in conversations about the text and new vocabulary they encounter. Interactive read-alouds should not replace our less formal "just-for-the-fun-of-it" read-alouds, but should coexist alongside them.

In their May 2007 *Reading Teacher* article, "Repeated Interactive Read-Alouds in Preschool and Kindergarten," Lea M. McGee and Judith A. Schickedanz describe a three-day procedure for reading aloud stories, in which vocabulary enhancement is one of the main components. This article is one of the best I've encountered on interactive read-aloud, and I highly recommend that K–3 teachers read it in its entirety. In addition to vocabulary, the article addresses the importance of providing extensive book introductions and scaffolding the analytical "how" and "why" questions we ask. See the "Interactive Read-Aloud in Action" box for how I used this approach to teach vocabulary explicitly while reading aloud.

Linda Hoyt has also made a valuable contribution to how teachers implement interactive read-alouds, demonstrating how to align them to state standards and model comprehension strategies. Her series, *Interactive Read-Aloud: Linking Standards, Fluency, and Comprehension* for elementary-grade students addresses grades K and 1 (2006), grades 2 and 3 (2007), and grades 4 and 5 (2007).

Introducing Vocabulary Before Students Read   Generally, I don't preteach vocabulary before reading a book. Rather, I teach unfamiliar words as we encounter them. However, there are times when it's necessary for students to know what a word means before starting out. For example, when reading Peter Brown's *The Curious Garden* (2009), it would be foolish to begin reading without first clarifying the meaning of *curious*, since in this title curious means "odd" or "unusual," and not "eager to know something," its more commonly used definition.

The other exception is when I'm working with struggling readers or English language learners who may not have enough background knowledge to determine the meaning of a word from context.

First-grade teacher Sara Flores and I planned to read aloud and discuss *Penguins Are Water Birds* (Taberski 2000), the big book I authored with my first-grade class. (Please note that while this text is big-book formatted, we used it as a read-aloud since our focus was on *content*, not on word-related skills and strategies that typically dominate a shared reading experience.) We wanted her children to learn about penguins and knew that this text with its gorgeous photographs and grade-appropriate text features would give her students access to valuable and interesting information.

However, Sara was concerned about a group of English language learners in her class who, she felt, would be unable to understand key words and concepts in the book, such as *flippers*, *webbed feet*, and *streamlined* without some preliminary exposure. So we arranged for this group to meet the morning of the whole-class read-aloud to read and discuss a synopsis text that Sara and I had prepared (Figure 5-6). This also got students to examine the photos and text features in the big book as they discussed the synopsis text.

Then Sara read the book to the whole class, called attention to the photos, and gave children opportunities to talk and ask questions about what they were learning. Sara was thrilled with the response and enthusiasm of her ELLs, as evident from the poignant email she sent me that evening (Figure 5-7.)

Interactive Read-Aloud in Action

Here's a description of how I implemented McGee and Schickedanz's interactive read-aloud recommendations while reading aloud Don Freeman's *Earl the Squirrel* to a class of first graders. My instruction was explicit, not incidental, since I preselected words that I considered important for students to know, and followed up on day 2 and day 3 with additional exposures to help children become more familiar with the words. However, I didn't expect the children to master the words upon completion of this three-day read-aloud sequence. It was simply an opportunity to introduce them to new words in the hope of forming a hook in their brains on which they would hang additional encounters.

Day 1: Before I read the book aloud, I identified the words *yank*, *spoiled*, *scampered*, *scold*, *scattered*, and *absurd* as the focus words that mature language users need to know. I added the word *determined* (even though it wasn't in the text) since it's one I used repeatedly to discuss Earl's resolve to find his own acorns and not rely on the help of his neighbor.

During Day 1 of the read-aloud, I was more concerned about helping children understand the story in its entirety than I was with the vocabulary *per se*, so I held back on my verbal explanations of words and focused on the expressiveness of my reading and ways to call children's attention to the meaning of words with bodily and facial gestures. Thus, I *scampered*, *scolded*, and *yanked* my way through the first reading.

Day 2: During the second read-aloud, I provided verbal explanations of the focus vocabulary. These weren't lengthy explanations, just brief asides that extended my more expressive and dramatic vocabulary interpretations of the previous day. Since the students already knew the story, I was confident that my verbal asides would not interfere with their overall understanding and appreciation of the narrative.

Day 3: I continued to combine verbal definitions of the focus words with pointing to the pictures and dramatic gestures. I also related some of the focus words to situations with which students were more familiar, e.g., "When you're playing outside you might become angry if a friend *yanks* the ball out of your hand."

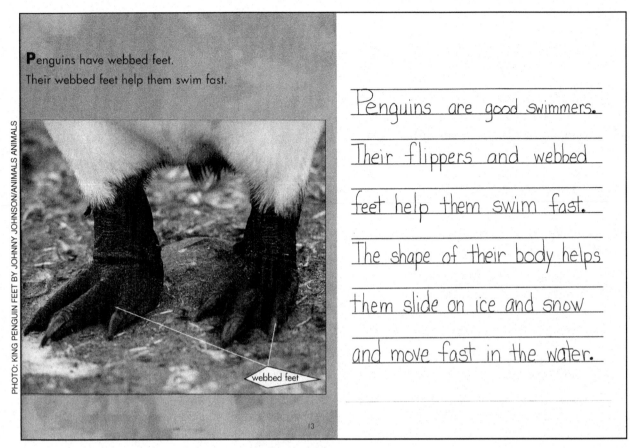

Figure 5-6. Page from Penguins Are Water Birds *and Synopsis*

Hey Sharon,

So today I tried out the synopsis that we put together yesterday and it went awesome! I met with the small group during developmental play for about 10 minutes. We read the synopsis and I explained what flippers and webbed feet are. They were really excited when I told them I was going to tell them about a section of the book before reading and no one else.

Then I read the section to the whole class. I swear to you every one of the students from that small group had their hands up volunteering as we looked at the pictures first. The confidence they showed as they shared their ideas and thoughts was so great. They made me want to cry because usually only one or two of them raise their hands and most of the time the child that I call on says something that is irrelevant to what we are doing. They even used the language that was used in the synopsis. They were so engaged during the reading as well.

So I'm going to try it some more to see if it holds up. It was a good day…

Thanks again,
Sara

Figure 5-7. Sara Flores' Email Letter to Me

Ten Tips for Helping ELLs Acquire Social and Academic Vocabulary

1. Introduce words in context, never in isolation. If you think your students may not understand the context of a story or book you're reading, provide examples that relate to their own lives and experiences to ground them.

2. Frontload lessons by introducing children to unfamiliar vocabulary and background knowledge at the start of a lesson, or reinforce what's been taught at the end.

3. Bring in real-life objects to demonstrate words and concepts. For example, when I read *Earl the Squirrel,* I brought in a bag of acorns and a nutcracker to link the concepts to the words.

4. Use pictures to illustrate what words mean. Even clip art helps.

5. Use your hands, your body, and your voice—be dramatic. If you want children to know what *scowl* means then scowl, if you want them to know what *peer* means then screw up your eyes like you're looking hard at something.

6. Read aloud to kids—a lot. Make sure the books you've selected don't overload them with too many unfamiliar concepts or vocabulary. The problem with many textbooks is that they include too much information and too much challenging vocabulary, making the content less accessible. As you read, point to a picture (if there is one) that demonstrates what the word means.

7. Use alphabet *concept* books, with easily recognizable pictures, to represent the letters, and alphabet *content* books to introduce vocabulary related to specific topics, e.g., fruits and vegetables, the library, or geography. Some examples can be found in the Effective Practice: Using Alphabet Books to Develop Children's Vocabulary in Chapter 8.

8. Reread, reread, reread. All children, but especially ELLs, thrive on repetition. Each time they revisit a text, it's from a stronger, more informed stance.

9. Read wordless books to your ELLs and be deliberate in the words you introduce in your rendition and discussion of each page. Then give them opportunities to read and retell the story on their own.

10. Convene a small group of your needier students for interactive read-aloud or shared reading where you can give them more personalized attention.

Helping Kids Infer the Meaning of Words Readers can infer the meaning of approximately 60 percent of all English words from the surrounding context (Block and Mangieri 2005). And as Linda Gambrell and Kathy N. Headley (2006) state in "Developing Vocabulary by Learning Words Through Context" (in *The Vocabulary Enriched Classroom: Practices for Improving the Reading Performance of All Students in Grades 3 and Up*), there's a back-and-forth movement between using context to determine a word's meaning and learning more about a word from the contextual clues that are given:

> The information derived from the surrounding text helps the reader infer meaning of an individual word and, therefore, better comprehend what is being read. Thus, the meaning of a word can emerge from context, and context can also give the reader a richer, expanded understanding of the word. (p. 20)

To infer a word's meaning it's important to show students how to use their prior knowledge and any illustrations present in combination with the text that comes *before* and *after* the unknown word. Prompt students to:

1. Use all they know to figure out the word—their background knowledge of the topic, what's happening in the story or text, what they know about the word itself, e.g., Does it look like any word they know? Do they know the meaning of parts of the word—the prefix or root?

2. Substitute other words that might make sense. For example, a child not knowing the meaning of *burrow* in the passage, "The female lizard digs a burrow deep in the sand. She lays two to four white eggs in the burrow," may realize that *hole* would make sense and learn that this is, in fact, what *burrow* means. (At least, it's what the noun *burrow* means.)

3. Use pictures or text features as tools to figure out the meaning of a word. For example, children can see from this illustration in Gail Gibbon' *Horses!* (2004) (Figure 5-8) that *walk*, *trot*, *canter*, and *gallop* represent a series of gaits from slowest to fastest. And that *trot* and *canter* mean to move faster than *walk*, but slower than *gallop*.

Figure 5-8. Page from Gail Gibbons' Horses!

The Gradual Release of Responsibility Model

Gradual release of responsibility is a research-based instructional model developed by P. David Pearson and M. C. Gallagher (1983). The goal is for instruction to move gradually and over time from where there's high teacher support and little to no control from students, to where the students are in control of the learning task with the teacher providing little to no support.

As such, the goal of vocabulary instruction is to gradually move from where the teacher is selecting the words students should learn and providing the verbal explanations or definitions, to where the students themselves identify words they consider important or interesting and want to learn more about. This often involves students keeping a separate vocabulary notebook or designating a section in their reading notebook for vocabulary, where they list words with which they're unfamiliar and feel they need to know. Students might:

+ Write the word and the sentence in which the word was found along with other context-related information, such as the book's title, genre, and topic or theme.
+ Predict what the word means based on their background knowledge and the context in which it is used.
+ Look the word up in a dictionary to see if they are correct, revise their prediction, and learn additional meanings of the word.

 For a strategy sheet to help children self-select vocabulary, see Appendix 9 online. In addition, I recommend reading Cathy Collins Block's *The Vocabulary-Enriched Classroom* (2006), a wonderful resource for teachers of third grade and higher wanting to help students become more independent in their vocabulary acquisition. It's filled with ideas from leading researchers and practitioners for developing vocabulary through word building, learning content-area words, learning words through context, etc. It also has chapters addressing the special vocabulary needs of ELLs, gifted students, and struggling readers.

+ + +

Bottom line—children need to engage in purposeful, high-level talk with one another to more fully understand, appreciate, and remember what they're learning. They need to enlarge their thinking and get ideas for how they might respond to texts in the future.

We need to reflect on how we come across to students. Do we crowd out their thoughts with our own talking? Do we do enough to find picture books and other texts by the gifted wordsmiths of our day so we develop the child's ear for the sheer beauty of words put together in the right order? Do we go wonderfully overboard in our delight about science, social studies, and math—the "content" of the world—so that children pick up on the idea that intriguing *concepts* matter to us, not just mastering tricky words? We love every detail of the butterfly's transformation from chrysalis to their night flight to Mexico—not the million-dollar word *metamorphosis* for its own sake.

The ways into vocabulary development are many. I often envision a Chinese checkers game where we jump over shiny colorful marbles to get from where we are to where we need to go. Words help us connect the dots of our understanding, they help us to infer, inform others, name what's in our head. Words, whether spoken, read, or written, must be the currency of our classroom.

Part Two

Refining Our Teaching

Accurate Fluent Reading
Principles and Practices

CHAPTER **6**

"In order to ensure that readers have enough attention available to understand texts adequately, it is necessary for them to develop decoding to the point that each word is recognized instantaneously. Once readers have established such automaticity, they will have freed up the attention to focus on meaning." (p. 130)

—Melanie R. Kuhn in "Fluency in the Classroom: Strategies for Whole-Class and Group Work" (*Best Practices in Literacy Instruction*, Second Edition, 2003)

Accurate, Automatic Word Reading and Comprehension

Tommy beams up at me during a guided reading group, calling out *pond*, the word that stumps some of the kids in his group. "You know how I know?" (He confidently twice-taps the picture of the pond into which Little Lion is staring and then taps the word itself.) "It starts with p. /p/ ... /p/ for pond. And that's a pond."

In contrast, in the midst of a citywide reading assessment done the previous week, first-grader Emma hesitantly reads "Jill is a pill," a puzzled expression coming across her face. "I think it says *pill*, but that doesn't make sense." Some other students opted for "Jill is a *pal*," a version that makes sense to them but doesn't match the letters.

This opening sentence, obviously written for the –*ill* spelling pattern, confuses these kids, who can't be expected to know that *pill* means Jill was being moody. It exemplifies a commercial test-maker's tendency to shoehorn in a word to see if the kids know the pattern, at the cost of obscuring a text's meaning. A frustrating and unwise trade-off.

We don't need a steady diet of "Jill is a pill" types of text in our classroom to develop accuracy and automaticity. We do need to build in more time for explicit instruction and independent practice to help readers consolidate their newly acquired skills and strategies.

> *Note to Readers:*
> Chapters 6 through 10 each contain a Foundational Principles section that demonstrates how the ideas presented in Chapters 1 through 5 relate to the comprehension strand featured in that chapter. Following each Foundational Principles section is an Effective Practices section describing procedures for bringing these principles to life.

Foundational Principles for Building Word Recognition

We want students throughout the elementary grades to learn to recognize words accurately and automatically, whether they're emerging readers just beginning to differentiate one word from the next, developing readers who can identify most basic words automatically, or more advanced readers who need to fine-tune their word skills to include derivational and inflectional affixes, homophones, etc. The following foundational principles support this goal.

Know the Big Picture of Phonics Instruction and What Your Class Needs

A while back I attended a seminar by Stephen Krashen on second-language acquisition. While he was brilliant on the topic of English language learners, it was his advice about phonics instruction that was most memorable. In response to a question about whether or not phonics is important, Krashen said: "Of course phonics is important. And we should teach it to the extent that it makes text more comprehensible." I admired how he so naturally linked phonics with comprehension since that's *why* we teach it in the first place—to help children learn words accurately and automatically to free up space in their brain for comprehension.

We need to hone in on the skills we've determined our students most need to learn and then teach those skills wisely and well at each grade, recognizing, of course, that *each* class of first graders, third graders, etc., is likely to look quite different from the next. Then we have to differentiate even further—teaching to the middle level during whole-class instruction and addressing the specific needs of all readers (from lower-, to middle-, to higher-achieving) in small groups and one to one.

Here are some skills children need to develop accuracy and automaticity. (But remember, where you "enter" and which set of skills you target will depend on the assessed needs of your students):

+ Children need to develop phonemic awareness, the ability to hear, identify, and manipulate phonemes (the smallest units of sound). See Figure 6-1 for ways to develop children's phonemic awareness and Appendix 10 online for how to work with Elkonin boxes.

+ Children need to know the *letter names* and *sounds*. They need to know the names of the letters so we can engage them in conversations about letters and the sounds they make and help students locate them in words. However, children don't need to know all the consonant and basic vowel sounds *before* they start reading real texts, since they'll learn many new sounds while participating in shared reading, coauthoring language-experience charts, reading just-right books, and writing their own texts.

Phonemic Awareness Activities

There are basically five types of phonemic awareness activities: rhyming, isolating and identifying phonemes, blending phonemes, segmenting phonemes, and manipulating phonemes. Here are some ways to develop children's phonemic awareness:

- Sing songs and recite nursery rhymes together as a class. Ask students to continue the rhymes.

- Read and reread poems and books with rhythmic patterns and encourage children to participate.

- Use Elkonin boxes to isolate phonemes or syllables. Begin by modeling this for the class and then work with a small group of students to help them distinguish the different phonemes in oral words. (See Appendix 10 online.)

- Make up alliterative sentences, e.g., "The famished fox found food." Ask students what sound is being repeated and have them work with a partner to compose their own alliterative sentences.

- Play word games with students. For example, "Say *mat* without the /m/" or say "*stay*" without the /st/." You can play word games like these while lining up, walking in the hall, or during any downtime. You can do this with beginning and ending sounds or with single letter sounds or blends. Students might take turns leading the game.

- Have students clap out the syllables in their names and/or difficult words.

- Say multisyllable words with a one or two-second pause in between each syllable and see if students can say the whole word. For example, "ap pe tite" or "dif fi cult." You can also do this with individual sounds. For example, ask students what word the following sounds represent /b/ /e/ /d/.

Figure 6-1. Phonemic Awareness Activities

+ Children need to develop their *sight word vocabulary*. They need to learn high-frequency words like the Dolch words to free up space in their working memory so they can work through the harder words and comprehend. See the Effective Practice: Learning Sight Words and Appendix 11 online for the five Dolch Word Lists.

Figure 6-2a. The CVC Pattern

+ Children need to *make words*:
  + They start with the basic consonant-vowel-consonant (CVC) pattern, such as in *tap* (Figure 6-2a), where they're introduced to short vowel sounds and where their consonant-sound learning is reinforced.
  + They learn about onset and rime and how by simply changing the consonant before the vowel in a one-syllable word, they can easily read and write many more words. For example, starting with the word *will*, by changing the *w* (the onset) that comes before *-ill* (the rime), they can make *fill, pill, sill, kill,* and *mill.* (See Figure 6-3 for Wylie and Durrell's 37 rimes and how to teach onset and rime.)

Onset and Rime Activities

Helping children become familiar with spelling patterns in words enables them to move beyond seeing isolated letters in words to seeing chunks of letters that make specific sounds. In 1970, R. E. Wylie and D. D. Durell identified 37 rimes found in 500 primary-grade words. In a single syllable word, the onset is the initial consonant or consonant blend before the vowel, and the rime is the vowel and any consonants that follow. For example, in the word *stick, st* is the onset and *ick* the rime. This list of Wylie and Durrell's 37 rimes offers us a place to start when teaching spelling patterns:

-ack	-an	-ap	-at	-ank	-ash	-ail	-ain	-ake
-ale	-ame	-ate	-aw	-ay	-ell	-est	-eat	-ill
-in	-ip	-it	-ick	-ink	-ing	-ide	-ine	-ice
-ight	-op	-ot	-ock	-oke	-ore	-ug	-uck	-ump
-unk

- Have students generate word lists with specific rimes.
- Work with spelling pattern sorts. Students can sort words based on their spelling pattern.
- Play spelling pattern concentration. Students can match cards with the same onset or the same rime.
- Identify rimes during shared reading. Make it fun and be explicit with students. Explain and demonstrate how it's easier to recognize a word when you look for patterns. Then you don't have to consciously sound out every letter because you are looking for and noticing groups of letters or patterns.
- Ask students to be rime detectives. While they are reading independently, have them jot down one or two rimes on a Post-it note and then share a few with the class.

Figure 6-3. Onset and Rime

- They learn about the CVCe pattern (Figure 6-2b) such as in *tape*, where they're introduced to how adding a silent *e* at the end of the CVC pattern sometimes changes the vowel sound from short to long.
- They learn the CCVC (*clip*) pattern that introduces initial blends and diagraphs, and the CVVC (*team*) pattern where they examine how two vowels together often make the long sound of the first vowel.

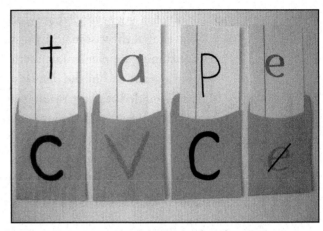

Figure 6-2b. The CVCe Pattern

- And, of course, they also need exposure to *r*-controlled vowels, variant vowel combinations such as *-ow* and *-ou*, diphthongs, inflectional endings, contractions, prefixes and suffixes, and so on.

We need to trust ourselves as teachers. We need to stop relying so heavily on the pacing guide or scope and sequence as the perfect way to cover learning objectives each year. While they do serve as a framework to orient ourselves in the direction our children need to go, they're not perfect because the classes we teach each year don't have identical needs. Furthermore, scope and sequence charts often give the false impression that when we teach something—once, twice, three times—kids will get it, and that's simply not so.

Overrelying on these tools at the exclusion of also looking closely at each individual student to determine what he or she knows and needs to learn also lulls us into a point of view that children *only* learn what we teach. Children are quite capable of figuring out parts of the print-code puzzle when they have enough parts (i.e., some letter-sound knowledge and some skills and strategies) and lots of time to read and write. In addition to the explicit and direct phonics instruction we provide, we also know that kids will eventually "get it" through wide, just-right reading experiences where they get to apply what we've demonstrated, and by providing plenty of opportunities for them to write their own texts.

The teacher certainly needs to see the big picture of phonics instruction from the start. But *where* she decides to enter with a particular class of students and *when* and *how* to teach each skill and strategy are decisions she'll make along the way. The beauty of immersing children in a print-rich environment, with real literature and flexible, instructional materials from the "best of the best" educational publishers, is that one after another, the skills and strategies that kids need to learn, the very same ones on our scope and sequence chart—adding *-ing* to base words, the *-op* and *-ack* spelling pattern, *ou* and *ow* vowel diagraphs, etc.—emerge naturally in the course of real reading and writing experiences. And, keeping the big picture in mind, if they don't surface, the teacher will make it happen.

There's no question that some kindergarten and first-grade students (perhaps as many as 20 percent) and a handful of second- and third-graders require phonics interventions beyond that which the classroom teacher can provide. Yet I'm convinced that the vast majority of students do not need these often excessive and time-consuming supplemental practices. Most children need explicit phonics instruction that's grounded in the demonstrations they receive during shared reading, word study, guided reading, reading conferences, and writing workshop, *along with*—and this is critical—opportunities to use these skills and strategies as they read and write on their own.

Use High-Quality Texts and Encourage Students to Read for Understanding

To help students develop their ability to read accurately and with automaticity, we need to use picture books, poems, nonfiction—a wide array of *real* literature as opposed to texts written specifically to teach phonics, which tend to have weak syntax and story lines. We should seek out the very best reading materials from educational publishers that provide appropriate and supportive texts for students who are just learning to read and more complex text features as children develop.

Texts that target spelling patterns over meaning can pose problems for a young reader's comprehension. Most children are perfectly capable of using what they know about letters and sounds together with pictures and structural supports to help them read—provided the texts make sense and our instruction guides them in this direction.

Children should be encouraged to monitor their reading for meaning. When Ben's mom skips pages in Gene Zion's *No Roses for Harry* (1996) and he insists she go back and read it the right way, or when Jamie reads "The pigs are in the *pan*" for "The pigs are in the *pen*" and then self-corrects, they're monitoring for meaning. Children are *entitled* to be in situations where they can ask, "Does this make sense?" and listen for "clunks" in their reading so they can intervene with fix-up or meta-cognitive strategies. But they can't improve their word recognition skills if what they're reading makes little sense from the start.

Along the same lines we must also make sure that students apply the meaning-making skills and strategies we're demonstrating in whole-class and small-group instruction to texts they're reading on their own. When children's independent reading texts are too difficult, they can't access meaning or use syntactical cues, leaving them to struggle letter by letter and word by word.

This means we may need to rethink the way our kids exchange books in their book bags—less independent book shopping and more reading conferences to help match them with just-right texts. We also need to provide mini-lessons to show students the type of books they should have in their independent book bag. (See Chapter 3 for more about just-right, "look," and easy books.)

Build Prior Knowledge

Prior knowledge is as important for figuring out unknown words as it is for comprehension in general. It adds to what students bring to texts to help them monitor their reading and allows them to use letter-sound information, meaning, and syntax together.

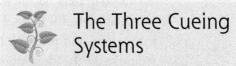

Children who speak English as a second language, those from less academically advantaged households, and other struggling students will need even more in the way of background knowledge and real-world experiences to help them bridge the gap between themselves and their higher-achieving counterparts.

For example, when I sat with English language learner Tahir to listen to him read an emergent level text about different foods that animals eat, he had trouble reading the word *carrot*. While he was able to sound it out letter by letter, *c-a-r-r-o-t-s*, Tahir was unable to blend the sounds together or identify the picture of the carrot on the page. Phonics alone was not enough to support his reading and comprehension. What will likely make it happen is the combination of the three cueing systems and a deep reservoir of experience and background knowledge.

> ## The Three Cueing Systems
>
> When referring to the three cueing systems— **syntax, semantics,** and **letter-sound information**—I don't always list them in that order, rather I sometimes list meaning first, sometimes letter-sound information, and sometimes syntax. I resist assigning primacy to any one over the other because each contributes something valuable to children's reading. When teachers favor one cueing system over the other two, young readers don't get the well-rounded approach to printed language that they need.

Therefore, when considering a plan of action for our struggling and second-language readers, we need to build in abundant opportunities for them to acquire language, life experiences, and background knowledge, and not simply immerse them in heavy-duty phonics programs at the expense of more meaningful and integrated instruction.

In Chapter 9, under the Reading-Writing Connections Foundational Principles, I'll discuss how the encoding students do as they *write* complements the decoding they do when they *read*. Then, in the Effective Practices section later in this chapter, you will find two instructional practices that, taken together, give children some of the explicit instruction and practice they need to develop accuracy and automaticity. (There are also two others that relate to fluency.)

Fluency

"Besides being able to decode automatically, fluent readers chunk or parse text into syntactically appropriate units—mainly phrases. This is important because often meaning lies in a text's phrases and not in its individual words. The ability to separate a text into phrases aids comprehension." (p. 32)

—Timothy Rasinski in *The Fluent Reader: Oral Reading Strategies for Building Word Recognition, Fluency, and Comprehension* (2003)

Fluent Reading and Comprehension

I listened closely as Peter read for me during his conference, ready to take notes about how to help: "*A blue tang fish lives here. The baby blue tang fish is yellow. As it grows it changes color....*" No need to have him read much further. I knew exactly the type of help I would give. Peter was reading the words accurately, but he was reading them word by word, with little expression or modulation to his voice. He needed to read more fluently with proper phrasing, intonation, and prosody. Not only would this make his reading sound better, it would make the ideas more comprehensible to him and those listening to him read.

During the conference I explained to Peter how he needed to chunk the words together into phrases instead of reading them one at a time. As I was going on about this, Peter looked up at me and asked, "But how do you know? How do you know which words go together?" His question was a revelation. I'd been explaining to kids since the beginning of the school year that they needed to chunk words together and I thought they understood what I meant! When I recovered from his question, I showed Peter by running my finger under the phrases in his text. I wrote him a note in his assessment notebook (Figure 6-4) that even chunked my message to him: "Be sure . . . to read . . . in phrases."

The next day during our reading workshop mini-lesson, I told the class about my conference with Peter:

> I had the most interesting conference with Peter yesterday, and he asked the most amazing question. I was explaining how he needed to chunk words together to make his reading sound more natural, and he asked me *"How do you know which words go together?"* Now was that a smart question, or what? And he got me thinking that there are probably a whole lot of you who would love to know the answer to that very same question. (The head nodding confirmed my suspicion.) So let me show you what I mean.

Figure 6-4. Note to Peter Showing Explicit Support

By sharing Peter's conference and astute question with the class during a mini-lesson, I showed that asking questions is a vital part of learning that I encourage and admire. The class picked up on this message loud and clear and, going forward, felt more comfortable voicing their own questions.

(I continued) "We've been reading this book for a couple of days (pointing to the enlarged-text edition of Nicola Davies' *Big Blue Whale* (2000) propped against the easel), and we've certainly learned a lot about whales. Let's reread a part of it today, and this time I'll sweep my pointer under each phrase to show you how I'm grouping or chunking certain words together because it sounds better that way, and it makes more sense. (I also read a couple passages where I chunked inappropriate words together to help them see the difference.)

This demonstration gave children something concrete to hold onto. All this takes time—and there's no one right time, or one-only time to do it. There's no place on our scope and sequence that signals: Now's the best time to teach "chunking words into phrases." Through one-to-one and small-group instruction, the teacher can best decide when children need what skill or strategy and how best to teach it.

Foundational Principles for Developing Fluency

The practices that follow will help you build fluency activities into your day-to-day instruction and help students transfer these skills and strategies to their independent reading.

Model Fluent Reading and Let Children Try It

Read-aloud and shared reading allow us to model how fluent reading sounds and how it enhances our enjoyment and shapes our understanding of a text. I often illustrate this point by comparing a more fluent-sounding rendition of a text (good intonation, phrasing, and prosody) to one that's bland and lifeless. The kids get it and from then on don't hesitate to let me know when my read-aloud and shared reading fall short. (See the tips below on how to read aloud well.)

Fairy tales, folktales, and animal "pourquoi" stories, with their predictability, characterization, dialogue, and repetition are especially good genres for demonstrating fluent reading, but any poem or story that has rhythm to its language and entertaining characters will work well too.

 ## Tips on Reading Aloud to Model Fluent Reading

1. **Love the books you read aloud.** It's difficult to read aloud a book well if you don't care for it in the first place. Consider, as part of your weekly planning, finding new and engaging read-aloud titles. You want to bring kids the best of what's out there from libraries and bookstores.

2. **Practice reading the book yourself before reading it to the class.** You should know in advance where you plan to pause to solicit feedback from the students or how much you plan to read on a particular day. (A word of advice: If at all possible, don't leave kids hanging by stopping just as a climax is approaching. Nothing turns them off more than that. Part of the fun of reading is building up suspense and then finding out what happened—preferably, all on the same day!)

   Tell the kids that you've read the story several times to get good at reading it. It's a message they need to hear.

3. **Read expressively—using your whole body.** Good readers don't just use their voice when they read. They use their eyes, facial expressions, and body movements to convey meaning.

4. **Read aloud nonfiction with as much attention and forethought as when you read fiction.** The author's purpose in writing is to convey information that she finds interesting. Let your voice express amazement at the fact that "the baby blue whale drinks between 50 and 100 gallons of its mother's milk each day."

5. **Consult professional books** such as Jim Trelease's *The Read-Aloud Handbook: Sixth Edition* and Mem Fox's *Reading Magic: Why Reading Aloud to Our Children Will Change Their Lives Forever* for more tips on reading aloud to students and some great titles to add to your collection.

Repeatedly read aloud the books that your class designates as favorites and leave them in a special "Favorite Read-Alouds" basket in the meeting area for students to read on their own. Kids love sitting in the teacher's rocking chair and reading a book to a friend or two during independent reading. And it's uncanny how they sound just like us!

Allow Children to View Fluency Cues Up Close

One of the benefits of reading big books and other large-formatted texts is that, unlike standard-size texts, children can see them up close as you point out cues the author (and illustrator) left for how to read them:

+ *Italicized or emboldened words* in fiction signal the reader to emphasize them. In nonfiction, bold print highlights concepts that require extra special consideration and directs the reader to the illustrations and glossary for additional information.

Figure 6-5. A Page from Benchmark Education's Little Red Hen

+ *Punctuation* cues readers about how a text should sound to the ear. Question marks signal the voice to rise, periods signal it to fall. Exclamation marks tell you to sound excited, and quotation marks alert you to the fact that a character is speaking and to try to match your voice to what he or she is thinking, feeling, or doing. You'd read the sentence "Your mother has been looking all over for you!" differently than you would the sentence "Let's take a walk."

+ *Illustrations* depicting the character's facial and bodily expressions can convey their emotional status. Help young readers discern whether a character is sad, exasperated, angry, or delighted by attending to his eyes, how he's holding his body, his head, or his hands. Take a look at Little Red Hen's face in Brenda Parkes' 2009 retelling of *The Little Red Hen* (Figure 6-5) as she digs a hole in the ground to plant her seeds. She's literally sweating it, her feathers are flying, and she's probably thinking unkind thoughts about her friends who refuse to help.

Provide Authentic Fluency Experiences for Practice

Despite the fact that I initiate Reader's Theater soon after the school year begins, I can never seem to schedule enough performances to satisfy my students. They love this dramatic activity that helps them focus on the quality of their reading.

Ever since becoming involved in Reader's Theater, Emily's been intent on rereading her books with expression. So I wasn't surprised when she asked for a conference so I could hear her read. She read beautifully, and I told her so and I asked if she wanted any new books. Emily declined, deciding to stick with the books in her bag a bit longer so she could practice some more.

This set a good example for Janice. Having observed what took place during Emily's conference, she decided to try the same expressive reading techniques. By the time I finished my round of conferences, Emily and Janice sounded as if they were auditioning for "Annie!" My only problem was getting them to read quietly enough so they wouldn't disturb the other readers in class!

More About Rereading

The more times students hear and read a story we've introduced, and the more they practice reading books from their independent reading bag, the better they understand the texts and bring their newfound interpretation back to the reading, thus improving both their fluency and *comprehension*.

It's not difficult to get emergent and early readers to reread. They understand that they didn't read it so well the first time, and welcome the opportunity to try again. Not so with transitional and fluent readers. They understandably resist rereading their chapter books, and therefore it's up to us to find authentic and alternate ways for them to practice.

For Emily's, Janice's, and all our students' sake, we must tap into our more authentic oral reading experiences such as choral reading, reading along *with* (not just listening to) books on tape, Reader's Theater, and so on to support children's expressive reading.

Professional Books That Address Fluency and Oral Expression

- *The Fluent Reader: Oral Reading Strategies for Building Word Recognition, Fluency, and Comprehension* by Timothy V. Rasinski

- *Goodbye Round Robin, Updated Edition: 25 Effective Oral Reading Strategies* by Michael F. Optiz and Timothy V. Rasinski

- *Comprehension and English Language Learners: 25 Oral Reading Strategies That Cross Proficiency Levels* by Michael F. Optiz and Lindsey M. Guccione

- *Reading Magic: Why Reading Aloud to Our Children Will Change Their Lives Forever* by Mem Fox

Effective Practice: Learning Sight Words

What Are Sight Words?

Sight words, otherwise known as Dolch or high-frequency words, are 220 of the most commonly used words in the English language. We encounter them with great frequency in trade books, textbooks, magazines, newspapers, and on-line resources. They are the service words—*they, said, under*—of our language. They include pronouns, adverbs, prepositions, conjunctions, adjectives, and verbs, but notably, they do not include nouns.

Children can't, as a memory device, attach a picture to words like *said* or *with*, as they can to words like *apple, boat,* and *tree*. This lack of a concrete reference is part of what makes learning sight words challenging for many children. In addition, because many of these words have an irregular spelling, they can't be sounded out using common phonics patterns.

There are five lists of Dolch words, ranging from preprimer and primer through grade 3, which account for between 50 percent and 75 percent of words found in texts for school-age children. Note that these "graded" lists are organized by the *reading level* of the books in which Edward Dolch, the lists' compiler, found them, and not by the grade at which they should be taught and learned. For example, list 4 (grade 2) was compiled after reviewing books read by children in second grade. (See Figure 6-6 for Dolch List 1 and Appendix 11 online for all five lists.)

Dolch List 1	
a	make
and	me
away	my
big	not
blue	one
can	play
come	red
down	run
find	said
for	see
funny	the
go	three
help	to
here	two
in	up
is	we
it	where
jump	yellow
little	you
look	I

Figure 6-6. Dolch List 1

Why Is Learning Sight Words Important for Reading Comprehension?

We all have a limited amount of brain capacity in our working memory. While our long-term memory can hold a seemingly unlimited amount of data, the "space" in our working memory is finite. Therefore, we want to teach our youngest readers to automatically recognize as many words as possible so their minds are freer to grapple with the more difficult words and the text's concepts.

Then, as children move farther into the primary grades, we want them to add many more words, more than just the basic 220 Dolch words, to their automatic word bank. At this point, we expand our definition of sight words to include *all* the words children recognize by sight. Those who acquire a large sight vocabulary have an easier time with comprehension than those who don't because they can direct more of their attention to understanding the text. By third grade, we want children to be reading most words automatically as sight words.

What's the Best Way to Help Children Learn Sight Words?

Giving children many opportunities to read and write each day is the most powerful way to build their automatic word recognition. Since sight words occur frequently in texts, children encounter them repeatedly during shared, guided, and independent reading. Valuable writing exercises to enhance learning sight words include language experience charts, children writing their own pieces during the writing workshop, and responding to text or recording what they've learned about content-area topics.

These repeated exposures to sight words, *along with* instructional practices that call attention to the letters in the words and how they're configured, help children develop automaticity in reading them. For example, when reading Margaret Yatsevitch Phinney's 2004 big book *A Trip to the City* (Figure 6-7), children encounter the words *no, going, under, the, too,* and *said* multiple times. As added reinforcement, we can highlight with tape the words we want to focus on. We can also initiate extension activities that spotlight targeted sight words.

After reading Flora McDonald's *I Love Animals* (1996) multiple times for the sheer pleasure of hearing how the words play out in a predictable pattern, children made a class book of things they "like" to do, patterned on McDonald's text, e.g., "I like ___. I like ___." Each child wrote a page, e.g., "Rosie *likes* to run," "Tim *likes* to swing," "Molly *likes* to jump rope." I showed them how the word *likes* (the Dolch word *like* with the affix *s*) is repeated on each page and how they also need to listen for sounds in words from the beginning of the word all the way through to the end. It's through "whole-to-part" activities like this that children most effectively add sight words to their automatic vocabulary. (See the box for some additional ways to help children learn sight words.)

We are going under the bridge.

Grandpa is going under the bridge, too.
"No, Grandpa, no!" said Grandma.

Figure 6-7. Pages from A Trip to the City *(Mondo)*

Other Tried-and-True Ways to Teach Sight Words

- Call children's attention to a word's "shape" by boxing it (drawing a frame around the outside of the word) to make visible the high and low letter formations.

- Provide magnetic and wipe-off boards for students to practice making and writing words.

- Use build-a-word pockets (Figure 6-8) where students use letter cards to make words.

- Give each student a word book of sight words, such as Mondo's *My Word Book* (Figure 6-9), to keep in their writing folder, and make additional copies available for reference during reading, math, social studies, and science.

- Make copies of the poems and short texts you've read and written during shared reading and shared writing, and keep them in a binder for children to reread during independent reading.

- Write each targeted sight word in a sentence or phrase to post in the classroom. For example, the written phrase, "our school" (accompanied by a quick sketch of a school) may help a child make an association for the word *our* that he may not have otherwise made.

- Play games with the sight words. There's a wide assortment of games available for purchase and others you can make on your own. Check out the Teaching Resource Center Web site: www.trcabc.com.

- Have children cut a sight word written on a card or sentence strip into letters, scramble them, and then rearrange them to make the word.

- Play riddle games with word wall words. Pose a riddle such as "I'm thinking of a word *(make)* that has four letters but only three of them make a sound." Provide additional clues as needed.

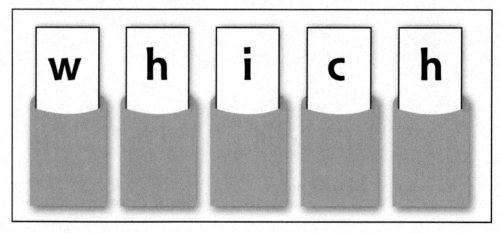

Figure 6-8. Build-a-Word Pockets

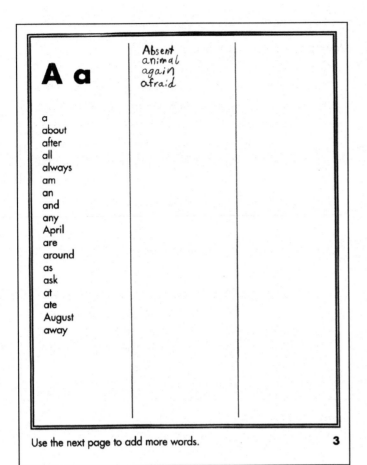

Figure 6-9. Page from Mondo's My Word Book *with a Student's Personal Words Added*

How Do I Help Children Learn the Harder Sight Words?

At the start of the year, I examine the Dolch lists for sight words I want children to learn and sort them into categories that suggest how I'll teach them. (See Figure 6-10 for how I sort Dolch words.) For example, some words such as *under* and *jump* can be readily sounded out and are more easily learned. I'm confident that as I teach letter-sounds, children will work out how to spell these more regularly spelled words and add them to their sight word bank. However, I have to make an extra effort to help children learn other more challenging sight words, such as *done*, *again*, and *want*, since they can't be sounded out as readily.

The "Look, Say, Cover, Write, Check" procedure is one way to help children learn to read and spell the more challenging sight words. Here's how it's done:

1. **Identify a word** from the word wall that children typically have trouble learning—*could*, for example. Remove the word card (which had been thumbtacked instead of stapled for easy removal) and tape it to a large wipe-off board propped against the easel at the meeting area.

2. **Look.** Tell the children to **look** carefully at the word *could* and ask them what they **see.** After doing this procedure several times, they understand what you're after and say things like: "I see five letters"; "I see a *c* at the

---

Sorting Sight Words into Categories

When deciding how to teach a specific word, it's helpful to sort Dolch words into categories:

- **Regularly spelled sight words.** Words like *keep, must,* and *cold* should be easy enough for children to learn once they know the letter-sounds and have abundant encounters with these words as they read and write.

- **Irregularly spelled sight words.** Words like *where* and *does* present more of a challenge to students and require them to focus on how words *look* as well as how they *sound*. The "Look, Say, Cover, Write, Check" procedure will help them do this. *Note:* I also include some of the more challenging *phonetically* spelled words such as *know* and *soon* in this category.

- **Words containing a common spelling pattern.** There are high-frequency words, such as *will* and *play*, containing a common spelling pattern (*-ill* in *will* and *-ay* in *play*) that can help kids learn other words with the same spelling pattern. For example, if kids can read and spell *will*, they'll also know *pill, Bill, still,* etc. To call attention to these words, I put highlighting tape on the spelling pattern before putting the words on the word wall. (See Figure 6-3 for Wylie and Durrell's 37 rimes.)

- **Color and number words.** Instead of writing "color" and "number" words on white cards like the rest of the words, I write "color" words like *red* and *yellow* on blue cards, and number words, like *eight* and *two*, on pink cards to help children find them on the wall.

Figure 6-10. Sight Words Sorted into Categories to Help Plan Your Teaching

beginning"; "I see *-ld* at the end"; "I see two vowels"; "I see two vowels in the middle"; "I see three consonants"; etc. Typically someone says something like "I see /k/" to which you reply: "No, you don't see /k/. You hear it. Right now we're **looking** for letters, not listening for sounds."

3. *Say.* Have children say the word slowly several times along with you. Remind them that now they're **listening** for sounds. Children might say: "I hear /k/ at the beginning of the word"; "I hear /d/ at the end" (here you'd note that they hear the /d/ but not the "l" and then someone most likely will say "I don't hear the "l""); "I hear /o̊/"; "I hear three sounds"; etc. The point is that children are distinguishing between letters they **see** and letter-sounds they **hear.** It always surprises them to realize that although *could* has five letters, we only hear three sounds. This recognition also helps them when they go to write the word.

4. **Cover and Write.** Cover the word with a piece of paper or your hand, and call on a student to come up and write the word on the wipe-off board from memory.

5. **Check.** After the child attempts to write the word correctly, compare the correct spelling of the word with what the child wrote. Children love this exercise, which alerts them to the fact that how a word sounds may not match how it looks.

Effective Practice: Letter and Sound Searches

What Is a Letter or Sound Search?

Letter and sound searches are fun explorations where children try to find words with specific letters or letter combinations, or words that contain specific sounds. You can launch letter and sound searches with an enlarged text, such as a poem written on chart paper, a language experience chart you and your children have written together, or a big book that children know well. It's easier for students to learn letter-sound relationships using a familiar text than it is to work with them in isolation.

What's the Difference Between a Letter Search and a Sound Search?

A letter search is when we *look* for letters or letter combinations in words, and a sound search is when we *listen* for sounds. Be precise when explaining this distinction to children because it's easy in the hustle and bustle of classroom life to phrase it incorrectly and tell kids to look for sounds or listen for letters, which will indeed confuse them.

How Does a Letter or Sound Search Work?

1. *Select a big book or enlarged text to read with students that contains several examples of the letter (or spelling pattern) or sound you want to teach.* For example, I chose Wendy Elizabeth Johnson's poem "Sledding" from Simon James' 2000 anthology *Days Like This: A Collection of Small Poems* (Figure 6-11) to initiate a sound search for the long /o/ because the poem contained several words with that sound.

2. *Introduce the letter or sound you're targeting.* After the children and I read through the poem several times, I give them some examples of words with a long /o/ sound that are not from the poem and explain that there are also words in the poem with that sound. Whenever possible, include class members' names that have the targeted sound, such as *Tony* and *Margo*, for the long /o/ sound.

3. *Identify words containing the letter or sound you're looking or listening for.* As the children and I read through the text line by line and find words containing the long /o/ sound, I put highlighting tape on the words and later write them on chart paper. I make sure

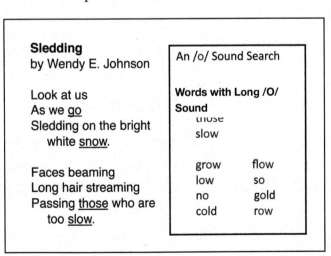

Figure 6-11. *Poem Used to Initiate a Long /O/ Sound Search*

to use a different-color marker for the letters or letter sounds I'm targeting so children can easily differentiate them from the rest of the word.

4. *Give children opportunities to search for the targeted letter, spelling pattern, or sound in books and environmental print.* I attach five blank Post-it notes to the "long /o/ sound" chart and tell students before they go off to read independently that if they find a word with that sound, they should write it on a Post-it and reattach the note to the chart so we can examine their findings the following day. (Children should write their names on the Post-it note.)

    Note: I recommend limiting to five the number of Post-it notes you make available each day. I used to leave the entire packet of notes out, only to return minutes later to find a forest of them attached to the chart. Besides the fact that I don't want students spending so much of their independent reading time searching for words to chart; it's impractical to try to list the contents of more than five notes, especially since children typically try to squeeze several words onto each one.

5. *The next day, review the Post-it notes and add new examples of the targeted letter, spelling pattern, or sound to the list.* As I do this, I review with the children the long /o/ sound we are focusing on and read through our growing list of words with that sound.

    Continue to attach five Post-it notes each day until your list of words is varied enough to sort. (By "sort" I mean to designate a column or page for each subcategory so you can add to these sorted lists as new words surface.)

6. *Sort words to fit the letter or sound you're teaching.* Since we were focusing on the long /o/ sound as we worked with the poem "Sledding," I sort our list according to words with a CVCe pattern (*those*), words with an open vowel at the end of a syllable (*no*), etc.

    If you're doing a sound search you'll want words containing a variety of letter combinations with that sound. If you're doing a letter search, you may want to demonstrate how the targeted letter or letters show up at the beginning, middle, and end of words, or to help differentiate among the various teaching points you might be making, e.g., a consonant can stand alone (*boil*) or blend with another consonant or consonants (*bread, street*).

7. *Keep adding to the sublists.* Once I feel children have acquired a better understanding of the letter or sound I'm teaching, I discontinue our formal search, but keep the charts available to reference or add to at a later time. However, I continue to explain to children how this attention to letters and sounds will help them read and write words more effectively on their own.

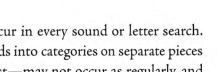

Note: Steps 1–5 are standard and occur in every sound or letter search. However, steps 6 and 7—sorting the words into categories on separate pieces of chart paper and then adding to that list—may not occur as regularly, and whether you do them or not would depend on the needs of your students and the amount of attention a pattern or sound requires. In cases where I decide to eliminate the word sort, I may instead box each word on the chart with the colored marker I've designated for each spelling pattern or sound.

How Many Days Does Each Letter and Sound Search Last?

That depends on the focus letter or sound, and the children's grade and prior exposure to that phonetic element. If it's a more substantive letter or sound search, such as searching for words that contain an /er/ sound, the search and sort may take a couple of weeks since it involves collecting words with the *-er, -ur, -ir,* and *-or* spelling pattern that make that sound. On the other hand, a simpler letter search for *d* may take just a couple of days.

How Can I Extend This Practice?

In addition to letter and sound searches, children can also do *word* searches where they search for sentences that contain homophones, such as *there-their-they're, to-too-two,* and *by-buy-bye.* The teacher selects a homophone to target, starts the list by recording on chart paper a sentence for each of the homophones, and calls children's attention to their different spellings and meanings. For *there-their-they're* she might write: 1. Put the box over ***there***. 2. Blue is ***their*** favorite color. 3. ***They're*** coming on vacation with us.

When children find a sentence from a book containing one of the targeted homophones, they copy the entire sentence on the Post-it note and attach it to the chart. (I still make only five Post-it notes available each day.) Then after school or the following morning before the children arrive, the teacher writes each new sentence on the chart, omitting the homophone and leaving a blank in its place. When children gather that day, they discuss which of the homophones fits the sentence and why.

Effective Practice: Fluency Is About Reading Well, Not Fast

How Is Fluency Typically Defined and How Should It Be Defined?

In recent years, fluency has come to be understood by many educators as reading fast, with accuracy and expression. The problem with this definition is that reading fast and reading with expression do not necessarily go hand in hand. When someone reads with expression, she may pause and slow down her reading to reflect meaning, using the cues the author has embedded. So it's facile to say that fast = fluent. Think of watching a play and how a nervous, novice actor may rush through his lines, where a seasoned actor is a master at appropriately paced speech.

The second problem with this take on fluency is that, I daresay, it's coming from the commercial marketplace rather than from the research, from the wisdom of teachers, and from the real reading of children. When the National Reading Panel released its report in 2000 citing fluency as one of the five essential components of effective reading instruction, some publishers rushed to market fluency programs and assessments and overplayed the role of speed to suit their products rather than children. These products took hold in schools and became "pedagogy," often leaving expression and prosody as little more than afterthoughts, especially when classroom teachers are required to time students' reading with a stopwatch.

To be sure, a child has to read at a certain rate, and not choppily, so that he has enough mental capacity in his working memory to understand the message the author is trying to communicate; I only want to caution that we must attend to children's comprehension more than their speed. Comprehension is at the core—speed is a by-product.

For example, take William's end-of-the-week reflection (Figure 6-12) indicating how proud he was with the number of pages he read in just minutes and how he was bent on "breaking the record of his fluency reading." (An odd goal for a child to set without outside prompting, wouldn't you say?) After reading William's comments, I asked to meet with him for a conference. Since he was new to our school I wanted to hear firsthand where he had gotten such ideas. (See the dialogue box for a transcript of our conversation.)

> **This week I was successful at:**
> Reading a Magic Tree House book! I read 3 pages in one minute. And 5 pages in 5 minutes. I also got to the sixth chapter. I am on the 8th chapter. I improved my reading alot. My teacher thinks I improved and so dose May. She is the asctint teacher. At breaking the rekord of My FlUency reading ✓
>
> **Next week I plan to:**
> Finish Viking Ships at Sun rise. That is a Magic Tree House book. And I want to be in the Magic Tree House book club agin. Next week If I don't finish Viking Ships at sunrise then I atleast want to get to a farther page. I realy think I'm going to finish the book I got too a far page! Realy far! ✓

Figure 6-12. William's Reflection Sheet

Sharon: I see on your reflection sheet that you try really hard to read quickly. Why?

William: Well...sometimes when I read, I read fast because my teacher in my old school said that when you're reading you should practice your fluency. Sometimes I read fast, and sometimes I read slow because I think I'm reading too fast.

Sharon: Why do you think your teacher wanted you to read fast?

William: Because sometimes I didn't do that good on my fluency test and sometimes I did.

Sharon: She gave you a fluency test to see how fast you could read? Why do you think she did that?

William: I don't know why. She just said to do it.

It's encounters with the Williams of the world that compel me to drive home the point that we are overdoing the "reading rate" side of things, and at great cost, and failing to convey to students the relationship between fluency and comprehension. Researchers such as Richard Allington in *What Really Matters for Fluency* (2009) offer a more balanced and instructionally sound definition of fluency as "reading accurately, with expression and comprehension," which recognizes that in most cases reading rate will be addressed as comprehension is attended to.

Some Reasons Why Students Lack Fluency

If a child is reading word by word and without expression and proper phrasing, it may be because:

- He's an emergent reader and still figuring out the basics—what a word is and pointing to keep his place. His fluency will likely improve once his word recognition skills and automaticity kick in, and when his teacher helps him differentiate between when he should point with his finger (i.e., when a book is unfamiliar, when he stumbles on a difficult sentence or word and needs to focus on fixing the problem), and when he should remove his finger and track print with his eyes.

- The book he's reading is too hard and, therefore, he's putting all of his attention to figuring out how to read the word. In most cases, this is the primary reason for a child's lack of fluency. When the book's a good fit, fluency naturally improves.

- He doesn't recognize that the speed at which he reads and the intonations in his voice are tools readers use to make and convey meaning. He needs opportunities to examine book passages with his class, such as the one from *Chicken-Chasing Queen of Lamar County* in the box on page 141, to heighten his awareness of cues authors leave for how to read the text. He also needs his teacher to model fluent reading and give him opportunities to practice.

Rachel's reflection sheet (Figure 6-13), attached to her Weekly Reading Log, demonstrates her developing confidence and savvy as a reader. Her goal, unlike William's, is to slow down—to take her time reading the Cam Jansen mysteries she's grown to love. And she's learning to understand what literacy is all about, setting her sights on integrating what she reads and writes because that's the natural thing to do.

This week I was successful at:

Taking my time to read a book. The book was called Cam Jansen and the School play mystery It was by David A. Adler. I Like to read Cam Jansen beacause I Love reading books with mysterys.

Next week I plan to:

Read more non-ficton I want to because Since we are Learning about birds I thout it would be a good idea.

Figure 6-13. Rachel's Reflection Sheet

How Do We Combine Fluency and Comprehension in Our Teaching?

We need to build into our teaching explicit demonstrations of how the *way* we read a piece is determined by what the author is trying to say. We read so that we can understand the ideas and information the author is sharing.

Where do we start?

1. **Make this fluency-comprehension connection when you read aloud.** Locate passages from stories and texts you're reading where phrasing, word choice, punctuation, *and* comprehension are interwoven—where it's obvious how *together* they convey the story's meaning and signal how it should be read. While it's true that these elements tie together in all texts, there are some books that demonstrate this point more explicitly than others. (See box for a list of such books.)

Books That Beg to Be Read Aloud

- **One Dog Canoe** by Mary Casanova
- **Hurty Feelings** by Helen Lester
- **Bed Head** by Margie Palatini
- **Kitchen Dance** by Maurie J. Manning
- **The Ghost-Eye Tree** by Bill Martin Jr. and John Archumbault
- **How Chipmunk Got His Stripes** by Joseph Bruchac and James Bruchac

- **The Boy Who Lived with the Bears: And Other Iroquois Stories** by Joseph Bruchac
- **The Chicken-Chasing Queen of Lamar County** by Janice N. Harrington
- **Some Dog** by Mary Casanova
- **Casey at the Bat: A Ballad of the Republic Sung in the Year 1888** by Ernest Thayer and illustrated by Christopher Bing

See the box below for a passage from Janice N. Harrington's *The Chicken-Chasing Queen of Lamar County* (2007) and how I "thought aloud" to demonstrate how the words, punctuation, and meaning work together. (When doing this with a class, I project the pages onto an interactive whiteboard or make overheads of them to view.)

TEXT from *The Chicken-Chasing Queen of Lamar County* by Janice N. Harrington	MY THINK ALOUD about using the text to inform my reading
I'm the Chicken-Chasing Queen of Lamar County.	*[Judging from the picture and these words, this little girl sure seems proud of her "title." I'd better read it that way and pause extra long at the end of the sentence to emphasize this even further.]*
Big Mama says, "Don't you chase those chickens. If you make those girls crazy, they won't lay eggs. You like eggs, don't you?"	*[Big Mama is trying to make a point. So I need to read this emphatically and pause a bit after she asks a question.]*
But I don't care. Soon as I wake up, wash away the dreaming, and brush my teeth whiter than a biscuit, I always do three things: eat breakfast, tell stories to Big Mama, and—when Big Mama isn't looking—CHASE CHICKENS!	*[There she goes with her attitude . . . I can't imagine doing anything fast in the morning, especially when I'm trying to "wash away the dreaming" and "brush my teeth whiter than a biscuit." So I'd better take my time reading it.]* *[When I'm stating things I have to do, I pause at the end of each one, so that's what I'll make this character do.]*
I go sneaking up on those chickens real slow, real easy, and the—freeze.	*[If she's sneaking up on chickens, she must be doing it very quietly and slowly, so my reading has to match this. Then I'll "freeze" my reading when she does.]*
I make myself as still as sunlight. And those chickens hold still, too: one leg raised in the air, just waiting to step off. "Pruck! Pruck"—which must be chicken for "What's she up to this time?"	*[Wow! Sunlight is really still so I have to make sure I show this in my voice. And if the chicken's leg is suspended in mid-air, my reading better show that too.]*

2. **Make this fluency-comprehension connection when you confer with students.** Conferences provide yet another opportunity to show students why it's important to match *how* we read a text with the message the author is conveying.

When I conferred with first-grader Ryan, who was reading Jenny Giles' *My Book* (Rigby 2000), a text he had read many times, I explained how his finger-pointing to words was making his reading slow and choppy. And how he needed to adjust his reading to show the excitement the little girl was feeling as she stumbled upon lots of misplaced toys while looking for her book. When she said, "Look! Here is my monkey!" or "elephant" or "tiger," the exclamation marks in combination with what's occurring in the story tell a reader how to read it. My explanation and Ryan having the opportunity to reread the book yet again under my guidance also led him to more fully express the character's somber mood at the start of the book when she set off to look for yet another misplaced possession.

3. **Make this fluency-comprehension connection when you read informational text.** Let children know that a writer of nonfiction finds the facts he's included extremely interesting and has worked hard to share them with others in an exciting way. And now it's their job to bring to the text as much wonder, background knowledge, and fluent reading techniques as they can.

    Show children how to: read section titles with emphasis to announce what topic will be addressed; pause momentarily after reading a question to anticipate the response that will follow; punctuate indicators such as *first, second, next, lastly,* and *in addition* with their voice to signal that a new point is being made that requires attention.

4. **Make this fluency-comprehension connection when children write.** Ask them to consider what they want the reader to know or understand. In mini-lessons, shared writing, and at share time, ask questions like, *Do you want your reader to linger? To clip along to the next scene? To pause to absorb the sadness of your character?* Ask them often whether or not their choice of words and punctuation convey their intentions. If a child needs help achieving this understanding, then during a mini-lesson bring his piece of writing to the class so that together the child and his classmates can work out a more effective way to present his ideas.

    One very simple activity to enhance children's awareness of fluency is to show them how to use speaker tags to slow down or quicken the pace: "'I don't want you to leave,' Tillie said slowly." Or, "'You're not my mother!' David hollered as he dashed out of the room."

Effective Practice: Reader's Theater

What Is Reader's Theater?

Reader's Theater is an activity where students:

- read or develop a script, which can vary from poems for two voices to short plays and speeches,
- practice reading it, using their voice to express the thoughts, ideas, or emotions the characters are experiencing, and
- perform it for an audience of classmates, schoolmates, or family, reading aloud from the script rather than reciting memorized lines.

The beauty of Reader's Theater is that young children can focus all of their attention on making their *reading* of the script come alive for the audience. No pressure to memorize lines, no stage sets or costumes to make.

How Does Reader's Theater Facilitate Reading Comprehension?

As students rehearse their lines, they try to make their reading express the ideas an author wants to convey, or the emotions and motives he has assigned to the characters. They get to "be" Johnny Appleseed or boastful Squirrel in "How the Chipmunk Got Its Stripes," which leads them to comprehend and bring new meaning, and even greater fluency, to their next reading of the script.

As children learn more about the importance of reading with expression, intonation, and prosody, they will bring their newfound understanding and skills to other texts they read, and enhance their overall comprehension.

What Are Some Other Benefits of Reader's Theater?

Reader's Theater is a great equalizer since it allows less proficient readers to work with students who are more fluent. While some Reader's Theater experiences enlist readers at similar stages of reading development, it is also possible to select or develop a script that encompasses a broader range of reading levels. Here, as an added bonus, the less proficient readers learn to read some of the more difficult lines because of their repeated exposure to them in a context that probes meaning.

When the teacher develops or adapts a script from a book that students have read and enjoyed, she can differentiate the parts so that there is something for everyone. Some publishers, such as Benchmark Education, provide scripts that include a range of reading levels. Brook Harris' *Working on the Railroad* (2008) has lines for readers at Levels A–G, and Gregory Brown's *Johnny Appleseed: An American Tall Tale* (2007) includes parts for readers at Levels F–M.

> ···········
> READER'S THEATER
> _____
>
> **Eagle:** *(proudly)* He has planted thousands of apple trees across this land. He's always clearing a spot for a new orchard.
>
> **Squirrel:** Was he born in these woods like we were?
>
> **Eagle:** Goodness no! Johnny was born in Massachusetts in 1774. He lived in a log cabin with ten siblings!

Figure 6-14. Page from Johnny Appleseed *(Benchmark Education)*

In addition to scaffolding struggling readers, Reader's Theater also supports English language learners, who need lots of practice in how English sounds, especially its intonations and cadence. By reading and hearing text read repeatedly—and well—children fine-tune their listening, reading, and oral language skills. Likewise, hearing a script read repeatedly and well enhances their vocabulary. For example, on page 4 of *Johnny Appleseed* (Figure 6-14) the words *proudly, orchard, cabin, sibling,* and the idiom "clearing a spot" would likely present a challenge to ELLs. However, because children work with this text over the course of a week, hear the teacher discuss some of the vocabulary, and then listen to classmates give their renditions, they're more likely to get the gist of what the words mean.

How Do I Find the Time for Reader's Theater?

In light of the potential Reader's Theater holds to nourish the fluency and comprehension of readers, a better question might be "How could I not make the time for something so important?" We need to weed out less effective practices to make room for ones that work well, as Reader's Theater most certainly does. Ask any teacher who's tried it. Kids love it, beg to participate, ask for additional time to practice reading their lines—and as a result develop better fluency and comprehension skills. You can't argue with success!

Although Reader's Theater typically occurs during reading time, often temporarily substituting for guided reading, we can also integrate it into our content-area studies and writing. For example, my students once performed their own Reader's Theater adaptation of Arnold Lobel's *On the Day Peter Stuyvesant Sailed into Town* (1971) during a social studies unit on New York City. Since this was a whole-class affair with an audience of families and friends as invited guests, I needed to make sure everyone had a good part. So we cast several narrators, "Peters," and crowds of townspeople. As students rehearsed the script, they also learned a whole lot about New York City's early days as New Amsterdam.

During the writing workshop, students can also write their own scripts to perform. These may be originals (I often find children writing plays once they encounter one while reading) or reworkings of a favorite read-aloud. (In Chapter 9, Reading-Writing Connections, I describe how students took what they learned from a Rosemary Wells' author study and wrote Reader's Theater scripts about a favorite character.)

How Do I Implement Reader's Theater?

Here are some things to consider when implementing Reader's Theater:

+ *Think small.* Even though Reader's Theater can be done with an entire class of students or with several groups working at one time, it's best to start off with just one group of five or six readers to test the waters. That way you'll feel more comfortable working out some of the kinks, and students will be more relaxed, confident, and receptive.

+ *Select an appropriate text.* The parts you assign students should be somewhat equitable, that is, there shouldn't be one or two very long parts while others are only one sentence or a couple of words.

   You also need to consider how well the text matches the reading level of the students. While readers can often handle scripts that are a little more challenging than their independent reading level, the texts shouldn't be so much of a stretch that children become frustrated. In addition, if your script has several exceptionally challenging parts, you may want to invite one or two guest readers to join the group for its duration. Doing so is a

---

A Typical Schedule for a Week-Long Reader's Theater

Plan on Reader's Theater taking a week from start to finish. Here's how the week might look:

- **Day 1:** Gather a group of five to six readers and give each of them the script. If this is their first time doing Reader's Theater, you will need to be very clear about what you'll be asking them to do. Introduce the script as you would any book. Let children know what it is about and who the characters are. Give them time to examine the script before you start reading it to or with them. Don't assign parts yet. That will come at the *end* of Day 2.

   For Day 1, listen in on where children's interests lie. They often surprise you. I've worked with children having meek, quiet voices who want to be the big, fierce (and loud) Bear. Other times kids just want to make sure they have as many lines as their classmates. You never know.

- **Day 2:** Read over the script several more times with the children to give them a growing sense of what it's about and a chance to try out different parts they might like. Stop periodically to discuss the characters, what they're like, how they're feeling, etc. Assign parts to students at the end of this session.

- **Days 3 and 4:** Now it's time for children to practice their parts. On Day 3, you can meet with the group to help them read through the script—accurately, with expression and comprehension. Then on Day 4, children can practice on their own and take the script home to practice with their family.

- **Day 5:** Finally, the children get to perform the script they've been practicing all week. Set up chairs in the front of the room or meeting area and invite the readers to take their seat (with their script in hand). Either you or one of the readers can introduce the group.

win-win situation. The more proficient readers love the attention, and less able readers learn from hearing their classmates read.

◆ *Avoid overexacting assessments of students' performances.* Reader's Theater should be fun. We want students to enjoy and learn from the experience, and they can't if they're worried we're evaluating their every move. I like to first give the readers themselves the opportunity to express how they feel they did and then hear from their classmates. Students might also write about the experience in their reading notebook.

What Resources Do I Need and Where Do I Find Them?

In addition to writing your own Reader's Theater scripts during the writing workshop and turning favorite books into scripts, here are some places to get free and for purchase materials.

Sources for Reader's Theater Scripts

- **Reading A–Z.com** (scripts for elementary grades with membership)

- **Benchmark Education Company** (a wide assortment of Reader's Theater booklets, including fairy tales, biographies, and science and social studies topics)

- **www.teachingheart.net/readerstheater .htm** (free scripts to download, many relate to children's literature titles)

- *25 Just Right Plays for Emergent Readers* by Carol Pugliano-Martin

- *Readers on Stage: Resources for Reader's Theatre, with Tips, Worksheets, and Reader's Theatre Play Scripts, or How to Do Simple Children's Plays That Build Reading Fluency and Love of Literature* by Aaron Shepard

- An Internet search can also help you find numerous other resources.

Background Knowledge
Principles and Practices

CHAPTER 7

"Nothing is of more importance to students' understanding of text than the knowledge they already have about a topic. This knowledge serves as a foundation for all future learning and provides the "hooks" on which students can hang their new learning about a topic." (p. 92)

—Barbara Moss in *Exploring the Literature of Fact: Children's Nonfiction Trade Books in the Elementary Classroom* (2002)

Background Knowledge and Comprehension

The use of informational texts for reading instruction in the primary grades is more common than it was a decade ago, but it's safe to say that fiction still remains the genre of choice for most teachers. For many decades, educators have operated with the premise that narratives provide young readers and writers with the voice, vocabulary, and structure they need—a natural progression from the bedtime stories they've heard at home or everyday oral storytelling they hear as grown-ups recount the events in their lives.

+ In This Chapter...

+ **Background Knowledge and Comprehension**

+ **Foundational Principles to Build Background Knowledge**

+ Expose Your Students to More Informational Texts

+ Select High-Quality Texts

+ Teach Children to Read Informational Text

+ Frontload Lessons and Fine-Tune When Necessary

+ Integrate Content-Area Work into Your Literacy Lessons

+ Demonstrate How to Use Background Knowledge

+ **Effective Practices**
  Using Companion Texts for Guided and Independent Reading
  Clustering Informational Text on the Same Topic
  Working with a Synopsis Text
  Content-Area Literacy Centers

Prior Knowledge and Background Knowledge Defined

Prior knowledge is the sum total of all that we've experienced throughout our lives. It's our total life experiences—the places we've visited, the friends we've made, the conversations we've heard, the books we've read. All of this is our prior knowledge, and it's what we bring to each and every new experience and encounter.

Background knowledge, as I define it in this book, has a related but distinct cast. Generally speaking, it's the knowledge of the world we've accrued through our formal education and our understanding of the world. It relates to academics, to all the content-area topics we study in school, and what we learn through our outside experiences with them as well.

True enough, our lives are narratives, full of characters, problems and solutions, and adventures. But just as our students can sit spellbound, enchanted by *The Princess and the Pea*, they are likely to be at the edge of their seats with wonder at our read aloud of Madeleine Dunphy's *Here Is the Arctic Winter* (2007). Facts can motivate and engage children and develop their reading and writing skills as much as fiction, and so in this chapter on background knowledge, we shall reckon with this and take a good look at our teaching and the materials in our classroom. (See the "Prior Knowledge and Background Knowledge Defined" box for how I define *background* and *prior knowledge*.)

Look at your classroom library. What percent of your books is fiction and what percent informational? Think of the books you read aloud. How many times a week do you read a nonfiction text or display one that you just can't wait to share? Think of the summer reading list you give to families or recommendations to your parent group for books to order for the book fair. Do they stack up heavily on the side of fiction?

And consider the informational texts that occupy our classroom library shelves and book baskets. Do they include the main categories of nonfiction—narrative-informational, expository-informational, and mixed texts, which blend narrative and expository elements? (See the following box for how Sharon Benge Kletzien and Mariam Jean Dreher describe three types of informational text.) And do our expository texts include titles from the various subgenres such as persuasive, procedural, and enumerative? Do we have books to adequately support the content-area topics we will address throughout the year? And even more basic—do we address science and social studies as rigorously as we should or have we allowed content-area studies to take a back seat?

Clichéd as it sounds, we have entered the information age. With one click, our students can see live-streaming video of lions roaming the African savannahs, trees being cut down in the rain forest, polar bears sitting on melting Arctic ice. They can correspond with children in Russia, biologists in Alaska, paleontologists in Peru. Within a few years (or even now since some schools and homes already have handheld devices and wired libraries), think of the gadgets that will bring all this print and visual

Different Kinds of Informational Texts

In *Informational Text in K–3 Classrooms: Helping Children Read and Write*, Sharon Benge Kletzien and Mariam Jean Dreher divide informational texts into three categories: narrative-informational texts, expository-informational texts, and mixed text that combine narrative and expository text.

1. *Narrative-informational texts* are written in a story format, where the author may (although not necessarily) use narrative devices such as character, setting, problem, and resolution to convey information about a topic. Examples are *Panda Kindergarten* by Joanne Ryder and *Tarra and Bella: The Elephant and Dog Who Became Best Friends* by Carol Buckley. Biographies and autobiographies, such as *The Boy Who Drew Birds: A Story of John James Audubon* by Jacqueline Davies, are also included in this category.

2. *Expository-informational texts* convey information about the natural world. They address a generic topic such as rocks and minerals and are generally written in the third person. Some text structures are compare-contrast, cause-effect, sequence, enumerative, and problem-solution. *The Construction Alphabet Book* by Jerry Pallotta and *Everything Bug: What Kids Really Want to Know About Bugs* by Cherie Winner are examples.

3. *Mixed texts* that include both narrative and expository features combine the best of both worlds. These blended texts typically embed true information in a fictional story. Examples include Charles L. Blood and Martin Link's *The Goat in the Rug,* and Amanda Lumry and Laura Hurwitz's *Safari in South Africa.*

Note: While there are three types of informational text from which to choose, Kletzien and Dreher recommend that *most* of the informational texts we bring into the classroom should be expository since their structure and text features demand a different kind of reading than what's required of narratives.

---

information directly to our students. We have to embrace the different information devices and methods in our teaching, for this is the currency of our young students' lives and clearly the future. Our goal should be to help students become more adept and engaged readers and writers—of nonfiction and fiction alike. On screens and on pages.

Fiction and nonfiction must stand alongside one another in our classrooms. Readers should be transported by the fictional worlds that books create, but also thrilled and amazed by the beauty and wonder of our actual world. By embracing both genres, we give children knowledge and ideas about the world so they are well prepared to discuss them, respond thoughtfully to texts, and write to communicate their knowledge, whether it's derived from books or other medium. They bring their burgeoning background knowledge to texts, making reading more rewarding and comprehension more readily achieved.

In addition to helping children better understand the informational texts they read, their knowledge of the world helps them enjoy and comprehend other genres as well. A few years ago I purchased Marilyn Singer's wonderfully entertaining *Antarctic Antics: A Book of Penguin Poems* (2003) for my first-grade class. I thought the poems were uproariously funny and expected the children to feel the same. But they didn't. They weren't even mildly amused. This response puzzled me, until I realized they lacked the background knowledge to appreciate these poems.

In contrast, the following year when my children were hard at work writing *Penguins Are Water Birds* (2002), a book we were writing for Mondo Publishers, Singer's poems had direct and immediate appeal. These first graders appreciated a poem like "Regurgitate" and the illustration of dad coughing up food for his youngster because by the time they read the poem, they already knew a whole lot about a penguin's feeding habits. They knew that the mom and dad penguin feed their chick by regurgitating a milky substance into their chick's open beak, and that it's not quite as gross as they first imagined!

And the beauty of the relationship between what you already know and what you are learning is its spiraling effect: The more you know, the more you understand. The more you understand, the more you read. And the more you read, the more you know. There's so much for children to know and learn—and it's important that we give them the chance to start early.

Foundational Principles to Build Background Knowledge

The following principles will set you down a path to include more informational texts in your classroom and in children's lives.

Expose Your Students to More Informational Texts

Researchers and educators alike pretty much agree that half of what students read, write, and are exposed to throughout the day should be informational text and the other half should be fiction. In the classrooms where I teach and coach, seeing this balance in action is rewarding. Once you bring more nonfiction into kids' lives, you recognize how readily they seek it out as readers and writers. As teachers, it changes the choreography of our day in positive ways, allowing us to move from a read-aloud of a tall tale to reading a fascinating account of animals that inhabit the different layers of the rain forest. Science, social studies, and math connections become easier; we can plan or improvise connections between picture books and nonfiction.

Creating an interplay between fiction, poetry, and nonfiction allows children to accrue background knowledge of a more intricate design. Like native American beadwork, our students' minds make connections book by book. José, a second grader I worked with, finished up a personal narrative about hiking in the Adirondacks one day, and a day later of his own accord began writing a fictional piece about two brothers becoming separated from their families while on a camping trip in the mountains. Allison drew pictures and made labels for a poster describing how Ben Franklin's inventions revolutionized modern-day society, drawing from both Dennis Brindell Fralen's *Who Was Ben Franklin?* (2002), a straight biographical account of Franklin's life, and Stacia Deutsch and Rhody Cohon's *Ben Franklin's Fame* (2006), a time-travel blended chapter book of kids trying to prevent the evil Babs from convincing Franklin to step down from his dreams so she could step in and become famous.

Our mini-lessons become more varied too, providing us with opportunities to spread our wings in terms of the genres we model. I've seen teachers who never quite liked modeling pieces about their own lives relish working on a collaborative persuasive essay. Third graders can take on issues that matter deeply to them, writing a piece defending—or decrying—John Audubon's right to kill the birds he painted so he could memorialize their beauty in paintings to share with the world.

So, let's return to the implications for our classroom library. For every fictional picture book you prop up to entice kids to read, sitting right alongside it should be an informational text that's every bit as exciting and motivational as its partner. Nell K. Duke and P. David Pearson go so far as to say that children should have opportunities to try their hand writing *each* of the nonfiction subgenres they're learning to read (Duke and Pearson 2002). If that were the case, think of all the information, organizational frameworks, and text features to which students would be exposed. Just think of it.

> *For every fictional picture book you prop up to entice kids to read, sitting right alongside it should be an informational text that's every bit as exciting and motivational as its partner.*

Also consider what literacy specialists Nancy Frey and Douglas Fisher say about background knowledge in *Background Knowledge: The Missing Piece of the Comprehension Puzzle* (2009):

> How much a reader already knows about the subject is probably the best predictor of reading comprehension. When readers engage with a text for which they have limited background knowledge, the text is much more difficult to understand than one for which they have ample background knowledge. So while the reading world is focused on leveling books and comprehension strategy instruction, research indicates that children continue to spin their wheels when they don't have the background knowledge required to understand much of what they're reading. (p. 2)

Every time we read aloud or share a book, every time we meet for guided reading or a one-to-one conference with a student, every time we help a child select a book for his independent book bag, we can make a decision that brings us one step closer to achieving our goal of more informational text reading, more background knowledge, and better comprehension.

Select High-Quality Texts

In addition to bringing a variety of informational texts into the classroom and providing opportunities for students to interact with them throughout the day, we need to make sure that the books we offer students are of the highest quality. Our choices are abundant, and so we should know how to differentiate between a "must have" informational book and one that's just "okay." The informational books and resources we offer students should be attractive, accurate, and accessible:

- **Attractive.** Informational texts, whether magazines or books, should be visually attractive, loaded with colorful photos and illustrations to enhance children's motivation and engagement. After all, when children select a book to read we want them to attend to the illustrations, the pictures, the charts, the maps, even before they read text. In nonfiction, the text and the text features work in concert, each providing what the other does not.

+ **Accurate.** The texts should be accurate and up to date, and written by an expert in the field or someone who has spent a considerable amount of time researching the topic. The author's credentials should be stated up front as should any bias he might have about a topic. Children need to become critical readers and part of this involves their growing ability to note and then consider an author's perspective and bias.

+ **Accessible.** Authors and publishers need to be considerate of young readers and appreciate that they are just starting out on their information-acquiring journey without a whole lot of background knowledge. Too many content-area books, especially the text-bookish type, try to cram too much information, vocabulary, and concepts into too little space. This demands a great deal of the reader, especially a novice one, often causing him to lose interest and walk away.

I just love the way authors Henrietta Bancroft and Richard G. Van Gelder present the concept of hibernation in their 1997 book *Animals in Winter* (Figure 7-1). The concept is beautifully rendered, the illustrations and text work together harmoniously, and the repetition is exactly what young readers need in order to understand. Bravo!

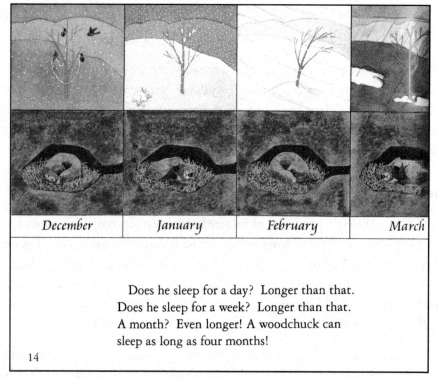

Figure 7-1. Page from Animals in Winter

Considering the Readability of Informational Text

Here are some things to consider when matching children with informational texts for independent reading:

- It may be advisable to drop a child down a reading level to accommodate the challenges he will inevitably face when reading nonfiction. Therefore, a child who is reading fiction at independent Level H might fare better with a Level G nonfiction book.

- If a child knows a lot about a topic and considers himself an expert of sorts, you may want to let him try reading books a bit above his independent level.

- If a child is interested in reading a nonfiction book that's far more advanced than her reading level, you may want to let her read it as a "look" book. She can gain information from the pictures, captions, labels, diagrams, etc.

Teach Children to Read Informational Text

Second-grader Isis began his conference by stating that he needed new books because some of the books in his bag were too hard, especially the one on sharks. He said it was a "grown-up" book and not for someone like him. While I might have agreed and let him select another book, I decided on this occasion to help him see that he could, in fact, get some cool information from this book. He just needed to read it differently. Not in the beginning-to-end, top-to-bottom way that he reads fiction, but in a more random, pick-and-choose, interest-driven way.

I showed him how he could look at the pictures and read the labels, and then read a sentence here and there. From the text we learned that a dwarf shark is just six inches long, not much longer than a goldfish, and from the scale drawing we learned that it's small enough to fit in the palm of your hand. Feeling newly confident and motivated, Isis decided to try this out for himself, and reveled in the information he was able to glean.

He learned the names of different kinds of sharks: the nurse shark, the great white shark, the mako shark, and that they have different kinds of teeth. The pictures of the sharks and the close-ups of their teeth formed a background knowledge platform from which Isis will, later on, explore how the size and shape of sharks' teeth help them get food and stay alive.

Isis learned a lot that day about sharks—and how we can read nonfiction differently than fiction.

Frontload Lessons and Fine-Tune When Necessary

Before you read aloud to students, consider what they know or don't know about the topic. You may find it necessary to frontload read-alouds, guided reading, etc., with an explanation of concepts children will discover as they read. Or you may even read aloud an easier and more basic book on the topic to lay the groundwork and facilitate students' understanding of the concepts and vocabulary. You may decide to write a synopsis text as Sara Flores did in Chapter 5, including some of the main concepts the book or section addresses, and read through it with students to give them some background on what's to come. (See the Effective Practice: Working with a Synopsis Text later in this chapter for how to do this.)

Helping English Language Learners

Students who are learning English as a second language may lack the language or the background knowledge to appreciate the topic you're teaching. While they may have acquired the social vocabulary to communicate with one another, they may not have the academic language to make sense of texts and information you share. Therefore you will need to adapt your lessons to meet their needs:

+ Bring in pictures that relate to topics they're learning and give them time to talk about them. This is a lot less threatening than having to deal with words only. Keep a file of pictures and add to it.

+ Use real-life objects to make concepts more concrete. Show them the bird's nest you found in your yard or the pinecone still holding tight to the seeds cradled within.

+ Relate what students are learning to what they already know. While this applies to all students, not just ELLs, it's even more important for kids just learning English. Even if you don't know Vietnamese or Spanish words to help kids make analogies, you can make English comparisons— a *longhouse* is like an *apartment building,* a *stable* is like a *barn*—and when they look puzzled, take it one step further and explain that a barn is like a house for animals. Starting with what kids know is always the best path to take.

Integrate Content-Area Work into Your Literacy Lessons

One surefire way to bring more informational texts into the classroom and provide more bang for the buck is to have children read about science and social studies topics during read-aloud, shared reading, guided reading, and independent reading.

+ **Read-Aloud**—Go through your science and social studies scope and sequence and list the main topics you plan to address. Get several large storage bags and label each bag with the name of one topic. Then add books to the bag as you come across them.

When the time is approaching to begin a science or social studies unit, start to read aloud books on that topic during your balanced literacy time of day, opening with the simplest, most basic one first and then moving to the more difficult titles to help your students acquire background knowledge to support their new learning. Be sure to include as read-alouds enlarged texts of informational books, such as Nicola Davies' *Big Blue Whale* (2000), so kids can see up close the illustrations and text features. Or read Julie Haydon's large-formatted *My Animal Scrapbook* (Rigby 2003) when beginning an animal unit to introduce students to each of the animal groups and their characteristics.

* **Guided Reading**—Gather sets of books at each of the various reading stages that address the content-area topics you'll study. For example, if you're studying weather, you should try to assemble a set of weather-related books for emergent, early, transitional, and fluent readers. Or at least target the stages that most represent the students in your class.

* **Independent Reading**—Children can read about content-area topics during their independent reading time. And if they can't read all the words, they can learn from the pictures. Make sure your books are of high quality.

* **Writing**—When children write about a topic they're studying, they're bound to need to read more on that topic. And thinking, gathering information, organizing it, and then writing it down to share with others helps them consolidate what they know. In addition, the books they write can be made available for their classmates to read. Student-authored books are among the favorites in most classroom libraries.

Demonstrate How to Use Background Knowledge

We use background knowledge to help us infer meaning. When a child approaches a text, he brings what he knows to figure out what he doesn't know. Daniel T.

Willingham, cognitive scientist and author of *Why Don't Students Like School? A Cognitive Scientist Answers Questions About How the Mind Works and What It Means for the Classroom* (2009), states that writers leave gaps for readers to fill in. If they didn't, the writing would become cumbersome, even unintelligible. Therefore, we have to teach students how to *use* what they know to make sense of what they're reading, and celebrate when they do.

During our study of Eastern Woodland Indians, the children and I read *The Sugar Bush* (Rigby 1999) by Winona LaDuke and Waseyabin Kapashesit, an enlarged text relating how a modern day Native American family makes maple syrup from the sap of the maple tree. The children learned about the long and laborious syrup-making process, which included the very important information that harvesters cannot begin collecting the sap until the end of February when the ground begins to thaw.

Then we read Connie Brummel Crook's *Maple Moon* (1999), a fictionalized tale of how maple sap was discovered by Rides the Wind, a Native American boy, who witnesses a squirrel licking maple sap from a tree branch, and then tastes it himself. By the time I got to the part where Rides the Wind returns to the forest late at night with his father and the tribal leaders to show off his discovery, and finds no sign of the sweet water, several children are wildly waving their hand: "I know what's going to happen! It's nighttime and the sap isn't going to be running. It's frozen because it's so cold at night. Everyone will think that Rides the Wind is lying."

The children were right. It wasn't until the next day when the earth warmed and the sap started running again that Rides the Wind was redeemed. The children's background knowledge and their understanding that they should apply what they know about collecting maple sap to this new reading experience supported their comprehension.

Background knowledge that comes from actual life experiences, books, and content-area studies is essential for children's growing ability to comprehend text. Bringing that background knowledge to bear on texts you're reading (i.e., making inferences) is a challenge for readers and should be a recurring topic for discussion throughout the elementary grades.

Here are some of the ways to show children how to infer:

+ Help them recognize the importance of monitoring their reading for when things make sense and when they don't. They need to listen for "clunks" that signal them to stop and fix what's broken, just as they do when they write. (See Chapter 9 for more about monitoring during reading and writing.)

+ Help kids see the difference between *subconscious* and *conscious* inferences. Subconscious inferences are those we make all the time without being aware that we're doing so. For example, when we read in a field guide that mallard ducks "migrate to warmer climates in winter to more easily find food," we infer they stay put in the warmer months. The conscious inferences are those where we intentionally pause because we don't understand what we're reading and must stop to figure things out. This "figuring things out"—using what we know to understand what we don't—is inferring.

+ Demonstrate how it's helpful to take a moment before starting to read to think about all you know about a topic, so that the information you've stored in your long-term memory is brought to the surface and ready to go. We might show children how to use anticipation guides or the "Building and Using Background Knowledge" strategy sheet described in Chapter 10 and shown in Figure 10-12 and Appendix 12 online.

+ Demonstrate how to make inferences by thinking aloud as you read. Children need to see us stop short as a passage puzzles us. They need to hear us think out loud about why it isn't making sense and what we'll do to get our thinking back on track. When this happens you might write your question on a three-column chart like the one shown in Figure 9-7, and later make a similar sheet (i.e., a strategy sheet) available for when students read on their own (Figure 10-16 and Appendix 13 online). This will help to make this process concrete: you use what's in the book (column 1) and what's in your head (column 3) to arrive at this new information (column 2).

+ Read several books, from easier to harder, on the same topic. Then show students how to use what they've learned from the easier books to understand the harder ones. Their comprehension is better because they have more background knowledge to fill in the gaps the author left.

Effective Practice: Using Companion Texts for Guided and Independent Reading

What Are Companion Texts?

I developed this companion text practice when I saw how much young readers benefited by having a way to swiftly apply what we were doing in guided reading lessons during the week to their independent reading. Merely encouraging children to practice the skill or strategy they'd worked on in guided reading with the books in their book bag wasn't enough; they didn't seem to gain enough traction with just any book they picked up.

But when I helped them select a book to read on their own that was on the same topic or theme, a book in the same series, or one that particularly supported the strategy or skill we'd been focusing on, the children's engagement and comprehension shot up. I'm convinced it's because they went into reading the companion text with relevant background knowledge and added confidence.

For example, I paired a Level K guided reading book, *Flash, Crash, Rumble, and Roll* (1999) by Franklyn M. Branley with Ann Herriges' *Lightning* (Bellwether Media 2009), a Level H book. Although both are expository, the guided reading selection is more challenging than its companion. Or with third graders reading at Level N–O, I'd feature the story *Computer Pigs* (2000 Mondo) by Josephine Selwyne in my guided reading lesson, and then offer the trade paperback *Mercy Watson to the Rescue* (2005) by Kate DiCamillo as a companion text because it's at an easier reading level—and also has a porcine protagonist!

At times I select a companion book that connects by way of the strategy I'm highlighting. For example, if in the guided reading lesson I'm focusing on using a glossary, I'd choose a companion book that also has a glossary. If I'm focusing on visualizing, I'd find a text that especially lends itself to that strategy because of its sensory-rich language. Or I might simply choose a companion text that's in the same series as the guided reading selection.

Which Book Is the Guided Reading Selection and Which Is the Companion?

For guided reading, I use the book that offers the most challenge in terms of level, genre, or text features. I use the text that's *easier* as its companion. The guided reading selection, read with teacher guidance and support, is at children's instructional level (90–97 percent word accuracy), and the companion text, which children read on their own, should be easier than that. Although I can usually determine which text is harder or easier by its assigned level, that's not always the case.

For example, I pair Ellen Doherty's *Ellis Island* (2004), which relates the experiences of European immigrants entering the United States through Ellis Island, with Doherty's *William's Journal* (2004), a fictional account of a young immigrant's journey from Ireland. Both are Benchmark Education books and have been paired and leveled (L) by the publisher, but the decision about *how* to use and sequence them is mine. Since *Ellis Island* is an expository text and the more challenging of the two, I designate it the guided reading selection and *William's Journal*, a narrative, becomes the companion. (See the "More Companion Text Pairing Advice" box for additional advice on pairing companions.)

The children read *Ellis Island* throughout our weeklong guided reading sessions, and I support them as they navigate this new and more challenging genre. I show them how to use the table of contents, index, glossary, captions, bold print, a "Who Came to America" chart, and "In Their Own Words" sidebars to access information. Then, at the conclusion of the guided reading group, I assign *William's Journal* as the companion, knowing that students will use what they've learned about Ellis Island to appreciate the experiences the fictional William records in his journal.

More Companion Text Pairing Advice

When working with transitional and fluent readers, it's often feasible to pair companion books that are at the same, or almost the same, reading level since these more proficient readers have acquired self-improving strategies to apply to unfamiliar texts. However, this is not the case with emergent and early readers.

Emergent and early readers need the companion text to be at least a level below the guided reading text selection. For example, if they're reading Katherine Scraper's *A Seed Needs Help* (Benchmark Education), a Level E book for guided reading, then the companion should be one step down from that and Level D, such as Jean Richard's *A Fruit Is a Suitcase for Seeds*.

Where Are Companion Sets Stored and How Do They Get into Kids' Hands?

I package six copies of a guided reading text and six copies of its companion text together in a plastic storage bag and house them in my guided reading bookcase (Figure 7-2). Emergent companion sets (Levels A, B, C, D) go on the top shelf, followed by a shelf of early companion sets (Levels E, F, G, H, I), a shelf of transitional sets (J, K, L, M), and, lastly, a shelf of fluent sets (N, O, P+). The range and distribution of companion set levels should reflect the grade you teach. For example, kindergarten teachers will have mostly emergent and a few early sets, while second-grade teachers will have a healthy collection of early and transitional sets and just a couple emergent and fluent ones.

I keep each companion set in a separate 9" x 12" book pouch that I purchase online from the Teaching Resource Center: www.trcabc.com. Since the front is clear plastic, I can easily identify the title.

+ At the start of the week, I remove the pouches I'll need for my guided reading groups and keep them in a plastic bin at the meeting area since this is where the students and I meet for small-group work. We typically work with the guided reading text throughout the week.

+ At the end of the week when a guided reading group disbands, I send each child off with a copy of both the guided reading text and its companion to

Figure 7-2. Guided Reading Bookcase

reread independently. I take a moment at the end of the last session to discuss the companion and how they might approach it.

How Many Companion Sets Do I Need?

In an ideal world, to account for the range of readers in your class, you'd want several companion sets at each level, but you and I know that's not going to happen. That's really all right because the *process* of assembling and working with even a handful of companion sets each year is valuable in and of itself:

+ You get to think carefully about books you most want to bring to students during guided reading and how you'll use them, and

+ Students see that chunking books by topic, genre, series, and strategy makes reading, thinking, and learning easier.

I recommend that you start by finding companions for only two or three of your *favorite* guided reading selections—ones that you can keep in your classroom as part of your core guided reading collection. (See the Effective Practice: A Teacher-Tailored Guided Reading Collection in Chapter 10.) Even if you gather only five companion sets the first year, you're off to a good start. And by going slowly you won't need to purchase so many book pouches at once, which gets costly.

When you're starting out I advise you to:

+ Assemble companion sets that target the middle of where your kids typically read. For kindergarten, this would most likely be Level B and C books. For first grade, the middle would be G and H, etc.

+ Give yourself time to explore book club offerings and book room titles, or splurge on trade books. There's a wealth of fabulous books available. Educational publishers such as Benchmark Education, National Geographic, and Mondo have an impressive line of guided reading materials. Ponder how you'd use a title and luxuriate in finding its mate. It's sort of like being a matchmaker—bringing together two singles that would not have otherwise found each other.

+ Work with grade-level colleagues to assemble some sets. Or it might be a fun activity to bring to a staff meeting. Imagine a first-grade team deciding to focus on the five main animal categories (birds, mammals, fish, reptiles, and amphibians) and each teacher bringing two or three guided reading titles (fiction, nonfiction, and poetry) to mix and match.

How Do Companion Sets Support Reading Comprehension?

Companion sets support reading comprehension in much the same way that series books do—by providing readers with background information to scaffold their reading. Since children have read the guided reading text with teacher guidance, they're better able to read and understand its companion on their own.

In addition, companion sets offer an alternative to time-consuming paper-and-pencil activities that are often assigned at the conclusion of a guided reading group. By giving children companion texts instead, they have more time—and more incentive—to keep reading.

What Do Companion Sets Have to Do with Background Knowledge?

Companion sets give children a chance to apply what they've learned about a topic or theme, genre, series, or strategy to an appropriate and related text—the similarity of which supports their efforts. They might compare the information in both, or how a theme is handled in various genres, or they might transfer a strategy they've practiced during guided reading to its companion.

For example, I pair Mary Pope Osborne's *Rain Forests* (2001) with its fictional companion *Afternoon on the Amazon* (1995) so that kids can apply what they've learned about rain forests from the research guide to Jack and Annie's time-travel adventures to the Amazon Rain Forest. When I meet with the guided reading group to introduce *Rain Forests*, I explain why I paired the books and give each student a bookmark (Figure 7-3). The bookmark lists several concepts from *Afternoon on the Amazon* that would enhance children's reading of the book. So instead of reading *Rain Forests* from cover to cover, we first check the index for each word listed on the bookmark and go directly to the pages containing the information we're after. My goal is to build children's background knowledge and then have them use it to make *Afternoon on the Amazon* more enjoyable and comprehensible—and it works.

A Note on Trade Books in Companion Sets

You'll note that some of the companion set examples I've provided include trade books one would purchase from a bookstore or online, which I know means an outlay of money. While we may not be able to make up the majority of our companion texts this way, we should try to include some trade paperbacks in our companion set collection. These books can be surprisingly inexpensive and discounted online through book sites.

Amazon

canopy

understory

forest floor

camouflage

army ants

vampire bats

jaguar

piranhas

Figure 7-3. Concept Bookmark

How Do Topic and Theme Companions Work?

Topic companions are texts on the same subject as the guided reading selection. The *topic* is what the book is about—the solar system, dolphins, the life cycle of monarch butterflies. The author often includes an easily identifiable *thesis statement* at the start to signal the information or message she intends to convey.

Nonfiction authors may or may not intend a message beyond the information they're providing. For example, in Bobbie Kalman's *Endangered Elephants* (2005), the words and images are crafted with the overarching goal that we must act to stop elephants from becoming extinct. In contrast, David Bloom's photo-essay *Elephants: A Book for Children* (2008) beautifully conveys information about elephants, but doesn't have the same author-generated call-to-action.

When you choose a companion book that connects by theme, you're looking for one that has the same underlying message or big idea. To find a book's theme, ask yourself, "What's the lesson or moral?" For example, theme companions such as Patrick Sken Catling's *The Chocolate Touch* (2006) and the Greek myth *King Midas and the Golden Touch* illustrate that it's unwise to be selfish.

How Do Genre Companions Work?

Genre companions are written in a different genre or subgenre than the guided reading selection. Like the Effective Practice: Clustering Informational Text on the Same Topic described later in this chapter, genre companions invite readers to compare and contrast how information and ideas "live" in different genres. For example, to augment a straightforward guided reading book on maple sugaring in Vermont, I'd select *Old Elm Speaks: Tree Poems* (2002) by Kristine O'Connell George. Two multicultural books I'd pair up are Barbara M. Flores' *Mud Tortillas* (Bebop Books 2005) and Michelle Freeman's *Making Tortillas* (National Geographic 2003).

I love when students take the initiative to pair books on their own. I learned during a reading conference that Jared paired Mary Pope Osborne's *Twisters on Tuesday* (2001) with her *Twisters and Other Terrible Storms* (2003), and *Mummies in the Morning* (2001) with *Mummies and Pyramids* (2003). Granted, these are obvious companions, but the fact that he independently applied this strategy from guided reading to his own reading is quite remarkable. (See Figure 7-4 for the note I wrote in Jared's assessment notebook to myself and Jared.)

How Do Series Companions Work?

Fiction series companions are the easiest to assemble because the author and publisher have done the work for you. All you need to do is find out which titles your kids would enjoy. Frog and Toad, Houndsley and Catina, Pinky and Rex, Tabby and Mr. Putter, Katie Kazoo Switcheroo all make fabulous fictional series companions that offer readers a world of support. Children are likely to read them successfully since they can easily transfer what they've learned from the guided reading selection about the characters, their personality, their friends, and home life to other books in the series.

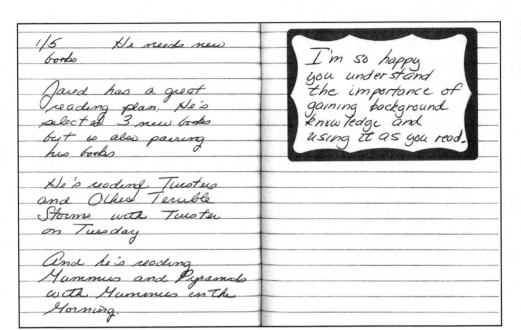

Figure 7-4. Notes in Jared's Assessment Notebook

Nonfiction series companions may not be a good idea for beginning readers since the topics and information vary from book to book and would require the reader to manage these challenges on his own. However, nonfiction series companions are likely to work out just fine for more proficient readers. Here are some nonfiction series suggestions: The One Small Square series by Donald Silver; A Picture Book of . . . series by David Adler; Who Was . . . series by Geoff Edgers; ABC series by Jerry Pallotta; the Adventures of Riley series (blended text) by Amanda Lumry and Laura Hurwitz, and the If You . . . series by Ellen Levine.

How Do Strategy Companions Work?

There are several ways to approach strategy companions. First, one might argue that strategies, per se, are generic and should be viewed as such. When a reader sits down to read he should be able to apply any of the strategies to any text: he might set a purpose for reading, use prior knowledge, ask questions and wonder, visualize what he's reading, etc. In this case, it wouldn't matter which two books go together, and whatever strategy the teacher may have demonstrated during guided reading should be what the student tries out when reading the companion. All true.

However, there are some texts and situations that seem to lend themselves to particular strategies. If students have learned about a topic, *weather* for example, in an earlier grade or earlier in the year, wouldn't it be wise to pair two books on that topic so the reader could access what he knows and apply it to the new text he's reading? Or if a book has gorgeous imagery and language, wouldn't it be powerful to pair it with another sensory-rich text so that children could naturally visualize its images and linger over its language? Also true. So it appears that both scenarios work and should be considered when assembling strategy companions.

Effective Practice: Clustering Informational Text on the Same Topic

What Does Clustering Books Mean?

I often cluster informational books by gathering two or three books on the same topic and storing each set or cluster in a plastic bag so children have easy access to them during independent reading. This not only makes it easier for students to learn more about a single topic, adding breadth and depth to their thinking, it also allows them to compare the way related texts are organized, the information they convey, and the text features they contain.

I try to include different types of informational books in each bag. For example, in a bag of panda books, instead of only including expository texts, such as Gail Gibbons' *Giant Pandas* (2004) and Marcia S. Freeman's *Giant Pandas* (2004), I might also add Joanne Ryder's narrative-informational *Panda Kindergarten* (2009) that chronicles a day in the life of panda cubs at the Wolong Nature Preserve in China and contrasts with the two enumerative titles.

How Does Clustering Books Improve Children's Reading Comprehension?

All learning is a process of connecting the known to the new. As children read or learn about a topic for the first time, a hook forms in their brain upon which they begin to build a schema. Then as they continue to read more about that topic, they can access their background knowledge, making it easier to comprehend and remember new information.

So rather than having students read only the assortment of just-right and "look" books in their bags, I often encourage them to select a bag of clustered books to browse through and read. Not only do children gain information by looking at the pictures, reading the labels and captions, etc., this practice helps to extend the length of time children can read on their own.

In addition, when children are selecting new books for their book bag, I encourage them to look for several books on one topic to pull together for a couple weeks, rather than an assortment of books on a range of topics.

Where Are Clustered Bags Kept?

I keep the clustered bags of books, labeled by topic (Figure 7-5), in a basket in one of my small meeting areas. I might select books from these bags to read aloud or to use for reading and writing strategy demonstrations. Having these clustered sets assembled and ready to go is also a great boon to children's writing. It not only gives them ideas for writing topics, but it's also comforting to know that once they do select a topic, there are several other books from which they can get information.

Figure 7-5. Clustered Bag of Books on Sharks

How Are Clustered Books Used for Teacher Read-Alouds?

I often use clustered books during read-alouds to demonstrate why it's important to build background knowledge. Here's what I do:

First, I identify a topic about which my kids would love to know more. When teaching second or third grade, I can usually determine these hot topics by observing their book selections during the first independent reading time when they can read any book that interests them. (See the "Two Important and Different Independent Reading Times" box for an explanation of how these two independent reading times of day play out in a second- and third-grade reading workshop.)

For example, if I notice children vying for the eagle or shark books, I might gather books on one of those topics for a clustered bag and center my read-alouds

Two Important and Different Independent Reading Times

- During the **first independent reading,** which occurs during the first twenty minutes of the day in second and third grade, children can select any book they want. Too easy, too difficult, just right. It doesn't matter. What matters is giving them the opportunity to try out different levels, genres, and topics.

- During the **second independent reading** while I'm conferring with students or meeting with small groups of readers, the children read books from their book bag that I've helped them select. They might also read from the clustered books for a portion of this time.

around them the following week. Or I might select a content-area topic, such as *life cycles* or *colonial times*, and gather books on that topic to read.

At the start of the week, I explain that instead of reading a book on a different topic each day, e.g., *spiders* on Monday, the *seasons* on Tuesday, we will read shark books throughout the week since I've noticed that many of them are interested in that topic.

Then I place three books from the clustered shark set, from easiest to hardest, along the easel so that children can see the cover of each book I plan to read. I explain that I'll begin by reading aloud the easiest book to gather some basic information. And from there we'll move on to the next hardest text, and the next, being more selective as we go regarding how much and what parts of the book to read.

Children quickly learn that they're likely to find some of the same information, concepts, and vocabulary in books on the same topic, and because they've been introduced to an idea, concept, etc., in one book, it will be easier for them to read, understand, and remember that information when they encounter it again. These explicit demonstrations have clear payoffs for our young students.

How Does Clustering Books Help Develop Vocabulary?

As I mentioned in Chapter 5, Warwick Elley's research demonstrates how children acquire vocabulary from listening to stories—how hearing books reread and vocabulary explained several times helps develop their word knowledge. These multiple exposures to words also occur when we read aloud several informational texts on a single topic or encourage students to read them on their own. The content vocabulary becomes part of their background knowledge of a topic (Willingham 2009).

Content vocabulary that children encounter in the first and easier books of a clustered set are likely to show up in other books in that set. For example, if a text is describing the parts of a bird's body, it's certain to mention that their bones are *hollow* since this physical attribute contributes to the lightness of their body and their ability to fly. Children reading several books on birds will meet the word *hollow* repeatedly. These multiple exposures contribute to their vocabulary acquisition and their comprehension.

How Does This Practice Support the Development of Comprehension Strategies?

Let's examine how clustering informational texts relates to each of following comprehension strategies:

+ **Access and Use Prior Knowledge**—When children read several books on one topic, rather than move from one topic to the next, they build their background knowledge about it. The more they know about a topic, the easier it will be for them to read, understand, and recall information.

+ **Summarize to Determine Knowledge**—Children who have read several books on a topic begin to notice the broad categories that keep recurring. *Habitat, life cycle, appearance, raising their young* pretty much show up in one form or another across-the-board in books about animals, while *water cycle* and *cloud formations* are likely to surface in weather-related books. This observation alerts students to the fact that these subcategories should be focal points when summing up what they've learned about a topic. Children might work together on a data chart, graphing the information about these subcategories to compare the information each book provides (Figure 7-6).

+ **Set a Purpose for Reading**—As children see the teacher demonstrate how she reads the easier text first to get some basic and general background information on the topic, and then how she alters her purpose and reads the second and third book to locate specific information or to answer students' questions, they learn that we read books for different purposes. And that one might even read the different subgenres of informational text for different reasons, such as biographies to learn why a person is famous, procedural texts to learn how to do something, enumerative texts to locate information to include in a piece they're writing, and so on. They begin to see value in setting a purpose for reading and adjusting their reading to meet that purpose.

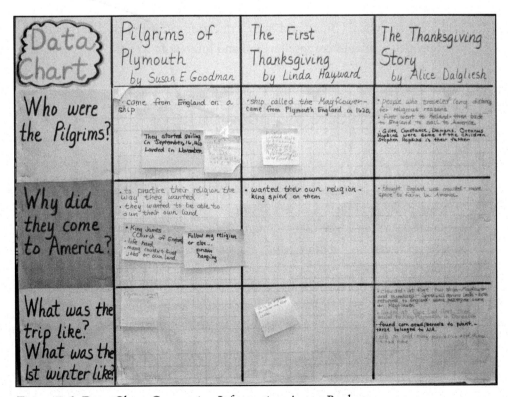

Figure 7-6. Data Chart Comparing Information Across Books

+ **Consider Text Structure**—Children reading several books on one topic become aware that books on the same topic may be structured differently. For example, Mike Venezia's *Georgia O'Keeffe* (1994) combines a chronological account of O'Keeffe's life and a handful of her well-known paintings with his own cartoons of key events. By contrast, Kathryn Lasky's *Georgia Rises: A Day in the Life of Georgia O'Keeffe* (2009) imagines the famous artist through a biography-based, but fictional, narrative, followed by a succinct traditional biography at the back of the book.

+ **Visualize to Experience**—Children know that it's important to create a mental image as they read. When they peruse a cluster of books on a single topic, they can't help but be struck by how authors illustrate the same topic differently. Children begin to envision facts from the literary details of the text, becoming taken with phrases like "a stegosaurus' back probably felt like a spiky pineapple" vs. the more straightforward, "the stegosaurus had a double row of plates sticking up along its back . . . ." Children also develop a comfort level with how pictures, photos, charts, and other text features augment their visual experience of the topic.

+ **Ask Questions and Wonder**—The more students know about a topic the better they're able to ask important questions. With only limited background knowledge, children tend to ask factual and lower-level questions since they haven't had the opportunity to go deeper in their thinking. However, when students know more from the books they've read, they can ask more analytical ("how" and "why") questions. It's this kind of thinking that propels students' comprehension and interest in a topic.

Clustered vs. Companion Texts

- **Companion texts** are two titles paired by topic or theme, genre, series, or strategy. The guided reading title is more difficult than the companion. The texts are packaged together in sets of six of each title and kept in the guided reading bookcase. They're used during guided and independent reading.
- **Clustered texts,** on the other hand, are read during independent reading and writing, or by the teacher as a read-aloud. Students select a clustered set because they're interested in the topic. The books are packaged by topic without regard to level. If the text is too difficult, the pictures, labels, captions, etc., provide children with plenty of interesting information.

Effective Practice: Working with a Synopsis Text

What Is a Synopsis Text?

A synopsis text is a very brief, written summary of a picture book or other text (or a portion of them) that I plan to read aloud or share with the class. Its purpose is to scaffold instruction for students who struggle with reading, special needs students, or English language learners needing extra support with unfamiliar concepts, vocabulary, and English language structures. Synopsis texts, as described here, relate to nonfiction.

I began to write these simple summaries when I noticed that my struggling readers often had overwhelmed expressions on their faces when I read aloud or did a picture book-based lesson. The concepts and vocabulary were coming at them too fast. Or maybe the pace, or their classmates' swifter responses, intimidated them. No matter how hard I tried to respond to them then and there, I knew I wasn't quite meeting their needs.

By creating this opportunity for readers to interact with the big ideas, key concepts, and vocabulary they would later encounter during the whole-group lesson, I gave them a needed leg up, enabling them to get the gist of what's being read, participate in class discussions, and become motivated to learn even more.

How Do I Write a Synopsis Text?

* Read through the book or portion of the book you plan to share, jot down the important concepts you'll teach, and note any vocabulary words you want to highlight. Consider ways to break the text into smaller, more manageable sections.

* To help you write the synopsis in a custom-tailored way, clarify your goals for this particular group of readers who need this boost. Your synopsis text, along with references to the original text, might help:
    * build background knowledge
    * present big ideas, key concepts, and vocabulary
    * enable students to infer in places where young readers need to fill in the gaps the author left
    * map how a text is organized
    * connect new information to what students already know
    * expose students to text features that help clarify and extend information, such as charts, diagrams, emboldened words, etc.

* On chart paper, write an abridged version of the text you're focusing on so that students can see it up close as you read it aloud and as they read along with you.

The length of each synopsis should reflect the grade you teach. In addition to several sentences conveying the key ideas, synopsis texts for kindergarten and first-grade students might take the form of pictures and diagrams you sketch on the chart paper and then label. Synopsis texts for second- and third-grade students might look like the one in Figure 7-7 that compares the learning tools students have now with what they had long ago.

Figure 7-7. Synopsis Text and Pages from Children Past and Present

How Do I Share the Synopsis Text with Students?

When I'm ready to work with this small group of readers, I gather them to read and discuss the synopsis text I've prepared. I always explain *why* we're doing this and how it will help them understand and remember what they've read. I also have on hand the book or text from which the synopsis originated so that I can point out pictures or text features that would further develop their understanding of the texts' key concepts.

For example, I wrote the synopsis in Figure 7-7 to accompany a portion of the enlarged text *Children Past and Present* (2009 Benchmark Education) that I planned to read with a class—several of whom were English language learners—the following day. When I gathered the students together, we discussed vocabulary and concepts I felt they might have a hard time understanding, like *tools*, *slates*, and *quill pen*. To help explain, I referred to the illustrations in the book and sketched what a quill pen looks like.

When Do Students Meet to Work with the Synopsis Text?

It doesn't matter when you gather your group as long as it's *before* the whole-class lesson. Sara Flores (in Chapter 5) met with her small group of readers first thing in the morning during their developmental playtime, and then she read the book with the entire class later that day. In the example above, I gathered my small group the day before I planned to share the book with the class.

It's unavoidable that the children who need this text preview will miss out on whatever it is the rest of the class is doing, and this can seem a difficult choice to make at times. My best advice is to keep in mind your end-of-year goals for students, and then do what's needed to achieve them. Ask yourself, what will best get them where they need to go—this week, this month, this year?

And as I write this, I'm compelled to add that we always have to take the whole child into account in these daily decisions about teaching and learning. Children's academic success isn't 100 percent about literacy. For example, the student who recently arrived from El Salvador or Taiwan and speaks no English might be better served at this moment in time by working in the block area and interacting with classmates as they create the "highest tower ever built!" Then next week, a synopsis text instead of blocks. These are decisions that only you can make.

Effective Practice: Content-Area Literacy Centers

What Are Content-Area Literacy Centers and Why Are They Important?

Literacy centers, commonplace in many elementary classrooms, typically focus on helping students acquire reading strategies and word skills. Giving them a nonfiction spin—calling them *content-area* literacy centers instead—refreshes the center concept and brings desperately needed content into the classroom. I first came across this type of center while working in Millie Velazquez's first-grade classroom. Millie always had at least two, sometimes three, nonfiction centers up and running on current or upcoming topics she and her students were studying.

As I watched Millie and her students, I was bowled over by how these centers built children's background knowledge, and impressed with the way Millie had brought together an eclectic mix of reading and writing materials, ranging from *Time for Kids* articles, to books spanning a range of genres, to papers in an assortment of colors and shapes. You name it, she had it. Visually pleasing posters, photos, and poems written on charts helped to define the space. It was like walking into a top-notch bookstore or children's museum.

Nonfiction centers, as Millie called them, dedicated to bringing knowledge of the world to children, are designed to invite several students to sit, linger a while, and read, write, talk, and draw about what they are learning—totally brilliant. I came to call them content-area literacy centers to drive home the point that they integrate science and social studies with reading and writing, but the idea is all Millie Velazquez's.

Many of Millie's centers feature animals from the animal groups her kids need and want to know about, such as *horses* (mammals), *ladybugs* (insects), *penguins* (birds), *frogs and toads* (reptiles and amphibians), and *sharks* (fish). These centers meet the first-grade science standard, "Living things have different structures and behaviors that allow them to meet their basic needs." Millie's Dinosaur Center (Figure 7-8), while not addressing a curriculum standard head on, was always a winner as far as the kids were concerned.

Millie makes a new center every summer and now has more than a dozen that enrich and enliven her students' learning throughout the year. She collects books, posters, pictures, magazines,

Figure 7-8. Millie Velazquez's Dinosaur Center

stuffed animals, games, puzzles, and real-life objects about each topic, and adds in new resources as she comes across them. She stores them in her basement and brings them to school as various topics surface.

Content-area literacy centers like Millie's are rare. Walk into any K–3 classroom and for sure you'll see standard literacy centers galore. But content-area literacy centers—not so much. We need to change that and make room for them because so many of our children come to school with a dearth of background knowledge, and this undermines their reading comprehension. Research has consistently demonstrated that children's background knowledge plays a significant role in how well they read. The more students know about a topic, the better able they are to understand new information they encounter.

For example, as second-grader Declan read me several pages of his book on insects—a topic he loves and knows so much about—he stumbled on some basic words like *feelers* and *body* but had no trouble reading other more difficult words such as *antennae, mosquito,* and *dragonfly.* Clearly Declan's background knowledge not only helped him understand the text and learn even more about insects, it also helped him read words that a novice reader lacking his background knowledge might struggle with.

Most of all, Declan's knowledge gave him the disposition to seek out more knowledge through books. We teachers are not there to merely impart information. We work beside children each day, nurturing in them a mindset—an inquiring, openness to the world. Content-area literacy centers are powerful tools to do this.

How Do I Assemble a Content-Area Literacy Station?

I encourage teachers with whom I work to start by creating just one center. I'm confident that they'll be hooked once they witness situations similar to when I saw Luis sitting spellbound with his nose in Seymour Simon's *Big Cats,* not realizing his classmates had lined up for lunch and were halfway out the door, or another student like Madeline furiously listing on her "Fact Sheet" all she's learning about twisters, having witnessed one up close last year when visiting her grandpa in Iowa. And like Millie, they'll gradually create new and dynamic content-area literacy centers, adding more year after year.

Here's how to assemble a content-area literacy station of your own:

+ Review your science and social studies curriculum and your standards, and survey students to find which topics they care most about.

+ Select a meaty topic about which you'll be able to gather an assortment of books and materials—one that will keep children engaged for several weeks.

    Also consider topics that allow students to build on subjects with which they're already familiar. For example, if at the beginning of the year you put out a center on *plants,* or if that's a topic you've studied or even one the children studied last year, then it might be wise to assemble a center on *rain forests* or *savannahs* so students can apply what they already know about plant life to this new, but related, topic.

+ Gather materials you'll need for your center:
    + **Reading materials in a variety of genres and formats**—magazines, newspapers, big books, Internet printouts, any reading material that sheds light on the topic. (See "Magazines That Include a Variety of Genre on a Topic" box for children's magazines to which you can subscribe or invite families to bring in past issues they may have at home.)
    + **Fiction and poetry** related to the topic will allow students to compare how information is presented in each and discern the differences between genres, a common curriculum standard. Students also need to recognize that even books within a genre are organized and formatted differently. They may read Bobbie Kalman's *Endangered Sea Turtles* (2004), an expository-informational text, and then turn to *Turtle Tides: Ways of Sea Turtles* (2005) by Stephen Swinburne, a narrative-informational book that delivers information with beautiful language and a story.
    + **Paper in different sizes, shapes, and colors.** It's also fun to supply students with booklets (either teacher-made or prebound) or allow them to make their own. It's amazing how giving children different sizes and shapes of paper can transform a student's writing. What once was simply a *list* of facts about frogs becomes a *book* when a child writes each fact on a separate sheet of paper, illustrates them, labels the drawings, and binds them together. And that booklet idea might even turn into a comparison book, highlighting the differences between frogs and toads, with information about each animal on alternate pages.
    + **Tools for writing and illustrating,** such as pencils, crayons, markers, staplers, tape, and scissors. You can show students how each of these tools has their own strength. Pencils, for example, often do a better job of illustrating and highlighting different parts of an animal's body or rock strata than colored markers, which can obscure the details the student wants to convey.
    + **Miscellaneous materials,** such as puzzles, games, stuffed animals, and real-life objects are especially good for young readers and English language learners. For example, games and puzzles offer students a non-print way of learning about a topic and give them hands-on experiences, which many students so greatly need.

+ Decide where your content-area literacy center will go. There should be room for several students to gather and work. You might set a couple of chairs at this center, or your students might sit on a small area rug (with pillows for their backs, of course) and use clipboards to steady their writing. The important thing is to create a comfortable and welcoming environment that invites students to spend some time.

Magazines That Include a Variety of Genres on a Topic

- **American Girl Magazine**

  An ad-free, award-winning magazine created just for girls ages 8–12. *American Girl* provides an appealing age-appropriate alternative to teen magazines and features original fiction, lively nonfiction, party plans and projects, advice, quizzes, and more.

- **Highlights for Children**

  Highlights for Children delivers puzzles, science projects, and jokes and riddles that challenge young minds, while characters in regular features like Hidden Pictures, The Timbertoes, Goofus and Gallant, and the Bear Family repeat from issue to issue.

- **National Geographic Kids**

  An award-winning magazine that combines learning with fun. Features great stories on animals, science, technology, and accomplishments of kids around the world. For kids 6 & up.

- **Ranger Rick Magazine**

  Great for second and third graders. Each issue is packed with amazing facts, awesome photos, outdoor adventures, and discoveries that help kids sharpen their reading skills and develop a deeper appreciation for our natural world.

- **Nickelodeon**

  Nickelodeon is the award-winning entertainment and humor magazine from Nickelodeon TV. It's packed with fascinating facts, celebrity interviews, comics, pull-outs, puzzles, activities, and the inside scoop on Nick TV. For children ages 6–14.

- **Sports Illustrated Kids**

  Sports journalism appropriate for children in second grade and up. Interviews with sports heroes, hilarious comics, and lively action photos.

- **Cricket**

  It is a 48-page joyride of fiction, fantasy, folktales, adventures, poems, history, and biography. The stories are written by top-notch writers and illustrated by award-winning artists. For third-grade readers.

- **Ladybug**

  A children's magazine that opens the door to reading for children ages 3 to 6. Each 40-page issue of *Ladybug* is filled with page after page of enchanting stories and poems to read aloud. Issues also include games, songs, and activities.

- **Spider**

  Each 40-page issue offers its readers stories with recurring characters, articles, humor, games, activities, puzzles, and projects, plus multicultural folktales from around the world. It's the ideal story and activity magazine for former *Ladybug* readers and all 6- to 9-year-olds who love to learn and read.

- **Click**

  Led by Click the Mouse and his pals Amy and Martin, *Click* magazine takes children on a journey through science, art, nature, and the environment in 40 full-color pages that are filled with amazing photographs, beautiful illustrations, and stories and articles that are both entertaining and thought-provoking. Ages 3–6.

- **Appleseeds Magazine**

  A magazine of adventure and exploration. In addition to fascinating stories and interviews, kids get activities, maps, puzzles, recipes, and games that are related to the theme. Each 36-page issue helps kids do further research on a topic by giving them recommended books to read and Web sites to visit. For 6–9 year olds.

- **Ask**

  A kids' magazine about science, history, and more. Written with 6- to 9-year-olds in mind. Pieces in the magazine are written by award-winning children's authors and issues are filled with cartoon characters, activities, projects, and contests.

It's good to set up your center against a wall so that you can use the wall or bulletin board to post related materials. As you can see from Figure 7-8, Millie sets a three-partitioned foam board at the front of her desk—which she's never ever at—and pushes several student desks and chairs up against it. It's also beneficial to locate this station alongside a computer so kids can access Web sites to find additional information about a topic.

How Do I Connect the Center Work to the Rest of My Teaching?

Here's how:

+ **Independent Reading and Writing**—Children can work at these centers during independent reading, writing, and center time. Acquiring background knowledge on a topic sets in motion a spiraling effect—new information inspires students to read, write, and learn even more.

+ **Conferences**—A child may use the center to follow up on what you and he have discussed during a conference. For example, if you learn that he's been having trouble responding to books because he can't think of what to write, you might send him to the content-area center with a friend to read a book together and discuss it as a rehearsal for a response he may later write.

+ **Shared Reading**—After you've shared a big book, poem, or experience chart that relates to a center topic, you can store it at the center for students to read and explore on their own.

+ **Writing Workshop**—I can't think of anything more beneficial to students' writing than to have access to a basket of books and materials on a topic about which they may want to write. And if the topic is expansive, *ocean animals* for example, you can sort the books into individual bags on *penguins*, *whales* and *dolphins*, *octopuses*, etc., so that a child can grab the bag he wants and read, read, read.

What If Students Can't Read the Books at the Content-Area Literacy Centers?

We should make every effort to provide a range of reading materials at the content-area literacy center so that there's something for everyone. We might also buddy-up a less able reader with a partner who's stronger. In addition, we should continue to show kids how to get information from pictures and text features as well as from running text. Therefore, it's wise to plan on providing several mini-lessons on how to do this.

When's a Good Time to Introduce a New Content-Area Literacy Center?

Content-area literacy centers should be introduced a week or so before formally introducing a topic to students, giving them a heads up on what's to come. Let's say you plan to begin a unit on the human body the following week, then you would begin to show children, throughout the prior week, materials you've gathered at the center to pique their interest. You might also read some basic books on the topic to help build background knowledge. This way when the study formally begins the kids will know enough to ask good questions that will propel their learning.

 CHAPTER 8 Oral Language and Vocabulary

Principles and Practices

"Children need to talk a lot to develop oral language fully— and playfulness may be the key element in this process. In a playful, purposeful environment of talk, talk, talk, children learn more than in classrooms where only the teacher's voice is heard. Put another way, oral language development cannot be a spectator sport. A lively hum of focused conversations in a classroom is a sign that talk is valued." (p. 15)

—New Standards Speaking and Listening Committee in *Speaking and Listening for Preschool Through Third Grade* (2001)

Oral Language, Vocabulary, and Comprehension

Just as emergent readers need to sub-vocalize so they can hear and process what they're reading, students throughout the elementary grades need to get their thinking out into the open. They need to *hear* their ideas, have them confirmed or disconfirmed, and then reflect on, refine, and extend what they know.

They also need to hear what others have to say and consider new ways that they themselves might think in the future. By engaging in conversations and dialogue, students expand their thinking and their world and are exposed to new ideas, perspectives, and vocabulary. But all too often, children's voices are hushed and ours are the only ones heard.

Fortunately, this is not the case at the Manhattan New School where I taught for almost twenty years. At MNS children speaking their mind is the norm, with teachers nudging students' thinking along by encouraging them to say more, and asking them to explain what they mean and how it relates to the topic being discussed. Helping children learn to love language and the way words feel on their tongue, and how words help them conceptualize their world, is what teachers at MNS seek to achieve. The Manhattan New School is progressive and, at the same time, nurtures conditions that are so very *basic* to human nature and learning.

After all, what's more basic than apprenticeships? Teachers working alongside students, showing them how to read, helping them infer the meaning of words from context, demonstrating the connection between what they read and what they write. Isn't this how, centuries ago, Mayan girls were taught to weave baskets? Or how young apprentice millers of the Middle Ages learned to process grain and wheat?

> *By engaging in conversations and dialogue, students expand their thinking and their world, and are exposed to new ideas, perspectives, and vocabulary.*

Lucky for me, my classroom was right across the hall from principal Shelley Harwayne's office, where there always seemed to be clusters of kids, parents, and visitors coming and going. I learned from Shelley, in an "apprenticeship-once-removed" sort of way, the joyfulness of language and its appeal. Although I could have shut my door to keep out the noise, most often I didn't because it was good, joyful noise and comforting like a child falling asleep to the muted conversation arising from the kitchen where company has gathered.

Shelley loved chatting with children, asking them about their day, and really and truly wanting to know. She'd post poems along the walls so kids could stop to read them as they walked to the washroom or cafeteria. She'd drop into classrooms, often interrupting math and writing lessons, just to read to kids. "Oops," she'd apologize . . . and then proceed to gather children around her like the Pied Piper, inviting them to luxuriate in language and words. "Isn't this fun?" she'd ask. Shelley, insisting that she'd never ever hire a teacher unless he or she was someone with whom she'd want to have dinner and share a lively conversation, was a constant reminder of the power of talk.

Lucky for me, Joan Backer's room was right next to mine. Joan is famous for the conversations and problem solving in which she'd engage students. Having trouble at recess? Let's call a meeting and talk about it. Can't figure out a math problem? Let's ask the class for help. There was nothing Joan liked better than bringing her fourth graders together to share ideas and work out the wrinkles in their lives and learning.

Lucky for me, Isabel Beaton was down the hall and Paula Rogovin on the third floor. I'll always remember walking into Isabel's room to find her covering a low table at her meeting area with a lovely gingham tablecloth on which young Rebecca would set her beloved toy bunny she'd brought for show-and-tell. And seeing Paula marching several of her first graders to Shelley's office each and every morning, not because they were in trouble, but to recite a poem they'd memorized. The Manhattan New School was one grand celebration of oral language and its embedded vocabulary. We all talked, we all laughed, and we all learned from one another. We surely, as James Britton once described literacy, "floated on a sea of talk."

It's puzzling, though, how this level of interaction appears difficult to replicate in so many schools and classrooms around the country. It's odd that we often think things are going well when *we're* doing most of the talking and the kids are quiet, instead of the other way around. Especially since theorists, researchers, and educators have identified oral language and the words it embodies as powerful contributors to children's learning to read and comprehend—or for that matter, their ability to reason and learn at all.

In *Thought and Language* (1986, newly revised edition) psychologist Lev Vygotsky asserts that children make sense of their world by internalizing the dialogue they hear, and then later using it in other interactions and in their thinking. He maintains that oral language gives shape and definition to our mental constructs, and that it's through interactions with adults and peers that ideas and learning are born.

Researchers Isabel Beck, Margaret McKeown, and Linda Kucan link vocabulary to comprehension by pointing out that we don't learn words to simply deposit in our vocabulary word bank and leave them there. We use them to expand our thinking and our comprehension. In *Creating Robust Vocabulary: Frequently Asked Questions and Extended Examples* (2008), they caution: "enhancing students' meaning repertoires is not an end in itself. The major purpose of having a large meaning vocabulary is to use it in the service of reading comprehension and writing" (p. 2).

Franki Sibberson, educator and author of several professional books including *Beyond Leveled Books, Second Edition* (2008), prides herself in the amount of talk that occurs in her classroom each day. She understands that children learn by talking. In fact, she gets kids talking the very first day of school and doesn't let up, nurturing their conversation and watching it develop.

Children need to hear beautiful language, informative language, explanatory language so they can speak it in their lives. And it's our job to make this happen every day.

Foundational Principles for Oral Language and Vocabulary

Oral language and vocabulary, despite their recognized and essential role in helping children learn to read and comprehend text, often have a hard time making their way into our daily classroom routines. The following foundational principles should help to remedy this.

Create a Safe, Nurturing Environment

If we want our students to interact more—with us and their classmates—to speak what's on their mind, even when they're not certain they're right, then we have to create a safe, welcoming environment that encourages self-expression and dialogue. Consider some of the questions in the "Does Your Classroom Environment Nurture

Oral Language and Vocabulary?" box for ways your environment can support children's oral language and vocabulary development.

We have to get kids sitting up close to us and alongside one another if we want them to talk. Let's face it, it's scary to sit in the back of the classroom, raise your hand to comment or answer a question, and hear your voice project all the way to the front of the room while classmates turn their head to look at you. And more often than not these long-distance exchanges are simply question-answer sessions and not actual conversations. In fact, I'd be hard pressed to recall a single stimulating discussion I've heard unfold between students and their teacher, or among students, working from opposite ends of the classroom.

We're looking for kids to exchange ideas, to dialogue, to think deeply and carefully about things. And it feels safer to give this a try when you're huddled together shoulder to shoulder on the carpet.

Does Your Classroom Environment Nurture Oral Language and Vocabulary?

- **Is your classroom attractive and inviting?** Our classroom speaks volumes about the expectations we set and how we regard our students and our teaching. It feels great to spend the day, a year, in a classroom that's been prepared aesthetically with attention to detail. When children see how we've thoughtfully provided pillows in each of the meeting areas so that they can be comfy when working with classmates, or when they see a comment box labeled "I'd Like to Hear from You" placed at the meeting area, they see the classroom as a friendly place to speak up and out.

  When Bebe, a recent alumna of my class, popped her head into the classroom to tell me she "missed this class," she wasn't referring to me or to her classmates; she was referring to the *room* itself. Spend time making your classroom attractive and comfortable. Your kids will appreciate it and so will you—for the community it helps to create.

- **Is your classroom environment conducive to conversation?** Desks lined up in rows facing the front can easily be misinterpreted by students to mean: I'm the teacher; you're the

kids. What I have to say is more important and more likely to be right. Even arranging desks in clusters scattered widely across the room is likely to inhibit the whole-group conversations you're after. Ideally, desks or tables should all be in one zone of the room.

  Make sure you have a large carpeted meeting area where all your kids can gather to talk, discuss, and even disagree, and provide additional meeting areas around the classroom for groups of three or four children or partnerships to gather. And don't forget the pillows, clipboards, and baskets of books—all equally important. See Figure 8-1 for one of my small meeting areas.

- **Is your schedule flexible?** It's hard to get the kids to talk more if you really and truly don't think you have the time. If *you* don't think there's time, your kids won't either. So when you plan your day, build time into each of your balanced literacy components for unhurried conversation and dialogue, even if it means not getting to everything you had hoped. And then—bask in the realization that what you've done, you've done well.

Figure 8-1. Small Meeting Area

Be Explicit in Your Interactions with Students

To respond thoughtfully and deliberately, children must understand the reasoning behind our instructional decisions and the questions we ask. When our purpose and reasoning is obscure or ambiguous, it's hard for kids to know what to say.

I wasn't always explicit in my teaching. In fact, I honed this skill while orienting the many visitors to my classroom at the Manhattan New School. Since these visitors lacked the context to immediately grasp what the children and I were doing (after all we had been together since the start of the school year and they'd just arrived) I found myself explaining things to them *through* the children, declaring our purpose at the outset of a lesson or recapping what we had done that morning or the day before:

> Boys and girls, we've been working very hard trying to learn which letter combinations make the /er/ sound and have been adding words to our list as we come across them. [Pointing to our chart.] We've listed words with *-er, -or, -ir, -ar, -ur*, and some words with less common patterns, like *-ear* in *learn*, and *-ure* in *picture*. I've even made these five Post-it notes available each day so that you can find new words to add from your reading and writing.
>
> So let's look at some of the words you found yesterday and add them now. It's really important that you learn these spelling patterns so that you can recognize new words as you read and spell them correctly when you write. Then you'll have room in your brain to think about what the text means.

While this may seem like a lot of words, they're words that describe how things work and why it's important to proceed one way and not another. They're words that ground children's thinking and learning. In contrast, years ago I might have just said: "Okay. Let's add these new /er/ words to our list" and proceeded to list the words the children had written on the Post-it notes. But that would have been so much less effective since children need continual reminders about what they're doing and why. They need to hear repeatedly the purpose—*how* this will help to improve their reading and their writing. Effective teaching is explicit.

The more information children have at the start of a lesson or the more they understand the reasoning that led you to ask a particular question, the easier it is for them to respond. I just love how Lea M. McGee and Judith A. Schickedanz, in their 2007 *Reading Teacher* article "Repeated Interactive Read-Alouds in Preschool and Kindergarten," make the point that when pre-K and kindergarten teachers ask a "how" or "why" question, they need to preface it with an explanation of what led them to ask it in the first place.

For example, instead of simply asking why Annabelle (the heroine of Amy Schwartz's 1988 *Annabelle Swift, Kindergartner*) hid from her teacher and classmates that she was a math wiz instead of boasting about it as her sister Lucy advised, scaffold your question by first letting children in on your thinking. Say: "I'm noticing that when Annabelle did as Lucy suggested and introduced herself as "Annabelle Swift, Kindergartner" and used fancy words, like *blue desire*, to name the color of the light blue lollipop, her classmates and teacher thought this strange. So why do you think that now she's . . . ." This way they can answer the question with more knowledge and insight, combined with their own school-start-up experiences.

While McGee and Schickedanz recommend we provide this kind of scaffolding for pre-K and kindergarten students, I'll take it a step further and suggest that all primary-grade students need this type of support.

Design Your Conversations to Get Students to Elaborate

Before we can ever hope to engage students in spirited conversations, we have to get better at the questions we ask. If we're asking question upon question because that's how we think it's done (teaching, I mean), we have to discard that misguided notion and look for ways to ask fewer questions and make those questions more purposeful. And if kids see us reading questions from a spiral-bound book, they won't buy that either. The more genuine and heartfelt the questions, the more thoughtful their responses will be.

So now suppose you've asked a good question, one you think has the potential to generate a lot of response, and the kids still have little, if anything, to say. Don't fret. Most students are so used to getting by with one-word or one-phrase answers that it's likely to take a while for them to realize that this will no longer fly. Finally, after what seems to you a very long time, someone raises his hand to speak and has only one sentence, at best, to offer.

It's your turn now to ask him to "say more." At first, he might look at you a bit confused, but you'll reiterate: "Tell me *more* about what you just said. Can you give an example? What led you to say that?" You may have to wait him out but, hey, no worries, you've got time.

And after he does finally elaborate a bit, take this opportunity to explain what you're up to. Tell the children you really want to hear from them, that you don't want to do all the talking and all the learning, and that we *all* increase our understanding of what we know when we teach it to someone else. So now it's their turn to get smart.

Surefire Techniques to Get Kids to Elaborate

To get kids to elaborate, we have to demonstrate what we mean. We might "fishbowl" this for children with the help of a student volunteer. (*Fishbowl* means that we demonstrate this interaction for students either in front of the class or sitting in the middle of a circle of students.) The child will ask you the question you've prepared in advance, and you will demonstrate what a good response might be, compared with the more typical one-liners. Of course, your question will have to be one that elicits elaboration. "Who," "what," "when," "where" questions won't cut it. "Why" and "how" questions will.

The "Say More" Strategy

"Say More" builds on Kathy Short, Jerry Harste, and Carolyn Burke's "Say Something" strategy for getting kids to connect to text, described in *Creating Classrooms for Authors and Inquirers*. "Say Something" is simple enough.

After students are paired, one child reads aloud a portion of text to his partner, to which the partner "says something" in response. The response might involve a critique, a personal connection, or relay an image the words helped create. Then the children alternate roles. "Say Something" is effective and nonthreatening. It doesn't prompt kids to "say something smart" (although they inevitably do)—just to say *something*. Now I just want students to "Say More."

When a child responds to a question you've asked with one word or a one-liner, ask him to "say more" rather than ask him to state his answer in a complete sentence. "Saying More" has to do with ideas, not sentence grammar. Ask if there's anything else he might want to add. If he says there isn't, but you feel there is more to be said, ask him to explain *why* he thinks this, *how* it relates to what you're learning. (Notice,

I'm asking "how" and "why," and not "who," "where," "when," or "what" questions.)

Then ask the rest of the class if they have anything to add or ask. This is where it's important to get kids to use the interactive speaking skills you've been encouraging: They should look directly at the person they're addressing, use his or her name, and confirm they've heard what he expressed, before adding their own comment: "Alex, I understand what you're saying. You think that John Audubon should not have killed the birds to paint them. But think about all the people that now get to see what the birds look like."

At this point you might ask this second speaker to say more about what he means. If it feels odd to keep asking kids to "say more," here are some other prompts that will yield the same result:

- Can you give me an example?
- What's your reason for saying that?
- What made you think that?
- Can you be more specific?
- How did you arrive at that conclusion?

The "Say More" strategy helps readers and writers elaborate, think in a more logical and concrete way, internalize some of questions and prompts to consider as they read, write responses to texts, and participate in literature discussion groups. The boxes examine how this strategy relates to literature circles and students' writing.

How "Say More" Relates to Literature Circles

One of the difficulties teachers face when implementing literature circles is that often the children don't speak up. They've read the book, have opinions on it, but are hesitant to express them. This may be because they're not used to doing this and fear they have nothing of substance to contribute. If we can get our students to "say something" and then "say more" in whole-class sessions, they'll undoubtedly gain confidence to voice their ideas and opinions in small-group literature circles.

I often initiate literature circle discussions by asking students who have read the same book to each take a turn saying something about the book. From there, we select one idea to help grow from those the children put forth. I want them to elaborate on the focus idea to see where it leads. Here their ideas become bigger and more substantial than when they were first voiced.

How "Say More" Relates to Children's Writing and Their Written Responses to Text

There are few things as intimidating to a writer as a blank page. Helping students elaborate on their ideas *orally* is one way to move their written language forward. A child who is regularly asked to say more about ideas he expresses orally is likely to internalize this prompt and apply it to written responses to text and his writing workshop pieces.

In addition, this elaboration is helpful throughout other curriculum areas. For example, when I took my class to the Museum of Natural History, I asked them to come away with a few things they learned because when we got back to class I was going to ask them to write more about one of them. I wasn't interested in them cataloguing all that they'd learned. I wanted them instead to select one thing and elaborate a bit. See Figure 8-2 for what Ben wrote in his content-area notebook about the fishing nets used by Native Americans.

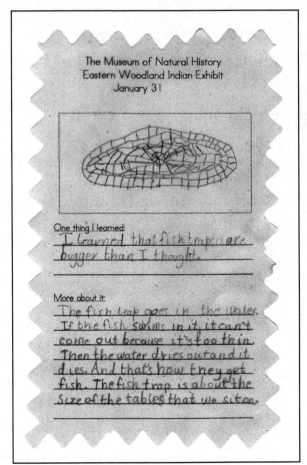

Figure 8-2. Ben's Content-Area Notebook

Weave Robust Vocabulary Throughout Your Balanced Literacy Components

Teachers, like the rest of humankind, use language to negotiate the world and make sense of things. Consider all the words we use each day during our exchanges with students—our dialogue with a student to get at why she chose to write about a trip to Disney when we were rooting for the piece on her *abuela's* recent visit from Argentina. Or our explanation of why it's important for children to edit their writing as they go and not wait until they've completed 15 pages! Not to mention all the rich on-the-fly exchanges we have each day. So let's exploit that opportunity—look at children's vocabulary development as something we can enhance far beyond attending to words in books.

Have children turn words they're learning into characters— *Mrs. Boisterous lived on a bumpy road, in a bright purple house with loud music blaring. She owned 10 romping puppies and loved to go to her neighbor's parties to laugh and dance.* Or happen upon enjoyable rituals that reinforce a love of words. Dramatically drop a nickel into a jar anytime someone uses a word that makes the class "ooh" and "aah," like when Samantha bounded in late from recess, saying, "I feel delirious!" when she was winded from running up the stairs. Use the merriment to look up the word, discover its meaning together, and maybe post it on some word wall.

The point is, we learn words through *many* exposures, so we need to seed our literacy block with myriad and multisensory opportunities for children to rub elbows with lots of words. Deliberately, explicitly, and with a touch of pizzazz.

Think-Turn-Talk: What It Is and Could Be

Most teachers know about "think, turn, and talk" or "think, pair, and share"—although quite often, they omit the "think" part and just have kids turn to one another and start talking. Not a good idea, since many children, especially the ones who struggle or who are just learning English, need time to consider what they themselves think before casting their ideas to the world. And although teachers know about this "think-turn-talk" procedure, I'm afraid that they don't do it nearly enough or throughout the day.

However, it may surprise you that I'm not going to recommend that you do it more often. Instead I want you focus on how to do it *better* as you read aloud to students. Once you get the hang of it and refine your practice during read-aloud, you can easily transfer these same principles to other parts of your day.

Here's how to improve "think-turn-talk" when reading aloud to children:

- **Give it time.** Instead of trying to fit read-aloud into a 10- or 15-minute time slot, give yourself plenty of time to do read-aloud and "think-turn-talk" well by giving yourself over to the book and to the conversation. Authors spend years researching and crafting their stories, and writing about topics they find fascinating. So honor the book, the author, and the reader by throwing away the clock—the metaphorical one that is—and asking kids to "say more."

- **Identify your stopping points.** Instead of stopping at any old place in a text to have children "think-turn-talk," read the book in advance and identify stopping points that will give kids opportunities to ponder what's happening, why a character may be acting a certain way, or how this situation might be resolved. Leave yourself Post-it note reminders so you won't forget.

- **Ask substantive questions.** Instead of asking unimportant questions or ones with obvious answers, like "Why are Billy's mom and dad going to the animal shelter after his dog died?" ask questions that foster deep thinking—"Why did Billy turn his back when his mom and dad brought home his new puppy?"

- **Let one response lead to another related one.** Instead of giving kids random turns to share their thinking, allow them to play their comments off one another. If Tommy says something, then Alice might comment on or add to what Tommy says, rather than overstepping his statement or question with one of her own. That's why, whenever possible, kids should sit in a circle, rather than face the teacher. I know this is often difficult to pull off, but it can make all the difference in the world in promoting interactive, energetic discussions.

- **Realize its potential.** Instead of just *doing* "think-turn-talk" because you've heard it's a good way to get kids talking, realize that it's actually great preparation for the literature circles in which children will use some of the same conversational moves, and for the written responses to text they'll be asked to make on their own. Children learn so much by *sharing* what they know and hearing what others have to say.

- Lastly, and perhaps most important of all, recognize that we needn't hear from each and every student or even most of them. And that we don't even have to ask *anyone* at all to share with the whole class what he and his partner were discussing. Sometimes, plenty of times, it's enough for children to just have the time to share their ideas with a partner.

Effective Practice: Using Wordless Picture Books to Support Literacy

How Do Wordless Books Help Teach Children to Read?

Wordless picture books offer readers, and soon-to-be readers, a unique opportunity to tell their own story based on a series of inviting illustrations. Because wordless picture books tell a cohesive story, i.e., the images are not random, the child is prompted to enact many important reading skills.

For example, readers have to find clues the author left to help them compose a narrative that makes sense, and they have to apply all they know about narratives to keep their version within the bounds of a story structure. And yet they get to use their own words and ideas in the telling. The tale they tell isn't wrong or right, it can be fantastical and whimsical. And although it's fun and unfettered by worries that their interpretation is going to be scored or graded, they know reading isn't a free for all and happily rise to the occasion.

Take a good look at a few wordless picture books and notice how they require children to do a great deal of interpretation and inferring, the very same high-level thinking skills readers use to comprehend texts. As readers interact with wordless books, they must attend to detail, follow the sequence outlined in the pictures, and apply their prior knowledge to develop the story they're telling.

For example, to tell the story on this page from Barbara Lehmen's 2007 *Rainstorm* (Figure 8-3), the reader must begin at the upper-left hand corner, move along to the right, then make a return sweep to the left, continuing on until he gets to the bottom. He must look carefully at all the places the little boy is trying out the key. As he does this, the reader is wondering, as he imagines the character is wondering, what mysteries might this key unlock? He may even make a few predictions here and there.

In addition to activating these reading skills, children must use their oral language and vocabulary to communicate what they think is happening. This spoken language component is especially important for young readers and English language learners who need extensive practice orally communicating their ideas. A whole lot of learning awaits children who sit down to read these wordless books—and a whole lot of fun, too.

Figure 8-3. Page from Rainstorm

How Do I Introduce Wordless Picture Books in My Classroom?

Start by simply putting out a basket of them for the kids to read—and see what happens. Think of it as a literacy center, or better yet, think of it as play where there are no academic expectations, but where abundant learning occurs. When kids play at the block area or at another dramatic play area, the conversations they engage in are masterful. They use language and learn language in ways that could never be replicated if someone set out formally to teach them to converse. The setting makes it happen.

The same is true of wordless books. The books themselves hold the magic. Give the kids the books, let them sit alongside one another, and let the talking start! They might take turns reading pages or they might assume the role of different characters. The story will most definitely change from reading to reading and their language will surely develop. All because you made the move to hook them with a book, and perhaps a partner, and gave them the time to read and talk.

You'll need to gather a healthy assortment of wordless books for the book basket or center. There are the basic beginning books, like Tomie dePaola's classic *Pancakes for Breakfast* (1978) and, at the other end, books like David Weisner's fanciful *Sector 7* (1999). In between there is a range of texts that all kids will be eager to get their hands on. The list I've provided in the "Some of My Favorite Wordless Books" box gives you some good titles to check out.

With a bountiful collection of wordless books, you'll be able to offer one to every child for his book bag. No worries here about whether a book is at the child's just-right level—because it's wordless and to a very large degree the child himself is the author.

Some of My Favorite Wordless Books

From Simpler to More Complex

- *Change, Changes* by Pat Hutchins
- *Rosie's Walk* by Pat Hutchins
- *Fly Little Bird* by Tina Burke
- *Pancakes for Breakfast* by Tomie dePaola
- *Clown* by Quentin Blake
- *Last Night* by Hyewon Yum
- *South* by Patrick McDonnell
- *The Surprise* by Sylvia van Ommen
- *School* by Emily Arnold McCully
- *First Snow* by Emily Arnold McCully
- *The Lion and the Mouse* by Jerry Pinkney
- *Beaver Is Lost* by Elisha Cooper
- *Rainstorm* by Barbara Lehman
- *The Red Book* by Barbara Lehman
- *Museum Trip* by Barbara Lehman
- *Trainstop* by Barbara Lehman
- *Lights Out* by Arthur Geisert
- *Hogwash* by Arthur Geisert
- *Time Flies* by Eric Rohmann
- *Anno's Journey* by Anno Mitsumasa
- *Anno's USA* by Anno Mitsumasa
- *Zoom* by Istvan Banyai
- *Free Fall* by David Wiesner
- *Tuesday* by David Wiesner
- *Flotsam* by David Wiesner
- *Sector 7* by David Wiesner

Can I Read Wordless Books to the Whole Class?

Of course you can, but the challenge here is to provide texts that the whole class can *see*. The last thing you want is to have 25 students climbing over one another, straining to see the picture you're going on about. If you've got an interactive whiteboard or document camera you're all set. You can show any page with a flick of a switch. But if not, you'll need to be a bit more creative. After an extensive search for appropriate wordless big books, I found only two that are readily available—*Best Friends* (1999) by Rhonda Cox and *Little Turtle* (2001) by Valerie Sommerville (both published by Richard C. Owen).

The next best thing to having a collection of wordless big books is to mask the text in the big books you already have. If you do this, I suggest using books where the words are placed consistently at the bottom or top of the page or always on the left-hand page to make it easier for you to cover them. Many of the Lap Books published by Richard C. Owen work well for this purpose. They're larger than standard-sized books but smaller than big books.

And then, of course, kids can go through the same process and develop oral language skills and vocabulary by explaining or telling a story about a single picture.

How Do I Read Single Pictures with the Whole Class?

1. Before you try reading a wordless big book with students, work with a poster-size photograph. You can use the posters that accompany student newspapers and magazines, such as *Weekly Reader* and *National Geographic*, or go directly to the publishers' catalogues to check out their giant-sized pictures and posters. I often use Mondo's *Let's Talk About It* (2004), a collection of 30" × 22" photographs designed to get kids talking and interacting.

2. Explain to children that since there are no words to go with the picture, they will have to look at the picture carefully to notice all the details that help them figure out what might be happening. It's also important to help children recognize that readers use *both* the picture and their prior knowledge.

3. Always *think aloud* so students can hear where your ideas are coming from and can think along with you. When discussing the photo in Figure 8-4 from Carmen Crevola and Mark Vineis' *Let's Talk About It* (Mondo) materials, I might say: "I see a chipmunk sitting in a tree and his cheeks are stuffed with food. I bet it's bird seed. Chipmunks love them. I always see them under my bird feeder gathering seeds that the birds have dropped."

4. Later, after you and the children have determined what the picture is about, you can turn your description into a narrative, beginning with a story opener something like this: "One day, Chippy the Chipmunk was sitting in a tree feeling quite lucky and content. He had found so many nuts and seeds to save for winter. If only he knew where to store them."

Or you might model an expository text about how chipmunks prepare for winter by gathering seeds, nuts, and berries. In this case, your narration would take a nonfiction turn: "Chipmunks gather seeds, nuts, and berries in the fall. They need to store food for the long winter months."

Give children plenty of encounters like this—showing them pictures and asking them to make up a story or describe what's happening. You may want to jot down what they say so that you can read back some of their responses. You will certainly want to help them see the similarities *and* differences between what they and classmates are thinking, and that no one version is right or wrong. Each reader brings his own experiences and perspective, and their story and description will reflect this.

PHOTO: EASTERN CHIPMUNK BY GERLACH NATURE PHOTOGRAPHY/ANIMALS ANIMALS

Figure 8-4. Chipmunk Photo in Let's Talk About It

How Do I Help Children Transition to Reading an Entire Wordless Book?

In transitioning from reading single pictures to reading an entire wordless book, you first need to recognize the difference in the amount and type of reading that's required. The difference in sheer volume alone calls for deciding in advance how you're going to divide up the reading. Will you introduce the book the first day and begin reading on Day 2? Or will you start reading on Day 1 and pull the parts together as you go? I favor starting to read right away, but you'll have to decide which option works best for you and your students. Deciding on how many days to spend with the book will depend on the complexity of the book you're reading and children's age and attention span.

After students have had several opportunities to work with a large single photo, it should be easy enough for them to transition to a wordless big book or one shown on an interactive whiteboard. Here are the steps:

1. Introduce the wordless book as you would any other. Read the title, examine the cover, and discuss with students what the book might be about.

2. Explain that to tell the whole story, in addition to carefully examining each picture as they did when they read single pictures, they will also have to consider how what's happening in each picture relates to what came before and what comes after. If it's fiction, they will have to think about story grammar, i.e., character, setting, etc. If it's nonfiction, they'll have to describe what they're learning.

3. Walk the children through the book to give them an idea of where it's headed, and let them help you name what they see on each page rather than trying to tell a story the first time through. That's a step you want to leave for the students on subsequent reads.

4. Once children have a general sense of the book, they can try to craft it into a story. Ask several children to tell what they think is happening on the first couple of pages where the character is introduced and the plot is set in motion. Decide on one "intro" and stick with it. (You may even want to chart these first few sentences so that you can later read them over when the children's storytelling wanders and you need to pull them back.) The challenge here is getting the kids to work together to tell *one* cohesive story, not myriad bits and pieces that don't connect.

5. Children will have to pay attention to the details and the sequence. So pepper your discussion with words like *first*, *next*, and *then* to help them think sequentially.

How Do I Use Wordless Books with a Small Group of Readers?

When working with a small group of readers you can go full steam ahead. You might work with one text, and because the kids can see the pictures up close, they can talk about their interpretation as they look through it and tell the story together.

Or you might have several copies. In this case, introduce the book, spend time looking at the cover and title, partner children in the group so each child has someone to talk and share ideas with, and then give them time to read the book together. You might want to direct them to only read up to a certain page and then stop so you can hear what they're thinking.

How Do I Use Wordless Books for Independent Reading?

Wordless books are a wonderful resource to add to children's independent reading bags as long as they're conceptually a good match for the child's age. I wouldn't give a five-year-old David Weisner's *Flotsam* (2006) for his independent reading book bag (although he and his mom or dad might have great fun digging into it at bedtime). A child in kindergarten would fare much better with Emily Arnold McCully's *School* (2005) or *First Snow* (2003) because the content is better suited to the prior knowledge and experience a child of that tender age brings.

When reading a wordless book, I encourage children to work with a partner during independent reading so they can talk about what they think is happening. This way they get to exchange ideas and consider possibilities they may not have thought of themselves. It's also fun to buddy-up kids in your class with older students. Sit and listen in as the older child points out nuances his younger buddy would likely miss, and celebrate when your student shares his coauthored story with the class.

How Is Children's Vocabulary Enhanced When They Read Wordless Books?

Since the books are wordless, the high-end vocabulary you want to expose children to will have to come from you. As you discuss a picture with students or introduce a book, you will want to use words that students would unlikely provide on their own. For example, when reading the page from *Rainstorm* in Figure 8-3 I might say, "This boy must be very *frustrated*. He keeps trying and trying all different places the key might work, and it doesn't. But look how *determined* he is. He just won't give up." It's likely that later the words *frustrated* and *determined* will pop up in children's conversations as they get to read these books on their own.

How Might Wordless Books Enhance Children's Writing?

Imagine a student day after day saying he has nothing to write about, that he has nothing to say. And imagine this same child coming off reading a wordless big book with his class, or reading one in a small group, or with a partner during independent reading, and then giving him a copy of the book he's been talking about for so long. This same child who once had "nothing to say" will be flooded with ideas about how he could put his words, written words this time, to paper. He's likely to write and write, and then want to share what he's written.

And because you've just witnessed this child's "IQ" palpably jump in minutes, you may want to include a file of pictures alongside the markers and paper in the writing area to trigger all of your children's imaginations as they write. Pictures of a bear making his way to a campsite looking for food, a child weeping because she's dropped her ice cream cone, a bald eagle perched high on a treetop scouting the river for food. The world is full of images and ideas about which kids can write. We just have to show them.

Effective Practice: Using Alphabet Books to Develop Children's Vocabulary

What Do Alphabet Books Have to Offer?

It used to be that when you shopped for an alphabet book the only ones you'd be likely to find were *Dr. Seuss's ABC*, Richard Scarry's *Chipmunk's ABC*, or *Chicka-Chicka-Boom-Boom*. Now there are literally hundreds to choose from, including a variety of subgenres ranging from the narratives and puzzle books to topical or thematic alphabet books. And no longer are they used primarily to teach our youngest readers *about* the alphabet—its letters and their sequence, and letter-sounds associated with each letter. Their scope is broader, and as a result they can be put to wider classroom use.

Among other things, alphabet books can enhance children's speaking and listening vocabulary and provide content vocabulary as they learn fascinating information on a range of topics—fruits and vegetables, composting, parts of the human body—in an alphabetically sequenced way. Their predictable structure is intrinsically comforting to children in K–3 who are just learning to read and understand texts.

For the purpose of this effective practice addressing vocabulary, I'll sort alphabet books into two main categories:

+ alphabet *concept* books that focus on teaching the alphabet and words associated with each letter, and

+ alphabet *content* books, which are topical or thematic in nature, and whose goal is to present content information and vocabulary using an alphabetical sequence.

What Are Alphabet Concept Books and How Can I Use Them to Teach Vocabulary?

Alphabet concept books help teach children basic features of the alphabet, just as color concept books teach about color, and number concept books teach about numbers and counting. In their purest and most fundamental form:

+ There are one or two letters to a page.
+ The pages are uncluttered.
+ The pictures that represent the letters are common, everyday objects.
+ The illustrations are simple and clear.

Whimsical Alphabet Concept Books

- *Dr. Seuss's ABC: An Amazing Alphabet Book* by Dr. Seuss
- *Superhero ABC* by Bob McLeod
- *Pigs from A to Z* by Arthur Geisert
- *AlphaOops! The Day Z Went First* by Alethia Kontis
- *Curious George Learns the Alphabet* by H. A. Rey
- *Alphabet Under Construction* by Denise Fleming
- *Alphabeep! A Zipping, Zooming ABC* by Deborah Pearson
- *Alphabet Rescue* by Audrey Wood
- *The Alphabet Room* by Sara Pinto
- *Max's ABC* by Rosemary Wells
- *ABC T-Rex* by Bernard Most
- *Tomorrow's Alphabet* by George Shannon
- *ABC I Like Me* by Nancy Carlson
- *Q Is for Duck: An Alphabet Guessing Game* by Michael Folson

See the following pages for further descriptions of whimsical, alphabet concept books.

+ The beginning letter-sound of the word represents the featured letter's most common sound.

These most basic concept books are best for children who haven't yet cemented their understanding of the alphabetic code. *Bruno Munari's ABC* (2006) is a prototypical example. Figure 8-5 shows one of two *N* pages (the other shows a *newspaper* caught in the tree branch). The *nest*, the *nuts*, and the *nail* are clearly illustrated, and kids sitting with a partner should have no trouble identifying these *N* words. Unfortunately, there are not many basic alphabet trade books, like Munari's, available for elementary-age students. Most of them are now published in board book format, which, understandably, doesn't sit well with the school-age crowd.

However, there are scores of other alphabet concept books that are more whimsical and well suited to young readers. (See the box on the previous page for some of these titles.) In addition to their focus on teaching upper- and lowercase letters of the alphabet, letter sounds, ABC order, etc., the authors engage children in word play and give them riddles and puzzles to solve and narratives to enjoy. Examples are Alethea Kontis' 2006 *AlphaOops! The Day Z Went First* (Figure 8-6) where Z, objecting to his last place in the alphabetical lineup, demands fairness, setting off an alphabetical romp not soon forgotten, and George Shannon's *Tomorrow's Alphabet*

Figure 8-5. Page from Bruno Munari's ABC

Figure 8-6. Page from AlphaOops! The Day Z Went First

(1999) where *A* is for *seed* (tomorrow's *apple*), *B* is for *egg* (tomorrow's *bird*), *C* is for *milk* (tomorrow's *cheese*).

I also want to mention alliterative alphabet books, despite the fact that they're not alphabet books in the strict sense of walking the reader through the entire alphabet letter by letter. However, they do highlight specific letters and their sounds and conjure up vocabulary around them in an amusing, engaging, and reinforcing way. See Figure 8-7 for a page from Pamela Duncan Edwards' *The Worrywarts* (2003). In the box are some of my favorite alliterative alphabet books.

Figure 8-7. Page from The Worrywarts

Alliterative Alphabet Books

- ***Some Smug Slug*** by Pamela Duncan Edwards
- ***Clara Caterpillar*** by Pamela Duncan Edwards
- ***Four Famished Foxes and Fasdyke*** by Pamela Duncan Edwards
- ***The Worrywarts*** by Pamela Duncan Edwards
- ***Rosie's Roses*** by Pamela Duncan Edwards
- ***Walter Was Worried*** by Laura Vaccaro Seeger
- ***Bashful Bob and Doleful Dorinda*** by Margaret Atwood
- ***Willie's Word World*** by Don L. Curry

How Can I Use Alphabet Books to Enhance the Vocabulary of English Language Learners?

Alphabet books expose English language learners to new vocabulary, and new vocabulary is precisely what they need. English language learners must acquire vocabulary from which to build a new language and a way of communicating. Imagine what it must be like to come to a new country—sometimes only weeks or days before school starts—not knowing the customs or the language the rest of the kids in class speak and to be expected to join in the activities, lessons, and discussions. It must be awfully hard.

English language learners often don't know Tier 1 words like *feather, bone,* and *clock* that native English speakers use so effortlessly. Therefore, we must begin their vocabulary instruction with these more basic words that occur regularly in their social and academic interactions, and it's here that vocabulary concept books can help build children's listening and oral vocabulary.

While it may be hard to find 10–15 *basic* alphabet concept books, such as Bruno Munari's, it's worth keeping a look out for them and gathering what you can in a basket. Give children opportunities to read the books with a partner, taking turns naming the words and discussing the featured letter and representative pictures, *banana, bench, bug,* etc., on each page.

You can certainly collect some of the simpler, more straightforward alphabet books though, such as Rosemary Wells' *Max's ABC* (2008) or Bernard Most's *ABC T-Rex* (2004) and let kids interact with these. (In the "Alphabet Books for ELLs" box are some alphabet books that are good for ELLs.)

As you gather books for English language learners consider how closely they match some of the characteristics of the more basic concept books, i.e., number of words on a page, easily recognizable pictures, etc. The puzzle and word play books won't fare well with English language learners at the beginning stages of English language acquisition. They need to learn the basics and, in this case, the simpler the alphabet books the better.

Alphabet Books for English Language Learners

- *Amazing Animal Alphabet* by Brian Wildsmith
- *Farm ABC: An Alphabet Book* by B. A. Hoena and Gail Saunders-Smith
- *School ABC: An Alphabet Book* by Amanda Doering and Gail Saunders-Smith
- *Food ABC: An Alphabet Book* by Amanda Doering and Gail Saunders-Smith
- *ABCs at the Zoo* by Sandy Seeley Walling
- *ABC Drive* by Naomi Howland
- *Miss Spider's ABC* by David Kirk
- *Abcdz: Alphabet Book* by David Ross
- *Max's ABC* by Rosemary Wells
- *ABC T-Rex* by Bernard Most
- *ABC I Like Me* by Nancy Carlson
- *On Market Street* by Arnold Lobel
- *Girls A to Z* by Eve Bunting
- *A, My Name Is Alice* by Jane E. Bayer
- *An A to Z Walk in the Park* by R. M. Smith
- *Alligator Arrived with Apples: A Potluck Alphabet Feast* by Crescent Dragonwagon

To help English language learners build their vocabulary by using alphabet books, consider the following strategies:

+ Put the books in a basket in a prominent place in the classroom where a child can go with a friend to look through and discuss what they see.

+ Partner up an English language learner with a native English speaker, or better yet a child or adult who speaks both English *and* the English language learner's native language, and give them ten minutes each day to read and talk together.

+ Set aside several minutes a day to sit alongside an English language learner or a small group of them, and look through an alphabet book and talk about what's on each page. You might even plan to work on a different letter of the alphabet each day and bring in real-life objects from home that match the pictures, e.g., a nut, a nail, a newspaper, so the child can connect this word to something concrete.

+ Set up a table where you feature one letter a day from the alphabet book on which you and your English language learners are working, and ask students in class to bring in objects that begin with that letter.

+ Have students make alphabet picture boards (Figure 8-8) and Appendix 14 online. In each box they sketch a picture of a word beginning with the featured letter and label it.

+ Have students make their own alphabet books to share with students in another class or grade. In this instance, the basic concept books like *Bruno Munari's ABC* would serve as a model for students on how to make their own book. Several students might work together, which would be even better since they can talk as they work.

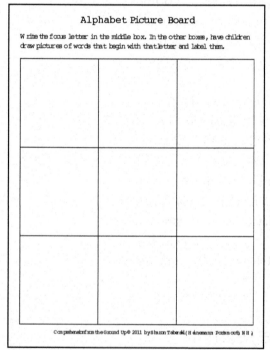

Figure 8-8. Alphabet Picture Board

What Are Alphabet Content Books and How Can I Use Them to Teach Content Vocabulary?

Alphabet *content* books are nonfiction texts that use alphabetical sequence as a framework for conveying information about a topic. In some instances, the information is broad and factual, such as in Jerry Pallotta's 1987 *The Bird Alphabet Book* (Figure 8-9) where the reader is introduced to a wide variety of birds, and at other times the focus is narrower and more conceptual as in Esther Hershenhorn's 2009 book *S is for Story: A Writer's Alphabet* (Figure 8-10) where the author offers advice on how to become a better writer. The "Alphabet Content Books" box contains examples of books in this alphabet content book genre.

Figure 8-9. Page from The Bird Alphabet Book

Figure 8-10. Page from S is for Story: A Writer's Alphabet

Alphabet Content Books

- ***Appalosa Zebra: A Horse Lover's Alphabet*** by Jessie Haas
- ***B Is for Bookworm: A Library Alphabet*** by Anita Prieto
- ***The Bird Alphabet*** by Jerry Pallotta
- ***Museum ABC*** (The Metropolitan Museum of Art)
- ***S is for Story: A Writer's Alphabet*** by Esther Hershenhorn
- ***Compost Stew: An A to Z Recipe for the Earth*** by Mary McKenna Siddals
- ***C Is for Caboose: Riding the Rails from A to Z*** by Traci N. Todd and Sara Gillingham
- ***All Aboard! A Traveling Alphabet*** by Chris L. Demarest
- ***Gone Wild: An Endangered Alphabet*** by David McLemans
- ***Country Road ABC: An Illustrated Journey Through America's Farmland*** by Arthur Geisert
- ***M Is for Masterpiece: An Art Alphabet*** by David Domeniconi

Alphabet books can support the development of students' content vocabulary as you work with them throughout the reading workshop in the following ways:

- Begin a new science or social studies unit by reading aloud an alphabet book on your content-area topic. Since these books usually provide broad introductory information, it's a great way to draw students into the study as well as to give the class a shared supply of content vocabulary to support discussion about that topic. During or after the read-aloud, you can make a chart of the new content vocabulary words and keep adding to the list as your study progresses.

- Read an alphabet book to four or five children and provide time for them to talk about what they're learning. It's okay if there's only one copy because the children are sitting up close to the book.

- Give children opportunities to read alphabet content books on their own. The book's structure and focus on one topic or theme help them learn *categories* of words and concepts, such as words about the solar system, animal adaptation, and feelings.

- Develop an alphabet book writing unit where each child creates his own book on a topic the class is studying, or

Storing Alphabet Books

Alphabet *concept* books should be stored together as ABC books, and alphabet *content* books should be kept with the informational texts. However, if a teacher is asking students to write alphabet books, she should combine the concept and content books to give kids easy access to them as they study the genre.

Alphabet Books Inspire Kid's Writing

Alphabet books provide a wonderful outlet for children to express their knowledge of a topic. The alphabet book format helps kids "stay in lane" with the details they want to share, without veering off topic or becoming overwhelmed by the prospect of organizing and writing an entire report.

For example, children know they can write several sentences about the "A Is for Alligator" entry, and they naturally deliver a topic sentence and supporting details and feel successful. And if they don't, it's easy enough for us to demonstrate how to begin with a general statement and move to the specifics with the several sentences they've written. So it's an obvious foreground to writing paragraphs too.

where children are working together to create a class book. This will give them the chance to use the vocabulary, information, and concepts they're acquiring.

My students once wrote a class alphabet book on reptiles and amphibians. We used the entire back bulletin board as a storyboard to display their work at various stages of completion. Each student was responsible for one letter and was assigned a space on the board to hang her written draft. In doing so, students acquired a great deal of background knowledge and content vocabulary about amphibians and reptiles as they researched their topic and listened as classmates shared what they'd written.

Effective Practice: "Words Words Words" to Learn Tier 2 Vocabulary

Amiable, exaggerate, flutter, preposterous, erode—these words are not the unsung heroes of our language like Tier 1 words *elbow, clock, yellow, table.* No, *ambiable* and its comrades in Tier 2 have a little more pizzazz and demand more of kids both conceptually and in terms of decoding. For these words, in addition to the exposure children get to them as they read widely, also need to be explicitly taught so children can eventually understand them with ease as they read on their own.

"Words Words Words" is one such approach to explicitly teaching Tier 2 words that I've adapted from an idea found in Isabel Beck, Margaret McKeown, and Linda Kucan's *Bringing Words to Life: Robust Vocabulary Instruction* (2002). As you will see, it really fires kids up to take on new words and find them in written text and conversations. (See Figure 8-11 for a description of Tier 1, 2, and 3 words.)

Tier 1 words are those that are used frequently and whose meaning is highly recognizable. Teachers do not need to teach students the meaning of words like *baby, book, truck,* and *horse,* except of course if their students are English language learners. In that case, English language learners need to know the English word for concepts they already know and understand in their native language, and may need scaffolding through the use of pictures, real-life objects, and practices that address the specific needs of English language learners.

Tier 2 words are likely to show up with high frequency in a mature language users vocabulary and include words like *fortunate, desperate,* and *alienate.* They're words that teachers need to use when speaking with students and focus on when teaching vocabulary.

Tier 3 words are low-frequency words that show up primarily in content-area studies, but not in everyday conversations. For example, when studying the solar system, we would expect children to read and use words such as *meteorite, galaxy, constellation,* etc., but wouldn't expect them to surface while reading fiction or when they're on the playground.

Figure 8-11. Three Tiers of Vocabulary

Why Is Explicit Vocabulary Instruction Necessary?

It's true that children learn words primarily from context; first through the words they meet in oral conversations and then through oral language experiences combined with words they read. However, it's also essential for children to receive explicit vocabulary instruction. Here's why:

+ Before third grade, young readers typically don't encounter Tier 2 words in texts they're able to read on their own. Up until then, their reading vocabulary is much more basic.

+ Students who don't read well or who don't read a lot may seldom have access to books that contain an abundance of Tier 2 words.

+ Students from lower socioeconomic families or from homes where English is not spoken are unlikely to hear Tier 2 words used in their daily interactions with family members.

Therefore, teachers must do their part to ensure that all students acquire the vocabulary they need to succeed.

How Does "Words Words Words" Work?

The six-step procedure is actually quite simple. Steps 1–3 occur after you read a book aloud, and steps 4–6 are integrated into your daily morning routine:

1. From a book you've read aloud, identify three Tier 2 words you want students to become more familiar with and eventually own. To "own" a word, they will need to interact with it repeatedly over time until they understand what it means when they read or hear it spoken, and can use it in oral and written expression. (*Note:* Do not select new Tier 2 words with each and every read-aloud. A realistic goal is to add three new words to the "Words Words Words" chart each week. This will be a step in the right direction to children acquiring the several hundred that they'll need to learn each year.)

2. Write each word on a sentence strip that's been precut to fit the width of your "Words Words Words" chart (Figure 8-12).

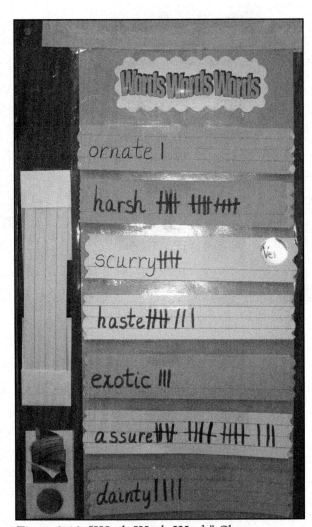

Figure 8-12. "Words Words Words" Chart

3. When adding a word to the chart, reread the sentence from the book in which the word was found and discuss its meaning. Give students a sample sentence or two that contains the targeted word and also ask them to think of a sentence with that word. Call on several students to share.

4. Attach these word strips to the chart and explain to students that they should be on the lookout for them as they read, write, and hear others engaged in conversations. If they find one of the Tier 2 words in a book they're reading or use one of the words in their writing, they should mark the page with a Post-it note. And, if they use or hear a word in conversation, they should write the sentence down.

   Children should bring their book, piece of writing, or paper with the oral sentence they've recorded to subsequent whole-class meetings to share. Some children love to find and use these words and they share a lot, while others prefer to just sit back and let their classmates take the lead. That's okay since all children are exposed to the words once they're shared.

Figure 8-13. Kolbein Tallying His Word

5. Ask several students each day to share *one* of their "found" words. Each child comes to the front of the meeting area and reads his sentence, omitting the targeted word and leaving it up to his classmates to fill in the blank.

6. Once the missing word has been identified, place a tally mark alongside the word. (Figure 8-13 shows Kolbein tallying his word.) Always ask the student who supplies the omitted word to explain why he chose that word over the others. This helps children realize that they should consider the context in which a word is used to determine its meaning.

How Do We Retire Words?

After the "Words Words Words" chart (which has 13 "slots") is full, the children and I select several words to retire. At this stage, we need to remove three cards each week to make room for three new ones. These are usually words that I'm confident the children know the meaning of since they've been found and shared more times than the others (as can be determined by counting the tally marks). In addition, we often retire words that seldom show up in texts the children read. Perhaps they were a poor choice to begin with.

To "retire" a word I place a new word strip over the one that's being retired, taping it along the top edge with clear packing tape so that the sides and bottom of the card remain unattached, and the words can be flipped through to see the words beneath.

The thirteen words that are visible are our "active" words, and the ones that have been covered over are the "retired" words. I've pragmatically set the number of "active" words at 13 since that's how many fit on my closet door where the chart hangs.

What Happens to Words That Have Been Retired?

Retired words are not forgotten; rather they are listed on a "Retired Words" chart that's posted alongside the "Words Words Words" chart. Children understand that even though they are no longer actively searching for these retired words to share with the class and tally, these are still important words to know.

In addition, families are informed each week of new words we have added to our active list and are encouraged to use them at home when talking with their children and while helping them with their homework.

What's So Good About "Words Words Words"?

Besides the fact that it's a great deal of fun, "Words Words Words" aligns with the research Beck, McKeown, and Kucan report on in *Creating Robust Vocabulary* (2008). According to this research cited in Chapter 5:

1. **Children must receive more than several exposures to a word.** In the "Words Words Words" procedure, children encounter the targeted words multiple times as they read them in texts, write them, and hear them in conversations. They receive additional exposures when classmates share examples they've found and challenge one another to figure out which of the words on the list best fits the sentence they're reading.

2. **Children need to consider both definitional and contextual information about the words.** Before a word is added to our chart, I read the sentence from the book in which the word was found so that kids can see how it was used in the story or text. Then I provide some sample sentences containing that word and ask children to supply a couple of their own. It's not unusual for us to also consult a dictionary or Google the word to learn how it's more formally defined.

3. **Children need to be engaged in active and deep processing of the word.** Kids are definitely engaged when working with "Words Words Words." In fact, their families report that they've never seen anything quite like it. "What are you doing," they ask, "to get kids so interested in words?" "Jonathan was at the dentist yesterday and was motioning to me while the dentist was checking his teeth because his dentist used the word *reluctant*—one of his vocabulary words."

   Children also enjoy learning how targeted words relate to other words they meet or need to know. For example, we often web our words to see what other words relate. It's empowering for children to know that if they know one word, *vary*, for example, then they have a place to start when considering what *variety*, *various*, *variation*, and *variegated* mean.

Recommended Professional Books

For ideas on various vocabulary practices to try out, I recommend:

- *Bringing Words to Life: Robust Vocabulary Instruction* and its sequel *Creating Robust Vocabulary: Frequently Asked Questions and Extended Examples* by Isabel Beck, Margaret McKeown, and Linda Kucan
- *Learning Words Inside and Out: Vocabulary Instruction That Boosts Achievement in All Subject Areas* by Nancy Frey and Douglas Fisher
- *What Really Matters in Vocabulary: Research-Based Practices Across the Curriculum* by Patricia Cunningham
- *The Vocabulary Book: Learning and Instruction* by Michael F. Graves
- *The Vocabulary-Enriched Classroom* by Cathy Collins Block and John N. Mangieri (eds.)

How Many Tier 2 Words Will Students Learn Using This Procedure?

Nagy and Anderson (1984) have estimated that students from kindergarten through grade 12 need to acquire around 700 Tier 2 words (i.e., different word families) a year. Recognizing the enormity of the task at hand, Beck, McKeown, and Kucan (2002) assert that "attention to a substantial portion of these words, say, an average of 400 per year, would make a significant contribution to an individual's verbal functioning" (p. 9).

However, I've never been able to reach anything near that 400-word target using this approach alone. Therefore, it's necessary to combine "Words Words Words" with other explicit vocabulary practices. See the box for professional books on other ways to explicitly teach vocabulary.

How Does "Words Words Words" Work with Kindergarten and First-Grade Students?

Kindergarten and early first-grade students can engage in a modified version of this practice.

1. Identify three Tier 2 words as described above in the full version of "Words Words Words" and write them on sentence strips. When working with young readers, it's up to the teacher to carefully select age- and grade-appropriate Tier 2 words and use them repeatedly since children aren't yet reading higher level books on their own.

   For example, after reading aloud Roger Duvoisin's *Donkey-donkey* (2007), I selected *clever, resemble,* and *unfortunate* to highlight, as it seemed likely we'd encounter these words in other read-alouds, and because I could easily weave them into conversations with students. (See Figure 8-14 for a list of Tier 2 or *interesting* words, as I sometimes refer to them, found in *Donkey-donkey*.)

It's exhilarating to see how much vocabulary we can expose children to simply by reading aloud high-quality literature.

2. Make a color copy of the book's cover and fasten it and the three word strips to a piece of 24" × 16" chart paper that's posted on the bulletin board (Figure 8-15). By displaying these vocabulary charts around the room, children's attention is drawn to both the read-aloud selection and the targeted vocabulary. These charts also remind us to use the words when addressing children.

3. When you hear, meet, or use one of these words, call students' attention to the chart and make a tally mark alongside the word. You'll need to deliberately use these words in conversations with students to give them as many exposures to the words as possible.

As with older students, these words can become the basis for additional "If . . . Then . . ." word work. For example, if children know the meaning of *unfortunate*, then they also know *fortunate* and *unfortunately*. The key, of course, is in the words you select to highlight.

Some Tier 2 (or Interesting) Words in *Donkey-donkey*	
dear	expression
master	stable
thistles	unfortunate
stream	wounds
ridiculous	healed
clever	pierced
advice	consult
resemble	attentively
trotting	grievances
colt	suspect
bandaged	practical
pulse	ashamed
impressed	inconvenience
fetch	brooding
dainty	perched
flattered	astonished
disposition	unpleasant
doubtful	

Figure 8-14. Some Tier 2 Words in Donkey-donkey

Figure 8-15. Linking Vocabulary to Cherished Books

How Can I Extend This Practice So My Proficient Readers Achieve More Independence?

You can move students in grade 3 (and some of your more proficient second-grade readers) from this whole-class "Words Words Words" procedure to one where they identify *personal* words to learn from their independent reading. Figure 8-16 and Appendix 9 online include a form where students identify and learn personal vocabulary in much the same way that a class of students learns about Tier 2 words from "Words Words Words."

If you do "Words Words Words" well, you'll:

- *help develop children's vocabulary*
- *help children use content to figure out the meaning of unknown words*
- *support students' comprehension development*
- *motivate students to pay attention to words*
- *help children consider multiple meanings of words*
- *attend to word roots and affixes*

Name _____ Date _____

My Words: Words I Want to Learn

1. _____ 2. _____

The sentence where I heard or read the word, and what I think it means:

1.

2.

Dictionary Definition:

1. _____

2. _____

Ideas for how to learn the words:

_____

_____

Figure 8-16. My Words Vocabulary Sheet

Reading-Writing Connections
Principles and Practices

"[T]he brain is a natural pattern seeker and synthesizer and actively searches for patterns to categorize, organize, synthesize information, code it into memory, and then retrieve it." (p. 22)

—Carol Lyons in *Teaching Struggling Readers: How to Use Brain-Based Research to Maximize Learning* (2003)

Reading-Writing Connections and Comprehension

When it comes to reading-writing connections, the wiring of our brain is not the warmest, most literary image to conjure, and yet this quote about pattern and synthesis is so evocative to me of children in grades K–3 who are consummate pattern seekers. Reading and writing are both still new for them and are often hard to learn, so their minds are working overtime to organize all the complex literacy concepts coming at them. How can we make it easier for them to learn each one?

We can read poignant picture books and beautiful nonfiction as mentor texts and uncover the bones of beautiful writing so our children can then recreate this craft in their writing. Sure. That's the most common iteration of the reading-writing connection. But in this chapter I want you to entertain this connection a little differently because of how it plays out with primary-grade children, and because it requires something different of teachers and instruction.

So here goes: Whenever I think of the reading-writing connection, the notion of systematic teaching comes to mind. Not the kind where our moves are scripted by packaged programs where we're told what to teach first, second, and third. No, I mean the organic, systematic teaching that arises when we teachers know what we need to accomplish our goals—and recognize how the various parts of our balanced literacy program work together to achieve them.

We plan. We know our objective going into each lesson and interaction. And yet, because in each moment we keep in mind the foundational framework of literacy (the nexus of reading, writing, and content-area concepts), we are also open to the serendipitous moment that makes us realize, wow, *now* is the time to teach this . . . or wow, given how engaged kids are, I'm going to bump my plans for tomorrow and carve out more time to keep this going. There was one occasion, in particular, where I even surprised myself. Where I had to step back and say, "This is so cool! So *this* is what it means to teach systematically, to teach smart!"

I had been reading aloud several of Rosemary Wells' picture books. Not simply reading them, talking about our favorite part, and then moving on, but helping kids learn what each of the characters is like, Noisy Nora, Shy Charles, Yoko, Timothy, Fritz—the whole gang—and then using that to better understand and enjoy the story. (See Figure 9-1 for some of the character webs we made to accompany the read-alouds.)

It didn't worry me that onlookers might think these picture books too juvenile for my readers, and it didn't seem to bother the children either. In fact, I think they secretly delighted in taking a breather from all the reaching they are accustomed to these days. And I was confident that we were doing reading work that would last a lifetime. The fact that the main characters had easily recognizable personalities and that the books were short, lending themselves to be reread as often as needed, made them just perfect . . . and now the drumroll . . . in preparation for my reading aloud Wells' *Timothy's Tales from the Hilltop School* (2004), a collection of short stories geared for more proficient second- and third-grade readers about these same delicious characters that we'd come to love and know so well.

I had been chomping at the bit to read these short stories ever since finding the volume in the bookstore, but had held back from merely

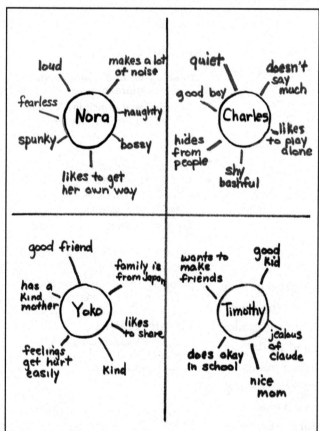

Figure 9-1. Character Webs for Some of Rosemary Wells' Characters

reading story upon story upon story (checking each off mentally as I did). I wanted instead to put this experience to far greater use. I wanted to show the children that by thinking about and mapping out Charles' and Nora's and Claude's and Dora's personalities—any character's, for that matter—they could position themselves to read, comprehend, and enjoy the story more fully. (By now you're probably wondering when I'm going to get to the "writing" part of this dynamic duo. Soon, trust me.)

When it was finally time to read "The Buried Treasure," our first short story featuring none other than Nora, the girl (the mouse actually) who can get away with being naughty when my children can't, I wasn't the only "chomper." The kids could hardly contain themselves. For here, Nora wants to buy Yoko an expensive birthday present at Gimbel's Gift Gallery and becomes quite upset when her mother tells her she can't. As expected, Nora acts out as only Nora would dare—*banging* food into the shopping cart, *shouting* in exasperation when her mother tries to calm her down, and *slamming* her feet as she walks down the supermarket aisles. (See where I'm headed?)

In the story "Charles Stands Tall," Charles (also known as "Shy Charles"), who seems to be breaking out of his shell and becoming a bit more assertive, wants to be a bald eagle for "Bird Week," but is too shy to ask out loud. So he draws a picture of an eagle on the chalkboard to let Mrs. Jenkins know he wants the part. And of course, Claude (the bully who tormented Timothy in *Timothy Goes to School*) wants the same part, giving Charles a hard time: "You're too small and too shy to make the bald eagle screech." In the end, Charles, who actually is too shy to screech like an eagle, realizes that he can make an even better eagle sound—"the sound of *five* screeching eagles at once"—by jumping up and down on the nurse's not-feeling-so-well cot. "SQUEAKITY SKREEKITY SKREEK!" go the springs.

And all the while we read these short stories, the children were giggling and shaking their heads in affirmation: "Yep, that's Charles! Yep, that's Nora! Yep, that's Claude! That's just how we expected them to act!" And as intended, the children understood and enjoyed the story more fully because they already knew these characters so well. After we read each story, I reminded the children to carry what they learned about character over to the books they read on their own and also to the stories they write. As highly acclaimed children's author Kate DiCamillo advises in "Character Is the Engine," a chapter in *What a Character! Character Study as a Guide to Literary Meaning Making in Grades K–8* (2005): "Start with a character, and the story takes care of itself" (p. 30).

Lina Pasquelina, my assistant teacher with a background in theater, thought it might be fun to have children write a story about either shy Charles' or noisy Nora's first day of school and then transform the stories into Reader's Theater scripts. The characters' opposite personalities, Lina reasoned, would help kids understand how a character's personality drives what happens.

Michelle, in her story of "Charles' First Day of School," captured his bashfulness by having him "not want to go to school," use a *whisper* instead of *talk*, and *cling* to his mother when introduced to classmates. The other characters also stayed "in character" in her portrayal: Claude and Doris, still antagonists, but nonetheless loveable, predictably laughed at Charles and made fun of him when he spilled the fruit punch. And as expected, Timothy and Yoko came to Charles' rescue, warning Claude and Doris that it was "a good thing they apologized to Charles" (leaving the "Or else!" unspoken but looming). And at the end, Yoko showed all of them how to do origami.

When I think of all the times I've tried to get children to write fiction and failed, and recall how well students did in this instance, I'm convinced that it was partially because I never spent the time—or enough time—helping them develop their characters before starting to write.

Days and days passed as Lina and I helped children turn their stories into scripts and rehearse them. Some children opted out, preferring to put their writerly talents to other pieces that were beckoning. But on the day of the Reader's Theater performances, all eyes were on the readers—and all children understood how this reading-writing connection process had played out. First, by reading and studying Rosemary's (as they now referred to Ms. Wells) picture books, and then her short stories. Next, working on their own "First Day of School" stories about Charles or Nora and turning them into scripts. And finally, reading their script to the class. Reading, to writing, and back to reading again. Perfect. Simply perfect.

These reading-writing connections lie just below the surface in our classrooms. However, if we're not tuned into their presence, or if we fail to call children's attention to them, we aren't maximizing their potential.

+ When children seem especially amused or moved by a picture book you read aloud, take notice: might you "effortlessly" turn around and use this same story for a writing mini-lesson the following day?

+ When children sound out words as they write, they're using the very same coding skills they use to transform print into spoken or "read" words.

+ When children take the time to think about what the title of a book or chapter they're reading may be about, they're doing the same kind of thinking as when they decide on a title for a piece they're writing.

+ When children look to the table of contents in a nonfiction text for what's there, this prepares them for one they will have to prepare for the expository piece they're writing.

Reading and writing. Writing and reading. When the two of them work together, children consolidate their understanding of what it means to be a reader who writes and a writer who reads. I can't think of anything more important or more empowering for children to experience.

Foundational Principles for the Reading-Writing Connection

Teachers who help children recognize the synergy between reading and writing have an easier task of teaching both sets of skills and strategies. Consider how the following foundational principles can help you enliven the interplay between these meaning-making processes.

Make the Reading-Writing Connection Explicit

The chart below lists some ways in which reading and writing relate to one another. Note that I've listed writing *before* reading because that's the chronology that helps children understand: Ideas and information have to be written before they can be read.

What *Writers* Do	What *Readers* Do
Writers attend to conventions of print by making their words go from left to right and top to bottom, leaving spaces between words, etc.	Readers attend to conventions of print by reading from left to right and top to bottom within a given chunk of text, noting spaces between words, tracking print, etc.
Writers encode words from sounds they hear in the word they're trying to write to letters that represent the sounds.	Readers decode words by associating sounds with the letters and spelling patterns in words they're trying to read.
Writers convey ideas and information through illustrations and graphics such as charts, maps, and photos.	Readers use the pictures and graphics the illustrator (who is sometimes also the author) has provided to get meaning and expand upon what's written.
Writers convey ideas and information through the text they write.	Readers acquire and interpret the ideas and information the author has communicated through the text he has written.
Writers use conventions such as spelling, capitalization, and punctuation to convey meaning.	Readers attend to the writing conventions the author has included to get meaning.
Writers organize their ideas to make them more accessible and comprehensible to a reader.	Readers look for how the author has organized his piece, knowing this will help them access information and remember what they read.
Writers attend to language and word choice to communicate precisely what they want to say.	Readers attend to an author's language and word choice for how it holds the key to meaning.
Writers monitor their writing—often by reading it out loud—listening for "clicks" and "clunks" to determine whether or not what they've written makes sense.	Readers listen for "clicks" and "clunks" as they read to determine whether they can keep going or should stop to smooth things out.
Writers anticipate their audience and consider this when determining how much and what kind of information to give their reader.	Readers make inferences to fill in the necessary gaps the writer has left. Without those gaps, the writing would be cumbersome and boring.
Writers use meaning-making strategies to help their reader understand, such as including a table of contents, illustrating ideas and information through pictures, scale drawings, and charts, moving from general to specific information, and defining a concept that may be confusing.	Readers use meta-cognitive strategies, such as *visualizing, summarizing, considering text structure*, when a text is likely to be difficult or when meaning breaks down.

Here are some ways to make the connection between writing and reading more explicit in your work with students so that they can make new connections on their own:

+ **Whenever possible schedule your reading and writing workshop back-to-back.** It's easier for you to highlight reading-writing connections when one workshop follows the other. Connections like, "You see how when we read, we paid attention to how the author used dialogue and quotations marks? You need to try the same thing in your writing. Get your characters talking to one another." Or "I just love this picture you drew of a chameleon—its bumpy skin, bulging eyes, long tongue. I can see it's getting ready to zap a fly. Isn't it fascinating how much information we can show in our pictures? Let's share this picture with the class during our reading mini-lesson."

    I remind the kids that when they love a book, it's for all the same reasons they love a classmate's piece of writing—or their own. The reading-writing connection needn't be a lofty theoretical thing in their lives. Have it come down to the elements of funny and endearing characters, beautiful language, sentences, and ideas that make them wonder and imagine.

+ **Use the same book for a reading mini-lesson and for a writing mini-lesson.** If during a reading mini-lesson, you're using a book to demonstrate how the table of contents, the index, the subtitles, etc., can help you access ideas and information, then during a writing mini-lesson, use the same book to make a similar writing point—that children should include these text features in their own writing to help their reader get information, access ideas, etc.

+ **Make on-the-spot "Wow! Connections."** Stop what you're doing and be amazed at how reading and writing connect. "Jamie, look here. This ellipse that Helen Lester used to show time passing is what *you* just did in this piece of writing. You wrote, 'The girl looked and looked . . . for a very long time.' You and Helen Lester did the very same thing!" Or when reading a student's piece, ask if you might share with the class a striking connection he's made—whether it's his use of beautiful language, a funny setting like one you just read in a book, and so on. Chart and post these examples and keep adding to the list.

+ **Prompt children to make their own links between their reading and their writing and provide time to share them.** Second and third graders might also keep a personal list of these connections in their reading notebook. It doesn't matter how profound or mundane the connection. What's important is that children start to make them.

Demonstrate the Role of Visuals in Writing and Reading

Children so often get the mistaken notion that reading and writing are all about the *words*, and given the natural emphasis in K–3 on letters and other word-level aspects of composition, it's not difficult to see how this may have happened. But we need to be mindful not to minimize the role of *visual literacy* in supporting children's literacy development.

From birth, a child learns largely by attending to the visual images he sees. Mom's ear-to-ear grin when she greets him in the morning, the maple pods that twirl in the air on stroller walks. The world is teeming with amazing sights!

Research supports what we know intuitively from watching children develop: We learn better through pictures than through words. In his book *Brain Rules: 12 Principles for Surviving and Thriving at Work, Home, and School*, John Medina (2008) writes:

> Text and oral presentations are not just less effective than pictures for retaining certain types of information; they are way less effective. If information is presented orally, people remember about 10 percent, tested 72 hours after exposure. That figure goes up to 65 percent when you add a picture...Vision is by far our most dominant sense, taking up half our brain's resources. (p. 234)

What are the implications for our teaching? How might we use pictures to enhance kids' understanding of the reading-writing connection? Clearly, we want our young readers to attend closely to the pictures for the information and ideas they hold, for how they may actually say more and say it more comprehensibly than if the same information were presented through text alone.

In the same vein, we want our young writers to include in their own written pieces illustrations that enhance and extend their words. We want Lauren's picture of a male and female tree swallow (Figure 9-2) and Michael's clever now-you-see-it-now-you-don't drawing of a bobcat camouflaging on the side of a tree (Figure 9-3) to shout out to kids and adults alike: "This here is why pictures are so important for writing—and for reading too!" For those darling and astute pictures really do speak thousands of words that convey all the concepts children really and truly know.

By tapping into kids' pictures, we help them elaborate. They can import the salient details that make their writing most resemble the picture books and nonfiction they adore. And when their writing resembles a satisfying text, they are motivated to read it and reread it again and again, which builds comprehension. This is yet another facet of the reading-writing connection. The boxes on pages 217 and 219 describe some visual literacy strategies for writing and reading.

In her book, *In Pictures and In Words: Teaching the Qualities of Good Writing Through Illustration Study*, Katie Wood Ray (2010) explains why it's important for writers in K–3 classrooms to hone in on the illustrations in texts they read: "Illustrators

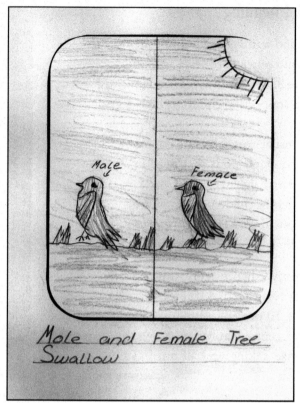

Figure 9-2. Lauren's Drawing of a Male and
Female Tree Swallow

Figure 9-3. Michael's Camouflage Drawing
of a Bobcat

make meaning with pictures, and writers make meaning with words, but they both
make meaning, and rich curriculum lies in understanding all the ways their decisions
intersect" (p. 72).

And in *Engaging the Eye Generation: Visual Literacy Practices for the K–5
Classroom,* Johanna Riddle (2009) has aligned some common first-grade literacy
standards with their corresponding visual literacy component, revealing how
visual literacy can help us reach the reading and writing standards we've set out
to meet. (See Appendix 15 online for an adaptation of Riddle's Shared Language
Arts and Visual Literacy Standards.)

Now let's turn to the "flip side" of using pictures to enhance children's development as writers to examine how pictures can enhance children's reading.
Following are strategies for harnessing the power of visuals to develop children's
reading comprehension.

Show Readers and Writers How to Monitor for Meaning

Children need to listen for "clicks" and "clunks" as they read over their own writing
or when they read texts written by others. When things are going smoothly and
making sense, they hear a friendly click-click-clicking sound, indicating all's well.
However, when meaning has broken down, a warning "clunk" signals them to stop
and fix what's wrong. Here's how to help kids do this.

Visual Literacy Writing Strategies

- **Use Expository Text to Demonstrate How the Illustrations and Text Features _Together_ Convey and Enhance Information.** Pictures and text go hand in hand, and we need to continually let kids know this. Read them the text from Andrew Collins' _Storms_ shown in Figure 9-4 explaining why tornadoes form _without_ showing them the illustration at the bottom of the page, and then ask them to explain what they learned. I bet they have a hard time. What does it mean by "cold air trapping in the warm air"? How does something "spiral upward?" Left to this task, children are likely to have many more questions than answers.

  Now let them study the illustration, and then once again read them the text. Bet they get it this time. Thanks to the text _and_ the pictures.

- **Give children time to elaborate on their pictures.** It's tempting, I know, to rush kids through their illustrations to get to what we've always perceived as the "good stuff"— the writing. But considering what illustrations can add to a piece, it's important to give kids ample time to express their ideas through their pictures first.

  Of course, if a child is taking days to complete her picture, and it's becoming her MO (where she's literally creating embossed pictures on the reverse side of her writing papers from all the attention she's giving them) then, by all means, tell her to move on.

- **Let children share and discuss their pictures with the class.** Too often we think of share time as a time for kids to simply share _texts_ they've completed. Let's also acknowledge the role that their drawings play in rehearsing their ideas and information and provide time for children to share them as well. Their classmates' comments and the questions about their picture may fuel a student's ideas for what to write and how to further elaborate on his text.

  That's why I often bump share time up to the beginning of the writing workshop instead of having kids share at the end. This way the children who share will have time to include some newfound ideas, and their classmates may get additional ideas of what to write.

Read Work Aloud

Look for opportunities to demonstrate how reading a piece aloud is an effective way for writers to notice sections where readers might be confused or lose interest. So much of good writing is in how it sounds to the ear. Getting students to read their pieces out loud can help them pinpoint what needs fixing. Even kids as young as second grade can hear the sentences where the energy goes slack due to confusing details or a lack of interesting words.

For example, when I conferred with Allie on her Baltimore Oriole piece, I read it out loud to help me _hear_ what may not sound right, problems that might otherwise go undetected. In the midst of all the "clicking" (nice voice, sensible structure, relevant information), I heard a "clunk." There was a section that didn't mesh with the full-of-voice writing I had experienced up to that point. The clunky part

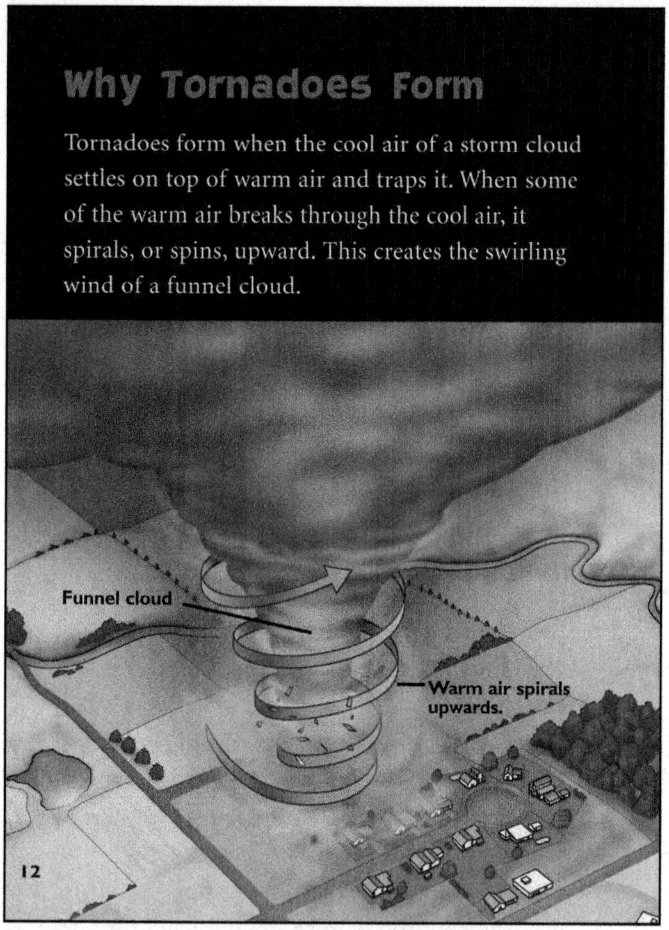

Why Tornadoes Form

Tornadoes form when the cool air of a storm cloud settles on top of warm air and traps it. When some of the warm air breaks through the cool air, it spirals, or spins, upward. This creates the swirling wind of a funnel cloud.

Funnel cloud

Warm air spirals upwards.

12

Figure 9-4. Page from Storms *(National Geographic)*

sounded too deliberately informative and contrived. Too researchy. Too "lifted" from a book.

When I pointed this "clunk" out to Allie, she didn't hear it at first, but later admitted that she sensed something was wrong. She wondered whether young children (her intended audience) would know what "tone" and "bars on their wings" meant—if the language was something little kids would understand. (*Note:* I never made a big deal—or in fact any deal at all—about her taking a passage from a field guide to include in her piece. We shouldn't make kids feel badly about "borrowing" another author's words without attribution, although it is something to discourage from a fairness point of view and teach at another time: "Boys and girls, authors work so hard at their writing, you know how that is. It isn't fair to take someone else's words and say that they're yours." Kids have a pretty healthy sense of fairness—no need to frighten them with warnings of plagiarism. This reminder about "fairness" is all you're likely to need to say about this in the primary grades.)

Now let's look at how this listening for clicks and clunks crops up during reading. When I was reading aloud John Peterson's *The Littles* (1993), I realized I left out a line. So I stopped, and instead of correcting myself and moving on, I said, as an aside, that "this happens a lot to readers, you're reading, reading, reading and things are going fine and all of a sudden something is wrong and needs to be fixed." In this case, I just needed to be more careful and perhaps take my time, but in other cases the "fix" may require active problem solving. (*Note:* Only occasionally do I insert an aside as I did above. Doing so frequently would interfere with children's enjoyment and understanding of the story.)

You've got to take time to show students that when they're really puzzled by what they've read (they read it correctly, they didn't leave out any words or lines—they simply didn't understand it), they've got to stop to figure things out. Children need to understand that they can't just skip over the troublesome passage (at least not too many of them); they have to first recognize they have a problem, and then stop to fix it. See the fix-up strategies boxes that follow to share with children about how to clarify words and ideas that give them trouble.

Visual Literacy Reading Strategies

- *Honor* picture reading. In addition to reading aloud to students, we should also present illustrations and photos that show what's happening. Children who are just learning to read need to be reminded to start with the picture and use what's there to read the words. And even as they advance, they'll need to use those same pictures to confirm the words they've read.

  More proficient readers, whose chapter books may no longer contain pictures and who now need to imagine the story the words create, still need to learn to use nonfiction illustrations and text features, e.g., illustrations and photographs, charts, maps, and scale drawings, to access information. In fact, they ought to consider them first, even before attempting to read the text.

- **Teach children *how* to read the pictures.** Don't assume children know how to mine the pictures in their storybooks and informational text; you have to show them. Before you start reading a fictional text, spend time examining the cover, thinking about the title and how the picture relates. Explain how this gives you an idea of where the story is headed.

  Or if you're reading a nonfiction piece, show children how your procedure may be even more prescribed: you read the title of the book or the section title and think of what it might be about, then you look at the pictures and read the captions. If you see a bold-print word you might look to see which of the illustrations relate to that word and take a moment or two to study it. *Then* you read.

- **Use pictures to teach.** Make a point to include more pictures in your teaching. When introducing a new topic, the rain forest for example, spend a day or so showing children pictures of a rain forest and recording on a chart what they're learning—just by *looking* at what's there. Then when kids go off to read, they can do so from an enlightened stance.

- **Use even more pictures when working with English language learners.** Children who are just learning to speak English need as many pictures as you can muster to help make new concepts and vocabulary more concrete. So front-load your lessons with opportunities for them to explore, examine, and discuss pictures of what they'll be learning.

- **Acknowledge graphic literature as a viable school and home genre.** Children of all ages love reading graphic literature, which is often comic, i.e., graphic novels and manga, and we mustn't downplay their role in children's literacy development.

  You can see why kids like them. They have cool graphics, they're usually part of a series, they can feel less imposing than page upon page of running text. In fact, it's often reluctant readers (or those who were once reluctant) who are their biggest fans. However, don't let the comic book appearance fool you—they're not all that easy to read and require a great deal of inferring.

  Kids should be allowed to read comic literature in our classrooms, as long as it's not *all* they read. What's more, we'd be wise to teach them how to read it.

continues

Visual Literacy Reading Strategies, *cont.*

- **Attune children to characters' facial expressions and body language.** Facial expressions and body language reveal a great deal about what a character is thinking or feeling. For example, in Margaret Rey's *Spotty*, Spotty's mom and Aunt Eliza (see Figure 9-5) are discussing whether or not Spotty—born to an all-white family of bunnies—should be allowed to attend Grandpa's birthday celebration. After all, warns Aunt Eliza, seeing Spotty like this would greatly upset Grandpa. Can you tell which is Spotty's mom and which is Aunt Eliza? Of course you can. Their facial expressions and body language are dead giveaways. Kids need to be encouraged to tune into visual information like this for how it can enhance their comprehension and enjoyment.

Figure 9-5. Page from Spotty

Fix-Up Strategies for Reading That Help Clarify *Words*

- Reread the sentence. You may say the word correctly the next time around.

- Read to the end of the sentence or even the sentence that follows. Sometimes this will give you the information you need to get the word from the context.

- Study the word. You might be able to apply the letter-sound information you know. Or you might recognize a prefix, suffix, or word root.

- Think about what makes sense. Maybe even try to substitute another word for one that's causing you trouble.

Fix-Up Strategies for Reading That Help Clarify *Ideas*

- Reread the confusing sentence or passage. Perhaps you read it too quickly the first time.

- Identify precisely what's confusing you. Do you know enough about the characters, where the story's taking place, the problem the main character is facing? Is the topic one you know little about? Recognize that different problems call for different solutions. So it's important to first identify the problem, and it's likely the solution will flow from there. See Figure 9-6 for some problem-solution scenarios.

- Consider whether one or more of the metacognitive strategies, such as *text structure*, *visualizing*, and *summarizing* might help. (See Chapter 10 for more on helping children acquire a repertoire of meta-cognitive strategies.)

If . . . Then . . .

If I'm having trouble . . .	Then I might try . . .
If I'm on the first chapter and I'm having trouble understanding what's happening . . .	reading the chapter over, slowing down a bit, thinking more about what's happening, or even reading on a little more to see if things become clearer.
If I'm having trouble keeping track of the characters . . .	starting a character web for the main ones where I list all I'm learning about each character and keep adding to it as I read.
If the story is taking place in a time period or place with which I'm unfamiliar . . .	reading up on the time period and location to beef up my background knowledge. I might record some of this information in my reading journal to see how it compares with what the author has written. Or I might sketch how I'm imagining the setting to look in my own mind.
If I get to the end of a passage and find I'm confused . . .	reading over the part that's giving me trouble or take a peek at the passage that follows to reorient myself.
If the meaning of a passage seems to hinge on a word with which I'm unfamiliar . . .	using contextual cues or word-related cues, such as affixes and word derivatives.
If the book I am reading has a lot of dialogue and I'm getting confused . . .	reading the dialogue aloud with different voices or slowing down to make sure I know which character is saying what.

Figure 9-6. "If . . . Then . . ." Scenarios

Teach Readers and Writers How to Infer

We infer all the time. We take an umbrella to work with us. We cross the street if we anticipate a passerby might not be trustworthy. We see a child smiling as she bounds up to a mature-looking woman at the train station and guess it's her grandma. We read in the paper that housing prices are holding steady and figure the stock market will go up that day. We make thousands of inferences every day!

Readers Infer

When we begin reading a short story and in the opening paragraph a horse-drawn carriage clippety-clops up cobblestone streets, we think, *Hmmm, not the twenty-first century.* As we read. "Maggie steps out, her brow furrowed." *Must be upset about something,* we think, as we piece together the clues the writer has planted for us. Reading is one big, satisfying act of inferring! The author tells us a lot, but the richness is between the lines.

However, all inferring does not require the same level of effort, and as teachers we need to know the difference. In contrast to the "effortless" reading of that story about Maggie in her carriage, there are times when readers have to make bigger inferential leaps to *keep* understanding. In these instances, the proficient reader intuitively knows she has to figure out something in the text that's become murky. Maybe the author didn't do a good job of making it clear. Maybe the reader doesn't have all the information she needs to make a decision or clarify what's puzzling her, so she has to intentionally draw on her prior knowledge (all her past experiences) and her background knowledge (her factual and procedural knowledge of the world) to pull up the information that might help.

For example, second-grader Isa was reading a nonfiction book on sea life. She read a detail about whales needing to come up for air every hour or so, but she didn't know why. Don't fish *live* in water? she wondered, puzzled. She was resourceful enough to pause and think back to the chapter opening and its details about fish gills vs. whales' blowholes. She activated other background knowledge about seals being mammals that nurse their young. Ah! She used this deliberate thinking to infer that whales are mammals, not fish, and that's why they need to come up for air.

Readers are required to make *conscious* inferences all the time. In *Why Don't Students Like School? A Cognitive Scientist Answers Questions About How the Mind Works and What It Means for the Classroom*, Daniel T. Willingham (2009) states:

> Reading comprehension depends on combining the ideas in a passage, not just comprehending each idea on its own. And writing contains gaps—lots of gaps—from which the writer omits information that is necessary to understand the logical flow of ideas. Writers assume the reader has the knowledge to fill in the gaps. (p. 23)

Children fill some of these gaps quite effortlessly when they have enough information to do so. But there are times when they're stumped. Perhaps they're just beginning the book and need to give themselves time to become oriented to the characters and the problems they're facing. Maybe they don't know the meaning of a word that's central to their understanding of the story and that's what's holding them back. In instances like these, where children's understanding of the story or information piece is flailing, we have to teach them to infer.

But how? How do we help a child combine what's *in the book* and *in his head* to arrive at new information? My advice is that when working with K–3 readers it's essential to make interfacing between book and head as concrete as possible. Here are some examples:

- **Thinking Aloud.** We need to make our thinking visible to students to help them understand what occurs when we *consciously* bring together what's in the book with what we know to figure out something that puzzles us. I sometimes use a book page icon with an arrow pointing to a line of text to represent "what's in the book" and a lightbulb to represent "what's in my head"

(Figure 9-7). I laminate these 9" × 11" sheets (see Appendix 16 online) and leave them on my easel so I can easily show kids when I'm doing each.

Let's say I'm reading Dan Yacarrino's *The Birthday Fish* (2005) and want to point out that Cynthia, who never wanted a fish in the first place—she desperately wanted a pony—asks the fish (who's turned out to be magical) if he'd like her to stop off at the store to get him something to eat on her

way to set him free. (That's the deal—she sets the fish free and he grants her wish for *two* ponies!) I might say, "That's so odd. How come all of a sudden Cynthia's being nice to the fish and is offering to get him food?"

And then, pointing to the book page icon on the easel, "Let's think for a moment about what's *in the book*." And so the children and I talk about (and find in the book) how up to now the *fish* has been asking Cynthia

Figure 9-7. Icons for "What's in the Book" and "What's in My Head"

to be careful—pleading with her to go more slowly so he doesn't bump around so much in his fish bowl, telling her to cross the street to avoid a menacing-looking cat, etc.—and now *she's* tending to his needs. Why?

Next we turn to the "in my head" icon to try to piece this puzzle together using all we know about stories having happy endings, about the character learning a lesson or becoming a kinder person, about times the children themselves have changed the way they felt about something. Here we're putting together what's in the book and what's in our head to arrive at a new conclusion about what's up with Cynthia.

In addition, these inferring icons can sit on the easel as a reminder to let kids in on our thinking. Or just point to one icon or the other as you work your way through something that puzzles you: "See (pointing to the page icon) I'm thinking about what the book said" or (pointing to the lightbulb) "now I'm using what's in my head." You want kids to realize how we deliberately, and often, need to make conscious inferences when we read.

♦ **We can use graphic representations and strategy sheets.** It's always helpful to offer students something tangible on which to hang their thinking. Graphic representations and strategy sheets can help. We can give children a strategy sheet like the one in Figure 9-8 where they're directed to use the information they've recorded in the "In the Book" column with information in the "In My Head" column to find the answer to something that puzzles them. (*Note:* We have to be mindful to not overdo our use of strategy sheets. Having children work out their thinking like this indiscriminately would likely interfere with their reading and their comprehension. We don't want that.)

A useful practice is to model these strategy sheets on chart paper to show kids how making inferences works as I did when reading Ben Kahn's "Cheeseheads" article in National Geographic's *Midwest Today* (2000). See Figure 9-9.

♦ **We can use picture books to teach inferring.** While children will need to infer with any book they read, it's also helpful to have a stash of books that particularly lend themselves to these demonstrations. Eve Bunting's *Sunshine Home* (2005) is one such book.

When seven-year-old Timmie visits his grandma in a nursing home for the first time, he realizes that both his Mom and Gram are trying hard to pretend nothing's wrong. But Timmie can sense (as can the reader) the sadness and anxiety that lies just below the surface by how his mother speaks in a "cheery and chipper" voice he's never heard before about how nice and clean the place is when it actually smells "like mouthwash, or the green bar that Mom hangs in the toilet bowl. The one that works for 500 flushes." Or when at dinnertime a nurse ties a bib around Gram's neck and she embarrassingly jokes that Timmie's dad should try using one to keep his ties clean. See the "Ten Books to Teach Inferring" box for some books you might use to teach kids how to infer.

Name _____   Date _____

Title: _____

Making Inferences

A Question I Still Have Is...

In the Book ➡	Something New	In My Head ⬅

Comprehension from the Ground Up © 2011 by Sharon Taberski (Heinemann Portsmouth, NH)

Figure 9-8. Three-Column Inferring Strategy Sheet

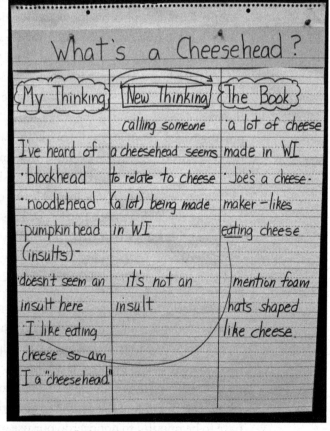

Figure 9-9. "Cheeseheads" Chart

Ten Books to Teach Inferring

- **Seven Blind Mice** by Ed Young
  A new take on the old Chinese tale of the three blind men and the elephant. As you read the story, ask students to use what they know based on the pictures and words to understand what the mice have encountered as well as what the message of the story might be.

- **Sunshine Home** by Eve Bunting
  A beautiful story about hard decisions, family, and being honest. When Timmie visits his grandmother in a nursing home for the first time, students can infer what each character is really feeling by paying attention to the author's descriptions and word choice.

- **The Skull Alphabet Book** by Jerry Palotta
  A creative book that takes students on a hunt to figure out 26 different mammal skulls from anteater to zebra. By looking at the pictures or reading the clues, students try to figure out to what animal the skull belongs. An added layer of fun and keen observation includes hidden facts and animal names within some of the illustrations.

- **My Lucky Day** by Keiko Kasza
  How does a pig "outfox" a fox? Read *My Lucky Day* to find out and, as you do, students will delight in the playful illustrations and enjoy figuring out what the pig is up to. Even then, they'll be surprised by the ending.

- **Animals Should Definitely Not Wear Clothing** by Judi Barrett
  In this playful classic, students use the illustrations and background knowledge to fully understand the words the author chose and the varying reasons why different animals should *definitely* not wear clothes.

- **In the Snow: Who's Been Here?**
  by Lindsey Barrett George
  William, Cammy, and their dog take a walk down a snow-covered sledding hill. While walking they see signs of animals that have been there before. Using these clues and background knowledge, students figure out what animals have passed through. The illustrations are realistic and spectacular.

- **The Memory String** by Eve Bunting
  A story about how a young girl's relationship to her new stepmother develops. Throughout the story, students can infer the characters' motivations to understand the story's message and beauty.

- **The Memory Coat** by Elvira Woodruff
  A moving story about immigration, family, and the strength of the human spirit. In this historical fiction picture book, students can infer how characters might feel and predict what they might do when things don't go as planned.

- **Smokey Night** by Eve Bunting
  Based on what happened during the Los Angeles riots, this is a story about how differences should not separate us and how there are many layers of people's emotions and reasons for their actions.

- **The Stranger** by Chris Van Allsburg
  Who is the stranger that Farmer Bailey hit with his truck one night? And why does summer seem to last one week longer on the Bailey's farm since the stranger arrived? Children try to infer these answers as you read this beautifully crafted story that blends fantasy with reality.

Writers Infer

While it's true that writers need to leave gaps in their writing to keep the writing from becoming overloaded with details and events, children in K–3 more frequently need encouragement to elaborate—to say more about what they're writing. Their tendency is to assume too much of the reader. And then at other times they include information that distracts from their central theme or message.

To help children find that balance between what to include and what to leave out, let them share pieces they've written with classmates during the "share" portion of the writing workshop. And also bring some of their stories to the mini-lesson time of day and, as a class, decide what else might also be included to more clearly communicate the information and ideas.

A child sits in the author's chair to read a piece. First, he shows the pictures, and then he begins to read. At the conclusion, classmates make comments and ask him questions. Now here's where the teaching comes in: You have to do two things. First, teach the children to be *specific* about what they liked or didn't like, and then to ask questions that really puzzle them.

Very often young children simply make comments—which is fine for starters—as long as you direct them to comment in ways that help the writer and the piece. Telling an author you "like the pictures" will not help move his writing along or even understand how his pictures and text complement one another. Writers need to know precisely what's going well so they can do it again.

What to Include and What Can Be Inferred   So how do writers subconsciously or deliberately leave "gaps" for their reader to fill in? For K–3 students, the "show, don't tell" maxim is a tangible way to teach them. If a writer pens, "Ben was sad when his puppy was sick," the reader feels cheated. On the other hand, *showing* Ben is sad lets the reader have the fun of inferring from the telling details: "Ben looked at his listless puppy on the couch and gently folded the plaid blanket up to the puppy's chin so she'd stay warm. His mom said softly, 'Puppy will be okay. We'll keep watch tonight.'"

Beyond revisiting "show, don't tell" in mini-lessons throughout the year, here are two powerful ways to help writers determine what information to include and what information to leave out for readers to infer:

+ **Have children read their piece to a friend.** Give them a check sheet with just a few prompts, such as: *What part was your favorite? Did you get the story's problem? Was there a section that went on too long? Did anything confuse you? Tell me about my character's personality. Do you know enough? Want to know more?*

+ **Ask a child to share his piece with the class to focus on a question you had as you read over the piece.** List a couple questions on chart paper and provide time for the children to discuss them and consider whether additional information would be helpful or distracting. Send the writer off to fix what he can.

Have Children Write About Their Reading

One surefire way to help children see and live the reading-writing connection is to create opportunities for them to write about what they're reading. This not only aligns with the recommendations of the Carnegie *Writing to Read* Report (see Chapter 4), it offers students some much needed downtime from their reading. Children can take a break from their reading and still engage in an activity that will enhance their reading experience and make them better comprehending readers.

When children write in response to their reading in the K–1 and 2–3 reading workshop as described in Chapter 4, they can reflect on and make sense of what they read. In addition, this tangible record of their reading is one they can reread, revise, and share with classmates.

However, when deciding how often to ask students to respond in writing, we need to weigh how much of their time we want diverted from reading itself. Since helping children acquire stamina for reading is my top priority, I make sure that children devote a healthy portion of the reading workshop to reading, just reading.

The frequency and type of written responses children make to text differs in K–1 and 2–3 classrooms. In kindergarten and first grade, children are just beginning to acquire both reading and writing skills, so it will take them longer to do both. Children's drawings often substitute for or supplement brief written responses (Figure 9-10). In second and third grade where children can write more fluently, it's possible for them to write more routinely about their reading, and perhaps jot some notes down daily. And even here, I encourage children, who wish to do so, to include illustrations that elaborate on their ideas and information (Figure 9-11). It just depends on the grade, the children, and my goals.

Figure 9-10. Reading Response Sheet

In any case, here are some questions to consider when making your decision:

+ **Am I giving children enough opportunity to read, or is too much of their independent reading time spent on other activities?** In *What Really Matters in Response to Intervention: Research-Based Practices*, Richard Allington (2009) advises:

> When it comes to comprehension while reading, volume is also critical. It is during high-success reading activity that readers have the opportunity to begin to consolidate all those separate reading skills and strategies. (p. 66)

We'd do well to heed this advice.

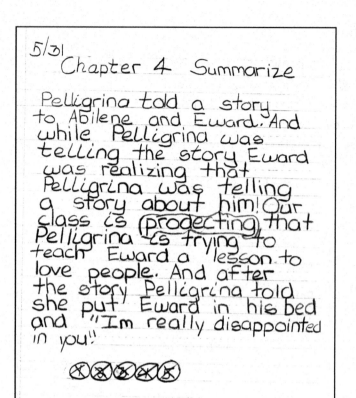

5/31
Chapter 4   Summarize

Pelligrina told a story to Abilene and Eward. And while Pelligrina was telling the story Eward was realizing that Pelligrina was telling a story about him! Our class is (prodecting) that Pelligrina is trying to teach Eward a lesson to love people. And after the story Pelligrina told she put Eward in his bed and "I'm really disappointed in you!"

Figure 9-11. Page from a Reading Notebook

• **Are the responses I ask children to make open-ended, or do they imply one right answer?** It's a good idea to develop a few response openers that encourage divergent thinking. Prompts such as "Imagine a different ending to the story…" "Did this book remind you of an event in your own life?" "What was the most fascinating information you learned, and why?" "How did the character change from the beginning of the story to the end…and suppose he hadn't?" These might be posted in the classroom for children to reference.

• **Do I model repeatedly what effective reading responses might look like?** Don't assume that children will know how to answer the prompts you suggest without your modeling them first and often. Children typically need to see responses modeled repeatedly to get the hang of what's being asked of them.

• **Do I give children time to share their responses with classmates and receive feedback?** Not only should children be given time at the end of the reading workshop to discuss what they've learned about themselves as readers and their favorite books and authors, they can also share written responses they've made to text. This helps to broaden their perspective and puts them in touch with the variety of responses they can make.

• **Do I vary the response requirements to provide for the individual needs of readers?** Regardless of the grade you teach you're likely to have a range of readers who will need reading responses tailored to their needs. You might ask children who are newer to reading to respond less frequently since it takes them longer and you want to make sure you've provided enough time for them to read. You might also give them a response sheet with a designated place for their pictures. More fluent readers might respond more frequently in a reading notebook.

Encourage Children to Write About Learning in the Content Areas

Children need to write throughout the day—not only during the writing and reading workshop. They should write about what they're learning in math, science, and social studies to make sense of new ideas and information and help commit them to memory.

Imagine your children are learning about different cloud formations and you give them a moment to reflect on how the clouds they see in the sky give a hint as to the weather. Or you're reading about colonial America and you give kids time to think and write about how life was different then than now. Or you just tell them to write about what they're learning during a math lesson. Linda Hoyt calls these cross-curricular scaffolds "power-writes." On an Internet posting that I saved, she states:

> When they [children] write in every subject area, every day, they apply the academic vocabulary related to the content, solidify understanding, and broaden the range of text types they control as a writer. Informational writing is a well-proven support system to effective reading and a survival skill for life.

I recommend providing children with content-area notebooks—composition notebooks with unlined pages—to record information about curricular topics. I prefer unlined pages because they give children more flexibility when describing their learning. When my class learned that Eastern Woodland Indians relied heavily on squash for survival, I brought in several varieties so kids could see the differences and determine which squash lasted the longest, an important consideration for native people in the absence of refrigeration. Figure 9-12 shows how the unlined pages allowed Alex to use the entire page to illustrate the squashes, creating a picture glossary of sorts. These notebooks can be sectioned off by subject area, or a teacher can decide to limit the notebooks to several broad topics that she and the children will explore in depth.

In my second-grade class, we sometimes focused on only two topics in our notebooks, e.g., Native Americans and birds. Since the composition notebook pages were blank, we could access them from either the front or the back. On the front cover of each notebook, we pasted a photograph of the "forest walk" (Figure 9-13) my class and I took on a trip to the Bronx Botanical Gardens to give children a sense of what the woodlands were like when inhabited by the Algonquin Indians. Then we flipped the notebook over and upside down and, on the back cover pasted a postcard of a bird to mark an entry into our bird information.

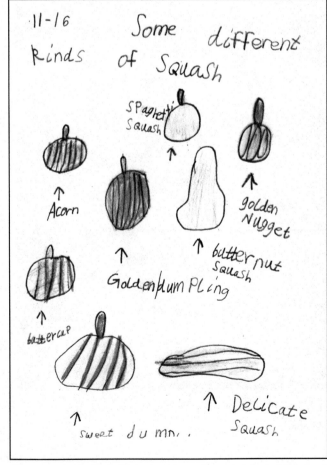

Figure 9-12. Alex's Squash in Her Content-Area Notebook

Content-area notebooks serve the same function as clustering books on the same topic, or packaging sets of guided reading books together as companions. We put ideas and information alongside one another in the hope that they interact—that their proximity helps students consolidate learning and make connections between ideas.

The sky's the limit in terms of what can go into content-area notebooks. You can ask children to:

+ write what they know about a topic before, during, or after an investigation
+ respond to a question (Figure 9-14)
+ write what they learned from a read-aloud
+ write about topic-related field trips (Figure 9-15)
+ write about a question they have
+ consider the meaning of some of the academic vocabulary (Figure 9-16)
+ illustrate what they're learning

Figure 9-13. Cover of Julian's Native American Notebook

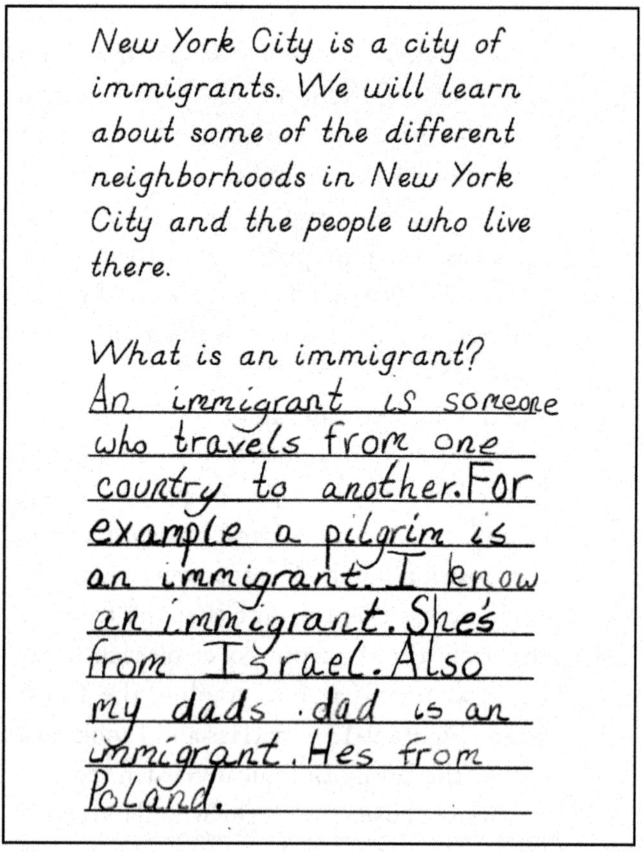

New York City is a city of immigrants. We will learn about some of the different neighborhoods in New York City and the people who live there.

What is an immigrant?
An immigrant is someone who travels from one country to another. For example a pilgrim is an immigrant. I know an immigrant. She's from Israel. Also my dads .dad is an immigrant. Hes from Poland.

Figure 9-14. Sabrina's NYC Content-Area Notebook Entry

Figure 9-15. Alex's "Learning" from Her Trip to See Kanata Dancers

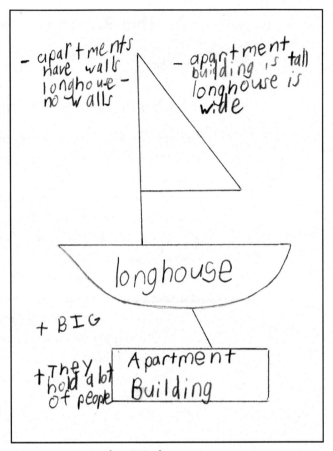

Figure 9-16. Anchor Words

Effective Practice: Using a Personalized Editing Checklist

What's a Personalized Editing Checklist?

Editing checklists typically list several items the teacher expects *all* students to address in their writing and check for correctness, e.g., use capital letters and periods at the end of sentences, look for spelling errors, and such. And herein lies the problem. These generic, grade-level checklists fail to differentiate among students. They hold *all* students accountable for *all* the listed items regardless of whether or not a student is ready and able to discern the task and assume this responsibility.

It makes little sense to require a student to put a capital letter at the beginning of a sentence and a period at the end when his writing indicates that he doesn't yet have a sense of what a sentence even is. Or to require a student who can't yet read basic high-frequency words to find the ones that are misspelled in his writing and correct them. However, when a student has demonstrated that he's capable of doing an editing task somewhat consistently, it makes all the sense in the world to now hold him accountable for doing it all the time. He "gets it" and with a bit more focus, effort, and practice, he'll be able to perfect this skill.

The personalized editing checklist I'm describing here, in contrast to the generic, grade-level checklist, holds a student accountable for *only* the items he has demonstrated he's capable of doing somewhat consistently and on his own. Its purpose is to differentiate editing tasks for students at various stages of writing development to help them fine-tune and consolidate the skills they're acquiring so they can move on to learn new ones.

A Note About the Editing Checklist

Except for item 1, the items on this checklist are more mechanical than creative. While I certainly post a chart listing the qualities of good writing that I hope children include in their piece and check for, I don't hold them accountable for acquiring them in the same way I'm describing my work with more mechanical edits. I want all students to strive for qualities of good writing in response to the mini-lessons I provide, but understand that these skills will develop over a long period of time and a writer seldom feels he has a grasp of them—they're something he's always working toward.

How Does This Checklist Work?

You'll notice that the circles (which are yellow) on the class editing checklist (Figure 9-17) are numbered to refer to the five editing items this checklist addresses. Also note that the editing circles on the inside pocket of each student's writing folder (Figure 4-8) are also yellow circles. This color and shape matching is to draw students' attention to the fact that the yellow circles in their folder (and later the numbers written on these circles) correspond to the editing tasks shown on the class editing checklist.

If a child "has" numbers 1, 2, 4, and 5 (as the folder in Figure 4-8 indicates), he is responsible for: 1—rereading for meaning; 2—underlining and correcting misspelled high-frequency words; 4—putting periods, question marks, and exclamation marks at the end of sentences; and 5—capitalizing the first word in a sentence, but not 3—circling and correcting other misspelled words (and here the number of words I ask students to correct varies from student to student).

When a child begins a piece, he enters "his numbers" in the editing bubbles (the circles) at the bottom of his lined sheet of writing paper that I've prepared (see Figure 9-18). If he's writing in a notebook or on a piece of paper where there are no premade bubbles, he makes his own by drawing five circles at the bottom of his page. Then he can write "his" numbers in the corresponding bubbles. Figure 9-11 shows a page from Amanda's reading response notebook where she's made her own editing bubbles at the bottom of the page and has entered 1, 2, 3, 4, and 5 inside the bubbles. However, if a child has only been assigned 1, 4, and 5, then these are the numbers she would write. Then after she completes the page, she reads over her writing to check for each editing item and crosses out the numbers in the bubbles at the bottom of the page to show she's edited for those items.

As children write longer pieces over several days, it's likely they'll have to revisit these editing items several times as they reread their piece. Therefore, I advise students to lightly pencil-in check marks for each rereading and editing, but then to indicate the final editing with a colored *X* or an asterisk inside the bubble. Having students edit only once at the end of a piece would give the mistaken impression that this is how editing occurs in real-life writing when, in fact, writers edit continually. It's a recursive process that often leads them to make substantive idea-related revisions.

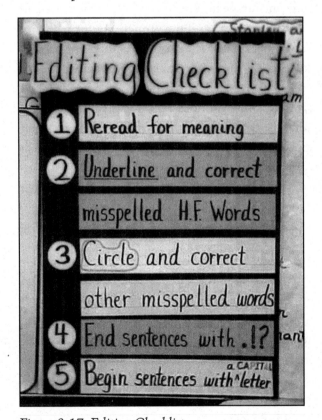

Figure 9-17. Editing Checklist

Figure 9-18. Writing Paper with Editing Bubbles Numbered

When and How Do I Assign Editing Numbers?

Although I introduce the class editing checklist early in the year once I establish my writing workshop routines, I hold off with the personalized checklists for a couple more months. Before I can assign personalized editing items, the children first have to do quite a bit of writing, and then I need to confer with each student to review the writing in his folder to see which editing items need addressing.

Here's how I assign editing items:

1. A couple of months into the school year when the children are familiar with the class checklist and I'm ready to begin assigning personalized editing items, I schedule a writing conference with each student. At the start of the writing conference, I place five yellow circle labels on the inside pocket of each child's writing folder. Then I look through his pieces of writing for evidence of how well he is naturally performing each item on the class editing checklist.

2. I assign the student personalized items by writing on the five yellow circles the item numbers that correspond to the item numbers on the class editing check-list. For example, if a student has demonstrated that he's somewhat consistent in rereading what's he's written to check for meaning (item 1 on the checklist in Figure 9-17), capitalizing the beginning of each sentence, and including end-of-sentence punctuation, I write 1, 4, and 5 on the circle labels on the inside of his writing folder.

   Although I would certainly encourage him to try his hand at items 2 and 3, I would consider these playful attempts and not something for which to hold him accountable. Eventual mastery of these skills requires me to provide ongoing and explicit instruction, and many more opportunities for the student to write and apply the skills he's trying to acquire.

   The absence of 2 and 3, or any other number, reminds me that I have to ratchet up my teaching a notch or two and alert the student to the fact that this is an area needing improvement. (Note that item 3—identifying mis-spelled words and then finding the correct spelling of the words in a dictio-nary, in books, or in environmental print—is a challenging task for most students. Thus, it's typically the last item a student is assigned. And even then, I don't require him to find the correct spelling of every misspelled word that's circled, only a couple.)

3. Although it takes me two or three weeks to meet with each student and assign individual editing items, they know that once I've met with them they're good to go. From then on they're responsible for performing each of these editing tasks on all pieces of writing they do. When I make strategy sheets, reading logs, and response sheets on the computer, I include the editing circles at the bottom of the page. But in situations where I can't, such as when a student is writing in a notebook or a piece of loose-leaf paper, students make their own editing bubbles at the bottom of the page.

4. Then, as I confer with students throughout the year, I'm on the lookout for how they're doing with their editing and call them on it when I think they're slacking off. Sometimes students ask for a conference because they think they're *ready* to be assigned a new item. So, in that case, we look over their writing to see if, in fact, they are. If their writing shows that they're somewhat consistent in performing a skill, then I'll write the number inside the yellow circle on the inside of their writing folder. The kids know that from here on in, they're responsible for doing what the items says.

One of the benefits of this personalized checklist is that it helps students transfer the skills they're learning in the writing workshop to each piece of writing they do throughout the day. Simply by making the five editing bubbles on the bottom of their response notebook pages, science sheet, homework paper, etc., and following the same procedure as during the writing workshop, they recognize editing for the meaning-making tool that it is and begin to apply it automatically to all their writing.

What If Kids Don't "Do" the Items They're Assigned?

The children understand that if they don't perform an editing task they're assigned, I'll remove the numbered circle and replace it with a blank one. And since they don't like to lose stickers—any kind of sticker!—they try to avoid this at all costs. However, they also know that they can easily earn the sticker back (and its accompanying responsibilities) by carefully attending to their writing.

What Are the Next Steps on the Class Editing Checklist?

You can differentiate this editing checklist even further for children who are more advanced in their editing and ready for more challenging tasks. For this phase 2 editing checklist you might use blue circle stickers instead of yellow ones and list items that are extensions of the phase 1 items. See the box on the next page for an example of how skills in phase 2 build on the phase 1 items: The first item in phase 1 and 2 relate to meaning, the second to spelling high-frequency words, the third to other misspelled words, the fourth to punctuation, and the fifth to capitalization.

How Does the Editing Checklist Relate to Comprehension?

The first item on any editing checklist should focus on *meaning*. Children need to make sure that what they've written makes sense. That they haven't inadvertently added or omitted words or ideas. That their ideas hang together as a cohesive whole. And by also making sure that what they've written is clear to their reader in terms of punctuation, capitalization, and spelling, they cross over the reading-writing line to where they're writing with an acute awareness of their reader. The next and natural step, of course, is to apply what they've learned from writing to their reading.

Phase 1 Checklist Items	Phase 2 Checklist Items
• Reread for meaning.	• Think through your writing before you start, e.g., make a table of contents, web your subtopics, set your purpose, etc.
• Underline and correct misspelled high-frequency words from the basic list.	• Underline and correct the more advanced misspelled high-frequency words from the advanced list.
• Circle and correct other misspelled words (from three to five words).	• Circle and correct other misspelled words (from five to eight words).
• Put a period, exclamation mark, or question mark at the end of sentences.	• Use more advanced punctuation such as commas, colons, semicolons, and quotation marks appropriately.
• Capitalize the beginning of sentences.	• Capitalize proper names, places, things, book titles, etc.

Effective Practice: Idea Books

What's an Idea Book?

An Idea Book is a teacher-made, spiral-bound booklet in which a student collects pictures, words, artifacts, lists, snippets of text, photographs, newspaper clippings, etc., that might one day jump-start a story, poem, or informational piece. Students keep their Idea Book in their personal writing tray with their Ta-Da Publishing Book and pieces of writing they're no longer working on.

I make the Idea Books by machine-binding together 25 pieces of copy paper, a cardstock front and back cover, and, for protection, an acetate sheet on top of both the front and back cover. Once children paste their photo on the cover, the Idea Books are finished and ready to go (see Figure 9-19).

Why Idea Books and Not Writer's Notebooks?

I choose to have students keep an Idea Book instead of a writer's notebook because Idea Books seem to be a more age-appropriate, idea-gathering tool for K–3 writers. My experience with writer's notebooks dates back to the 1980s when the idea of children keeping a writer's notebook was first conceived. The reasoning was that since adult authors and writers use notebooks to record, gather, reflect upon, and connect their ideas, why not give students access to the same tool?

Many years ago I tried to implement writer's notebooks with my second-grade students. No matter how hard I tried to get these seven- and eight-year-olds to mill through their entries to make connections and find something of significance to write about, they weren't buying. They preferred a more playful approach. (Note this page in Figure 9-20 from Madison's Idea Book where she lists and illustrates some mostly whimsical topics she may want to write about—"The Human Dog," "The Automatic Soccer Ball," "The Penguin Who Could Talk.")

My kids wanted to begin a lot of pieces and *end* them. They wanted to staple together papers in an assortment of colors and sizes to make books—and a lot of them. They wanted to illustrate the books. They wanted to gather a group of friends to write a "series" of books, each writing a different book in the series. (Step aside—Mary Pope Osborne!) This type of writing didn't mesh with the more

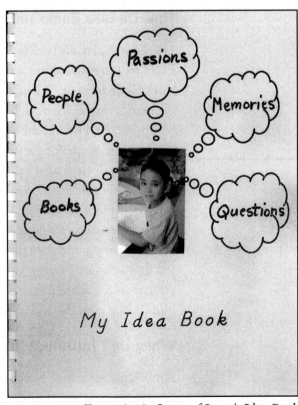

Figure 9-19. Cover of Jason's Idea Book

Figure 9-20. Madison's Idea Book Topics

reflective and substantive pieces that typically grow out of writer's notebooks.

Keeping a writer's notebook and then mining it for that gem that might eventually be published and celebrated required more stamina, investment, and delayed gratification than either my students or I could muster. But don't get me wrong—the writer's notebook can be a great tool for older students. For a helpful and beautifully crafted book on using a writer's notebook with upper-elementary-age students consult Aimee Bruckner's *Notebook Know-How: Strategies for the Writer's Notebook* (2005).

For K–3 writers, I harness the power of their passion to collect things. My goodness, most youngsters have been happily collecting rocks, sea shells, marbles, and baseball cards for years. The Idea Book, as I conceive of it, resembles the child's cherished shoebox or top drawer that houses a prized collection. It is a place to gather ideas and store them in one trove to go to whenever they need inspiration for what to write. However, the developing and drafting occur on sheets of paper in their writing folder.

How Do Idea Books Impact Student Writing?

Do children actually turn to these Idea Books over time? You bet. A child is far more likely to write well about a topic he knows and cares about than one in which he shows little interest. When a child is interested, even passionate about a topic, he's likely to bring experiences, background knowledge, vocabulary, and voice to a piece of writing. And he's far more likely to work hard at making it better.

In addition, making entries in an Idea Book gives kids something to do when they're plumb tired of writing and drained from the arduous work of composing. They can set aside their writing and peruse their Idea Book, add to it, and ponder their next piece of writing. Writers do this, you know. They move back and forth between drafting, jotting ideas for a newly conceived piece, editing, drafting some more, rereading, and then perhaps thinking of ways to refine the topic idea they jotted down earlier. Writing doesn't progress in a straight line from the start of one piece to its conclusion. For the children, jotting ideas in an Idea Book is the start, the middle, and even the end of this important process.

When Do I Introduce the Idea Books?

After children's first burst of enthusiasm for writing subsides—that is, after they've written about their summer-time experiences, the problem of "I have nothing to write about" surfaces. Then I need to help them realize that they do, in fact, have plenty of things to write about. We just need to figure out what they are!

Until the Idea Books are ready (I often ask parent volunteers to make them), I give each student a Topic List sheet (see Figure 9-21 for Madison's and Appendix 17 online for a reproducible) to accompany my initial mini-lessons on topic selection. I copy these Topic List sheets on colored paper so that they're easily distinguishable from the "white" pieces of writing in students' folders.

However, no matter how clear I think I'm being about children not having to write about each and every topic on the list, that these are simply ideas they *may* want to consider, there are still many who go through this list item by item, writing about and checking off every topic they listed. Perhaps the fact that it's a *list* throws them. After all, when their moms and dads make shopping lists, they buy all the items on the list, not just some of them! Not so with this list. Kids need to be selective. It's a good reminder for me that there's so much for kids to learn about topic selection and so much for me to teach.

After working with Topic Lists for several weeks, it's time to transition to Idea Books. Children are usually quite excited to receive their Idea Books since they've sensed something special in the air by the flow of parent volunteers with questions about how to put the books together.

> Name **Madison** Date **9/15**
>
> *Topic List*
>
> 1. friends
> 2. favorites
> 3. stores
> 4. family
> 5. camp
> 6. friends and family
> 7. poetry
> 8. sharks
> 9. school

Figure 9-21. Madison's Topic List Sheet

What Goes into Idea Books?

Basically anything that can be written, drawn, or pasted can go in the Idea Book. Here are some of the main categories:

+ *Pictures*—Children frequently draw pictures in their Idea Books to represent things they know a lot about or things they're interested in learning. Sometimes, the pictures are statements of things they enjoy doing, important people in their lives, or topics that excite them. As they draw, they elaborate and include details about the people or topics. Hopefully, if they ever decide to write about that topic, these details will make their way into their written pieces.

+ *Word Lists*—Sometimes during a mini-lesson on topic selection, I explain to students that writers often keep lists of words that interest or appeal to them because of how they sound or look, or because of the memories they elicit. Just one little word may trigger a story, poem, or informational piece. *Pomegranate, splatter, mischievous*—you never know.

+ *Topic Lists*—Children can keep genre-specific topic lists for the various genres they may want to write, e.g., poems, stories, informational pieces (Figure 9-24).

+ *Snippets*—Students sometimes write short passages in their Idea Book just to try an idea out. Or they can write a memorable sentence or passage from a book they've read, or part of a conversation they've overheard.

+ *Artifacts*—Children often bring in two-dimensional artifacts from places they've visited or ones representing special times they've had, e.g., a ticket stub from a basketball game, a wild violet from a walk with their mom, or a postcard from Disney World.

+ *Photographs*—The photos children bring from home can be great story starters. Sit alongside a child and ask him to talk about one of his pictures, and chances are that within minutes, he'll have a story he's eager to write.

Do I Ever Direct Students' Idea Book Entries?

Absolutely. There are many times when I want children to follow up on a mini-lesson I've given by working in their Idea Book. It may revolve around a formal genre unit or support a mini-lesson on how to use the Idea Book.

Here's an example: During the reading workshop my class and I were considering how a character's personality traits impact a story's outcome, and reading books with strong, memorable characters, such as Mary Hoffman's *Amazing Grace* (1997), William Steig's *Brave Irene* (1998), and Kevin Henkes' *Lily's Purple Plastic Purse* (1996), to fuel our discussion. Then during the writing workshop a couple weeks later, I reminded students that they need to focus attention on the personal qualities of the fictional and real-life characters they choose to write about.

On chart paper I demonstrated that if I decide to write about someone I know well or find fascinating, I would first want to:

+ List all the words I can think of that describe him or her.
+ Identify and circle the one that most characterizes that person.
+ Then think about situations when this character trait shined through.

Note: I delay addressing writing strategies that are reciprocal to reading strategies, such as characterization, organization, and word choice, until we've worked with them in reading for several weeks, rather than addressing these topics concurrently in both the reading and writing workshop. This allows students a chance to try out these strategies in reading before having to produce them themselves in writing.

Figure 9-22 is a sample of the graphic organizer I give children to paste in their Idea Book. It includes a web hub for them to write the character's name, lines to list words that describe this character, and a "one time" and "another time" web to help them think through two occasions when this character exhibited that quality. (Jason is writing about his friend Jacob's "playfulness.") Figure 9-23 shows a second page where students draw a scene related to their "one time" and "another time" recollection (see Appendix 18 online). I'm not concerned with students recording

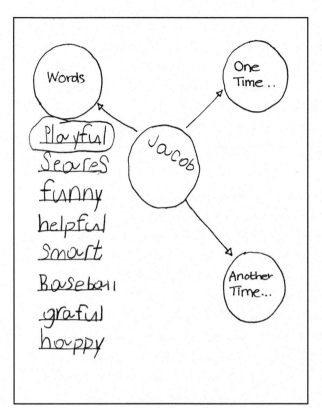

Figure 9-22. *Jason's Idea Book Web About Jacob*

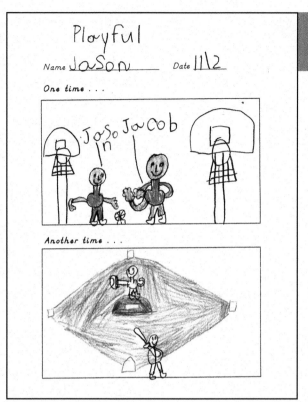

Figure 9-23. *Sheet Two Related to Jason's Idea Book Writing About Jacob*

their ideas in writing just yet. I first want them to rehearse and elaborate upon their ideas by drawing them. Writing their ideas in words comes later.

Anything Else I Should Know?

There are probably *many* other things you should know about Idea Books, which I'm confident you'll discover once you give them a try! Here are a couple of additional things to keep in mind:

- **Encourage students to turn to the Idea Books.** One of advantages of Idea Books is that they provide students with a meaningful writing activity when they're in-between pieces. It's not unusual for some students to work more quickly than others and to be finished with a piece or an assignment before other students. By having an Idea Book to turn to, a student always has something to do that's productive and will lead to better writing. But initially, we need to keep cheerleading students to use them—so they really and truly know we consider it a good use of time.

- **Repeatedly point out patterns in books and writing.** As I said at this chapter's outset, young children seek out patterns as they make sense of their world. Idea books, mini-lessons, read-alouds—use all these practices to celebrate with students the patterns you see between the steps of writing and the steps of reading. Over time, they will follow your path, much like Hansel and Gretel followed those moonlit white pebbles home!

By wondering aloud about all the decisions authors must have made as they organized their ideas—from deciding what information to include and what to leave out to deciding on a character's name—and by declaring when the author might have missed an opportunity for clarity, we help children see that writers the world over have to work as hard as they do to create readable books.

+ **Graze the Idea Books for timely mini-lessons.** My mini-lessons often grow out of what I observe students doing in their Idea Books. For example, I once noticed that the items children listed as possible topics for poems were very broad. (See Figure 9-24 for Jason's list.) Therefore, I decided to show children how they could write better if their topics were smaller. However, many of them initially mistook "smaller" to mean "in size." So the "dogs" became "cats" and smaller mammals. (You can laugh!)

After clarifying this, students then went on to list narrower, more specific topics that would lead to more detail and with that a better image for the reader to hold on to. Figure 9-25 shows one of the revised lists where "Chocolate" became "Reeses," "New York City" became "Yorkville" (a neighborhood on Manhattan's upper eastside), and "My Cousins" became "My Crazy Cousins."

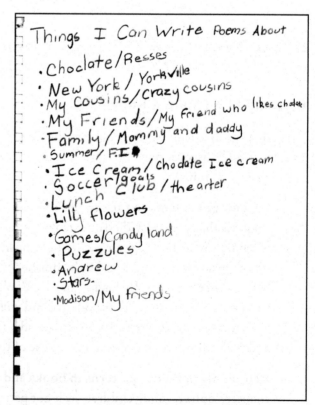

Figure 9-24. List of Topics for Poems

Figure 9-25. List of Narrowed Down Topics for Poems

Effective Practice: Ta-Da Publishing Books

What Are Ta-Da Publishing Books?

Ta-Da Books are blank books in which students publish four or so pieces of writing over the course of the year. I named these publishing books after the TADA! Youth Theater in New York City where one of my students was taking an after-school class. The minute I heard "Ta-Da!" I knew it would be the perfect name for our celebratory publishing books. Figure 9-26 shows the cover of Julia's book.

The Ta-Da Books have a sturdy hardcover, and their 8.5" x 11" dimensions provide room enough for children's handwritten pieces. (I order one for each student from Treetop Publishing, reasonably priced at under $3.00.) The students keep their Ta-Da Book in their personal writing tray along with their Idea Book and pieces of writing they're no longer working on.

How Do I Get Started with the Ta-Da Books?

The first entry in my students' Ta-Da Books is usually a personal narrative, which we start to publish in early October. Here's why: During the first few weeks of school when I'm introducing the writing workshop (see "The First Few Weeks of the Writing Workshop" box), I don't have time to guide students through a formal genre study. Therefore, I have students write about anything they want, and most of them just naturally choose to write about themselves, their family and friends, and experiences they've had. After a couple of weeks into the writing workshop, they've accumulated quite a few personal narratives in their writing folder.

The mini-lessons I offer in these few weeks leading into the Ta-Da Book publishing generally focus on getting the kids to "say more" or, conversely, moving them away from writing "bed-to-bed" stories to becoming more specific about a particular part of a larger experience, e.g., "It's better to write about the ostrich pecking grain from your hand—how it looked up close and how the experience made you feel—than to try to include everything that happened from the time you arrived at the zoo until you exited the gate to leave." If I notice that students' ideas are scattered and lack organization, I try to point this out as well.

Figure 9-26. Cover of Julia's Ta-Da Book

The First Few Weeks of the Writing Workshop

- I start the year by asking children to write an introductory piece about themselves, as a kind of "getting to know you" activity. The children can either write an "all about" piece where they really do tell all about themselves—their family, fun things they like to do, their favorite subject in school, etc., or they can select one thing about themselves, such as a recent family move to a new town or their all-time favorite thing to do for fun. However, if their favorite thing involves computer games, I explain that this is an "off-limit" topic and have them choose another.

- I call on three children a day to sit in the author's chair and share their pieces at the end of the workshop. Their classmates question them about what they've written or anything else they'd like to know. It takes about two weeks before everyone has been formally "introduced."

  After each child shares, I collect this first piece to keep as a baseline writing sample, and I make a copy for him to keep in his folder. It's fun and informative to periodically have students compare their current writing with what they did at the start of the year. Sometimes they're pleased with their improvement, and other times it serves as a wake-up call to be more careful and attentive to their work.

- Then, the following day, I schedule a writing conference with the three children who shared the day before, i.e., the children who shared on Monday will confer with me on Tuesday, etc. During this first writing conference, I give each child a blue writing folder, an assessment notebook, and a topic list, and

I explain how to use them. (See Chapter 4 for a description of materials I include in this folder.)

We also discuss how they feel about writing in general, what genres they prefer, what topics they like to write about, and I record this information in their assessment notebook. It takes about two weeks for me to meet with all the students.

- During these first few weeks, my mini-lessons are generic and often focus on what I see the students doing or struggling with as they write. For example I might address workshop routines and materials, writing about what you know, keeping to one topic, or narrowing a topic rather than writing bed-to-bed stories.

- I also read children books that sound like personal narratives, such as *School Bus* by Donald Crews, *When the Relatives Came* by Cynthia Rylant, and *Every Friday* by Dan Yaccarino. Since personal narratives are generally children's default genre, I want to give them some noteworthy examples.

Note: I call this genre *personal narrative*, not *memoir*, because that's what the pieces are. To me, *memoir* is a rather sophisticated form of writing by someone who has lived years and looks back over his life to cherry-pick significant events and tie them together. *Memoir* has a reflective "layer" or perspective that doesn't sit naturally in K–3 development, at least not with the younger writers in these grades. I've met teachers who use the term *memoir* because their kids like the fancy, grown-up connotation, but I prefer to call these writings what they are— personal narratives.

Here's the first page of a personal narrative (and its accompanying illustration) that Julia published in her Ta-Da Book about a new apartment into which she and her family had recently moved (Figure 9-27). Looks pretty good, right? Her ideas go together, the piece has a beginning, middle, and end. However, Julia's initial version of this piece was quite disorganized. She jumped around from facts about her bedroom, to the living room, to the kitchen, back to her bedroom, and then to stating that she lives on the twenty-second floor!

Name Julia _____ Date _____

Title: My New Apartment

My new apartment is big. I like my new apartment better than my old one. When we moved in, it was a mess. The floor I live on is 22B. I live with my family.

The livingroom is big. There is a big T.V. in the livingroom. We watch T.V. in the livingroom. There is a big couch and table in the livingroom. We eat in the livingroom. There is a little table in the livingroom where we sometimes eat on.

This is my livingroom.

Figure 9-27. Pages from Julia's Ta-Da Book

During a conference I explained to Julia that she needed to cluster her ideas and arrange them in a more logical order (a difficult task for students to undertake once their ideas are down on paper). Therefore, I gave her an "Organizing Sheet" (see Appendix 19 online) on which to rewrite the piece, sentence by sentence, and then had her cut the sentences apart and reorder them so that her piece would make better sense.

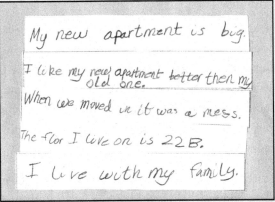

My new apartment is big.

I like my new apartment better then my old one.

When we moved in it was a mess.

The flor I live on is 22B.

I live with my family.

Figure 9-28. Julia's Reorganized First Paragraph

After Julia did this, she copied her new version onto a sheet of paper, which she then cut and pasted in her Ta-Da Book. And then she illustrated her text.

During the first few weeks of school I don't focus on teaching qualities of good writing during mini-lessons, such as word choice and organization because I'm introducing the writing workshop routines and materials and addressing basic writing skills. However, I will often select several students to work more closely with on one quality of good writing (as I did with Julia when I helped her reorganize her piece) to help them get a few steps ahead of the others. This gives me some samples of student writing to show the rest of the kids later in the year as they write and revise their pieces.

To introduce the Ta-Da Books, I show children a blank publishing book and explain how it works. I invite them to choose one of their personal narratives to publish, and I explain that they are going to revise and edit this piece. Of course, I use my mini-lessons from this point on to show them how.

Early in the year I'm just looking for their pieces to make sense, and I help them iron out the rough spots as we confer. After they have a draft they like and do whatever editing they can, they copy it over, and then I help them paste it into their books.

Frankly, it often makes me anxious at the start of the school year to think of all there is for me to teach and for the students to learn. I have to keep reminding myself that we have the year together, and that it's better to do fewer things deeply and well than to race through many items in a superficial way.

How Does the Actual Publishing Work?

After I've pasted a photograph of each child on the front cover of his or her Ta-Da Book, labeled it "Ta-Da! Julia's Publishing Book," and placed it in a plastic bag to protect it during months of use, I select two or three children to begin our first round of publication. By staggering children's publication start-ups, I keep it manageable, avoiding the chaos that would ensue with 25 children trying to begin publishing at once. In addition, this provides a model for the rest of the students for what they will soon get to do when they publish.

I meet with these first-round students at the conference table to explain the process:

- First, copy the final draft onto lined paper. (I've prepared this paper so that when the paper is trimmed and pasted onto the page, there's room left on the book page for a decorative border.)

- Next, trim each page of text or paragraph/section to fit onto the Ta-Da Book page and paste them in the book, making sure to leave room for illustrations. (*Note:* Paste the first page of the piece on page 5 of the Ta-Da Book. Page 2 of the book is the dedication page, page 3 is for the table of contents, page 4 is temporarily left blank, but will later contain an illustration to accompany page 5, which is the right-hand page and the first page of text.)

- Lastly, illustrate the piece with crayons or colored pencils. (I don't allow children to use markers since they show through to the backside of the page.)

Seeing their classmates' Ta-Da Books take shape excites and motivates children who are working at a slower pace to finish revising and editing (mostly editing at this point in the year) so they, too, can get to the "fun" part. By the end of October, all students will have published their personal narrative in their Ta-Da Book.

What Other Genres Are Published in the Ta-Da Books?

In addition to the first personal narrative Ta-Da Book entry, the children publish three more pieces at the conclusion of each formal genre study. These include:

1. several poems, written during a poetry study,

2. an informational piece on a topic we're studying in science or social studies, and

3. one additional piece, such as a persuasive text or pourquoi tale. We never know exactly what form or genre this last entry will take until we stumble upon it during our studies.

For example, a few years ago my second graders happened upon a topic as we were studying birds that led to a persuasive writing unit. The children read about John Audubon and how he spent a lifetime painting birds of North America so that people could enjoy and appreciate these amazing creatures. Then "the other shoe dropped" when they realized that he had to kill them first! Well, this stirred up quite a controversy, with students taking sides—"yes," it was okay for him to kill birds for this greater cause or "no," birds should never be killed. The irony was, that as these young animal-rights advocates were making impassioned pleas on the birds' behalf, they would soon be marching down to the lunchroom to chow down chicken nuggets! (Naturally I kept this observation to myself.)

Commentary: While four formally published pieces may seem a meager number when compared with the number many school districts insist their students publish each year, I truly can't imagine doing more and reaching the same level of quality. My more than 35 years of working with student writers tells me it isn't healthy to rush from one writing unit to the next to the next. Not only does this compromise the quality of student work and put extreme pressure on everyone (teachers, children, families) to get through these units, it fails to provide what I like to think of as "downtime" writing and opportunities for students to explore topics about which they're most interested in writing. Rushing takes the playfulness out of the writing—neither wise nor healthy.

It takes time to write well—a lot of time—so if we want students to experience the challenges and rewards of writing, we must allow them to go through the process of sitting for a day or so not knowing what to write and feeling the exuberance when an idea finally "arrives." (For that's how it really feels—like a gift, one you've worked hard for, but a gift nonetheless.)

If we want students to understand that a text's organization is central to both writing (you're writing so someone can understand you) and reading (you want to learn what someone else has to say), we need to give them time to work with their piece and experiment with how it should go. This doesn't happen in a few minutes or a few days. It happens through a great deal of hard work, hearing what classmates have to say, trying it out, scrapping that attempt, and trying again—and perhaps yet again. We need to help our youngest writers learn this valuable stick-with-it process.

Do Students Write Other Pieces in Addition to the Ones They Publish?

While only four pieces of writing are formally published in the Ta-Da Book, there's a lot of other writing and teaching that goes on as well. Just as we know students need to read widely to improve their reading, the same holds true for their writing.

Children need to write voluminously if they hope to get better at it. The time children spend writing and publishing their Ta-Da Book pieces, together with the teaching units involved, accounts for just about half of all the writing they do throughout the year. So in a typical school year, five months are spent on Ta-Da Book pieces and the other five months are devoted to children's "own-choice" writing.

Not only is it important that students be encouraged to write volumes, it's equally important that we give them plenty of whole- and small-group lessons and one-to-one conferences on how to write. Along with voluminous writing go daily mini-lessons to accompany the Ta-Da Book genres and other pieces they write between formal units. There's so much to learn and do, and it's so much fun to see all of what needs to be done surface as kids engage in lots of writing.

How Do I Integrate Ta-Da Books into the Day-to-Day Writing Workshop?

Thankfully, we've moved away from the regimented writing assignments of old where children selected and rehearsed a topic on Monday, drafted it on Tuesday and Wednesday, revised and edited it on Thursday, and published it on Friday. A healthy and rigorous workshop is more mixed, with children working in the various stages of the writing process at different times.

Working with Ta-Da Books actually helps with the management of the writing workshop. When children have completed a segment of the writing process, e.g., drafting or editing, or simply need a break from the more rigorous work of first draft writing and revision, they can turn to their Ta-Da Books to finish an illustration, work on the end pages, etc. And don't for a minute think that when they're illustrating a published piece, they're not considering what a classmate recommended they do to fix their story or thinking ahead to what to write next. After all, it's a process.

Keep in Mind Your Students' Capabilities

Obviously, this Ta-Da Book effective practice isn't well suited for kindergarten students. Some first graders might even have difficulty with it. You know your students and their capabilities, so follow your instinct.

That said, I urge you to consult Ann Marie Corgill's *Of Primary Importance: What's Essential in Teaching Young Writers* (2009) where she dedicates an entire chapter to "Publishing Possibilities: Tips and Techniques for Sharing, Showcasing, and Celebrating Student Writing." In this chapter, Corgill describes how to publish self-portrait collages, poetry posters, class poetry anthologies, how-to books, content-area museum displays, and many other genres. Her book won't disappoint and will provide a multitude of publishing options for your more novice writers.

Repertoire of Strategies
Teach in a Simplified, Sensible Way

CHAPTER 10

"The cumulative effect of teaching comprehension strategies from kindergarten through high school is powerful ... Each year teachers build on strategies the kids already understand, emphasizing a common language and how to use strategies flexibly with a variety of texts. We can teach all the strategies in developmentally appropriate ways to kids at all grade levels." (p. 29)

—Stephanie Harvey and Ann Goudvis in *Strategies That Work: Teaching Comprehension to Enhance Understanding, Second Edition* (2007)

Repertoire of Strategies and Comprehension

When you think about relaxing with a good book, the notion of your brain making all sorts of mental calculations isn't part of the picture. That's because as proficient readers, so much of what we do is as automatic as breathing. But the fact is readers, young and old alike, are using many cognitive strategies as they take in a text.

For some children, learning to read—and read well—occurs easily. Reading is intuitive, and all the strategies we talk about, whether inferring, rereading, or visualizing, seem to kick into play naturally. But for many others, learning to read well is a harder climb. They need more time and much more explicit modeling of what it means to read for understanding.

In addition, no matter how well versed children are reading fiction, they will likely need to apply strategies to informational texts or fictional texts that are conceptually challenging. For these types of texts, children benefit from us providing them with a repertoire of comprehension strategies they can draw on. For children to acquire and refine these strategies under our guidance and support, we need to make time to first introduce them and demonstrate how they're used.

At times, and especially at first, strategy instruction simply involves a teacher showing children what she does. The teacher names the strategy and demonstrates how it works, without having students try it themselves. In these instances, she's "getting the strategy out" in anticipation of more formal and focused instruction as students move up in the grades.

At other times, the teacher's approach is more comprehensive and spans a few instructional settings. For example, she might demonstrate for the class a strategy within a strategy unit itself, then in small groups or individually support students'

Differentiating Between Skills and Strategies

Although the terms *skills* and *strategies* are often loosely defined and used interchangeably—as I've done throughout this book—it's helpful in this repertoire of strategies chapter to define each term more precisely. In their February 2008 *Reading Teacher* article, "Clarifying Differences Between Reading Skills and Reading Strategies," Peter Afflerbach, P. David Pearson, and Scott G. Paris propose:

> Reading strategies are deliberate, goal-directed attempts to control and modify the reader's efforts to decode text, understand words and construct meanings of text. Reading skills are automatic actions that result in decoding and comprehension with speed, efficiency, and fluency and usually occur without awareness of the components or control involved. (p. 368)

Simply put—skills are automatic and strategies are deliberately applied. Take, for example, putting a capital letter at the beginning of a sentence, a skill we expect students to be able to do. However, before the skill is mastered, a student employs various strategies such as noting end-of-sentence punctuation (as a reminder to begin a new sentence with a capital letter) or rereading a text upon completion to make sure she hasn't overlooked any instances where she should have beginning-of-sentence punctuation.

What was initially a difficult task for a nascent writer becomes automatic over time with instruction and practice. One might say that at this later stage, the writer is skilled at capitalizing the first word at the beginning of a sentence, and no longer has to deliberately consider whether or not she's beginning a new thought or note the presence of any end-of-sentence punctuation that indicates a new sentence to follow. She has moved from deliberately applying a punctuation strategy to becoming skilled in its use.

efforts to try it out (perhaps even giving them a strategy sheet on which to record their thinking), and then reconvene in a whole-group meeting to process how it went. Or a teacher may show students how to refine their use of strategies and how to move from strategy to strategy within a given text. (We'll examine these three facets of comprehension strategy instruction later on in this chapter.)

Decide on a Repertoire of Strategies to Teach

Here are six strategies I consider essential to children's developing reading comprehension:

- Set a purpose for reading.
- Access and use prior knowledge.
- Consider text structure.
- Ask questions and wonder.
- Visualize to experience.
- Summarize to determine importance.

I choose to focus on these six strategies because students don't have a hard time understanding why they're important or how to use them as they read. They're kid-friendly.

These strategies may not be identical to the reading strategies you're currently focusing on, and that's okay. The six highlighted here are no doubt part of the DNA of whichever strategies or terms you or your school select. The important thing is to target a small, core set of strategies over the course of the elementary grades and present them deeply and well in age- and grade-appropriate ways. On school visits I've seen schools try to work with overly complex, ambitious lists of ten or more strategies—to say nothing of lengthy writing strategy lists—and this doesn't seem productive or in synch with elementary-age students.

Set a Purpose for Reading

Children don't initially realize that we read texts differently depending on our purpose. The world of print is new to them and often quite scary. At the start, they're so bent on figuring out each and every word, each and every sound, that they don't yet see the whole. However, as we read to them and with them during read-aloud and shared reading, and as their reading develops and matures, we can demonstrate why it's important to set a purpose for reading and show them how it's done.

We need to expose children to a variety of genres, and then prompt them to consider why they're reading a particular story, poem, or piece of nonfiction. Is it to get information? Is it to examine how an author's language creates powerful and memorable images?

Monitoring for Meaning and Making Inferences

I don't include monitoring for meaning or making inferences as separate strategies in the repertoire because they're *thinking* processes that are pervasive across the strategies, and as such are facets of *each*, like breathing is to walking or resting or talking. We breathe no matter what we do.

Readers need to *monitor* their reading for meaning. They need to listen for clicks and clunks as signals for whether they sufficiently understand the information and ideas a text conveys or whether they should read just to get back on track. The same is true of *making inferences*. Readers must fill in the gaps the author left, knowing that unanswered questions prompt readers to use what's in the book and what's in their head to draw new conclusions.

Our job is to show students how to routinely monitor their reading for meaning and make conscious inferences when they *expect* a text to pose problems or when something is confusing. When reading, this step of anticipating or expecting a problem often arises early on; so in this instance, see how monitoring is a facet of *set a purpose for reading?* To address monitoring our confusion or misunderstandings, we think aloud and demonstrate how we're always deciding whether or not to interrupt our reading to get our thinking back on track. We may be reading about penguins and realize that one book says there are 19 kinds of penguins and another says there are 17. Which is it? (In this case, this question posing as we monitor our understanding is actually a facet of *ask questions and wonder.*) This may lead us to consult an additional book or two or Google it to see if we can break the tie, or we may put the question on hold feeling that it doesn't really matter—17 or 19—they're in the same ballpark.

Or let's say we finish reading aloud the short article "Cheeseheads" from National Geographic's *Midwest Today* (that we've projected on an interactive whiteboard so kids can see the text and the text features) and we still don't know what a "cheesehead" is. The article describes the triangular foam hat (that looks like a block of Swiss cheese) Green Bay Packers fans wear to cheer their team on. It explains that Wisconsin produces more cheese than any state in the country, and that as a young boy John Widmer, a cheesemaker from a long line of cheesemakers, loved cheese so much that he would devour a chunk of blue cheese like it was a chocolate bar. Yet, the text doesn't state explicitly what a "cheesehead" is. We've heard of *blockhead, noodlehead, puddinghead*—all derogatory terms—but somehow since *cheesehead*, the article's title, is never used disparagingly, we conclude it must be an affectionate nickname for someone from Wisconsin, a state whose livelihood depends on cheese production. Here, notice that the monitoring and inferring functions are used as a facet of the access and use prior knowledge strategy.

Throughout our efforts to support the development of children's inferring skills, we let kids know that good readers actively wonder about things that are not explicitly answered in the text. So we have to combine what's in the book with what's in our head to answer questions we pose. Helping children draw new conclusions should be demonstrated throughout all components of balanced literacy and as we address each and every repertoire strategy. Clearly, monitoring for meaning and inferring are part of *all* our strategy work with students.

Children need us to orchestrate situations where they're exploring various purposes for reading a text as well as reading different types of texts. We need to help them see that, depending on our purpose, we read texts differently. For example, I might demonstrate how I:

+ Flip through a cookbook making a choice based on just the ingredients list, but then read the entire recipe carefully once I've made the choice.

+ Read the first page of the newspaper. Headlines first, then the first few paragraphs of each story, and finally choose one to read all the way through. I tell them how my husband has a whole different approach.

+ Read a poem quickly at first to get the gist of it, and then reread it several more times so I understand it better.

+ Read captions and sidebars in nonfiction before the main text to give myself an overview and background knowledge of what's to come.

In other words, we have to show students tried-and-true, effective approaches for locating information, but we also have to show them how individualistic we are in setting purposes. We need to demonstrate what we do as readers once our purpose is set. In time, we get good at covering the basics and then showing children the variations. For example, I confessed to a group of third graders that I have a favorite fiction author and every time she publishes a new novel, I dive right into reading the first chapter without reading the jacket copy or the reviews. When I read an article in *National Geographic*, I have a habit of looking at all the photos first, kind of circling the act of reading before I jump in.

Access and Use Prior Knowledge

Readers access and use their prior knowledge before, during, and after they read. While prior knowledge most definitely includes children's academic background knowledge—their knowledge of the world and how it works—it's more expansive. It encompasses everything they've experienced from birth to present. Every thought, every experience, every encounter is tucked away as prior knowledge. And it's the full range of this prior knowledge that children must access and bring to bear on texts they read.

Prior knowledge grounds children's reading. It helps them confidently navigate and understand a text by hooking its content to *all* they already know—not only about the topic at hand, but myriad associations and concepts that help them connect to and comprehend the text more fully. It allows them to accept or question the information or experiences they're reading about.

Prior knowledge helps a child consider whether a character's attempt at solving a problem is reasonable or just plain silly. It helps him predict the happily-ever-after ending of a fairy tale or the resolution of a mystery's cliffhanger. Prior knowledge helps readers intuit whether information an author presents rings true in light of what they already know or think they know about a topic. It becomes the framework for new learning, helping children become savvy readers.

Consider Text Structure

Good readers consider how a text is organized. Most of us do it quite automatically, but young children need to be shown what to do when they first encounter a text. If they can see its bones, they'll have a framework on which to connect new ideas and information. And they'll be able to understand and remember more of what they read.

Expository texts and fictional stories have different structures. Stories center around character, setting, problem, main events, and resolution. Readers become accustomed to how authors play these elements off each other and adept at knowing and empathizing with characters in order to "get lost in the story world" (Wilhelm 1997).

Understanding expository texts, on the other hand, requires different cognitive moves. Readers approach these texts on the lookout for road signs indicating how they're organized. Texts might be organized chronologically or sequentially. They may be enumerative (with subcategories housed under larger ones) or conceptual (with ideas grouped by concept such as "what animals do in the winter to survive"). Taking into consideration how a text is structured gives readers a way to organize the ideas and information they're learning. We need to help children see and understand these structures through think-alouds, mini-lessons, and across all the content areas.

Caution

One word of caution: Avoid making this or any strategy an end in itself that gets in the way of reading. Make the process explicit to students, with the goal that before too long they will take it underground—that is, children will use the strategy naturally in their own reading. In too many classrooms this cognition skill gets reduced to a snazzy wall chart of questions, divorced from the real goal of having our young readers know how to engage with texts. We want them to learn to formulate questions only as needed—to guide their thinking as they read and to nurture their curiosity.

Ask Questions and Wonder

Children need to assume an active stance toward reading. Unless they generate questions and wonder, it's unlikely they'll fully comprehend, enjoy, or remember much of what they read. We need to inspire and model this active behavior for our students.

For example, a reader might wonder: *Hmmm, he seems nervous. I wonder what's making him feel this way?* Or: *The author keeps including the image of the black cat. I wonder what that means? Hmmm.* Or: *Do sharks live as long as whales? I'm going to read on to find out . . .* These questions fuel our curiosity, engage us with the text's ideas and information, and help us infer to find the answer.

As children progress through the year and through the grades, they gradually transition from group-initiated questions to ones they generate on their own. This move from whole group to small group, then to independent questioning, and requires much time and practice. Children have to become good at identifying what genuinely puzzles them. It's our job to provide the time, books, and demonstrations that cultivate students' ability to ask questions and wonder as a core reading strategy.

Visualize to Experience

We often ask students to close their eyes to get a picture in their mind of what the author is saying. But what exactly does that mean and why is it important? When we visualize we combine our life experiences with the words on the page to create an image in our mind. This image is a powerful contributor to comprehension as it transforms text into a vicarious reality. We take what the author has presented and make it our own.

> *When we visualize we combine our life experiences with the words on the page to create an image in our mind. This image is a powerful contributor to comprehension as it transforms text into a vicarious reality.*

Sometimes an author's language is so compelling that it practically forces an image upon us. Her fresh or surprising language helps paint a picture in our mind—one that makes the reading come alive. When we're engaged in this way it's almost as though we're watching a movie and the scenes are just flying by.

There are also times when readers have to work a bit harder at creating these images. For instance, if we have little experience with a topic or we're reading about an unfamiliar situation; if we're reading about a historical period about which we know little; or if we're reading about places we've never visited or situations that are new to us, then we'll have to work extra hard to visualize and bring these texts to life.

Summarize to Determine Importance

We read to understand, and that involves making a host of decisions along the way. Decisions about what's important and what's not—about what we need to hold on to and remember and what we can put to the side. These decisions lead us to find the gist of the passage, the story, or the poem.

When children read informational text they must determine the main idea of each passage or section. Often this can be challenging. At times an author will assist by writing the topic sentence in bold print or boxing it to make it pop. At other times children will need to work from the section titles, the illustrations, and the written information to glean the important points.

Again, as good readers, this summarizing occurs with speedy automaticity—flickering thoughts and mental pauses—to confirm we still understand and are still engaged. Some examples of these fleeting checkpoints while reading nonfiction might be: animal camouflage occurs in many species, but some animals lose their camouflage when they aren't so defenseless. Or when Abraham Lincoln was young, he always worked hard at everything he did. Or Rosa Parks sure was brave.

When we read fiction we have to consider and then reconsider, often again and again, what's happening and how things will end up. Readers have to determine what's central to a story's theme, character development, plot, and what's secondary. As each chapter unfolds, new information must be integrated with the old as new summaries are shaped and predictions made.

Differentiate Comprehension Strategy Instruction Across the Grades: A Three-Faceted Approach

Throughout this book I've emphasized the need for teachers to be attuned to their students' developmental levels and individual needs. The principles and practices, skills and strategies, are all tools in the artisan teacher's hands, to be used to create something unique to her students, something she contours and shades differently month to month or year to year. Similarly, in this final chapter, I urge teachers to customize what I offer—but I'm adding something to the mix so that a haphazardness of strategy teaching doesn't spin out of control through the grades. A pleasant paradox: I urge uniqueness and yet believe that each teacher's yearly plan needs to be part of an overall design—a schoolwide vision.

Helping children acquire a repertoire of comprehension strategies to use as needed will not happen overnight. Children must accumulate experience, knowledge, and expertise over time.

I propose that each school or district establish a schoolwide repertoire of comprehension strategies to teach students across the elementary grades. Teachers and administrators decide on the meta-cognitive strategies they want students to become facile with by the time they graduate, and teachers at each grade level implement strategy instruction to fit the developmental needs of their students. Having this shared vision across the grades allows teachers to do their age- and grade-appropriate part to achieve this goal by the end of the elementary grades.

In addition, the strategies in this repertoire should be uniformly stated across the grades so that all teachers, kindergarten, third-grade, fifth-grade, etc., could help children *visualize, summarize, ask questions,* and so on with the same terminology. However, the strategy demonstrations and what's asked of students should look quite different across the grades and reflect students' age- and grade-appropriate needs. For example, in kindergarten *visualize* might involve students drawing a picture of their favorite part of a story, and in fifth grade students might copy powerful passages from a text and describe why they're so evocative. First graders might work together as a class to summarize a read-aloud while third graders might be asked to go it alone.

Helping children acquire a repertoire of comprehension strategies to use as needed will not happen overnight. Children must accumulate experience, knowledge, and expertise *over time.* Depending on their age, grade, and stage in reading, they need opportunities to engage in a variety of developmentally appropriate meaning-making experiences throughout the elementary grades.

Just as we wouldn't ask a kindergartner or first grader to decide which vocabulary words in a text he thinks are personally relevant and then figure out ways to make them his own, we shouldn't adopt a one-size-fits-all approach to teaching our repertoire of meta-cognitive strategies. All instruction, whether it relates to strategy instruction or children's accurate fluent reading, background knowledge, oral language and vocabulary, and reading-writing connections, needs to reflect what children are like at different stages of development. For this, we need a schoolwide plan to ease children's movement through the grades and stages of reading—one that's reasonable and easy to implement. (See Figure 10-1 for a synopsis of this three-faceted approach.)

We need to simplify comprehension instruction and learning so that we're clear about what needs to be accomplished by the time children leave the elementary grades and understand our grade-specific role in helping them get there. The schoolwide approach to comprehension-strategy instruction I'm proposing involves:

- comprehension-facilitating experiences
- focus strategy units
- integrated strategy units

Comprehension-Facilitating Experiences (K and Grade 1, and extending across the elementary grades)	Focus Strategy Units (Grades 2 and 3)	Integrated Strategy Units (Grades 4 and 5)
As a teacher reads to students or with them during shared reading, she thinks aloud about how she is making sense of text and the strategies good readers use. However, she doesn't hold students accountable for trying out the strategies on their own. Instead she names them in a grade-appropriate way and demonstrates how they work. She knows that in time students' reading will advance to the point that they will be independently applying these strategies to texts they read. The teacher is also aware of how children's comprehension is enhanced simply by giving them opportunities to read a lot of just-right books, write texts for others to understand, and engage in thoughtful conversations, and she provides abundant opportunities for them to do so.	Teachers in second and third grade divide the schoolwide repertoire of strategies between themselves—each grade assuming responsibility for explicitly teaching half of the strategies and implementing a unit of study for each one. Each focus strategy unit, which is two- to three-weeks long, centers on one strategy. Throughout the unit, the teacher demonstrates the focus strategy repeatedly throughout the literacy block to call students' attention to how it is used. She also prompts students to try the strategy out, guides their practice, and gathers them to process how it went. Teachers continue to call students' attention to all six strategies in the repertoire outside the focus strategy units as they surface in the course of children's reading, writing, and content-area studies.	In addition to helping students refine their use of each individual strategy, fourth- and fifth-grade teachers show students how to apply a variety of strategies within a single text. During integrated strategy units, students must determine whether or not they need to use a strategy, which one to use, and how to move among the strategies as they read. Rather than applying one strategy to a text as occurred during focus strategy units, students must consider how they might use any of the repertoire strategies to maintain or regain meaning. A teacher may decide to do several integrated strategy units throughout the year. Each one lasts two- to three-weeks.

Figure 10-1. Three-Faceted Approach to Comprehension Strategy Instruction (A Synopsis)

Comprehension-Facilitating Experiences in Kindergarten and First Grade

Every time a teacher picks up a book to read aloud, every time she gathers a group of children for guided reading, every time she sets out to teach a mini-lesson at the start of the writing workshop, she has an opportunity to demonstrate that both reading and writing are about making meaning. And if she's explicit about the strategies she's demonstrating, then these experiences are purposeful and provide the foundation for future comprehension work.

Unlike focus strategy units, which concentrate on one strategy over the course of a two- to three-week unit, and integrated strategy units, which show children how to move from strategy to strategy within a given text as the need arises, *comprehension-facilitating experiences* begin in kindergarten and are ongoing throughout the grades. They are also unrelated to any specific strategy unit. At times the opportunities to show students what proficient readers think and do as they navigate a text appear serendipitously, and at other times lessons are planned in advance. Much of the foundational principles and effective practices featured in this book can be "done" as comprehension-facilitating experiences.

For example, a comprehension-facilitating experience might play out like this: Before reading aloud Gail Gibbons' *Ducks!* (2001) a teacher would think aloud about what he already knows about ducks and show students how this helps orient his reading. While reading, he may pause to consider the difference between *domesticated* and *wild* ducks using the divided frame illustration in Figure 10-2. During a reading

Domesticated ducks can be seen and sometimes touched or fed at petting farms and zoos. Wild ducks can often be seen in parks.

Figure 10-2. Page from Ducks!

conference, he may show a student how attending to the bold print in an informational text helps focus on key concepts. And during a mini-lesson or guided reading group, a teacher may demonstrate how thinking about a text's structure helps readers organize their thinking and remember important information.

Whether these experiences are serendipitous or planned, they are all comprehension-facilitating experiences and part of the "comprehension-acquisition" process (Smolkin and Donovan 2000) because they call students' attention to the meaning of what's being read. This helps lay the groundwork for the more formal strategy instruction that begins in second grade with focus strategy units. (*Note:* Laura Smolkin and Carol Donovan's 2000 CIERA Report, "The Contexts of Comprehension: Information Book Read Alouds and Comprehension Acquisition," was instrumental in helping me consider how comprehension should be taught across the elementary grades. And I thank them for spear-heading my thinking.)

Focus Strategy Units in Second and Third Grades

Let's say a school decides to focus on the repertoire of strategies I've described in this chapter. In that case, the second- and third-grade teachers would divide up the six repertoire strategies, with second-grade teachers developing and implementing three strategy units throughout the year and third-grade teachers doing the same with the remaining three. They might plan one strategy unit for late fall and the remaining two after the first of the year. See the "Focus Strategies" box for how this might play out.

It makes sense to divide the strategy unit workload between second- and third-grade teachers. This way teachers at each grade assume responsibility for organizing and implementing three strategy units and doing them deeply and well, rather than trying to develop a unit for each of the six strategies. Not only is it more reasonable and

Focus Strategies

Second Grade	Third Grade
• Visualize to experience.	• Ask questions and wonder.
• Think about text structure.	• Summarize to determine importance.
• Access and use prior knowledge.	• Set a purpose for reading.

Note: In addition to the focus strategy units, a second- and third-grade teacher also demonstrates less formally, as comprehension-facilitating experiences and not part of a strategy unit, the entire strategy repertoire as children read, write, and talk throughout the reading and writing workshop and content-area studies. These opportunities surface as she reads aloud, engages children in shared reading, confers with students, and leads guided reading groups.

doable, it's more pedagogically sound since it leaves time for other important instruction and learning, such as accurate fluent reading, reading-writing connections, etc., which contribute equally to children's developing ability to comprehend text.

Throughout each unit, teachers use read-aloud, shared reading, guided reading, conferences, and independent reading to highlight the focus strategy with the expectation that children will then try it out themselves and process how it went.

An Example—Preparing and Implementing a Visualize to Experience Unit

A second-grade teacher, planning a unit on visualizing, begins to think through the components of balanced literacy to decide how she might use each component to demonstrate this strategy and gathers materials for the unit.

For example, she might first decide to read aloud Alexander McCall Smith's *Akimbo and the Elephants* (2005) and demonstrate how readers are better able to understand a story about a place and situation with which they have no firsthand experience by creating mental images as they read. Since children typically know little about Africa, helping them visualize scenes set on an African game reserve enhances their comprehension. And it appears the author concurs, as the opening paragraph of *Akimbo and the Elephants* urges readers to:

> Imagine living in the heart of Africa. Imagine living in a place where the sun rises each morning over blue mountains and great plains with grass that grows taller than a man. Imagine living in a place where there are still elephants. (p. 1)

When demonstrating a focus strategy during a read-aloud:

+ Use the first 15 minutes of children's independent reading time following the strategy demonstration for them to try out the strategy you've just demonstrated. For example, I made each child a visualizing booklet to use as I read aloud *Akimbo and the Elephants* by binding together a page for every chapter in the book. After reading aloud a chapter, I gave children time to draw an image or scene they felt was worth noting. Figure 10-3 shows Jason's picture of an elephant being eaten by vultures.

+ Send children off to read for the remaining 25 minutes of their independent reading time. Encourage them to try out the strategy as they read on their own. (*Note*: This abbreviated workshop time, down from 40- to 25-minutes, occurs only during focus strategy units to build in time for the guided practice students need after a strategy demonstration.)

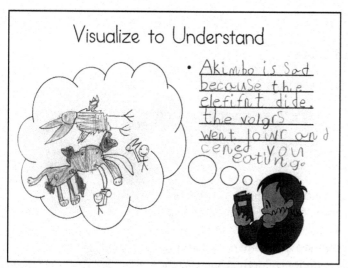

Figure 10-3. Jason's Picture of an Elephant Being Eaten by Vultures

+ When children reconvene at the end of the reading workshop, allow several of them to share their image from the strategy sheet and explain how visualizing helped them to better understand the chapter you read aloud. (The visualizing booklet remains in childrens' reading folder throughout the unit and serves as a reminder of this key strategy.)

During this *visualize to experience* unit, the teacher might also redemonstrate the focus strategy throughout other parts of the balanced literacy program. For example, she might select guided reading texts that help children understand how the author and illustrator combine efforts to help the reader "see" the information they're trying to communicate. She might demonstrate how the illustrations and text in a fiction book work together, and how in nonfiction the combination of text, photographs, charts, maps, diagrams, etc., contribute to their overall comprehension. For example, the diagram in Figure 10-4 from Aliki's *Corn Is Maize: The Gift of the Indians* (1986) illustrates how corn is pollinated, a concept that's difficult to explain and understand through written text alone.

The teacher might also call children's attention to the imagery that's created by an author's text comparisons. In *Big Blue Whale* (2001), Nicola Davies uses similes

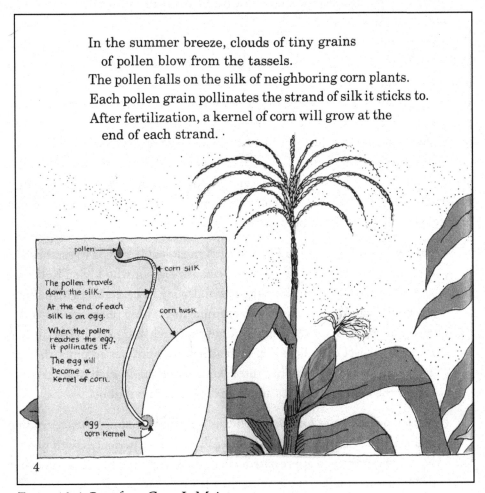

In the summer breeze, clouds of tiny grains
　of pollen blow from the tassels.
The pollen falls on the silk of neighboring corn plants.
Each pollen grain pollinates the strand of silk it sticks to.
After fertilization, a kernel of corn will grow at the
　end of each strand. ·

pollen
corn silk
The pollen travels down the silk.
At the end of each silk is an egg.
When the pollen reaches the egg, it pollinates it.
The egg will become a kernel of corn.
corn husk
egg
corn Kernel

Figure 10-4. Page from Corn Is Maize

to compare new information the children are learning with what they already know. She describes a blue whale's skin as "springy and smooth like a hard-boiled egg" and "slippery as wet soap."

In summary, the goal throughout a focus strategy unit is to provide as many demonstrations as possible of one repertoire strategy and opportunities for children to try it out themselves and to process how it went.

Integrated Strategy Units in Fourth and Fifth Grades

In the upper elementary grades, the units take on a new name and face. They're now called *integrated strategy units*, and instead of students' applying one strategy to a text they're reading, as was the case with focus strategy units, students must determine whether or not they need to use a strategy and move among strategies within a given text.

Since kindergartners and first graders have heard their teacher explain why she's using a particular strategy and have seen her demonstrate how to go about it as one aspect of comprehension-facilitating experiences, and second and third graders have explored each focus strategy in depth, fourth and fifth graders can now delve in more deeply. They can better comprehend how proficient readers vary their use of strategies within a text to meet their changing needs.

More mature readers understand that when reading for pleasure, we don't typically set out to visualize our way through an entire text as was done with *Akimbo and the Elephants*. If the book is just-right and engages us, we simply read, understand, and enjoy it. We get what it means. However, when a book is more challenging, we may need to intervene intermittently to gain a fuller understanding of the text. And visualization is just one of several strategies readers use.

For example, when reading Leslie Garrett's *Helen Keller: A Photographic Story of a Life* (2004), there are several strategies children might use to learn about and appreciate Helen Keller's life and contributions. The teacher needs to demonstrate how to move back and forth between strategies:

+ *Set a purpose for reading:* First and foremost, readers need to establish their purpose for reading. A general curiosity about who Helen Keller was and why she's famous may be the initial driving force. Readers may skim the book, pausing occasionally to examine interesting photographs and read the captions. Or they may be doing research and need information on a specific aspect of Keller's life, such as her early life, her accomplishments, and her relationship with her tutor Annie Sullivan. In each case they might review the table of contents and index for relevant sections.

+ *Access and use prior knowledge:* If this is a child's first experience reading about Helen Keller, she may need to call up past experiences with persons having disabilities to appreciate Keller's determination to prevail over her deafness and blindness. If a child already knows something about her, she would combine what she already knows with what she's learning, creating for herself a unique reading experience.

+ *Consider text structure:* Readers expect biographies to be laid out chronologically and this photographic story is no exception. An observant reader hones in on the timeline at the back of the book and, as she reads, relates what occurs in each chapter to that timeline.

+ *Ask questions and wonder:* Readers may wonder how Keller, who was both deaf and blind, could rise above her disabilities and inspire so many others to do the same. They may want to learn more about how her tutor Annie Sullivan contributed to Keller's success. A timeline tells us that Annie died in 1936 while Helen lived until 1968. Readers may wonder how she managed without Annie and whether or not someone else stepped in to take her place. Then, of course, readers would need to find answers to these questions or infer answers that are not explicitly stated.

+ *Visualize to experience:* The photographs, as intended, add great interest and power to the text. Children will continually navigate between the text and the visuals.

+ *Summarize to determine importance:* Children may want to pause periodically as they read to sort through what they've learned. In doing so, they'll need to differentiate between what's not important (in relation to their purpose for reading) and what may be relevant to the task they've set out to accomplish.

More often than not, fourth and fifth graders use reading notebooks instead of strategy sheets to record their thinking about texts. They record personal connections to texts they're reading, analyze a character and a problem he's experiencing, consider a change that's occurred from the beginning to the end, pose questions, and then use the information they bring to text and what's in the text itself to infer an answer—all of which contribute to their comprehension. Although it's possible that within these responses one can determine how a specific strategy or a combination of strategies may have helped jumpstart or consolidate their thinking, the most important thing is not a reader's use of a specific strategy or a combination of strategies, but that they *understand*.

Explicit Support for a Repertoire of Strategies

Even though I've identified six comprehension strategies that are critical for students to learn, I want to emphasize that no two readers are alike. Each of us will use the strategies differently, incorporating them into our own way of thinking, experiencing, picturing, and connecting our life to the lives and ideas an author has conjured on the page. What we're doing here is giving children the basic moves so they can create their own unique reading habits and interactions with texts.

It can take years for students to become skilled at using these six strategies. Over time and taken together—along with explicit demonstrations and opportunities for students to try them out—these strategies become the repertoire children rely on to understand and enjoy what they read.

Effective Practice: Strategy Sheets

What Are Strategy Sheets and How Do They Support Comprehension?

Strategy sheets are templates that scaffold a child's use of a comprehension strategy he's trying to acquire or refine. By recording his thinking on a strategy sheet, a reader makes his thinking explicit and concrete, allowing him to revisit and perhaps revise what he first thought.

Although strategy sheets may resemble worksheets, their purpose is quite different. Worksheets are *text*-specific and given to students *after* they read to reinforce learning and measure progress. Strategy sheets are *strategy*-specific and given to students to use before, during, and after they read a text. They're also generic enough to be used with a wide range of texts. Each strategy sheet described in this chapter can also be found in the Appendices online.

All Appendices are available online for classroom use.

Strategy Sheet Do's and Don'ts

Strategy sheets can help familiarize readers with the comprehension strategies proficient readers use. However, if they're overused or used indiscriminately, they can interfere with children's comprehension, rather than support it.

For example, we don't want students thinking they should *routinely* interrupt their reading to copy a passage from a text and draw the mental image it helps create as they do with the "Get the Picture" strategy sheet (Figure 10-17 on page 272). This would inappropriately direct their attention away from the text rather than acquaint them with a strategy to help them appreciate how visualizing can enhance their overall reading experience, and how each reader's image varies according to the experiences he brings to a text. Once they understand the goal—to pinpoint passages that might enhance their comprehension—we need to remove the scaffold (the strategy sheet) and encourage children to incorporate the strategy in more authentic ways.

So as you use strategy sheets, ask yourself these questions to determine how wisely you're using them:

- Are you requiring children to use a strategy sheet each and every time they read a book, or are you offering them on an as-needed basis?
- Are you conferring with students about how to use the strategy sheet?
- Are you asking students to explain why a sheet was or wasn't helpful?
- Are you revisiting the strategy sheet in whole-class lessons to demonstrate how to use it more effectively?

Remember the strategy sheets are temporary scaffolds that help students internalize the complex thinking proficient readers do automatically. Conferring with children is the best way for you to assess whether the sheets are helping them move toward automaticity or distracting them from that goal.

How Do Children Across the Grades Use Strategy Sheets?

Strategy sheets can be used in the following ways:

+ Kindergartners and first graders use strategy sheets in very basic ways and under the support and direct guidance of their teacher. In this context, strategy sheets help our youngest readers envision how a text is organized, record a question they have, or illustrate a scene from a text they particularly liked. In other words, strategy sheets at this age help students understand that the goal is not reading quickly and finishing, but understanding, savoring, and reflecting on what they read. See Figure 10-5 for a "Beginning, Middle, and End" strategy sheet a teacher might do *with* students as she reads a book aloud.

+ Second and third graders might use strategy sheets in conjunction with a focus strategy unit. As readers direct their attention to a specific comprehension strategy, the strategy sheet helps them differentiate one strategy from the next. A summarizing "Main Events" strategy sheet (Figure 10-19), for example, is noticeably different from one used to set a purpose for reading (Figure 10-9). This difference helps children conceptualize a repertoire of strategies they will eventually apply automatically.

    Additionally, second- and third-grade teachers use strategy sheets to differentiate instruction. A teacher might notice that a particular student is not giving himself enough time to consider the text and its meaning. In this case, the teacher might give the student a "Main Events" strategy sheet to use while reading his book. This helps him slow down and take notice of the important events or facts within the text.

+ Although fourth and fifth graders typically respond to texts and reflect on their process in reading notebooks, a teacher may occasionally find that a strategy sheet more effectively illustrates how proficient readers integrate their use of strategies. For example, the "Integrating Strategies" sheet (Figure 10-6) makes clear to readers, who are also given the opportunity to share what they record with classmates, that within a given text they'll likely move from strategy to strategy as the need arises. Or, on the other hand, an absence of entries may indicate that they immediately understood what they read and therefore didn't need to use a strategy.

Name _____ Date _____

Title: _____

Beginning, Middle, and End

Draw and write what happened at the beginning, middle, and end.

BEGINNING	
MIDDLE	
END	

○   ○   ○   ○   ○

Comprehension from the Ground Up © 2011 by Sharon Taberski (Heinemann: Portsmouth, NH).

Figure 10-5. Beginning, Middle, and End Strategy Sheet

Name _____ Date _____

Title: _____

Author: _____

Integrating Strategies

Strategies:

1. Set a purpose for reading.
2. Access and use prior knowledge.
3. Ask questions and wonder.
4. Consider text structure.

5. Visualize to experience.
6. Summarize to determine importance.
7. (Others)

☐ _____

_____

_____

☐ _____

_____

_____

☐ _____

_____

_____

○   ○   ○   ○   ○

Comprehension from the Ground Up © 2011 by Sharon Taberski (Heinemann: Portsmouth, NH).

Figure 10-6. Integrating Strategies Sheet

How Are Strategy Sheets Introduced and Used During a Focus Strategy Unit?

Strategy sheets can be used during a second- and third-grade focus strategy unit to help readers practice the strategy you're demonstrating. Here's how:

1. Once you've decided on your focus strategy, select a text to read aloud that particularly lends itself to the use of that strategy. Then select a strategy sheet that will help make the strategy demonstration more explicit. For example, when introducing the strategy *consider text structure*, I read from Carol Fenner's *Snowed In with Grandmother Silk* (2005) and used the "Thinking About Text Structure—The Story Elements" strategy sheet (Figure 10-13) to show students how key elements of a story—character, setting, problem, main events, and resolution—work together. When reading aloud Sylvia M. James' *Dolphins* (2002), I used the "Parts of the Whole" strategy sheet (Figure 10-14) to demonstrate how informational texts often include and describe various subcategories within a main topic.

2. Introduce the strategy sheet by projecting it on an interactive whiteboard or overhead projector, or by making an oversized representation of it on chart paper as a way to record a reader's thinking about the focus strategy. Explain to children how using this strategy sheet will help them gain a better understanding of what they're reading.

3. After reading aloud the first chapter or section of a text, decide with your students what to write on the model strategy sheet and record this thinking. When reading *Snowed In with Grandmother Silk*, I asked children to identify which of the story elements listed along the left-hand side of the sheet (see Figure 10-13) was most central to the chapter. They agreed that in this first chapter they learned a lot about Rudy and Grandmother Silk, their personal qualities, and so we circled the "character" box.

   Instead of drawing a picture as they typically would, we made a character web in the box of Rudy and Grandmother Silk to show what we learned— that Grandmother Silk has "designer hair," wears high-heel bedroom slippers, hates loud noises, etc., and Rudy, well Rudy, has never liked visiting Grandmother Silk who's not fun like his Granny Nancy. We also wrote a couple sentences about this chapter on the lines below the box.

When reading *Dolphins,* I read the introductory section "What Is a Dolphin?" on the first day and recorded some information we learned in the upper left quadrant of the "Parts of the Whole" strategy sheet (Figure 10-14).

4. On the following days—and once you're confident students understand what to do—give each student a strategy sheet to work on after you read a chapter, and allot the first 10 to 15 minutes of children's independent reading time for them to work on their strategy sheet.

5. Each day gather students at the end of the reading workshop (the reading share time) to share and discuss what they recorded. See Figure 10-7 which shows Lauren's thinking about what occurred in Chapter 2. She decided that "problem" was the key story element of the chapter—Rudy was upset that he had to spend Halloween weekend with Grandmother Silk while his Mom and Dad went on a cruise. Figure 10-8 shows what Danny learned from Chapter 2 about the parts of a dolphin's body.

6. Throughout the focus strategy unit as children work in small groups or on their own, revisit the focus strategy and the strategy sheet. Reinforce the strategy that you introduced during read-aloud by giving children the opportunity to practice during guided reading. And when you think students are ready to go it alone, make copies available for them to use during their independent reading time.

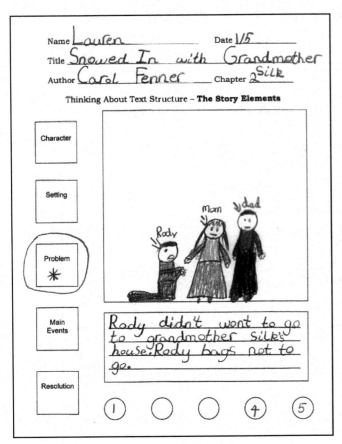

Figure 10-7. *Lauren's Thinking About Chapter 2 of* Snowed In with Grandmother Silk

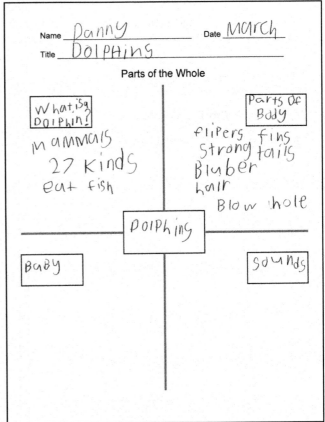

Figure 10-8. *Danny's Parts of the Whole Strategy Sheet As He Read Chapter 2 of* Dolphins

What Are Some Strategy Sheets That Correspond with Your Repertoire of Strategies?

When demonstrating a new strategy to students, I like to have a couple strategy sheets available for guided practice and for students to use when reading on their own.

SET A PURPOSE FOR READING

We read texts differently according to our purpose. It's important to show children how setting a purpose for reading can help them develop a plan for how they'll read a text.

"I'm Reading to . . ." Strategy Sheet

This strategy sheet (Figure 10-9) encourages readers to take a moment to determine their purpose for reading a text and then reflect on how they might adjust their reading to fit their purpose. For example, if a child's purpose when reading a nonfiction text is to learn some basic information about an unfamiliar topic, he may decide to first attend to the illustrations, captions, sidebars, bold words, etc., before attempting to read the text. This will ground his reading and help him focus on the information that's most important.

"My Purposeful Reading Log" Strategy Sheet

To get students in the habit of setting a purpose for reading, have them use this reading log/strategy sheet (Figure 10-10). It prompts them to consider their purpose

Name _____ Date _____
Title: _____

I'm Reading to . . .

My Purpose	How I Will Adjust My Reading:
How It Went:	

○ ○ ○ ○ ○

Comprehension from the Ground Up © 2011 by Sharon Taberski (Heinemann: Portsmouth, NH).

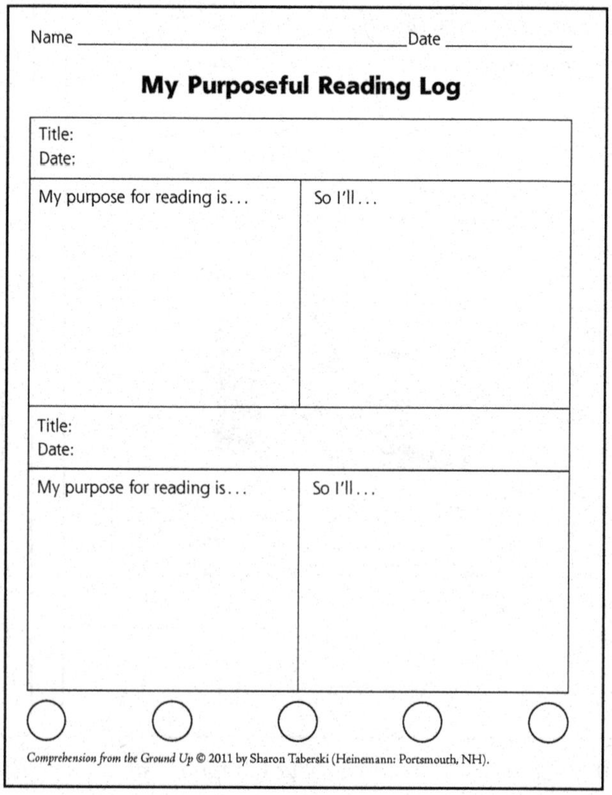

Name _____ Date _____

My Purposeful Reading Log

Title: Date:	
My purpose for reading is . . .	So I'll . . .
Title: Date:	
My purpose for reading is . . .	So I'll . . .

○ ○ ○ ○ ○

Comprehension from the Ground Up © 2011 by Sharon Taberski (Heinemann: Portsmouth, NH).

Figure 10-9. I'm Reading to . . . Strategy Sheet   *Figure 10-10. My Purposeful Reading Log Strategy Sheet*

for reading and how it will affect their handling of a text. If a reader wants to acquire specific information, he may go directly to the table of contents and index to find where to look. If he wants to simply enjoy a good story from a familiar series he may just need to recall at the start what he already knows about each of the characters.

ACCESS AND USE PRIOR KNOWLEDGE

Before children can use what they know to help them understand what they're reading, they need opportunities to access their prior knowledge. It's wise to encourage students to take a moment to think about what they already know about a topic so that they'll be better able to integrate it with the new information they're learning.

"Building and Using Background Knowledge" Strategy Sheet

Before reading a text ask students to think about what they already know about a topic, and record in the left-hand column of the strategy sheet (Figure 10-11) some content vocabulary they think they might encounter. For example, if students are reading a book about rocks and minerals, they might expect to find *sedimentary, igneous,* and *strata* in this new book. Then as students read, they check off the box alongside the words they find.

Ask students to record new content vocabulary they encounter during and after reading the text. Then have them select one of the words to write more about at the bottom of the page.

Name _____ Date _____

Building and Using Background Knowledge

Title: _____

Words I Expect to Find	Unexpected, but Interesting
☐ _____	_____
☐ _____	_____
☐ _____	_____
☐ _____	_____
☐ _____	_____
☐ _____	_____
☐ _____	_____
☐ _____	_____
☐ _____	_____
☐ _____	_____
☐ _____	_____

Next time I read about _____, I'll expect to

find the word _____ because _____

_____

_____

Comprehension from the Ground Up © 2011 by Sharon Taberski (Heinemann: Portsmouth, NH).

Figure 10-11. Building and Using Background Knowledge Strategy Sheet

"Before and After" Strategy Sheet

Before students read a text, have them draw or write what they know about a topic (Figure 10-12). Then after they read the book or section, have them draw or write what they learned. The goal is to help them see that reflecting on what they know at the onset makes it easier to read and understand new information.

THINK ABOUT TEXT STRUCTURE

Thinking about the overall structure of a piece supports children's efforts to work through it. Since they know "the whole," their goal becomes to consider the parts and how they work together.

"Thinking About Text Structure—Story Elements" Strategy Sheet

Before students begin reading have them take a look at the strategy sheet (Figure 10-13) so the various story elements are fresh in their minds. After each chapter, ask them to consider the five elements listed along the left-hand side of the sheet and circle the one that most directly relates to the chapter they just read. For example, "character" and "problem" are most likely to be circled as students read the beginning chapters of a book, and "resolution" is identified at the end. Then have students draw a picture that relates to their story element choice and write about it on the lines below the picture.

Name _____ Date _____
Title: _____

BEFORE and AFTER

(Draw a picture or write.)

BEFORE I read the book I knew:

AFTER I read the book, I knew:

Comprehension from the Ground Up © 2011 by Sharon Taberski (Heinemann: Portsmouth, NH).

Figure 10-12. Before and After Strategy Sheet

Name _____ Date _____
Title: _____
Author: _____ Chapter: _____

Thinking About Text Structure—The Story Elements

Character

Setting

Problem

Main Events

Resolution

Comprehension from the Ground Up © 2011 by Sharon Taberski (Heinemann: Portsmouth, NH).

Figure 10-13. Thinking About Text Structure Strategy Sheet

"Parts of the Whole" Strategy Sheet

Children need to consider the subtopics under the main topic of their informational texts, and then find supporting details that help to fill out the picture. Ask students to write the topic of the book or section in the center of the strategy sheet (Figure 10-14) and then the subtitles in each of quadrant boxes. As they read, they can record information about each one.

ASK QUESTIONS AND WONDER

Questions, both our own and those posed in the text, direct our thinking to find an answer. Our job is to encourage an active questioning stance in our young readers, and then help them know the difference between pertinent questions and inconsequential ones so that the direction of their thought stays focused on a text's big ideas and doesn't go off route into dead-end streets of unimportant or unrelated details.

"Turn Titles into Questions" Strategy Sheet

When reading informational text, children can easily turn a section title into a question that will direct their reading and their thinking. Have them write the section title on the strategy sheet (Figure 10-15) and then reframe it as a question. Then as children read, have them find the answer to the question and record it in the box. They can include an illustration as well.

Name _____ Date _____

Title: _____

Parts of the Whole

Comprehension from the Ground Up © 2011 by Sharon Taberski (Heinemann: Portsmouth, NH).

Figure 10-14. Parts of the Whole Strategy Sheet

Name _____ Date _____

Title: _____

Turn Titles into Questions

Section Title:	Section Title:
Question:	Question:
Answer:	Answer:
Section Title:	Section Title:
Question:	Question:
Answer:	Answer:

Comprehension from the Ground Up © 2011 by Sharon Taberski (Heinemann: Portsmouth, NH).

Figure 10-15. Turn Titles into Questions Strategy Sheet

"Making Inferences" Strategy Sheet

It's up to readers to fill in the gaps that writers leave. To make these inferences, they need to bring together what's in the book with what's in their head. I like to use this strategy sheet (Figure 10-16) when readers are having difficulty finding an answer to a question they still have upon completing a section, chapter, or short text—a question whose answer is not so obvious.

VISUALIZE TO EXPERIENCE

When children are just learning to read, they rely on the pictures to help them understand the text. First they look at the picture, and then they read. As children's reading advances, they use the text to create their own mental images. To become proficient, they need to be sensitive to the language that helps them create pictures in their mind.

"Get the Picture" Strategy Sheet

Have students identify a passage from a text they're reading that elicits a powerful mental image and copy it on the lines on the left side of the strategy sheet (Figure 10-17). Then ask students to sketch what this language helped them imagine. Children can talk among themselves or share with the class their strategy sheets and the image the words helped create.

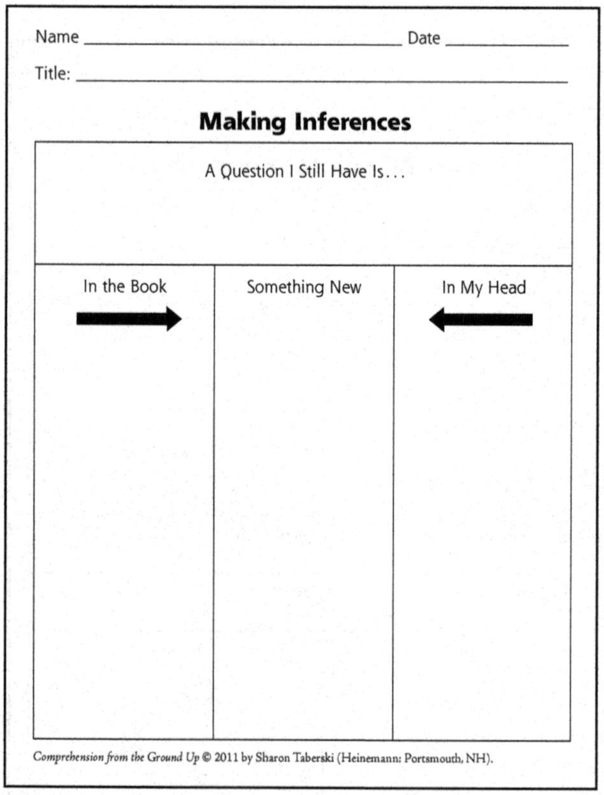

Figure 10-16. Making Inferences Strategy Sheet

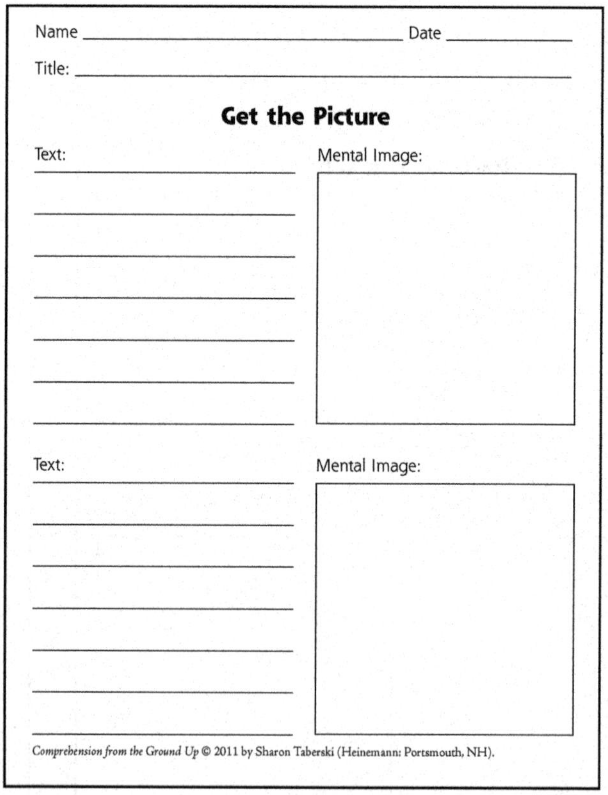

Figure 10-17. Get the Picture Strategy Sheet

"Sketch What You Learned" Strategy Sheet

A strategy sheet can be as simple as having children draw a detailed picture to convey what they learned from each section of a book (Figure 10-18). These sketches are not meant to be hastily drawn, but should be labeled and informative. This helps children understand how nonfiction illustrations are packed with information they need to mine to get the most from their reading experience.

Name ______________ Date ______

Title: ______________

Sketch What You Learned

1.	2.
3.	4.

Figure 10-18. Sketch What You Learned Strategy Sheet

SUMMARIZE TO DETERMINE IMPORTANCE

It's helpful for students to pause occasionally as they read to consider what's happened so far in the text or what they've learned before reading on. This serves as a platform for incorporating what will come next.

"Main Events: Fiction" or "Main Ideas: Nonfiction" Strategy Sheet

After students read a chapter of a fiction book or section of an informational text, have them summarize in two or three sentences what occurred or something important they learned (Figure 10-19).

Name ______________ Date ______

Main Events: Fiction

Title: ______________

Author: ______________

Chapter: ______

Chapter: ______

Chapter: ______

Name ______________ Date ______

Main Ideas: Nonfiction

Title: ______________

Author: ______________

Chapter: ______

Chapter: ______

Chapter: ______

Figure 10-19. Main Events: Fiction or Main Ideas: Nonfiction Strategy Sheets

Before students read on subsequent days, direct them to reread what they wrote on the strategy sheet to recall the events or ideas. This enables them to read the new chapters or sections from an enlightened stance.

"Getting the Gist" Strategy Sheet

After students read a chapter or section of a text, ask them to think about how they might summarize it in 15 words or less (Figure 10-20). As they do, children begin to understand how using precise phrases and vocabulary helps shorten the number of words needed to convey the gist of the text read. (This strategy sheet is for children in third grade or for some second graders at the end of the year.)

Name _____ Date _____

Title: _____

Getting the Gist

Comprehension from the Ground Up © 2011 by Sharon Taberski (Heinemann: Portsmouth, NH).

Figure 10-20. Getting the Gist Strategy Sheet

Effective Practice: A Teacher-Tailored Guided Reading Collection

What's a Teacher-Tailored Guided Reading Collection?

A teacher-tailored guided reading collection is a small collection of guided reading titles (with multiple copies of each title) that a teacher houses in her classroom so they're available when she needs them. These are titles she's selected herself because she knows them well, likes using them, and understands how they address the needs of her students. This in-class collection reflects the guided reading levels of the majority of readers in her class.

For example, a kindergarten teacher, recognizing that *most* of her children will require Level A–D books, would have several six-packs of books for each of these levels, e.g., five sets of Level A books, five sets of Level B books, etc. A third-grade teacher would do the same with Levels M–P. When a teacher needs guided reading texts for students whose reading falls outside this mid-range or to supplement titles in her in-class collection, she would check them out of the school bookroom collection.

This classroom collection does not eliminate the need for a bookroom; it complements it, and may be just what's needed to maximize the effectiveness of guided reading instruction and fine-tune our comprehension strategy demonstrations.

How Does Having a Teacher-Tailored Collection Improve the Overall Quality of Guided Reading?

We all know that using the right book at the right time can make all the difference in the world to our teaching. However, when we go to the bookroom to select guided reading books to use the following week, we have to choose from whichever sets happen to be available at the time. These titles may or may not be the ones we'd hoped for and know well, or the ones best suited to our children's interests and needs. In addition, all too often the publisher's teaching guides that originally accompanied the sets are no longer available, leaving us to fend for ourselves. This "hit-or-miss" approach can compromise the effectiveness of guided reading instruction.

If, on the other hand, teachers have a core set of books in their classroom that they know well and love using, they're better able to differentiate instruction. I know from experience that the more often I use a title, the better I know what it has to offer, and consequently, the more targeted my guided reading lessons become. I know what trips kids up and am ready to provide the necessary guidance and support.

When teachers don't know a book well, the guided reading lesson is more likely to be generic and bland, a scenario I've witnessed all too often: The teacher introduces the book and has students read the title, examine the cover, and make predictions. Then, she walks students through the book, discussing the pictures and what might be happening on each page as she inserts into the discussion vocabulary children might find challenging. And finally, the children read the texts.

Differentiation in Guided Reading

Differentiation in guided reading is more likely to occur when the teacher knows the book well. Having this teacher-tailored collection of texts can help teachers break loose from the generic guided reading procedures that can so easily dominate our teaching, and can help us implement practices that are more responsive to the collective needs of students in each group.

If students are emergent readers, they read the entire book once or twice, and then again the following day. If the text is longer, the book reading may take three or four days. And that's it. Occasionally a skill is taught and then reinforced, but not always. Students are given the guided reading book for their book bag to reread during independent reading.

In contrast, guided reading lessons should be varied and fresh, maximizing what the book has to offer. This is easier to achieve when the teacher can count on having a core set of self-selected materials in her classroom from which to draw.

How Does Having a Teacher-Tailored Guided Reading Collection Promote Strategy Instruction?

Readers who are grouped for guided reading are more alike than different. Therefore, it's wise to develop a *group* sensitivity toward guided reading that focuses on the strategies readers need to acquire at different *stages* of development rather than over-attend to what *individual* readers within the group are doing. (See Figure 10-21 for one of four guided reading sheets I use, which provides a space for me to record the *group's* activities, their movement and needs, rather than notes about each child and Appendix 32 online for all four guided reading sheets.)

It's not that individual needs are unimportant or that they don't factor into our lesson, it's just that we've got to be practical. We've got 15 minutes for kindergarten and first-grade guided reading lessons and 20 to 30 minutes for second- and third-grade lessons. Not much time at all. Therefore, it's better to address children's collective needs during guided reading and then direct our attention to their individual needs when we meet with them one-to-one for reading conferences. Of course, if something significant jumps out at us about a child's reading, e.g., that he's reading noticeably slower than the rest of the children in the group, we can jot that down on the sheet as well and then schedule a conference to check it out.

Figure 3-11 lists some characteristics of readers at different stages of development. From these characteristics we can deduce which skills and strategies will move students along the continuum to the next stage of development and make sure that we have books available to facilitate this process. For example:

- If our emergent readers need to learn to develop fluency with familiar text, we should include some Reader's Theater selections to encourage them to reread their texts with more expression.

- If our early readers need to begin reading longer texts in a variety of genres, then we can make sure to include a *range* of informational text subgenres, such as how-to books and biographies in our collection. It's also wise to include books that address a full range of content-area topics, such as

Guided Reading Sheet—Early Readers

GROUP	MONTH

Some Skills and Strategies for Early Readers

Basic Skills and Strategies:
Relying more on text than pictures
Adding to sight-word vocabulary and knowledge
    of letter-sound relationships
Expanding and consolidating word-solving skills
    and strategies
Self-monitoring for meaning
Beginning to read longer texts and a variety of genres

A Repertoire of Meta-Cognitive Strategies:
Visualize to experience
Ask questions and wonder
Think about text structure
Set a purpose for reading
Access and use prior knowledge
Summarize to determine importance

Names	Date: Book:	Date: Book:	Date: Book:	Date: Book:

Figure 10-21. Guided Reading Sheet for Early Readers

geography and transportation, and not just books on living things (Pentimonti et al. 2010). Giving children early access to a variety of text structures, vocabulary, and content knowledge can buoy up their learning.

+ If our transitional readers need to learn to maintain interest over an entire book, we can provide short, high-quality chapter books to support and scaffold their engagement.

+ If our more fluent readers need to move beyond the literal to a deeper understanding of text, we can select texts that encourage conversation about a character's motives, other actions he might have taken, etc., that will promote interpretation and multiple points of view.

(For a detailed description of readers at each reading *level* within a stage, consult Irene Fountas and Gay Sue Pinnell's *Guided Reading: Good First Teaching for All Children* [1996]).

How Do I Select Books for This Collection?

Once you've considered the range of books you need and have examined the characteristics of readers at each stage, the next step is to select several sets of books for each level within that stage. Aside from the fact that all books are not created equal (some are better written, more engaging, and of greater interest to students), certain titles are better suited to specific skill and strategy demonstrations and the guided practice you'll want to provide.

For example, if you're a second-grade teacher and know that your students learned about ants in first grade as part of their science curriculum, you may want to include a set of *Ants* (Daronco and Presti 2001) from Benchmark Education to drive home the point that it's important to activate prior knowledge before reading. Or if you're a third-grade teacher and have found that your high-end readers grow passive around mid-year, you may want to have on hand a title such as John Reynolds Gardiner's *Stone Fox* (1992) that you know from experience will generate passionate response and interaction. At this grade, the guided reading groups typically transition into literature discussion groups with an emphasis on interpretation rather than literal reading. However, reading nonfiction still requires guided reading procedures as do groups of readers not yet proficient reading grade-level fictional texts.

When assembling your in-class guided reading collection, you'll need to identify several titles at each reading level that will likely do a better job than others of supporting comprehension strategy demonstrations. For example:

+ *I can't imagine teaching kindergarten (Levels A–D)* without having a set of Mondo's *A Week with Aunt Bea* (Nayer 1997) at my disposal, a book that has been a mainstay in my guided reading collection for many years primarily because it's funny and immediately appealing to children. Aunt Bea comes to visit her niece for a week and as they visit the zoo, the playground, the circus, she outdoes herself with exhausting and embarrassing antics.

   As you can see in Figure 10-22, the text is simple and the structure repetitive, e.g., "On Monday we went to the playground. On Tuesday we went to the zoo," and so on. However, in addition to figuring out the unfamiliar word at the end of each line, the children have some serious comprehension work to do. It's only when they factor in Aunt Bea's antics as shown in the *illustrations* that they fully understand and appreciate the story. Even the monkeys can't figure her out!

On Tuesday we went to the zoo.

Figure 10-22. Page from A Week with Aunt Bea, *Level C*

+ *I can't imagine teaching first grade (Levels E–I)* without having *Watch a Frog Grow* (Pugliano-Martin 2007) from Benchmark Education at my fingertips. It's a life-cycle book that supports children's content-area science work. It's organized sequentially, rather than descriptively, prompting readers to follow a frog's development from egg to tadpole to frog (Figure 10-23) and highlights sequential signal words such as *first, then,* and *now.*

   In addition, there are supplemental materials I can use to give readers extra strategy support. There's Margaret McNamara's (2009) big book *The Life Cycle of a Frog* (Benchmark Education), which I can read to the whole class to give students some background knowledge about how frogs develop that will make them "smarter" when they work in guided reading groups. Knowing I have provided these readers with background knowledge *before* the group meets allows me to ask them to think of what they already know about frogs and expect they'll answer.

Then there's Benchmark Education's (Pugliano-Martin 2007) fictional *A Frog Someday*, the companion text that I package with *Watch a Frog Grow*. Here, Tadpole wishes to grow up and is reassured by her big brother that she will, in fact, be a frog someday. And once again, I can encourage children to bring their background knowledge about frogs to help them read this fictional text.

+ *I can't imagine teaching second grade (early transitional Levels J–L)* without a guided reading set of Daronco and Presti's *Ants* from Benchmark Education. I love the text features—the table of contents, glossary, emboldened words, and diagrams. The diagram of the parts of an ant's body (Figure 10-24) visually conveys the important fact that insects have three body parts. And I appreciate how the table of contents lays out the enumerative design of the text in a question/answer format that inspires active reading. I also know that throughout the book I can call students' attention to the bold print to help them focus their attention on key information, and have them use those words and related information found in the captions, diagrams, and photos to write about what they learned.

Then the front legs grow.
The tadpole still lives in the water.

▲ The tadpole grows front legs.

13

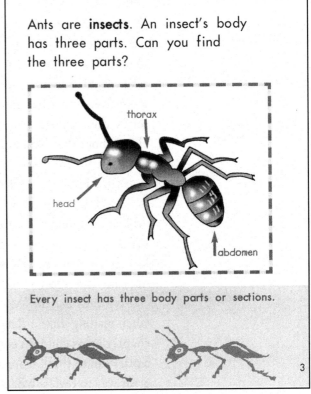

Ants are **insects**. An insect's body has three parts. Can you find the three parts?

thorax

head

abdomen

Every insect has three body parts or sections.

3

Figure 10-23. Page from Watch a Frog Grow *(Level F)*   *Figure 10-24. Page from* Ants *(Level J)*

How to Succeed in Guided Reading

There are three facets of guided reading that we need to incorporate into our weeklong guided reading plans:

- *Text Reading*—Giving children opportunities to read whole texts and discuss what they're learning should be the driving force in our guided reading instruction and should occur every time the group gathers. By focusing first and primarily on the ideas and information the text conveys, children can do a better job of thinking about the parts, the words, the letter-sounds, etc.

- *Word Work*—Guided reading instruction should also help children learn word skills and words they don't know. Some will be sight words—those they add to the bank of

words they can read automatically—and others will be words to which they need to apply the letter sounds they are learning.

- *Writing*—Children need to write about what they are learning. In fact, writing about text is a surefire way to support their reading comprehension. We can ask students to retell what they've learned, describe a key part of a story, and tell about their favorite part, and all the while be confident that this will also improve their reading comprehension. Even writing words on a wipe-off board can help students remember them, leaving more of their mental capacity for understanding what the author has to say.

+ *I can't imagine teaching third grade (Levels M–P), the late transitional stage, without having Mondo's* Take a Bow, Winky Blue *(Jane 1998) from the Winky Blue series, as part of my in-class guided reading collection. I like to use this book (see Figure 10-25) for guided reading instead of* No Way, Winky Blue *(1998), which is the first book in the series, because I often read the introductory title of a series to the whole class. Then later during guided reading, when the children are reading another book from the series, they can use what they've already learned from the whole-class read-aloud about the characters, the setting, etc., as they work their way through the guided reading selection.*

It's good that the book is short, just 56 pages, as it's problematic to attempt to have children read books that are too long within the confines of the desired weeklong guided reading framework. And even as short as this book is, I find I have to assign chapters for students to read on their own. I also love that each of the 10 chapters is short (only four to five pages with illustrations interspersed), which gives us time to talk about what we're reading.

I typically use the "Main Events: Fiction" strategy sheet (Figure 10-19) when reading *Take a Bow, Winky Blue.* Writing a brief summary after each chapter helps children consolidate and recall what they read and gives them a platform to think from as they read the remaining chapters. Also, it's a great way to review what's happened from day to day.

Winky Blue, Superstar

Early the next morning, Rosie opened her eyes and sniffed. The smell of warm cinnamon toast was floating down the hall from the kitchen. Rosie jumped out of bed and uncovered Winky's cage.

"Good morning, Winky," she said.

"No way!" said Winky grumpily.

This time he meant what he said. Winky was usually cheerful and good-natured, except in the morning when he first woke up.

"He's just not a morning bird," Aunt Maria always said.

8   9

Figure 10-25. Page from Take a Bow, Winky Blue *(Level P)*

Let's face it—guided reading is a challenging instructional component for teachers to orchestrate. The more we know our guided reading books, the easier it will be to develop expertise as guided reading teachers. Having an array of books at our fingertips is like a painter having easy access to a full palette of colors. It's to everyone's advantage to give us "at-the-fingertips" access to books that will make our instruction most effective.

Why Not Simply Select Books from the Bookroom Each Week and Learn What a Book Has to Offer During Planning?

It pains me to even have to address this question, but I will since I know that it may be in the back of some readers' minds. Simply put, it takes time—lots and lots of it—for teachers to do all that's asked of us. And it takes even more time to do things well.

Why shouldn't we have books in our classroom that we love and know well so that we have access to them when we need them? All too often the bulk of our school's funds is spent on expendable materials, such as workbooks and test-prep materials, and on programs that may sound good on paper, but don't give much "bang for the buck." It's more reasonable and cost effective to purchase in-class sets of guided reading books that we teachers have selected ourselves to enable us to get better at guided reading.

What If Your School Resists the Idea of In-Class Sets of Guided Reading Books?

Here are a few things you can try:

+ Begin your own collection by ordering multiple copies of titles using your book club points. Once you experience the value of having an in-class guided reading collection, you'll be better able to convince others to give it a try.

+ Ask your principal if you can form an exploratory group of three teachers to test the waters for half of the school year using in-class sets of books and see where this leads. You'll want to keep track of how having them at your fingertips has helped improve your guided reading instruction. The more documentation you have, the more likely you'll be able to make this trial run permanent.

+ Decide with grade-level colleagues to include a strategy "cheat sheet" inside each bag of books you particularly like that lists your school's repertoire of strategies and how the title can help to demonstrate one or more of them.

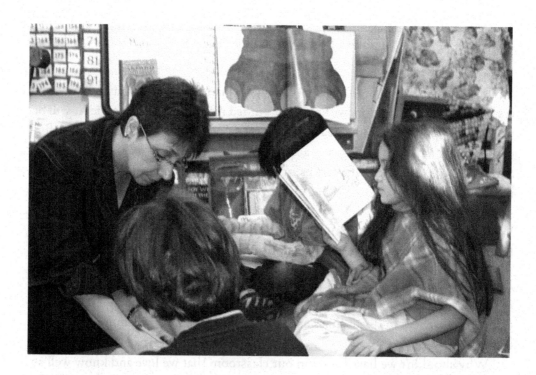

Effective Practice: "Putting Our Strategies to Work" Board

What Is the "Putting Our Strategies to Work" Board?

The "Putting Our Strategies to Work" board encourages students to apply a repertoire of strategies to texts they're reading on their own on an as needed basis and share what they've done with the class. I make the strategy board by gluing two rows of six library pockets to a 24" X 36" piece of foam board and labeling the pockets in each row with the names of the six strategies. (The library pockets along the bottom row are identical to those on the top.) See Figure 10-26.

Next, I place several blank 3" X 5" index cards, each labeled with the name of the strategy, in the corresponding pockets along the top row. Students may take a card from the strategy pocket that reflects the strategy they're using and write about it. However, when the children and I are involved in a focus strategy unit, I may decide to insert index cards in only the pocket of the strategy we're focusing on, alerting students to the fact that, for now, we're attending to this one strategy and not the other five.

How Does the Strategy Board Work?

When children are ready to share a strategy they've used, they take a card from the top row, record the title of the book, write a brief description of how they used the strategy, and write their name at the top of the card. When they're done, they return the card to the matching strategy pocket along the *bottom* row, which signals me that they're ready to share.

Figure 10-26. "Putting Our Strategies to Work" Board

Toward the end of the reading workshop, but before I ask children to put away their materials, I select two or three children to share. These children know to bring the card and the book they were reading to the meeting area. Each child reads and elaborates on what he's written and classmates ask him questions. (Notice how this effective practice combines reading, writing, and talking, the three essentials in our literacy teaching and children's learning.)

In addition, just having the board propped up against the easel throughout the day reminds me to point out strategies I'm using as I work with students. For example, when I'm reading aloud and find it makes sense to stop for a moment to think about what I've just read, I can simply point to the *summarize to determine importance* strategy pocket to show students that this is what I'm doing. Or if a child asks a question about a text we're reading, I can note this by referring to the *ask questions and wonder* pocket. The board helps to integrate strategy instruction into the daily working of our reading workshop and our work in the content areas.

Can My Students Use Strategy Cards That Relate to Strategies I Haven't Formally Introduced?

By the time children enter second grade, we can expect that they've been exposed (through comprehension-facilitating experiences and the like) to each of the repertoire strategies, and we can therefore encourage them to use these strategies as they read on their own. However, you may decide to start the year by reviewing each of the strategies one by one and, therefore, only place cards in the pockets as you reintroduce a strategy.

In addition, you will certainly be demonstrating strategies to students informally (that is, outside of focus strategy units) during mini-lessons and guided reading, as well as thinking aloud about strategies as you read aloud and confer.

Must All My Students Use the Strategy Board?

No. The strategy board is there for students to use if they choose to do so. I've found that some children love recording and sharing how a strategy helped them, while others do it occasionally or not at all. And sometimes there's a student or two who use the cards habitually, but inappropriately. You can tell by the sameness of their responses from one day to the next or by the fact that "what they did" doesn't ring true. In cases like this I explain to the student when I confer with her that she should tell me when she plans to use a card so we can talk over what she'll write.

What Are Some Benefits of Using a Strategy Board?

The strategy board is an effective way to call students' attention to the repertoire of strategies readers employ to help them understand what they're reading because it visually showcases the repertoire (presenting all six strategies *together*) and prompts conversations about how the strategies are used.

For example, Jared benefited by writing on his *visualize to experience* card (Figure 10-27) that when he read Mary Pope Osborne's *Day of the Dragon King* (1998), he "visualized the Chinese people making the Great Wall of China." But an even greater impact derived from the discussion that followed, allowing him to explain how this strategy actually helped. He told classmates that when I read them David Schwartz's *How Much Is a Million?* (2004) during our math workshop, he got a better idea of how large these numbers are. This helped him picture just how many people it took to build this 5,000 mile-long wall. Jared's classmates could relate to this as well because they too had heard the book and had "oohed" and "aahed" at numbers almost too grand to imagine.

The strategy board also reinforces for students the various junctures in reading or reflecting on a text when the use of a particular strategy might be called for. And it does so in an integrated way by presenting a visual menu of strategies, thus allowing for a different type of thinking than when a teacher focuses on one strategy for several days.

On any given day within a 5- to 10-minute period of time, students may hear:

Figure 10-27. Jared's Strategy Card

+ a classmate wondering why orcas, which are dolphins, are also considered killer whales and then share the explanation she came up with,

+ a student describe how he referred to the table of contents and index to find specific information he needed for his Baltimore Oriole project, and

+ another child who was reading Jon Scieszka's *Time Warp Trio: Knights of the Kitchen Table* (2004) admit that she knows nothing about that historical period and, therefore, had to work really hard in the first pages to create the scenes in her mind to give her something concrete to hold on to.

What Are Some Things to Watch Out for When Using the Strategy Board?

As with any learning endeavor, children's initial use of the strategy board is often less fruitful than after repeated practice. At first, children are so smitten with the board's novelty, they seem to be "playing at" using a strategy rather than seriously using it to engage with a text. Not to worry—in time, they'll use the board more effectively.

However, even this initial playful approach has its benefits since it reinforces the fact that there *is* a repertoire of strategies for them to use. It may also serve as a first step in learning to use the strategies more effectively. This gives us the chance to reinforce strategies we're teaching and explain them on different occasions in an integrated way.

Can I Introduce the Strategy Board to Kindergartners and First Graders?

The strategy board as I've described it above—its scope (the inclusion of all six strategies) and the size of its cards—is most appropriate for students in second and third grade. However, it is possible to introduce students to a modified version in first grade by designing individual boards for each of the strategies in your school's repertoire or only for those strategies you consider important and appropriate for your youngest readers (Figure 10-28).

For example, let's say you want to make a board to highlight *access and use prior knowledge.* You would make an individual strategy board for just that one strategy:

+ Take an 11" x 14" piece of foam board and attach a 10" x 13" manila envelope (with four inches cut from the top) to the front. Fasten the sides and bottom of the envelope securely with clear packing tape.

+ Label the pocket with an age-appropriate name for the strategy. For example, you might simply write "use what you know" to refer to the *access and use prior knowledge* strategy and then draw a picture of a child, with a thought bubble above her head, thinking about *fish* or *trees* or *airplanes.*

+ Insert several blank pieces of 9" x 12" oak tag in the pocket just as I described with the second- and third-grade model. Display the single-strategy board on the easel when you're demonstrating the strategy during read aloud or shared reading.

Figure 10-28. Individual Strategy Board

✦ Then, as you demonstrate that strategy, take one of these oak tag sheets and write a sentence or draw a picture of how you're using the strategy. For example, you might write or draw a picture (or ask a child to help you) showing what you already know. Or when demonstrating *set a purpose for reading*, you could simply write, "I want to learn a lot of facts about butterflies." When demonstrating *visualize to experience*, you might draw a picture of your favorite part of the book. (*Note:* I don't ask my youngest readers to independently apply comprehension strategies as they read on their own and then to share or write about how it went. Except for the most basic strategy application, such as drawing a picture of their favorite part of a book or something they learned, strategy instruction in kindergarten and first grade is best done in whole-class and small-group settings.)

Can I Use a Similar Strategy Board to Teach Writing Strategies?

I use a "Putting Our *Writing* Strategies to Work" Board (Figure 10-29) that's similar in design and function to the reading strategies board. It helps demonstrate that the strategies readers use to comprehend texts are similar to those writers use to make sense of texts they're writing. See the "Reciprocal Reading and Writing Strategies" box for how reading and writing strategies mirror one another.

This writing strategies board works in the same way as the reading board. The strategies are listed on the pockets along the top and bottom rows. A student takes a card when he is applying that strategy to a piece of writing. He writes his name on the card and how he's using the strategy. Then the card is placed along the bottom row to indicate that he is ready to share.

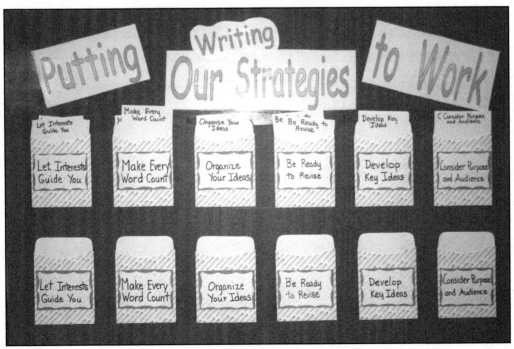

Figure 10-29. "Putting Our Writing Strategies to Work" Board

Reciprocal Reading and Writing Strategies

Reading Strategies	Writing Strategies
Set a purpose for reading.	Consider your purpose for writing and your audience.
Access and use prior knowledge.	Start with what you know or what interests you.
Consider text structure.	Organize your ideas so they're accessible to a reader.
Ask questions and wonder.	Write to learn.
Visualize to experience.	Create an image for your reader.
Summarize to determine importance.	Elaborate on your key ideas.

Once again, this practice gives children the opportunity to talk about how they're making sense of texts—this time texts they're writing. Of course, we eventually want children's use of strategies to go underground and be applied automatically, but there's an initial period where they need to explicitly write about what they're doing and talk it through. The strategy boards—both the reading and writing board—help on both counts.

Closing Thoughts

"It Takes a Lot of Slow to Grow"

Throughout this book I've demonstrated that to develop as readers, children need time to read, write, and talk. But children also need time to grow, and it's this last point I want to resonate above all. It takes time to learn strategies for reading and writing. It takes time to acquire background knowledge that will facilitate comprehension. It takes time to gain experiences that make them well-rounded individuals who can connect those experiences to text they read and write, and to conversations about their reading. In takes time to move from being an emergent reader who's scarcely aware of what a word is to one who's proficient and can critically reflect on what he's reading.

I'm reminded of the principal in Sharon Creech's *A Fine, Fine School* (2003) who learned this lesson from Tillie, a small girl who had the courage to speak up when she saw that more school and less play (downtime) weren't working. Tillie explained that ever since the principal extended school to weekends, holidays, and even summers, not everyone was learning. Her brother wasn't learning how to swing and how to skip, her dog wasn't learning to sit and jump creeks, and she wasn't learning to climb a tree and sit for an hour. Tillie knows and we educators know that children need time to experience things that will make them balanced, well-versed, educated adults. They need time to process what they're supposed to be learning. We know this, but are we in practice giving them and ourselves the time to learn deeply and teach well? I dare say in many classrooms we are not.

I'm not suggesting that we sit idly by, waiting for children to develop and become ready for the next step. We must actively provide the developmentally appropriate experiences that help children internalize the skills and strategies they need to acquire. Whether it's providing demonstrations of how to think and ask questions as they read or taking them to a museum to see the mummy display so that they can more fully appreciate and understand both fiction and informational texts related to ancient Egypt. Whether it's working on short vowel sounds in a whole-class setting so they have more phonics knowledge to bring to text or conferring with students one-to-one to match them with just-right books—it's our job to help children achieve success in the next step in their development, but not to push them there so quickly that we compromise the likelihood of this ever happening.

Creech's words should resonate in our minds and in our bones when, in our day-to-day teaching and administrative lives, we recognize that "good" things are being overdone. It's good to hold teachers and children accountable, but bad when it takes time away from the experiences that truly add up to learning. It's good to prepare children with test-taking routines several weeks before the test to make them more test-savvy, but bad to start in October. It's good to identify in general terms what's important for children to know, but it's bad to script what teachers must say, what materials they must use, what page they must be on Monday, Tuesday, and every other day. The principal in Creech's book heard and understood what Tillie said, and "he was very worried."

We should be worried, too, when testing and curriculum demands get out of hand in the push to reach higher and higher standards. When that happens our attention is diverted from what's truly important—teaching children to read, write, and talk in ways that make sense. Regardless of what policy makers think, we need to slow down and give our children and ourselves the opportunity to do things well.

Poet Eve Merriam, in her closing line of "A Lazy Thought," advises: "It takes a lot of slow to grow." She's right. It does.

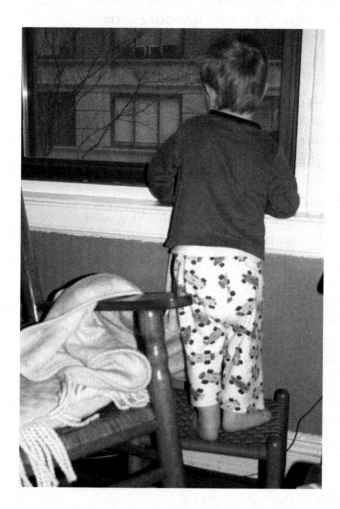

A Lazy Thought

by Eve Merriam

There go the grownups
To the office,
To the store,
Subway rush,
Traffic crush;
Hurry, scurry,
Worry, flurry.

No wonder
Grownups
Don't grow up
Any more.

It takes a lot
Of slow
To grow.

# Works Cited

Chapter 1

Dewitz, P., J. Jones, and S. Leahy. 2009. "Comprehension Strategy Instruction in Core Reading Programs." In *Reading Research Quarterly* 44 (2): 102–126.

Duke, N. K., and P. D. Pearson. 2002. "Effective Practices for Developing Reading Comprehension." In *What Research Has to Say About Reading Comprehension*, 3d ed. Edited by A. Farstrup and S. J. Samuels. New York: Guilford Press.

Graham, S., and M. A. Hebert. 2010. *Writing to Read: Evidence for How Writing Can Improve Reading*. A Carnegie Corporation Time to Act Report, Washington, DC: Alliance for Excellent Education.

Kuhn, M. R. 2003. "Fluency in the Classroom: Strategies for Whole-Class and Group Work." In *Best Practices in Literacy Instruction*, 2d ed. Edited by L. M. Morrow, L. B. Gambrell, and M. Pressley. New York: Guilford Press.

Moss, B. 2002. *Exploring the Literature of Fact: Children's Nonfiction Trade Books in the Elementary School*. New York: Guilford Press.

National Institute of Child Health and Human Development. 2000. Report of the National Reading Panel. *Teaching Children to Read: An Evidence-Based Assessment of the Scientific Research Literature on Reading and It's Implications for Reading Instruction* (NIH Publication No. 00-4769). Washington, DC: U.S. Government Printing Office.

Taberski, S. 2011. *Lessons from the Ground Up: Cultivating Comprehension in K–3 Readers* (DVD). Portsmouth, NH: Heinemann.

Willingham, D. T. 2006. "How Knowledge Helps: It Speeds and Strengthens Reading Comprehension, Learning—and Thinking." In *American Educator* (Spring) pp. 30–37.

Chapter 2

Ames, L. B. 1981. *Your Five-Year-Old: Sunny and Serene*. New York: Dell.

Peterson, R., and M. A. Eeds. 2007. *Grand Conversations: Literature Groups in Action*. Updated Edition. New York: Scholastic Teaching Resources.

Simpson, M. 1985. *Reading in Junior Classes*. Wellington, NZ: Learning Media Limited.

Stahl, S. A. 1999. *Vocabulary Development*. Newton Upper Falls, MA: Brookline Books.

Taberski, S. 2000. *On Solid Ground: Strategies for Teaching Reading K–3*. Portsmouth, NH: Heinemann.

Children's Works Cited

Henkes, K. 1996. *Lily's Purple Plastic Purse*. New York: Greenwillow.

McDonald, M. 1998. *Beezy at Bat*. New York: Orchard Books.

Chapter 3

Allington, R. L. 2009a. *What Really Matters in Response to Intervention*. New York: Pearson Publishers.

Allington, R. L. 2009b. *What Really Matters for Fluency*. New York: Pearson Publishers.

Anderson, R. C., P. T. Wilson, and L. G. Fielding. 1988. "Growth in Reading and How Children Spend Their Time Outside of School." In *Reading Research Quarterly* 23: 285–303.

Daley, A. 2005. *Partner Reading: A Way to Help All Readers Grow*. New York: Scholastic Teaching Resources.

Hancock, M. R. 2005. "Students Write Their Own Understanding of Characters—and Their Understanding Soars." In *What a Character! Character Study as a Guide to Literary Meaning Making in Grades K–8*. Edited by N. L. Roser and M. G. Martinez. Newark, DE: International Reading Association.

Howard, M. 2009. *RTI from All Sides: What Every Teacher Needs to Know*. Portsmouth, NH: Heinemann.

Jensen, E. 1998. *Teaching with the Brain in Mind*. Alexandria, VA: Association for Supervision and Curriculum Development.

McGill-Franzen, A. M. 2005. *Kindergarten Literacy: Matching Assessment and Instruction in Kindergarten*. New York: Scholastic.

Roser, N. L., and M. G. Martinez. 2005. *What a Character! Character Study as a Guide to Literary Meaning Making in Grades K–8*. Newark, DE: International Reading Association.

Strout, E. 2008. *Olive Kitteridge*. New York: Random House.

Taberski, S. 2000. *On Solid Ground: Strategies for Teaching Reading K–3*. Portsmouth, NH: Heinemann.

Willingham, D. T. 2009. *Why Don't Students Like School? A Cognitive Scientist Answers Questions About How the Mind Works and What It Means for the Classroom*. San Francisco, CA: Jossey-Bass.

Children's Books Cited

Athaide, T. 2002. *Pran's Week of Adventures*. New York: Bebop Books.

Carle, E. 1995. *The Very Busy Spider*. New York: Penguin.

Fotherby, L. 1994. *The Cat Who Came to Stay*. Stamford, CT: Longmeadow Press.

Hoff, S. 2000. *Sammy the Seal*. New York: HarperCollins.

Hubbell, P. 2010. *Cars: Rushing! Honking! Zooming!* Tarrytown, NY: Marshall Cavendish.

Kasza, K. 2005. *The Dog Who Cried Wolf*. New York: Penguin.

Katz, S. 2007. *Oh, Theodore! A Collection of Guinea Pig Poems*. New York: Clarion.

Osborne, M. P. 1999. *Buffalo Before Breakfast*. New York: Random House.

Phinney, M. Y. 2004. *A Trip to the City*. New York: Mondo.

Pugliano-Martin, C. 2004. *Little Lion*. Pelham, NY: Benchmark Education.

Smith, C. 2008. *Old Mother Hubbard's Hungry Family*. Pelham, NY: Benchmark Education.

St. George, J. 2005. *So You Want to Be an Inventor*. New York: Puffin.

Chapter 4

Corgill, A. M. 2009. *Of Primary Importance: What's Essential in Teaching Young Writers*. York, ME: Stenhouse.

Duke, N. K., and P. D. Pearson. 2002. "Effective Practices for Developing Reading Comprehension." In *What Research Has to Say About Reading Comprehension*, 3d ed. Edited by A. Farstrup and S. J. Samuels. New York: Guilford Press.

Graham, S., and Hebert, M. A. 2010. *Writing to Read: Evidence for How Writing Can Improve Reading*. A Carnegie Corporation Time to Act Report, Washington, DC: Alliance for Excellent Education.

Newkirk, T. 2009. *Holding on to Good Ideas in a Time of Bad Ones: Six Literacy Principles Worth Fighting For*. Portsmouth, NH: Heinemann.

Shillinglaw, S. ed. 2002. *John Steinbeck: Centennial Reflections By American Writers*. San Jose, CA: Center for Steinbeck Studies, San Jose State University.

Children's Books Cited

Krull, K. 2004. *The Boy on Fairfield Street: How Ted Geisel Grew Up to Be Dr. Seuss*. New York: Random House.

Lester, H. 1994. *Author: A True Story*. Boston: Houghton Mifflin.

Polacco, P. 1996. *Meteor!* New York: Putnam Juvenile.

Polacco, P. 1997. *Thunder Cake*. New York: Putnam Juvenile.

Polacco, P. 2001. *The Keeping Quilt*. New York: Aladdin (Simon and Schuster).

Seuss, Dr. 1961. *The Sneetches and Other Stories*. New York: Random House.

Chapter 5

Beck, I. L., M. G. McKeown, and L. Kucan. 2002. *Bringing Words to Life: Robust Vocabulary Instruction*. New York: Guilford Press.

Beck, I. L., M. G. McKeown, and L. Kucan. 2008. *Creating Robust Vocabulary: Frequently Asked Questions and Extended Examples*. New York: Guilford Press.

Biemiller, A. 2003. "Oral Language Sets the Ceiling on Reading Comprehension," In *American Educator* 27 (1): (Spring): 23, 44.

Block, C. C., and J. N. Mangieri. 2005. "National Study of the Effects of Research-Based Vocabulary Instruction on Students' Literacy Achievement and Attitude Toward Reading." Charlotte, NC: Institute for Literacy Enhancement.

Block, C. C., and J. N. Mangieri. 2006. *The Vocabulary-Enriched Classroom: Practices for Improving the Reading Performance of All Students in Grades 3 and Up*. New York: Scholastic.

Collins, K. 2008. *Reading for Real: Teach Students to Read with Power, Intention, and Joy in K–3 Classrooms*. York, ME: Stenhouse.

Elley, W. B. 1989. "Vocabulary Acquisition from Listening to Stories." In *Reading Research Quarterly* 24 (Spring): 174–187.

Hart, B., and T. R. Risley. 1995. *Meaningful Differences in the Everyday Experience of Young American Children*. Baltimore, MD: Paul H. Brookes Publishing.

Howard, M. 2010. *Moving Forward with RTI: Reading and Writing Activities for Every Instructional Setting and Tier*. Portsmouth, NH: Heinemann.

Hoyt, L. 2006. *Interactive Read-Alouds, Grades K–1: Linking Standards, Fluency, and Comprehension*. Portsmouth, NH: Heinemann.

Hoyt, L. 2007. *Interactive Read-Alouds, Grades 2–3: Linking Standards, Fluency, and Comprehension*. Portsmouth, NH: Heinemann.

Hoyt, L. 2007. *Interactive Read-Alouds, Grades 4–5: Linking Standards, Fluency, and Comprehension*. Portsmouth, NH: Heinemann.

Jensen, E. 1998. *Teaching with the Brain in Mind*. Alexandria, VA: Association for Supervision and Curriculum Design.

Johnston, P. 2004. *Choice Words: How Our Language Affects Children's Learning*. York, ME: Stenhouse.

McGee, L. M., and J. Schickedanz. 2007. "Repeated Interactive Read-Alouds in Preschool and Kindergarten." In *The Reading Teacher* 60 (8): 742–751.

Nichols, M. 2006. *Comprehension Through Conversation: The Power of Purposeful Talk in the Reading Workshop*. Portsmouth, NH: Heinemann.

Pearson, P. D., L. R. Roehler, J. A. Dole, and G. G. Duffy, 1990. "Developing Expertise in Reading Comprehension: What Should Be Taught? How Should It Be Taught? *Technical Report No. 512*. Champaign, IL: Center for the Study of Reading.

Pearson, P. D., and M. C. Gallagher. 1983. "The Instruction of Reading Comprehension." In *Contemporary Educational Psychology* 8: 317–44.

Stahl, S. A. 1999. *Vocabulary Development*. Newton Upper Falls, MA: Brookline Books.

Children's Books Cited

Brown, P. 2009. *The Curious Garden*. New York: Little, Brown and Company Books for Young Readers.

Clunes. 2003. *Who Lives in the Wild?* (Baby Sparkle). New York: Priddy & Bicknell (St. Martin's).

DiCamello, K. 2009. *The Miraculous Journey of Edward Tulane*. Somerville, MA: Candlewick Press.

Forest, H. 1998. *Stone Soup*. Atlanta, GA: August House.

Gibbons, G. 2004. *Horses!* New York: Holiday House.

Hooks, G. H. 2002. *Can I Have a Pet?* New York: Bebop Books.

Lester, H. 2004. *Hurty Feelings*. Boston: Houghton Mifflin.

Lumry, A., and L. Hurwitz. 2007. *Polar Bear Puzzle*. New York: Scholastic.

Lumry, A., and L. Hurwitz. 2007. *South Pole Penguins*. New York: Scholastic.

Sill, C. 2007. *About Birds: A Guide for Children*. Atlanta, GA: Peachtree.

Taberski, S. 2003. *Penguins Are Water Birds*. New York: Mondo.

Wells, R. 2000. *Timothy Goes to School*. New York: Puffin.

Chapter 6

Allington, R. L. 2009. *What Really Matters for Fluency*. New York: Pearson Publishers.

Fox, M. 2008. *Reading Magic: Why Reading Aloud to Our Children Will Change Their Lives Forever*, 2d ed. Updated and revised ed. Boston, MA: Mariner Books.

Krashen, S. 2003. Comments from a professional development seminar.

Kuhn, M. R. 2003. "Fluency in the Classroom: Strategies for Whole-Class and Group Work." In *Best Practices in Literacy Instruction*, 2d ed. Edited by L. M. Morrow, L. B. Gambrell, and M. Pressley. New York: Guilford Press.

National Institute of Child Health and Human Development. 2000. Report of the National Reading Panel. *Teaching Children to Read: An Evidence-based Assessment of the Scientific Research Literature on Reading and Its Implications for Reading Instruction*. NIH Publication No. 00-4769. Washington, DC: U.S. Government Printing Office.

Rasinski, T. 2003. *The Fluent Reader: Oral Reading Strategies for Building Word Recognition, Fluency, and Comprehension*. New York: Scholastic.

Wylie, R. E., and D. D. Durrell. 1970. "Teaching Vowels Through Phonograms." In *Elementary English* 47: 787–797.

Children's Books Cited

Brown, G. 2007. *Johnny Appleseed: An American Tall Tale* (Reader's Theater Folktales, Myths, and Legends 1–6). Pelham, NY: Benchmark Education.

Davies, N. 2000. *Big Blue Whale* (Big Book). New York: Random House.

Giles, J. 2000. *My Book*. New York: Rigby.

Harrington, J. H. 2007. *The Chicken Chasing Queen of Lamar County*. New York: Farrar, Straus and Giroux.

Harris, B. 2008. *Working on the Railroad* (Reader's Theater Nursery Rhymes and Songs). Pelham, NY: Benchmark Education.

Johnson, W. E. 2005. "Sledding." In *Days Like This: A Collection of Small Poems*, edited by S. James. Somerville, MA: Candlewick Press.

Lobel, A. 1971. *On the Day Peter Stuyvesant Sailed into Town*. New York: HarperCollins.

McDonald, F. 1996. *I Love Animals* (Big Book). Somerville, MA: Candlewick Press.

Mondo. 1999. *My Word Book*. New York: Mondo.

Parkes, B., and J. Smith. *The Little Red Hen*. Pelham, NY: Benchmark Education.

Phinney, M. Y. 2004. *A Trip to the City*. New York: Mondo.

Trelease, J. 2006. *The Read-Aloud Handbook*, 6th ed. New York: Penguin.

Zion, G. 1976. *No Roses for Harry*. New York: HarperCollins.

Chapter 7

Duke, N. V., and P. D. Pearson. 2002. "Effective Practices for Developing Reading Comprehension." In *What Research Has to Say About Reading Instruction*, 3d ed. Edited by A. E. Farstrup and S. J. Samuels. Newark, DE: International Reading Association.

Elley, W. B. 1989. "Vocabulary Acquisition from Listening to Stories." In *Reading Research Quarterly* 24: 174–187.

Frey, N., and D. Fisher. 2009. *Background Knowledge: The Missing Piece of the Comprehension Puzzle*. Portsmouth, NH: Heinemann.

Kletzen, S. B., and M. J. Dreher. 2003. *Informational Text in K–3 Classrooms: Helping Children Read and Write*. Newark, DE: International Reading Association.

Moss, B. 2002. *Exploring the Literature of Fact: Children's Nonfiction Trade Books in the Elementary Classroom*. New York: Guilford Press.

Willingham, D. T. 2009. *Why Don't Students Like School? A Cognitive Scientist Answers Questions About How the Mind Works and What It Means for the Classroom*. Hoboken, NJ: Jossey-Bass.

Children's Books Cited

Bancroft, H., and R. G. Van Gelder. 1997. *Animals in Winter*. New York: HarperCollins.

Bloom, D. 2008. *Elephants: A Book for Children*. New York: Thames & Hudson.

Branley, F. M. 1999. *Flash, Crash, Rumble, and Roll*. New York: HarperCollins.

Catling, P. S. 2006. *The Chocolate Touch*. New York: HarperCollins.

Crook, C. B. 1999. *Maple Moon*. Markham, ON: Canada: Fitzhenry and Whiteside.

Davies, N. 2000. *Big Blue Whale*. Somerville, MA: Candlewick Press.

Deutsch, S., and R. Cohon. 2006. *Ben Franklin's Fame*. Aladdin.

DiCamello, K. 2005. *Mercy Watson to the Rescue*. Somerville, MA: Candlewick Press.

Doherty, E. 2004. *Ellis Island*. Pelham, NY: Benchmark Education.

Doherty, E. 2004. *William's Journal*. Pelham, NY: Benchmark Education.

Dunphy, M. 2007. *Here Is the Arctic Winter*. Berkeley, CA: Web of Life Children's Books.

Flores, B. M. 2005. *Mud Tortillas*. New York: Bebop Books.

Fralin, B. D. 2002. *Who Was Ben Franklin?* New York: Grosset and Dunlap.

Frank, M. 2009. *Children Past and Present*. Pelham, NY: Benchmark Education.

Freeman, M. 2000. *Giant Pandas*. Mankato, MN: Capstone Press.

Freeman, M. 2003. *Making Tortillas*. Washington, DC: National Geographic.

George, K. O. 2007. *Old Elm Speaks: Tree Poems*. London, UK: Sandpiper.

Gibbons, G. 2004. *Giant Pandas*. New York: Holiday House.

Haydon, J. 2003. *My Animal Scrapbook*. Boston, MA: Rigby (Houghton).

Herriges, Ann. 2009. *Lightning*. Eden Prairie, MN: Bellwether Media.

Kalman, B. 2004. *Endangered Sea Turtles*. New York: Crabtree Publishing Company.

Kalman, B. 2005. *Endangered Elephants*. New York: Crabtree Publishing Company.

LaDuke, W., and W. Kapashesit. 1999. *The Sugar Bush*. New York: Rigby.

Lasky, K. 2009. *Georgia Rises: A Day in the Life of Georgia O'Keeffe*. New York: Farrar, Straus and Giroux.

Osborne, M. P. 1993. *Mummies in the Morning*. New York: Random House.

Osborne, M. P. 1995. *Afternoon on the Amazon*. New York: Random House.

Osborne, M. P. 2001. *Mummies and Pyramids*. New York: Random House.

Osborne, M. P. 2001. *Rain Forests* (Magic Tree House Research Guide). New York: Random House.

Osborne, M. P. 2001. *Twisters on Tuesday*. New York: Random House.

Osborne, M. P. 2003. *Twisters and Other Terrible Storms*. New York: Random House.

Ryder, J. 2009. *Panda Kindergarten*. New York: HarperCollins.

Selwyne, J. 2000. *Computer Pigs*. Australia: Macmillan.

Simon, S. 1994. *Big Cats*. New York: HarperCollins.

Singer, M. 2003. *Antarctic Antics: A Book of Penguin Poems*. London, UK: Sandpiper.

Swinburne, S. 2005. *Turtle Tide: The Ways of Sea Turtles*. Honesdale, PA: Boyds Mills.

Taberski, S. 2002. *Penguins Are Water Birds*. New York: Mondo.

Venezia, M. 1994. *Georgia O'Keeffe* (Getting to Know the World's Greatest Artists). Chicago, IL: Children's Press.

Chapter 8

Beck, I. L., M. G. McKeown, and L. Kucan. 2002. *Bringing Words to Life: Robust Vocabulary Instruction*. New York: Guilford Press.

Beck, I. L., M. G. McKeown, and L. Kucan. 2008. *Creating Robust Vocabulary: Frequently Asked Questions and Extended Examples*. New York: Guilford Press.

Crevola, C., and M. Vineis. 2004. *Let's Talk About It: Oral Language and Print Concept Development for Grades K–3*. New York: Mondo.

McGee, L. M., and J. Schickedanz. 2007. "Repeated Interactive Read-Alouds in Preschool and Kindergarten." *The Reading Teacher* 60 (8): 742–751.

Nagy, W. E., and Anderson, R. C. 1984. "How Many Words Are There in Printed School English?" In *Reading Research Quarterly* 19: 304–330.

New Standards Listening and Speaking Committee. 2001. *Speaking and Listening for Preschool Through Third Grade*. Pittsburgh, PA: National Center on Education and the Economy and the University of Pittsburgh.

Short, K. G., J. C. Harste, and C. Burke. 1995. *Creating Classrooms for Authors and Inquirers*. Portsmouth, NH: Heinemann.

Sibberson, F., K. Szymusiak, and L. Koch. 2008. *Beyond Leveled Books: Supporting Early and Transitional Readers in K–5*, 2d ed. York, ME: Stenhouse.

Vygotsky, L., and A. Kuzulin (eds). 1986. *Thought and Language*—Revised Edition. Cambridge, MA: MIT Press.

Children's Books Cited

Cox, R. 1999. *Best Friends*. Katonah, NY: Richard C. Owen.

DePaola, T. 1978. *Pancakes for Breakfast*. London, UK: Sandpiper.

Duvoisin, R. 2007. *Donkey-donkey*. New York: Knopf Books for Young Readers.

Edwards, P. D. 2003. *The Worrywarts*. New York: HarperCollins.

Hershenhorn, E. 2009. *S is for Story: A Writer's Alphabet*. Chicago, IL: Sleeping Bear Press.

Kontis, A. 2006. *AlphaOop!s: The Day Z Went First.* Somerville, MA: Candlewick Press.

Lehmen, B. 2007. *Rainstorm.* Boston, MA: Houghton Mifflin.

McCully, E. A. 2003. *First Snow.* New York: HarperCollins.

McCully, E. A. 2005. *School.* New York: HarperCollins.

Most, B. 2004. *ABC T-Rex.* London, UK: Sandpiper.

Munari, B. 2006. *Bruno Munari's ABC,* 6th ed. San Francisco, CA: Chronicle Books.

Palotta, J. 1987. *The Bird Alphabet Book.* Watertown, MA: Charlesbridge.

Schwartz, A. 1988. *Annabelle Swift, Kindergartner.* New York: Orchard Books.

Shannon, G. 1999. *Tomorrow's Alphabet.* New York: Greenwillow Books (HarperCollins).

Sommerville, V. 2001. *Little Turtle.* Katonah, NY: Richard C. Owen.

Weisner, D. 1999. *Sector 7.* New York: Clarion Books (Houghton).

Weisner, D. 2006. *Flotsam.* New York: Clarion Books (Houghton).

Wells, R. 2008. *Max's ABC.* New York: Puffin.

Chapter 9

Allington, R. L. 2009. *What Really Matters in Response to Intervention: Research-Based Designs.* New York: Pearson Education.

Bruckner, A. 2005. *Notebook Know-How: Strategies for the Writer's Notebook.* York, ME: Stenhouse.

Corgill, A. M. 2009. *Of Primary Importance: What's Essential in Teaching Young Writers.* York, ME: Stenhouse.

DiCamillo, K. 2005. "Character Is the Engine." In *What a Character! Character Study as a Guide to Literary Meaning Making in Grades K–8,* edited by N. L. Roser and M. G. Martinez. Newark, DE: International Reading Association.

Graham, S., and Hebert, M. A. 2010. *Writing to Read: Evidence for How Writing Can Improve Reading.* A Carnegie Corporation Time to Act Report. Washington, DC: Alliance for Excellent Education.

Hoyt, L. "Power-Writes: Cross Curricular Scaffolds." Presentation given at IRA Annual Convention, Chicago, IL, April 25–28, 2010.

Kahn, B. 2004. "Cheeseheads." In *The Midwest Today.* Washington, DC: National Geographic.

Lyons, C. 2003. *Teaching Struggling Readers: How to Use Brain-Based Research to Maximize Learning.* Portsmouth, NH: Heinemann.

Medina, John. 2008. *Brain Rules: 12 Principles for Surviving and Thriving at Work, Home, and School.* Seattle, WA: Pear Press.

Ray, K. W. 2010. *In Pictures and In Words: Teaching the Qualities of Good Writing Through Illustration Study.* Portsmouth, NH: Heinemann.

Riddle, J. 2009. *Engaging the Eye Generation: Visual Literacy Practices for the K–5 Classroom.* York, ME: Stenhouse.

Willingham, D. T. 2009. *Why Don't Students Like School? A Cognitive Scientist Answers Questions About How the Mind Works and What It Means for the Classroom.* San Francisco, CA: Jossey-Bass.

Children's Books Cited

Bunting, E. 2005. *Sunshine Home.* London, UK: Sandpiper.

Collins, A. 2002. *Storms.* Washington, DC: National Geographic.

Henkes, K. 1996. *Lily's Purple Plastic Purse.* New York: Greenwillow Books.

Hoffman, M. 1997. *Amazing Grace.* New York: Dial.

Peterson, J. 1993. *The Littles.* New York: Scholastic Paperbacks.

Rey, M. 1997. *Spotty.* New York: HMH Books.

Steig, W. 1998. *Brave Irene.* New York: Farrar, Straus and Giroux.

Yacarrino, D. 2005. *The Birthday Fish.* New York: Henry Holt and Co.

Wells, R. 2000. *Timothy Goes to School.* New York: Puffin.

Wells, R. 2004. *Timothy's Tales from the Hilltop School.* New York: Puffin.

Chapter 10 and Closing Thoughts

Afflerbach, P., P. D. Pearson, and S. G. Paris. 2008. "Clarifying Differences Between Reading Skills and Reading Strategies." In *The Reading Teacher* 61 (5): 368.

Fountas, I., and G. S. Pinnell. 1996. *Guided Reading: Good First Teaching for All Children.* Portsmouth, NH: Heinemann.

Harvey, S., and A. Goudvis. 2007. *Strategies That Work: Teaching Comprehension for Understanding and Engagement,* 2d ed. York, ME: Stenhouse.

Pentimonti, J. M., T. A. Zucker, L. M. Justice, and J. N. Kaderavek. 2010. "Informational Text Used in Preschool Classroom Read-Alouds." *The Reading Teacher* 63 (8): 656–665.

Smolkin, L., and C. Donovan. 2000. "The Contexts of Comprehension: Information Book Read Alouds and Comprehension Acquisition." CIERA Report 2-009. Ann Arbor, MI: University of Michigan School of Education.

Wilhelm, S. D. 1997. *You Gotta BE the Book: Teaching Engaged and Reflective Reading with Adolescents.* New York: Teachers College Press.

Children's Books Cited

Aliki, 1986. *Corn Is Maize: The Gift of the Indians.* New York: HarperCollins.

Creech, S. 2003. *A Fine Fine School.* New York: HarperCollins.

Daronco, M., and L. Presti. 2001. *Ants.* Pelham, NY: Benchmark Education.

Davies, N. 2001. *Big Blue Whale.* Somerville, MA: Candlewick Press.

Fenner, C. 2005. *Snowed In with Grandmother Silk*. New York: Puffin.

Gardiner, J. R. 1992. *Stone Fox*. New York: HarperCollins.

Garrett, L. 2004. *Helen Keller: A Photographic Story of a Life*. New York: DK Children.

Gibbons, G. 2001. *Ducks*. New York: Holiday House.

James, S. M. 2002. *Dolphins*. New York: Mondo.

Jane, P. 1998. *No Way, Winky Blue*. New York: Mondo.

Jane, P. 1998. *Take a Bow, Winky Blue*. New York: Mondo.

Kahn, B. 2004. "Cheeseheads." In *The Midwest Today*. Washington, DC: National Geographic.

McNamara, M. 2009. *The Life Cycle of a Frog*. Pelham, NY: Benchmark Education.

Merriam, E. 2005. "A Lazy Thought." In S. James' *Days Like This: A Collection of Small Poems*. Sommerville, MA: Candlewick Press.

Nayer, J. 1997. *A Week with Aunt Bea*. New York: Mondo.

Osborne, M. P. 1998. *Day of the Dragon King*. New York: Random House Books for Young Readers.

Pugliano-Martin, C. 2007. *A Frog Someday*. Pelham, NY: Benchmark Education.

Pugliano-Martin, C. 2007. *Watch a Frog Grow*. Pelham, NY: Benchmark Education.

Schwartz, D. 2004. *How Much Is a Million?* New York: HarperCollins.

Smith, A. M. 2005. *Akimbo and the Elephants*. New York: Bloomsbury Publishing.

Index

Entries followed by "OR" can be found in the Online Resources that accompanies this book.